RITCHIE BOY SECRETS

How a Force of Immigrants and Refugees
Helped Win World War II

BEVERLEY DRIVER EDDY

STACKPOLE
BOOKS
Guilford, Connecticut

STACKPOLE BOOKS

An imprint of Globe Pequot, the trade division of The Rowman & Littlefield Publishing Group, Inc.
4501 Forbes Blvd., Ste. 200
Lanham, MD 20706
www.rowman.com

Distributed by NATIONAL BOOK NETWORK

British Library Cataloguing in Publication Information available

Library of Congress Cataloging-in-Publication Data

Names: Eddy, Beverley D., author.
Title: Ritchie Boy Secrets : How a Force of Immigrants and Refugees Helped Win World War II / Beverley Driver Eddy.
Description: Guilford, Connecticut : Stackpole Books, [2021] | Includes bibliographical references and index. | Summary: "This is the story of the 15,000 immigrants and refugees who used their native language skills and knowledge of their home countries to help America to victory in World War II. Beverley Driver Eddy tells their story thoroughly and colorfully, drawing heavily on interviews with surviving Ritchie Boys"— Provided by publisher.
Identifiers: LCCN 2021005862 (print) | LCCN 2021005863 (ebook) | ISBN 9780811769969 (cloth ; alk paper) | ISBN 9780811769976 (electronic)
Subjects: LCSH: World War, 1939–1945—Military intelligence—United States. | Camp Albert C. Ritchie (Md.)—History. | Camp Albert C. Ritchie (Md.)—Biography.
Classification: LCC D810.S7 E35 2021 (print) | LCC D810.S7 (ebook) | DDC 940.54/867308691—dc23
LC record available at https://lccn.loc.gov/2021005862
LC ebook record available at https://lccn.loc.gov/2021005863

♾️™ The paper used in this publication meets the minimum requirements of American National Standard for Information Sciences—Permanence of Paper for Printed Library Materials, ANSI/NISO Z39.48-1992.

To Daniel Gross and Stephen Goodell,
who mentored me throughout
my writing of this book

CONTENTS

Foreword

Given the abiding interest in World War II, the slow emergence of Camp Ritchie and its trainees into similar prominence appears surprising. But now the silence seems to be history. After Christian Bauer's magnificent film and book *The Ritchie Boys* and Bruce Henderson's exciting book *Sons and Soldiers*, the media has discovered the astounding feats of a special intelligence unit. The film was directed and produced—of all things—by a German filmmaker, the second work by a seasoned best-selling chronicler of heroic, hitherto little-known deeds of a military unit or of individuals.

Now a book by Beverley Driver Eddy comes along, titled *Ritchie Boy Secrets: How a Force of Immigrants and Refugees Helped Win World War II*, and it looks as if it will achieve as much renown as the two earlier works. I felt honored when I was asked to write some introductory lines, since this topic was an important and ongoing part of my long life. Knowing that through works like this one more and more people will be interested in and discover the Ritchie Boys makes me proud of being one. Richly illustrated, there is scarcely an aspect of the camp's history that is not covered; Eddy documents the secret warfare at the European and Pacific theaters well. The same can be said about the multiple achievements of the Ritchie Boys, as we were nicknamed.

Eddy provides a surprisingly revelatory account of the ambience at Camp Ritchie, listing not only our foibles and follies but also our determination and devotion to the requisites of our mission. As one of those "boys" still around (at age ninety-eight, I scarcely deserve that appellation), I look forward to the spread of Eddy's book and am glad that my comrades in arms who went to war from that military institution will now earn further deserved recognition. Her book is undergirded by meticulous research. Well, we veterans of the "Great Invasion," in large number refugees from German-speaking countries, may still learn something.

Guy Stern
Director, Holocaust Memorial Center
Farmington Hills, Michigan

INTRODUCTION

ON JUNE 19, 1942, THE US ARMY OPENED A SECRET MILITARY INTELligence Training Center (MITC) at Camp Ritchie, Maryland, where, over the next four years, it produced some twenty thousand graduates—intelligence and language specialists—for service in the war.

Little has been written about the history of the camp, the training that was offered, and the programs that were mounted there, but, in the past sixteen years, a good deal of attention has been given to some of the camp's alumni. By now the term *Ritchie Boy* has entered the vernacular, popularized both through German filmmaker Christian Bauer's 2004 documentary film *The Ritchie Boys*, which earned an Academy Award nomination, and through historian Bruce Henderson's best-selling 2018 volume *Sons and Soldiers*, which traces, in some detail, the lives of six of the Ritchie graduates.

If one were to look to these works for a definition of the term *Ritchie Boy*, one might find it in the marketing material that accompanied Bauer's film. *The Ritchie Boys*, it said, captured "the never-before-told tale of a handful of German nationals who used their language and cultural knowledge to wage psychological warfare against the Nazis and to liberate Europe."[1] And, in looking at Henderson's book, we read in its subtitle that it presented the "untold story of the Jews who escaped the Nazis and returned with the U.S. Army to fight Hitler."

These works describe some, but not all, of the men who trained at Camp Ritchie. In this book, I have adopted a much broader definition of the term *Ritchie Boy*, one that includes a more diversified assortment of trainees. Ritchie Boy Daniel Thomas Skinner, for example, was an African American. He was born in Boston and, in 1938, graduated magna cum laude from Harvard with a degree in Romance languages. Because of his fluency in French, German, Italian, Latin, and Spanish, Private Skinner was brought to Camp Ritchie as a member of the seventh class and then graduated from Officer Candidate School as a second lieutenant. Because of his race, his talents could not be fully utilized in Europe; he served there as a driver and translator. Seventh class alumnus Frederic Maxwell Henderson was born and raised in Tucson, Arizona, where he grew up proud of his Apache Indian heritage. After graduation from Ritchie, he was recruited by the Office of Strategic Services (OSS) and sent behind enemy lines in Italy to rescue downed airmen and escort them across German lines to safety. Kiyoshi Yanaginuma was born in Oxnard, California; when the war broke out, he and his family were removed to the Gila River Relocation Center south of Phoenix, Arizona. Yanaginuma was recruited to army service from this internment camp. As a Nisei soldier, he could not join the war in the Pacific. He graduated from the MITC's twenty-ninth class and was made an instructor at Fort George Meade, Maryland, where he trained infantrymen for service in Japan.

These three men were all American born and are representative of the broad spectrum of American citizens from which the MITC at Camp Ritchie drew its soldiers. Their racial backgrounds—African American, Native American, Japanese American—indicate that Camp Ritchie trained many soldiers widely regarded at the time as outsiders or even "suspect" citizens. In general, the US Army reinforced the nation's biases. Black officers were not allowed to command white soldiers in the field, and Nisei could not be commissioned as officers. Many European-born soldiers were "suspect" because they came from Axis countries at war with the United States. At first the army had refused to enlist them, just as it refused for a time to allow Nisei into active service.

In addition, there was a high percentage of Jews at Camp Ritchie. During the 1930s and 1940s, Jewish refugees to the United States had discovered the existence of anti-Semitism in this country. While not as rampant as in Europe, it had been fueled on the radio throughout the 1930s by the weekly anti-Semitic diatribes of Father Charles Coughlin. Paradoxically, American anti-Semites linked Jews with the excessive greed of world banking as well as world Communism, both of which they regarded as threats to American democracy. Veterans of the Spanish

Civil War were also suspected Communists, as were all those people who had, early on, spoken out against Hitler and the rise of Fascism. To many Americans, these "pre-mature antifascists" were, at the very least, Communist sympathizers.

Camp Ritchie, then, was an idyllic spot for many of its soldiers, in terms of both geography and inclusiveness. It was a true melting pot of America where the mutual goal of defeating the Axis nations superseded everyday prejudice.

If we apply the term *Ritchie Boy* to the 11,637 students who successfully completed the camp's standard eight-week courses, we find that well over half of the men were born in the United States. The second largest group by far was German (15 percent), followed by Austrians (4.1 percent) and Italians (1.9 percent). As to their religion, Protestant Christians topped the list at 29.7 percent, followed by Roman Catholics (20.1 percent) and Jews (19.7 percent).

But there were many other foreign nationals who trained at the camp: Arabs, Jamaicans, Mexicans, Dutch, Greeks, Norwegians, Russians, and Turks. Two hundred Native Americans were stationed there as part of Camp Ritchie's training cadre. There were also two hundred from the Women's Army Corps (WAC). While most classes provided training for service in Europe, many of the Ritchie soldiers studied Japanese war tactics and were sent to the Pacific. Belgian-born Andrew Pelgrims, of Camp Ritchie's seventh class, had grown up in Djokjakarta, Indonesia. Because he spoke fluent French, Dutch, and Malaysian, he was sent to the South Pacific, where he was stationed in Merauke, New Guinea, to serve as the liaison between the American and Dutch armies. He, too, was a "Ritchie Boy."

Perhaps one can come to a better definition of the term *Ritchie Boy*, then, not by looking at the men's religion or nationality, but rather by comparing the various groups of men (and women!) attached to the MITC with the individuals associated with an academic university, such as the Massachusetts Institute of Technology (MIT). By these criteria, anyone enrolled in the standard camp curriculum who successfully completed some or all of its course work would classify as a Camp Ritchie alumnus, or "Ritchie Boy." This category would include the twelve WAC officers ("Ritchie Girls"!) who broke the gender gap by taking courses with the men. Those who came to Ritchie only for short, specialized courses would correspond to guest or graduate students, while all other people attached to the camp would correspond to university faculty, administrators, and support staff. Because they were essential to the success of the academic program, they are all part of this history. Even the war prisoners who passed through the camp must be included, since they were part of the camp's raison d'être.

Since the release of the Christian Bauer film, stories about Ritchie Boys have popped up like mushrooms. Through books, films, memoirs, museum exhibits, lectures, and veteran interviews, the public has come to know the individual stories of nearly 150 men who graduated from Camp Ritchie's Military Intelligence Training Center, or, as some of the men called it, "Military Institute of Total Confusion."

These stories of individuals or small groups of camp veterans are fascinating. However, the men's knowledge of the camp's training program is circumscribed by the class they attended and the particular specialty in which they were trained. And these veterans place far less emphasis on their training than on their actions in the war. As I looked at and listened to their stories, I could not help but notice a great variety in the men's wartime activities. And I asked: How were these men trained for their remarkable assignments? And how effective was this training when put into practice in the field?

In 1972, George Bailey wrote in his groundbreaking history *Germans: The Biography of an Obsession*, "If in the ensuing thirty-odd years Camp Ritchie has not entered world literature, it is only because the phenomenon of it has proved too difficult to grasp and transmit in any coherent way."[2] In this book I take up this challenge, while acknowledging other, earlier attempts to do the same.

In doing so, I recognize that the history of a war is written by victors and survivors. This fact is particularly true of Camp Ritchie. In the last twenty years, surviving veterans of the camp have been interviewed by volunteers at the United States Holocaust Memorial Museum, by veterans' associations, by Jewish organizations, by family members, and by schoolchildren. These interviews, coming at least fifty years after the events of World War II, rely of necessity on faulty memories and, frequently, distortions of facts. A historian I know once commented about the personal history related by a Camp Ritchie veteran, "I adore the man, but I also know he often doesn't let facts stand in the way of a good story." How, then, does one reconcile a veteran's statements with apparently conflicting "facts"? And where does one come by these facts?

In pursuing this study, I have used multiple sources. George Le Blanc's 1945 *History of Military Intelligence Training at Camp Ritchie, Maryland*, individual course histories, army records, officer reports, and training manuals certainly provide the most reliable research materials. Unfortunately, they do not capture the unique flavor of Camp Ritchie and the men who trained there. Here one must seek contemporary sources produced by individuals stationed at the camp: letters to family and friends, diaries, individual army reports, and contemporary newspaper articles. The letters written by Lawrence Cane, Alfred de Grazia, James Mims, and Alfred Diamant give lively, contemporary authenticity to the Ritchie experience. Still, these contemporary documents not only present a view that is limited to one man's perspective but also are constrained by the secrecy of the camp and of the men's missions in the war zone.

Veterans of the camp have also written memoirs; there are scores of these works. Those who acquired postwar fame had their memoirs published by commercial presses. Many others were published with subsidy presses or left in manuscript form, often as gifts to family members. These memoirs have already been "tainted" in part by the passage of time. There are errors of fact embellished by ego and by faulty memories. These present a good sense of the flavor of the camp but must be checked—and double-checked—for accuracy. We find here, for example, misspellings of names: the camp commander's name is remembered as "Banfield," rather than Banfill; the head of the German section Warndof is remembered as "Warndorf," and Master Sergeant Bartal is remembered as "Bartol." Entire teaching segments have been utterly forgotten, even as memories remain alive of important personages who never set foot in the camp. A good handful of veterans have distinct recollections of Henry Kissinger training at the camp, even though Kissinger himself denied ever having been there. One veteran even claimed to have gotten Kissinger a promotion during his supposed stay at Camp Ritchie. Here one must look at official army records to confirm or deny such claims, all the time realizing that many of these records are missing, incomplete, and themselves sometimes prone to error.

Another perspective on the Camp Ritchie experience is provided by biographers of veterans who trained there. Although one step removed from the veterans' experiences, most of them make a careful effort to document their sources and, where necessary, provide amplification and correctives to the subject's own narrative.

Meanwhile, a whole new aspect of the Camp Ritchie experience is provided by novels written by veterans of the camp. These fictional works change the names of soldiers and create figures who are conglomerations of several men, but they are, perhaps, best at capturing the raw emotions of the men who trained there. Here, of course, the camp itself plays a minor role, but these works masterfully portray the work of Ritchie men in the field, fighting, for example, with the French resistance (Fred Eden's *An Untold War Story*), coordinating with guerrilla fighters in Burma (Dean Brelis's *The Mission*), or working as a propagandist or an interrogator in the European Theater of Operations (Stefan Heym's *The Crusaders* and Hans Rosenhaupt's *The True Deceivers*). In more recent years, novels about the men from Camp Ritchie have been written by a younger generation of non-veteran authors: K. Lang-Slattery's *Immigrant Soldier* and Linda Kass's *A Ritchie Boy* come to mind. Both authors based their heroes' stories on those of real-life veterans.

Finally, there are the more reliable scholarly works that have been written by non-veterans about the camp and its trainees: Christian Bauer and Rebekka Göpfert's *Die Ritchie Boys* (2005), Bruce Henderson's *Sons and Soldiers* (2018), and Robert Lackner's *Camp Ritchie und seine Österreicher* (2020). A volume titled *Fort Ritchie: 1926–1998*, lovingly put together by Steve Blizard and Kathy Fotheringham and released in a limited edition, provides both textual information and photographic evidence of all phases of programming at the site.

I have studied all these variations on Camp Ritchie history, and in *Ritchie Boy Secrets* I endeavor to combine history with personal anecdote. Personal experiences give a sense of the flavor of the camp and show the men's perceptions of their teachers, their training, and their fellow students. Although they are often biased and based upon an individual's personal interactions, they add a human dimension to class numbers, program descriptions, and course content. These anecdotes are carefully identified as personalized accounts throughout the book, so as not to confuse the reader into mistaking these remarks for official camp history.

I encountered a new difficulty when I began to write of the Ritchie veterans' experiences in the field and to highlight some of their achievements. Here I was confronted with the problem of tying an individual's Camp Ritchie training with his wartime deeds. Many of the Ritchie Boys were absorbed into the Office of Strategic Services or the Counterintelligence Corps (CIC). How, then, can one claim that the skills they exhibited in the field were not developed at other training sites, rather than at the MITC? One cannot, of course. But, in reverting to my comparison of the US Army's MITC with academia's MIT, I would maintain that the basic eight-week course at Camp Ritchie provided the Ritchie graduates with something akin to an undergraduate degree. The fact that some men went on to other sites for further specialized training does not diminish the Camp Ritchie experience. Indeed, I found that this war training went two ways. US Marines, as well as men trained in OSS and CIC programs, came to Camp Ritchie for specialized work—the equivalent, one might say, of advanced graduate study. Not technically "Ritchie Boys," they were also Ritchie students who carried out their various war assignments in the European and Pacific theaters. I include both Ritchie Boys and Ritchie "graduate students" in my exploration of achievements in the field.

In his excellent study of the Austrian contingent of soldiers who studied at Camp Ritchie, Robert Lackner is careful to state that the intelligence efforts of the Ritchie Boys seem to have been minimally effective in the European campaign—they saved some lives but were not a decisive factor in winning the war. In this volume, I have tried to neither downplay nor overvalue the achievements of the Camp Ritchie veterans. I have looked at them instead as individuals. Some were heroes; some were victims on the battlefields of Europe and Asia. Some "pushed paper" in offices, some drove jeeps, and some repaired radio equipment.

Whatever their task, however big or small the achievement, each of them saw himself as part of a larger cause and did everything in his power to further it. In this respect, all those who passed through Camp Ritchie were heroic, just as all were members of the "greatest generation."

Throughout my work on this project, I have tried to examine the disparate materials by scholars and veterans with a skeptical eye. I have been aided immensely in my research by my colleagues Daniel Gross and Stephen Goodell. Both men have kept me honest by questioning and fact-checking my materials.

Dan Gross, who describes himself as a "Ritchie Boy Wannabe," has devoted many years of study to the camp and to all the men and women who passed through it. He was actively involved in the 2012 "Ritchie Boys" reunion and symposium held in Washington, DC. He has written individual time lines for more than six hundred Ritchie Boys, and he has put together tables of most of the classes offered at Ritchie, giving dates and student numbers for each. Some of these are included in the appendices of this book. Dan is the "go-to" man for information on nearly any aspect of Camp Ritchie, and I could not have written this book without him. I am especially grateful for his generosity in sharing with me books, articles, and research notes relating to the Camp Ritchie experience.

Steve Goodell served for many years as director of exhibitions at the US Holocaust Memorial Museum in Washington, DC, where he submerged himself in the Holocaust and in World War II history. From 2010 to 2013, he was the museum's liaison with US Army veterans. As he assisted in putting together the Detroit Holocaust Memorial exhibit *Secret Heroes* in 2011, he began a quest to find artifacts, documents, and photographs of Camp Ritchie and the Ritchie Boys. To date, Steve has scanned thousands of photos and assorted documents from the rich collections at the National Archives and Records Administration; he has shared many of these materials with me, including 251 photographs in the Signal Corps collection of "Ritchie Boys in Action." Most of the photographs in this book come from Steve's collections.

Although I have personally conversed with only sixteen Camp Ritchie veterans, Dan and Steve have met and interviewed many, many more, including the thirty-four who attended the Ritchie Boys reunion and symposium held in Washington, DC, in 2012. I will not mention all their names here; still, I must offer a special expression of gratitude to Ritchie Boy Paul Fairbrook, who most generously shared with me histories, documents, and reports relating to Camp Ritchie's Order of Battle program and the Military Intelligence Research Section (MIRS) operating at Fort Hunt, Virginia, and who gave my manuscript a careful reading. I must also thank Ritchie Boys Guy Stern, Richard Schifter, and Peter Burland for sharing their expertise with me and offering me their encouragement.

Kay Mitchell and Jennifer Marek, daughter and granddaughter of Ritchie instructor Theodore Fuller, have generously shared documents and photos relating to the Camp Ritchie Photo Interpretation program. Other generous people who shared personal papers, documents, and photos with me include Anita Boucher, Buck Browning, David Cane, Kasey Clay, Barbara Fredrickson, Ruth Horlick, Patricia Magee, Philip Pines, Ruth Schroeder, Florian Traussnig, and Joyce Yamane.

I would be remiss if I were not to mention the Facebook page "Ritchie Boys of WWII," a page developed by Erik Brun, Dan Gross, Bernie Lubran, and Leslie Braunstein, which works to provide information and connections to the "Ritchie Boys," their descendants, and others who trained at Camp Ritchie. Bernie Lubran has a large collection of memorabilia and artifacts related to Camp Ritchie and the Ritchie Boys, and he has called to my attention a number of Camp Ritchie resources that I might otherwise have missed.

To all the archivists, librarians, and staff members who have, in their professional capacities, provided information and service throughout the time I have been working on this project, I give an enthusiastic shoutout. These people serve tirelessly as unofficial research assistants to scholars everywhere, providing quick and efficient solutions to scholarly quandaries, making rare materials accessible via internet and snail mail, forwarding letters of inquiry to other knowledgeable sources, and passing on unexpected finds in their collections—and they perform these services with unending good humor. To name the libraries and museums that have been especially helpful during this period: the US National Archives and Records Administration, the United States Holocaust Memorial

Museum, the US Army Heritage & Education Center, the Leo Baeck Institute, the Washington County Free Library, the National Park Service, the Wisconsin Historical Society, the Fairfield Museum & History Center, the Stephen H. Hart Research Center at History Colorado, the Archibald S. Alexander Library at Rutgers University, the Jewish Federation of Greater Santa Barbara, the Rauner Special Collections Library at Dartmouth College, the library and research center at the Gettysburg National Military Park Museum and Visitor Center, and the archives of the Adams County Historical Society. I am especially indebted to the Inter-Library Loan Department of the Waidner-Spahr Library at Dickinson College for helping me obtain research materials with unwavering efficiency and speed.

Finally, I am everlastingly grateful to my husband, Truman, for his advice, encouragement, and steadfast support throughout this project. He has accompanied me on numerous site visits, listened patiently as I have obsessed about this work, asked the right questions, made the right suggestions, and helped me organize and refine my arguments.

In writing this work, I could not cover the deeds of all the men who passed through Ritchie. I have tried, instead, to take figures who are representative of all of them. To any veterans or veteran families who feel left out of my study, I apologize. I alone bear the responsibility for any errors or critical omissions.

CHAPTER ONE

Building Camp Ritchie

*Actually, it had been a Victorian vacation spot. . . . There was a lovely
lake . . . on which Mom and Dad used to go boating around World
War I. Lovely, large homes were scattered throughout the area—these
had been vacation homes at one time. By 1944 modern barracks were
up—a beautiful Officers Club by the Lake, large mess halls, horse
stables and warehouses.*[1]

NEARLY ALL THE SOLDIERS WHO CAME TO STUDY AT CAMP RITCHIE
remarked on the idyllic placement of the camp on two small, man-made
lakes in a hollow backed by wooded mountains. Even as a military
installation, it looked, many felt, more like a resort than an army camp.
And, in truth, that is how that area of Pennsylvania and Maryland—
Highfield-Cascade, Pen Mar, Blue Ridge Summit—had been developed.
John Mifflin Hood, president of the Western Maryland Railroad, had
envisioned the area as a popular destination site for wealthy Baltimor-
eans seeking to escape the summer heat and humidity. During the 1870s,
he oversaw the construction of a passenger line to service the area and
an amusement park in Pen Mar to entertain its visitors. In its heyday,
roughly from the 1880s to the 1920s, trainloads of day visitors came to
the area to hike, swim, fish, and socialize in a delightfully breezy setting.
In 1885, the Monterey Country Club was opened in nearby Blue Ridge
Summit, Pennsylvania, offering additional pleasures to those Baltimorean
blue bloods who chose to spend the summer there. Presidents Woodrow Wilson and Calvin Coolidge came there to golf. Trolley service

connected the amusement park with the villages around it, and soon a number of wealthy Marylanders constructed their own homes in the area. Others stayed in its colossal and more moderate-sized hotels, while those with less ostentatious wealth stayed in summer boarding houses. Wallis Simpson was born in Blue Ridge Summit in June 1896, while her mother was summering in a cottage directly across from the golf course. A Baltimore newspaper advertisement from 1915 led off with the headline "72° in the Blue Ridge Mountains" and touted the area as a "summer and health resort" offering "every form of amusement." It pointed out that Pen Mar Park now featured a "sensational mountain roller coaster, joyland, latest moving pictures (including Charlie Chaplin), boating and fishing, and a miniature steam railway."[2]

During this same period, entrepreneur Thaddeus Wastler took advantage of the local railway line by establishing the Buena Vista Ice Company on the future Camp Ritchie site. He constructed the two artificial lakes there, naming the lower, larger lake after his father-in-law, Samuel T. Royer, and the upper lake after himself (Lake Wastler). He also constructed eleven ice houses. A railroad spur was built alongside the southeastern shore of Lake Royer for transport, and, beginning in 1903, the natural ice harvested at the lakes was sold and used to preserve produce and dairy products during shipment to markets in Baltimore, Maryland, and points south.

Lake Royer became part of the recreational offerings in the Pen Mar area. The summer tourists could boat, fish, and swim there. In the winter, local children came there to skate. But the 1929 crash of the stock market, the rise in automobile travel, and the competition offered by new ocean-side resorts along the eastern seaboard all led to the eventual demise of Pen Mar Park and the fading grandeur of homes and hotels in the area. The Buena Vista Ice Company had already folded in the early 1920s. With its closing, the acreage encircling the Royer and Wastler lakes acquired a new purpose. The Maryland National Guard was attracted to the area by its proximity to the Western Maryland railway and telegraph line, and it decided to build a summer training camp there. Captain Robert F. Barrick, of the Army Corps of Engineers, was assigned the task of building the camp.

Barrick was thirty-three at the time. He was brought to the Camp Ritchie site in 1926 and would remain there through the duration of World War II as post engineer.

Even though he had only a seventh-grade education, Barrick was a self-taught engineer with a rare talent for putting theory into practice. He drew up plans and blueprints for the camp and supervised the construction of numerous stone buildings—headquarters, mess halls, kitchen facilities, and such—out of local timber and field stone, using local workers. Most of these buildings had a rather simple design, with gable roofs, decorative rafter ends, and prominent chimneys. The camp headquarters was the one standout building at the camp. Barrick based his design on the insignia of the Corps of Engineers, giving it a miniature castle facade with towers and parapet. The gates into the post shared the same castle-like form. Nineteen square kitchens originally constructed for the platoons of the First Maryland Regiment were soon modified by being extended into nineteen long and narrow "finger buildings" to serve as mess halls for the men. Additional buildings included Lakeside Hall, the headquarters company mess, administration facilities, a stable, and various bath houses. In addition to this construction, Barrick modified the natural landscape by laying out numerous roads and an expansive parade ground. Land was graded on the hill southeast of the finger buildings for the laying of 210 concrete slabs to serve as bases for the guardsmen's bivouac tents. The banks of Lake Wastler were shored up and reinforced, and a mountainside stream was diverted underground to feed it. Two tunnels were built from the brigade officers' mess hall: one was a passageway to a building at the top of the hillside, one a utility tunnel for access to electric wiring and pipes. In 1929, a beautification program at the camp included the planting of twenty-five thousand flowers, shrubs, and conifers.[3]

The camp was named for the current governor of Maryland, Albert Cabell Ritchie, and it served the Maryland National Guard until 1942, when the camp, now encompassing 638 acres, was taken over by the US Army to train army intelligence personnel.

This was not the first use that the US Army had made of the camp, however. Already in summer 1941 the State of Maryland had leased Camp Albert C. Ritchie to the federal government for $1 a year, so that the War Department could begin offering soldiers summer recreation programs at the site. Other organizations, such as the Boy Scouts, were also allowed use of the camp for summer programs.

Its multipurpose usage ceased with the army's establishment there of its new Military Intelligence Training Center. This center was formed at the initiative of General George C. Marshall, US Army chief of staff, who recognized that the United States had entered the war woefully ill prepared, in terms of both manpower and the quality of its intelligence gathering. The war in Europe had already been raging for two years, and still the United States had no programs for the specialized intelligence training of American servicemen.

Things changed after Pearl Harbor. In January 1942, the Army Air Force was approved for establishing an air intelligence school: first in space offered by the University of Maryland; then in government-purchased property in Harrisburg, Pennsylvania; and, finally, at Orlando, Florida. The training at this school placed great importance on photo intelligence. Army intelligence training was not approved until April 1942; in the weeks that followed, it was determined that this program should be carried out at Camp Albert C. Ritchie, under the 1941 lease agreement of $1 per year. The site was now closed off to the public, and its name was shortened to Camp Ritchie.

Soon construction was going on everywhere. The army faced the formidable task of transforming a summer training camp capable of housing three thousand men in tents into a year-round operation capable of housing six thousand. Funding of $5 million was provided for this task, which necessitated major work to provide adequate water and sewage facilities.

One hundred sixty-five assorted structures were built between June 1942 and January 1945. The concrete beds for the summer tents of the National Guard were removed, and two-story wooden barracks were constructed. These barracks were constructed not only at the old National Guard location but also on the hillside above the camp. Separate barracks, offices, and mess halls were constructed for the Composite School Unit, for a cadre of Black soldiers, for Native American soldiers, and for a prisoner of war (POW) camp for Italians. Barracks rose on the opposite shore of Lake Royer for army officers and for the Women's Army Corps

(WAC). In addition to the barracks, a post headquarters, a post exchange, a training headquarters building, a quartermaster building, and a post chapel were constructed of wood. New stone structures were added: a finance office, a theater, a signal office building, and a training headquarters supply building; a post gymnasium was built of brick. In 1943, a large hospital complex was erected on the west shore of Lake Royer. This involved a vast expansion of constructed buildings in that area. The hospital consisted of fifteen (later twenty-two) one-story wooden units connected by closed, heated corridors; these units accommodated 225 beds, 26 single rooms, physicians' quarters, and barracks housing for hospital personnel. In addition, it had laboratory facilities, a dental clinic, an X-ray department, and two well-equipped operating rooms.

The final tally of buildings constructed at Camp Ritchie included forty-four classrooms, forty-two enlisted men's barracks, eleven barracks for officers, nine buildings for WACs, five mess buildings, the twenty-two buildings of the Station hospital, and thirty-two miscellaneous structures. New construction continued throughout the entire period of the camp's existence, and, as post engineer, Robert Barrick saw to it that the camp maintained the integrity of his original landscape design. The soldiers frequently complained about the constant construction work, pointing out that, whenever it rained, the grounds turned into a sea of oozy, sticky mud. This "soft, brownish mud . . . stuck to our boots," one remembered, "yet the barracks had to be kept clean."[4]

The new Military Intelligence Training Center at Camp Ritchie was activated on June 19, 1942, in a brief ceremony overlooking the parade ground. Only six of the camp's new officers were present. A flag was raised, and, as commandant of the new center, Colonel Charles Y. Banfill delivered a few opening remarks. Following this, the camp adjutant, Major Joseph Hoffman, read the formal activation order and the Order of the Day. The camp's assistant commandant, Lieutenant Colonel Walter A. Buck, was also at the opening ceremony. He would have authority over the consolidated mess and troop supply, quartermaster section, the Detached Enlisted Men's List, ordnance section, military police section, training battalions, the Composite School Unit, the WAC detachment, and, eventually, the Pacific Military Intelligence Research Section. Buck had already served directly under Banfill in the Military Intelligence Division (soon to be renamed the Military Intelligence Service, or MIS). At Camp Ritchie, the two men would continue their close association.

Colonel Banfill was well equipped for the position of Camp Ritchie commandant. He was a tall and muscular Southerner whose military service coincided with the nation's development of aerial warfare. Born in Bonifay, Florida, in 1897, he had served in the First Field Artillery of the Louisiana National Guard before being sent for training at the School of Military Aeronautics at the University of Texas in November 1917; he followed this up with advanced training in pursuit flying at Kelly Field. During the 1920s, he worked as a flight instructor while also gaining experience and training in aerial observation and photography. By the end of the decade, Banfill had achieved recognition in the press as a noted stunt flyer. During the 1930s, Banfill had trained at the Air Corps Tactical School at Maxwell Field in Alabama; at the Command and General Staff School at Fort Leavenworth, Kansas; and at the US Army War College before being called to Washington, DC, for service in air corps photo-mapping for the Operations Section of the Office of the Chief of Air Corps. He had gone on to attend a special course in assault operation technique at Fort Belvoir, Virginia, and, in January 1941, had joined the War Department General Staff as chief of the geographic section, Military Intelligence Division (MID). No one could question his credentials. Despite his relocation to Camp Ritchie, Banfill continued to serve the MID, now reorganized as the Military Intelligence Service, as its assistant chief. These direct ties to the War Department permitted a speedy resolution of all questions of operation and instruction at Camp Ritchie. When Banfill moved to the camp, he brought with him his Piper Cub and his horses. Although he did not have a lot of day-to-day contact with the enlisted men, he kept a sharp eye on their programs and progress, made decisions as to who should go to Officer Candidate School after completing the course work at the camp, and made recommendations for the men's future deployment. Staff Sergeant Peter Burland recalled that Banfill "was a tyrant, a carbon copy of old George Patton. He could have written a dictionary of four-letter words."[5] During his service at the camp, Banfill was named temporary brigadier general. The enlisted men

He Passed through Camp Ritchie

When war broke out in Europe, Corporal **Renato Volpi** (1921–2014) became a member of Italy's Thirtieth Infantry Regiment of the Assietta Division. He was a musician and played the violin and the bugle for military fanfares. His unit was sent to Sicily on Christmas Day 1942; just before the Allied landings seven months later, he was transferred to the Twenty-Ninth Infantry Regiment. He was captured by the Americans at Prizzi, sent as a POW to North Africa, and then transferred to a Liberty ship, where he was jam-packed in the ship's hold. When he landed at Newport News, Virginia, twenty days later, he was emaciated and riddled with bedbugs. He spent a month in quarantine at Fort Meade, Maryland. During his stay, a priest gave him a violin donated by an Italian American family.

At the end of September 1943, Volpi was sent to Camp Ritchie, where he spent five months as a POW. Although kept under armed guard and isolated from news sources, Volpi felt "really well off" there, since the cooks were nearly all Italian, and they had access to the American mess halls and other food establishments at the camp.

After Italy's surrender, the Allies began a program of voluntary labor cooperation among Italian POWs who swore allegiance to the United States. Volpi agreed to collaborate and was sent to the Letterkenny Army Depot north of Chambersburg, Pennsylvania, to be integrated into an Italian Service Unit. Because of his former work as a typographer, he was assigned to work in the print shop in the battalion headquarters. At Letterkenny, the cooperating Italians had a great deal of freedom: they built numerous structures there, including their own oven for baking bread and a Catholic chapel to replace the barrack in which Catholic services had previously been held. On September 15, 1945, the Italian service program was closed, and Volpi returned home to Italy, where he became a technician with the Nestlé Corporation, got involved in local Italian politics, and became a councilman in his hometown of Abbiategrasso, near Milan.

were proud of the fact that this made Camp Ritchie the only post commanded by a general. He joined the war in Europe in January 1945 and was replaced at Camp Ritchie by Colonel Mercer Walter.

Banfill's assignment was to train soldiers for the interrogation of prisoners of war, linguistic interpretation, and translation, but all aspects of military intelligence underlay that training, from counterintelligence to map reading to close combat. His overriding principle was that the camp should replicate, as closely as possible, all aspects of warfare that its graduates would encounter on the ground in North Africa, Europe, and in the Pacific. A German "village" was constructed on the Camp Ritchie grounds, made of plywood and burlap, that could be used to demonstrate effective methods of street fighting and the seizure and occupation of buildings. It included mock homes, businesses, and even a bell tower. From this tower, German "snipers" could fire down on the Americans "to show these men what could happen when they came through a German village."[6] In addition, earthen fortifications were built, foxholes and an array of trenches were dug, and camouflaged enemy hideouts were constructed in the neighboring forests. As items became available through the African campaign, the camp acquired captured Axis uniforms, weaponry, and motorized vehicles. The main street of the camp was decked out with an array of enemy artillery pieces.

Lieutenant Colonel Shipley Thomas was made director of training at Camp Ritchie, and he and Major Theodore Fuller prepared the training program. Both men were well suited to the task. Thomas had served in World War I, first as a platoon commander and then as an S-2 (intelligence officer) in the Twenty-Sixth Infantry, First Infantry Division in France. He maintained that he had taken part in every engagement of the Twenty-Sixth Infantry, performing intelligence and reconnaissance work "on horse, foot, and belly." After the war, he had written two books: *The History of the A.E.F.* (American Expeditionary Forces, ca. 1920), and *S-2 in Action* (1940). This latter work was a how-to book for intelligence officers and provided a basis for the Camp Ritchie training program. He was a graduate of the British IV Army Sniping School, the French Photo-Interpreter and Order of Battle schools, the US Army Intelligence School, and the Command and General Staff College. He had a Silver

Star and Oak Leaf Cluster, the Legion of Merit, the Purple Heart, and a personal award of the Fourragère of the Croix de Guerre. He was fifty when he came to Camp Ritchie and remained there as director of training for the duration of the war.

Theodore Fuller was seventeen years his junior, but he, too, came to Camp Ritchie with sterling qualifications. He had had a commission in the US Army Engineer Reserves before being ordered to Fort Belvoir for duty on the staff and faculty of the Engineer School. There he wrote two field manuals—*Elementary Map and Aerial Photo Reading* and *Advanced Map and Aerial Photo Reading*—that would be used by the army throughout World War II. He also served as corrective editor on the manuals *Surveying* and *Camouflage*. His next assignment had been to write the *Photo Interpretation Technical Manual*; these five works were used as training texts throughout the war. Finally, he had taught two courses in photo interpretation at Fort Belvoir's Engineer School. These courses evolved into courses for photo interpretation offered by the US Air Force in Harrisburg, Pennsylvania; the US Navy in Quantico, Virginia; the US Marines at Camp Lejeune, North Carolina; and the US Army at Camp Ritchie, Maryland.

Thomas and Fuller's task of working up the complete training program for Camp Ritchie was, Fuller said, "a monumental task," since they were ordered to draw up a course "which would prepare intelligence specialist teams to serve from every echelon from regiment to Army Group."[7] Fuller also worked up the tables of organization and equipment for the entire post and school. During this period, he and Thomas were working in a temporary building across from the old Munitions Building in Washington, DC, which, in those pre-Pentagon days, housed the War Department.

Both Thomas and Fuller were present at the low-key ceremony that marked the opening of Camp Ritchie's Military Intelligence Training Center in June. A flag and first crest were created for the camp, showing a German military map set against a Silver Star, superimposed upon a wreath with the letters *MITC* and the motto "*Fas est et ab hoste doceri*," or "You must learn from the enemy." After the ceremonial opening, Thomas and Fuller found and rented houses in nearby Blue Ridge Summit. They then returned to Washington until mid-July, when they made the permanent move to Camp Ritchie. The first class began there on July 27, 1942.

View of Lake Royer and surrounding cliffs, prior to the construction of Camp Albert C. Ritchie. SOURCE: LIBRARY OF CONGRESS

Captain Robert F. Barrick, the army engineer responsible for the construction of Camp Albert C. Ritchie (1926–1929). SOURCE: WESTERN MARYLAND REGIONAL LIBRARY, MARYLAND STATE ARCHIVES

Army construction and expansion on the Camp Ritchie grounds.
SOURCE: NATIONAL ARCHIVES AND RECORDS ADMINISTRATION

Completed construction of the main campus of Camp Ritchie. SOURCE: NATIONAL ARCHIVES AND RECORDS ADMINISTRATION

Colonel Charles Y. Banfill, Camp Ritchie commandant (left). SOURCE: WESTERN MARYLAND REGIONAL LIBRARY, MARYLAND STATE ARCHIVES

CHAPTER TWO

The First Class

Inasmuch as Ritchie was unlike any other Army unit and was respon-
sible only to the War Department, we were not hampered by regula-
tions which governed other units. For this reason, [we] had a lot of
leeway for new ideas and innovations.[1]

COMMANDER BANFILL HAD HIS HANDS FULL WITH THE DEMANDS OF
setting up Camp Ritchie's new Military Intelligence Training Center (MITC). He had Shipley Thomas and Theodore Fuller to help in
designing the program, but that was only the beginning. Now he had to
find—and train—instructors qualified to teach the basics in its different intelligence components. Fortunately, some work in these areas was
already going on at various locations around the country, and he could
draw on instructors from these camps, such as Fuller himself, who had
been an instructor in reading aerial photographs at Fort Belvoir, Virginia,
and Charles Warndof, a senior instructor in interrogation techniques at
Camp Blanding, Florida, and at Camp Bullis, Texas. Warndof brought
his entire staff along when he transferred from Camp Bullis to Camp
Ritchie. Shipley Thomas, a proud and gregarious Yale graduate, sought out
qualified officer graduates from the Ivy League schools—Yale, Princeton,
Harvard—for the first class at Camp Ritchie, for, unlike all later Ritchie
classes, Banfill had determined that this first one should consist solely of
officers. It was his idea that most would serve as instructors at the camp
once they had completed their course work; they would be needed, since
classroom groupings in the later classes were not to exceed a total of

thirty-five officers and enlisted men. Because the program was beginning from scratch, Banfill determined that the entire first MITC class should not exceed that number. Of the five hundred plus officers who applied for acceptance into the program, thirty-six were accepted. Because two of them—Major William Black and Major Victor Klefbeck—were immediately assigned as instructors, and two others did not graduate, the number of successful first class graduates was thirty-two.

While Shipley Thomas handled recruitment of officers, Theodore Fuller worked on organization; he also developed a cadre of men whose assignment was to demonstrate German uniforms, vehicles, weaponry, and fighting techniques. His German vehicles included jeeps and half-tracks, and even bicycles and motorcycles, since the Germans used both for their smaller units. Scores of soldiers were brought in as military police (MPs) and as service personnel. Sixty Italian prisoners of war were also brought in to the camp and worked chiefly in the mess halls on kitchen patrol (KP) duty and as cooks. Lieutenant Alfred Diamant, of the thirteenth class, recalled the delicious meals in the officers' mess, "prepared by carefully selected Italian POW cooks, so it featured antipasto and other delights of Italian cooking."[2]

In addition to its demonstration cadre, the camp housed an equally important visual aid section and reproduction branch. Although these were less visible, they were critical to the success of the MITC teaching program, since these units produced all the camp's instructional materials. A photo section provided the photography used in the photo intelligence and ground forces classes, while its photostat unit created facsimiles of forms, documents, and visual aids at the rate of twenty-five thousand prints per month. The five mimeograph machines in the mimeograph section provided instructional aids at an average rate of 350,000 pages per month. And a photo-litho section, with its camera, layout, plate, press, and stock units, handled all photolithographic reproduction for the school and post. The publications that were produced here served both as instructional aids and as reference materials in the field. Each month this section produced roughly eight hundred thousand impressions.[3]

While planning the programming at Camp Ritchie, Fuller confessed later to one error in judgment: "To get away from the habit of Sundays,

I got the commandant to set up the eleven-day 'week.' Instead of resting on the Biblical seventh, we extended it to the eleventh. . . . But I found that the Lord was pretty smart about that seventh day to rest, because we became pretty fagged after a few months of eleven-day weeks."[4] Eventually, Colonel Banfill reduced the "week" to a more reasonable length. He remained convinced of the value of varying the camp days of "rest," however. Remembering that the attack on Pearl Harbor had occurred on a Sunday morning, Banfill introduced eight-day weeks, so that the men would not associate their day off with a specific weekday. By doing so, he introduced two new words into the camp vocabulary: *Ban-week* and *Ban-day*.

Originally the training program consisted of six sections, each headed by a chief officer in charge of instruction in that area. These were Terrain Intelligence (headed by Raymond Grazier), Signal Intelligence (George Le Blanc), Staff Duties (Arthur Jorgenson), Counterintelligence (William C. Piper), Enemy Armies (Charles Warndof), and Aerial Photo Interpretation (Theodore Fuller). In very short order, three sections were added to the mix: Military Intelligence (Delbert Pryor), Close Combat (Rex Applegate), and Visual Demonstration (George Weber). The last section added to the mix was Enemy Order of Battle, drawing upon material gathered by British intelligence and published under the name *Order of Battle of the German Army* in October 1942. It was the task of the section chiefs both to serve as teachers at Ritchie and to supervise the instructors assigned to their particular section. They did this by observing classes and by holding weekly meetings to discuss and critique both the program and the instruction.

Some of the section chiefs, such as Austrian-born Charles Warndof and Oregonian Rex Applegate, held their positions throughout the war. Others, such as Theodore Fuller and George O. Weber, entered active service in Europe. For his service in Italy, Weber would receive the Silver Star, Purple Heart, and Bronze Star with Oak Leaf Cluster.

Most of the section chiefs were lieutenant colonels, with a sprinkling of majors. The thirty-six members of the first class of students, by contrast, consisted of thirty-six second and first lieutenants and captains. The youngest, Henry C. Barringer, was twenty-two; the oldest, Young A.

Neal, was forty-seven. Twenty-six-year-old Captain Sterling Ryser noted that "most of us in the first class were native born Americans."[5] Ryser had participated in a Mormon mission to Germany from December 1936 to May 1939, and he had therefore been in a unique position, as an American, to witness the violently repressive anti-Jewish laws that led up to the "Night of Broken Glass," or *Kristallnacht*, and the burning and looting of Jewish-owned buildings, businesses, and synagogues. Only eight of his classmates were foreign born: Werner Fischer, Hanns Kurth, and Walter Rapp were born in Germany; Henry Staudigl in Austria; Robert Grosjean in Belgium; John Brinkerhoff Jackson in France; and Trygve Sandberg and Paul Birkeland in Norway. Rather surprisingly, one, Leroy H. Woodson, was a Black American. These men were all being trained for leadership positions in intelligence work, although eventually, as was the case with the section chiefs, these men might go on to fill a variety of assignments, with some being stationed at the front, others transferred to Washington or London, and a few retained at Camp Ritchie for the duration of the war.

Because Britain was already far ahead of the United States in military intelligence training, British colonel Thomas Robbins came to Camp Ritchie in June to provide instructional oversight. Robbins had been stationed at the British School for Interrogators of Prisoners of War at Cambridge University, and he was an expert in all areas of intelligence instruction. Under his guidance, the Military Intelligence Training Center at Camp Ritchie, in the first few months, developed a full spectrum of specialty classes. The basic class instruction now consisted of ten curricular components.[6]

First, the Ritchie Boys took a basic course, *German Army Organization*. All except those chosen for the Pacific theater of operations attended this course, which was conducted for a long time by Captain Ulrich Biel. Students were exposed to German vehicles, standard weapons, and uniforms. At the end of this course, students were expected "to know the rank, the branch of service, the medals and uniform parts that revealed an enemy's special training."

A shorter course, *Italian Army Organization*, focused on the breakdown of the Italian binary divisions.

A third component of the Ritchie program was titled *Order of Battle*. Here students were introduced to all the divisions and units that they would be likely to encounter in the European theater of operations, including, wherever possible, the names of the commanding officers. This material was constantly updated.

Next, students were expected to become proficient in *Morse Code*. A special classroom was equipped with keyboards and headphones for all the students; at the end of the course, they were tested in transcribing messages sent from a central control station.

The fifth component was *Terrain and Aerial Intelligence*. Students learned how to draw a topographical map indicating distances and elevations, and to interpret features of aerial photographs shown to them as stereograph 3-D images.

Students were also expected to *Read German Documents*, including those in Gothic print (*Fraktur*) or in the handwritten script known as *Sütterlin*. To the students already knowledgeable in German shorthand, Austrian-born Sergeant Bernard Tengood offered specialized training in the reading of shorthand documents in *Einheit* stenography.

All students participated in nighttime *Field Exercises*, in which they demonstrated their skill at map reading, regardless of language, and at finding their way to a designated gathering spot with only a map and a compass for orientation.

An eighth component involved instruction through film and practical exercises in *Close Hand-to-Hand Combat*.

The ninth component, *Visual Demonstrations*, offered dramatizations of all course components in the field, at the camp theater, at a mock German village, and at a cut-away house.

Finally, toward the end of their training, all students were sent on a forty-eight-hour exercise and then on an eight-day exercise outside the camp, where each of various stations on the exercise tested a different skill, such as interrogating prisoners or intercepting telephone conversations. They were also given a fifty-item identification test of uniform pieces and weaponry scattered around a huge meadow. This, one soldier remembered, was an "occasion of mental torture," adding, "I don't think anybody scored fifty out of fifty; I certainly didn't."[7]

The first class held at Ritchie began on July 27, 1942, and ran until September 19. Colonel Robbins followed the students' progress every step of the way and stepped in to teach classes in POW interrogation, order of battle, captured documents, photo interpretation, and night orienteering. Sterling Ryser probably spoke for many of his classmates when he remarked that Colonel Robbins was something of a "know-it-all."[8]

Ritchie's second class arrived at Camp Ritchie before the first class had completed its program. Its course work began on August 24 and lasted until October 17. Colonel Robbins remained at Camp Ritchie through the completion of the second class. This class was typical of the classes that followed, in that it was much larger than the first, had a higher percentage of foreign-born students, and contained a mix of officers and enlisted men. It was not typical in that of the 124 officers and 132 enlisted men in the class, only 49 percent completed the training program. Sterling Ryser, who was now teaching prisoner of war interrogation at the camp, explained this phenomenon:

Before the second class was to graduate, everything was abruptly frozen. No communication in or out whatsoever. Around 4:00 a.m., a convoy of about six trucks took half of the men stationed on base away with no explanation. . . . The allied invasion of North Africa was imminent and linguists were needed there for the interrogation of German prisoners.[9]

This was typical of men suddenly called into service. The blocked communications meant that the married men were unable even to call their wives and bid them farewell. While Lieutenant Vernon Walters could understand the need for secrecy, he could not understand the attitude of Colonel Banfill:

As we prepared to drive off, the commandant came out and watched us. I was shocked by the fact that he said nothing to bid us farewell or wish us luck. We were obviously not going to complete the course and were clearly on our way overseas, yet he had no word of encouragement or farewell for us. It was a lack of leadership that I was not to forget soon.[10]

As for Sterling Ryser, he was promoted to captain and remained at Camp Ritchie as an instructor until the end of January 1943. He was then sent to London to work in the Intelligence section (G-2) of the Headquarters European theater of operations. His task was to plan staffing and provide interrogators and linguist interpreters for the European theater. The army quickly adopted Ryser's proposed organizational plan—namely, to use six-man teams (two officers and four enlisted men), with two teams per division, three per corps headquarters, and four per army headquarters. Ryser became executive officer and then commander of their supervisory headquarters and oversaw POW interrogation teams in northern Europe while moving his headquarters to follow the progress of the war, from England to France to Germany. In April 1945, he was promoted to lieutenant colonel. For his service in cooperation with the Polish forces, he was awarded the Golden Cross medal of honor by the Polish government in exile.

Each of the officers from the first class at Camp Ritchie had a unique story to tell. Some helped pen materials crucial to the successful conduct of the war. Captain Christo T. Mocas helped produce books of foreign maps for the Military Intelligence Service, or MIS. Lieutenant Henry J. Staudigl was sent to Fort Hunt, Virginia, where he cowrote a hardbound manual, *Evasion and Escape*, for air force personnel. This book explained what the airmen could expect if captured and the kinds of interrogation methods that the Germans generally employed. Staudigl had experience working in Hollywood as a consultant and writer, and he put that expertise to use by assisting in the creation of a training film for airmen.

Fort Hunt was such a secret site that it was referred to throughout the war only as PO Box 1142. One reason for this secrecy was that it housed those German prisoners of war who were of particular interest to military intelligence. Captain John H. Brown served there briefly as an interrogator before being transferred to London to serve as an instructor in three-week courses in the identification of enemy and allied uniforms and equipment. There Brown assumed the role of a German soldier and

He Passed through Camp Ritchie

Master Sergeant **Frank S. Leavitt** (1891–1953), who is known in the professional wrestling world as "Man Mountain Dean," was born in New York City, enlisted in the army as a teenager, and saw action in the Border War with Mexico. In World War I, he was sent to France, where he fought in General George Patton's tank division. These actions led to his being awarded a ribbon for his service in the Border War and the Croix de Guerre with palm for his action in World War I. Then, after a brief stint in professional football, Leavitt turned to wrestling.

He had already begun wrestling during his army service, using the ring name "Soldier Leavitt." He used a number of other rubrics before meeting Doris Dean, who became his wife and manager and gave him the moniker by which he is known to this day. Leavitt grew a formidable beard, which, with his five-foot-eleven-inch height and three-hundred-pound weight, made him an imposing star in the wrestling world. He also took on the role of stunt double for Charles Laughton in the 1933 movie *The Private Life of Henry VIII.* Leavitt continued making films until 1938. He retired from wrestling in 1940 and moved to a farm in Georgia.

After the attack on Pearl Harbor, Leavitt tried to enlist in the army. He was unsuccessful until General Patton wrote a letter on his behalf, and, after acknowledging his excellent physical condition, the army waived the age requirement (Leavitt was fifty). He quickly rose to sergeant and was assigned to military police work for the US Armored Corps in training in Indio, California. Upon entering the army, Leavitt had bragged that "I've beat every Jap I ever wrestled, and I can still do it!" He went to Fort Bliss, Texas, to teach the GIs how to wrestle, and, as demonstration, he taught a 130-pound corporal how to toss him. The War Department was impressed, and Leavitt was brought to Camp Ritchie as first sergeant and instructor in hand-to-hand combat.

Leavitt completed his military service at Ritchie and then returned to Georgia, where he studied journalism and dabbled in politics.

wore the uniform of a German sergeant for his demonstrations. Lieutenant Colonel Hubert J. Plumpe and Lieutenant Robert E. Walker served in a different section of PO Box 1142, in its Military Intelligence Research Section (MIRS) that produced critical resources for unit commanders and interrogators in the European theater.

In their initial or early assignments, it appears that three of the first class graduates were assigned to MIRS; four were assigned to other duties at PO Box 1142; four were sent to London; four were assigned to the European theater of operations; and six were assigned to the Fifth Army.

In keeping with its original intent, the army retained seven of its first class graduates to serve as instructors at Camp Ritchie. Lieutenant Kenneth D. Koch became an instructor in Terrain Intelligence (Section 1), while Captain Christo T. Mocas served as an instructor in Military Intelligence (Section 7). Still, not a few Ritchie instructors were frustrated by their assignments as teachers. The foreign-born graduates were especially eager to get abroad to put their training into active service on or near the European theater of operations. An anonymous poem called "Ritchie-Bitchie" gave expression to this frustration:

> *Cheer up friend, the war is young yet,*
> *Maybe there will be a chance*
> *When the Second Front is opened*
> *And you do your stuff in France.*
>
> *Just sit tight and count your blessings;*
> *Maybe Ritchie will burn down,*
> *And you'll join the Great Invasion*
> *Far away from Hagerstown.*

The French-born captain John Brinkerhoff Jackson had composed the earliest version of "Ritchie-Bitchie" while enrolled in the first class. He had no problem getting his chance to "join the Great Invasion," however; he was sent to North Africa as an interrogator of German prisoners.

One graduate had particular reason to be frustrated in his desire to use his interrogation/interpretation skills in the European theater. Leroy

Henry Woodson, the sole African American enrolled in the first class, soon discovered that the army did not appear to know what to do with its Black officers. He was assigned to staff and faculty at Camp Ritchie, where he performed a variety of activities, first teaching the Terrain Intelligence course and then taking on such duties as being in charge of "Prisoner of War stories and personnel on all Intelligence problems" and assisting in writing and directing an Intelligence demonstration held in December 1942 for all G-2s (military intelligence staff) at Camp Ritchie. He then was sent from Ritchie to join the Black Ninety-Second Division as an assistant in the G-2 section. Here he assisted in setting up and teaching in the Division Intelligence School at Fort McClellan, Alabama, before moving to Fort Huachuca, Arizona, as intelligence officer in the Coast Artillery Corps, Ninety-Second Infantry Division Headquarters. After fifteen months of being shuffled around, Woodson declared himself "completely 'stymied' by a War Department ruling . . . to the effect that Negro Officers will not be promoted to positions where they will have command of white officers." Woodson pleaded that he be allowed to go overseas and serve in the European theater, protesting that his training was deteriorating in a setting where he had no opportunity to practice his German and French interrogation skills. He began to think that he might have a better chance of serving abroad if he were involved with air force intelligence. "I have a burning desire to get into the 100th Pursuit Squadron or subsequent all-Negro squadrons, where my training would be useful," he wrote to Truman Gibson, civilian aide to the secretary of war.[11] Gibson forwarded his letter to Air Intelligence, recommending that Woodson be assigned to a Negro bomber group or the 332nd Fighter Group. The petition was rejected.

But as the conditions of the war changed, so, too, did the assignments of the Camp Ritchie graduates. At last, in July 1944, the Ninety-Second Infantry Division was ordered to Italy, where, as the only Black infantry division to see combat in Europe, it served as part of the Fifth Army's Italian campaign. Following his war service, Woodson earned his doctorate from Catholic University and became a professor of German, but he also retained his position as an officer in reserve. During the mid-1950s, he returned to Europe, this time to serve the State Department as screening officer at the Paris embassy, where he decided the fate of refugees applying for permission to enter the United States.

Paul Maldal Birkeland served as an instructor at Ritchie for several months before receiving an assignment in Europe to serve as assistant military attaché at the American embassy to the Allied governments in exile in London. These exiled governments included Norway, Poland, Czechoslovakia, Holland, and Belgium. Birkeland was uniquely qualified, since he was the son of a US diplomat and, through his father's assignments, had grown up living in many European countries, including Poland. He worked with the intelligence staff of the Norwegian government in exile and, because of his near native fluency in the Polish language, also with the Polish General Staff Intelligence Service in the procurement of intelligence in support of the European war. For this he received two American and two Polish medals.

Birkeland spoke six foreign languages. His classmate Captain Henry C. Barringer also spoke six languages and would go on to a distinguished thirty-year career as a foreign service officer. After his graduation from Camp Ritchie, he was assigned first to the Military Intelligence Service, then later to Bletchley Park, England, where wooden huts had been constructed on the nineteenth-century estate grounds to serve as the Allies' principal center for code breaking. It was a British endeavor, with restricted access granted to its American Allies. Barringer was one of the very few Americans assigned to work there, as a translator of deciphered German codes. Later he joined General Patton's army as interrogator of German prisoners of war.

After V-E Day—May 8, 1945—many of the first class graduates continued their work on the Continent, although they were now interrogating German civilians, not POWs, to determine their eligibility for state positions. The Germans who did not fit this criteria were sent to denazification camps. One of the Ritchie graduates, Jovan M. Obradovic, died while performing this service. He had been assigned to the headquarters of the Nineteenth Corps for the duration of the war and had been awarded a Bronze Star for his service in France, Belgium, and Germany. But on July 13, 1945, two months after the close of hostilities, he "experienced a critical situation which resulted in loss of life." His death was described as "DNB," or "Died Non-Battle," and he was buried in the American cemetery in Normandy.[12]

Walter H. Rapp had been a lawyer prior to coming to Camp Ritchie; this made him a particularly effective interrogator. Among those he questioned was Hermann Göring, a man second only to Hitler in power and influence during much of the Nazi period. Later, from 1946 through 1948, Rapp functioned as a prosecutor by serving as the director of the Evidence Division at the Office of Chief of Counsel of War Crimes at Nuremberg, Germany. His classmate Benno H. Selcke served as his deputy, and as an officer of the Nuremberg Tribunal, when Rapp was promoted to the position of deputy chief of Counsel. Rapp retired from the army as a lieutenant colonel.

Once their work was wrapped up in Germany, some Ritchie alumni, such as Sterling Ryser, Paul Birkeland, and Hubert J. Plumpe, chose to remain in national service by either remaining with the army or entering the foreign service or the CIA; others, such as Jack Dabbs, Christo Mocas, and Erhart A. Schinske, became college and university professors. The GI bill enabled many of the men to study at colleges and universities, but otherwise it is hard to say how the jobs of those men who did not opt for continued national service were shaped by their wartime experiences. Without reading too much into his career choice, it is intriguing to speculate that Conrad Reining's groundbreaking anthropological work in African studies might in some small way have first been awakened during his war service in North Africa. Christo Mocas freely admitted that his hobby of collecting and studying foreign maps arose from his assignment to MIS.

There were, of course, those whose careers seem to have been unaffected by their war work. Arthur Curtis made his career in investments and securities, while Mario Manzone became vice president and administrator of a base metals research and development laboratory in New Jersey. Indeed, some first class graduates simply returned to the work they had interrupted for army service. Henry Staudigl returned to Hollywood as a dialogue coach, color consultant, and writer. And Edwin Ruprecht returned to his hometown in Iowa to work in the lumber and hardware business.

Theodore Fuller, who helped design the Camp Ritchie curriculum. COURTESY OF KAY FULLER MITCHELL

Camp Ritchie's first section leaders. From left to right: William C. Piper, Charles R. Warndof, Theodore Fuller, Raymond E. Grazier, Rex Applegate, George Le Blanc, George O. Weber, Arthur L. Jorgenson, Delbert A. Pryor. COURTESY OF KAY FULLER MITCHELL

Members of the first class at Camp Ritchie: (1) Thomas Robbins; (2) John R. Guenard; (3) George H. Rochman; (4) John B. Jackson; (5) Werner Fischer; (6) Mario G. Manzone; (7) Kenneth D. Koch; (8) John F. Parker; (9) Young A. Neal; (10) Theodore J. Roberts; (11) Henry J. Staudigl; (12) Benno H. Selcke Jr.; (13) Hanns G. Kurth; (14) Edwin L. Ruprecht; (15) Walter H. Rapp; (16) Paul M. Birkeland; (17) Arthur W. Curtis; (18) Erhart A. Schinske; (19) Sterling R. Ryser; (20) Robert E. Walker; (21) Jack A. Dabbs; (22) Christo T. Mocas; (23) Robert L. Grosjean; (24) Leroy H. Woodson; (25) Conrad Reining; (26) John H. Brown; (27) Henry C. Barringer. COURTESY OF KAY FULLER MITCHELL

Captain John H. Brown, in German uniform, instructs Allied soldiers in England on how to detach the barrel from a German machine gun. SOURCE: NATIONAL ARCHIVES AND RECORDS ADMINISTRATION

Captain John B. Jackson interrogates a German prisoner as a noncommissioned officer takes notes. North Africa, May 6, 1943.

Walter H. Rapp studies documents at Nuremberg for the International Military Tribunal (1946).

CHAPTER THREE

The Men at Ritchie

Vas you effer at Kamp Ritchie,
Der very schönste platz of all,
Vere die sun comes up like Donner
Mit recorded Bugle Call?

Where the Privates are professors,
And the Corporals write the books.
And the Pfc's scare Captains
With their supercilious looks?

Where the sergeants all talk Hoch Deutsch,
Hindustani, Czech, or Greek,
And they all are intellectuals
In whatever tongue they speak?[1]

THERE WERE TWENTY VERSES TO THIS POEM, WHICH WERE RECALLED and recited by Ritchie Boys decades after their period of service. The implications of this poem are clear: Camp Ritchie was an international camp, a good many of its soldiers were intellectuals, and the relationship between enlisted men and officers was not the same as at other training camps.

The entire camp was "somewhat on the unusual side," to quote the German novelist Klaus Mann. He remarked that "there are conspicuously many Europeans in this camp, also Americans who were 'over there' for a long time and can speak foreign languages. In the barracks, in the 'mess hall,' in the 'P.X.' one hears Italian, German, French, Polish, Czech, Norwegian; one hears correct American only in exceptional cases."[2] Klemens von Klemperer reported that he shared his barracks with a Russian White Army veteran, a Danish butcher, an Englishman "who knows all the languages of the Middle East yet regularly forgets the passwords," an Italian, and a Frenchman.[3]

Many of the immigrants stationed at Camp Ritchie had entered the army with only the bare minimum of English. Indeed, it was often hard to decipher the English of those who became instructors at the camp and spoke a "mishmash of German and English." When Sergeant Herbert Knoblauch instructed the men in close-order drill and calisthenics, for example, his troops would sometimes request a translation after he had issued an order, or else simply carry on and add to the chaos of the drills.[4] This linguistic situation confused many of the foreigners into believing that there were very few Americans in the camp; Lieutenant Hans Habe estimated that "about 80% of the Intelligence recruits were not yet American citizens; about half of them were refugees from Hitler, and less than 5% had been born in America."[5] Habe was quite right about slightly more than 50 percent of the men trained as specialists in German Interrogation of Prisoners of War (IPW) being refugees from Hitler. Many of these men were Jewish. Habe's estimates were very much off-kilter, however, when one includes in this count the men in other areas of training at the camp. Of the men enrolled in Camp Ritchie's thirty-one classes, 56.2 percent were American born, while 19.1 percent were born in Germany or Austria, and 19.7 percent identified themselves as Jews.[6] Still, since the men at Ritchie were selected for their language skills, the Americans who were fluent in German often spoke this language with the foreign-born soldiers, and German became "the second *lingua franca* in camp." Staff Sergeant George Mandler commented that "because of the amount of German being spoken, I at least had the impression of a large proportion of the trainees being German and Austrian refugees . . . but, once in the field, the preponderance was less obvious, if it existed at all."[7]

Although the German-born soldiers were the largest majority of foreign-born soldiers in the camp, Ritchie was, according to Private George Bailey of the ninth class, "a pool—not to say 'cesspool'—of language talent; it harbored every conceivable—and in some cases inconceivable—kind of immigrant: there were barracks housing Russians, Greeks, French, Italians, Spanish, Indians (American and Hindu), Icelanders, Laplanders, Mexicans, Albanians, Ruthenians, Macedonians, Slovenians, Wends, Hungarians, Welsh, Algerians, Syrians, Montenegrins, Ceylonese, Eskimos, Tunisians, Turks, Georgians, Azerbaijani, Uzbeks, Chuvash, Cossacks, Kozakhs, Mongolians, and Basques, to name but a few."[8]

Camp Ritchie's noncommissioned American soldiers also spoke a variety of foreign languages. Some were recruited from academe when the army's short-lived Army Specialized Training Program (ASTP) was closed down early in 1944. Camp Ritchie sent recruiters to campuses throughout the nation to recruit ASTP language students. In March, 419 of them were transferred to Camp Ritchie, where they became the bulk of the eighteenth and nineteenth classes.

Many of the other American students at the camp had grown up with a foreign language and spoke without any noticeable accent. Others had spent considerable time living abroad. Colonel Banfill even saw the value to psychological warfare in having some of the trainees speak German with a pronounced American accent. Still, the army occasionally made errors regarding the linguistic abilities of its students. Alfred Meyer recalled one such case:

> *In the camp PX one day I asked the sergeant who had served me a beer why he was at Camp Ritchie. "Because I was born in Berlin," he said.*
> *"So why are you now a bar keeper in the PX?" I asked him.*
> *"Because they discovered that it was Berlin, New Hampshire," he replied. Perhaps he was pulling my leg; perhaps it was true.*[9]

An even greater linguistic snafu at Camp Ritchie occurred when Private Baldwin T. Eckel reported for duty as a fluent speaker of Japanese. The sergeant at the desk informed him, "We don't have Japanese here," and assigned him to the German section—probably because of his German-sounding last name. Amazingly, Eckel was able to graduate from the sixth class without knowing any German at all. He managed this feat because his training partner, an Austrian, was able to help him out: "When it came to interrogation, I asked the questions. The Austrian would put them into German. The Austrian would give me the answers in English and we would write them down. Nobody complained, so we graduated with superlative ratings as interrogators after five weeks of study." Still, Eckel told a superior officer he did not know enough German to be of any use on a German interrogation team. When he continued to assert that he knew Japanese, not German, he was sent to the camp's psychiatric ward, because his ratings as a German interrogator seemed to belie his assertions. A civilian psychiatrist confirmed that Eckel was "delusional," and Eckel was not released until the former US military attaché to Japan intervened and got him transferred to the Army Japanese Language School at Camp Savage.[10]

The foreign-born soldiers looked especially favorably on their Mormon, or Church of Jesus Christ of Latter-day Saints, colleagues. These men—all Americans—had the benefit of having performed missionary service abroad and, through that service, having acquired both the linguistic and the cultural literacy that qualified them for service in military intelligence. They were well liked; as Second Lieutenant George Frenkel put it, they "were all exemplary people, very nice people, well behaved, good fellow soldiers. I can't say any unkind word about them."[11] Master Sergeant Hugh Nibley, of the seventh class, was one of these Mormon soldiers; he was particularly well qualified for intelligence service, since he "spoke sixteen languages tolerably well" and had a "nodding linguistic acquaintanceship [that] included twice that number."[12]

The vast number of languages spoken at the camp inspired a small group of soldiers to go to the Post Exchange, listen in on conversations, and identify all the languages they heard spoken there. A group of Ritchie pranksters decided to invent their own artificial language of some two hundred words, "enough for a limited conversation and just enough to pique the curiosity of [these] overhearers." Great effort was taken to avoid any similarities with European and Asiatic languages, and the men felt well rewarded by having the linguists come to them and "humbly ask which language was being spoken."[13]

The numbers of any given nationals fluctuated according to the immediate demands of the war. Norwegians were brought in to train for a possible invasion of the continent through Norway. The camp brought in Arabs as well, in preparation for an invasion through North Africa. Technician Third Grade David Chavchavadze noticed a Spanish section and guessed that its students must be there in case the United States would invade Spain, "or be allowed to pass through Spain to get at the Germans. They were all Puerto Ricans, they had an awful lot of rank, and most of them were named Rodriguez."[14]

Technical Sergeant Leon Edel recalled that during his time in Camp Ritchie (late 1943), "the Italian GIs showed much depression. Italy had come apart in 1943, and was being reconquered. It looked as if their linguistic proficiency might not be used. Back to infantry."[15] Sure enough, the Italians "did not last long. On the third day they marched out of Ritchie with real, honest-to-God M-1 rifles slung on their shoulders, waving at us with sheepish, unhappy faces, pointing at the weapons which had become so unfamiliar for Ritchie inmates. The Italians were needed in a hurry for the invasion of Sicily."[16]

The war's immediate needs could, in fact, change from one day to the next. This situation inevitably had an effect on the placement of camp recruits. Lieutenant William Sloane Coffin related a conversation he had one evening with his former German teacher:

He told me that two months before the camp had been invaded by Turks, in response to some order to rush all Turkish-speaking personnel to Ritchie. No sooner had they all gathered . . . than whatever it was Washington had in mind for them to do was canceled. That was why the motor pool was [now] run entirely by Turks. A similar reason accounted for the camp's laundry being handled exclusively by Arabs.[17]

In similar fashion, troops were sometimes returned to Ritchie from the front, to serve as instructors, to enroll in one of the Ritchie classes, or to serve as "enemy combatants" in the demonstrations put on by the camp's Composite School Unit. Native Americans were sent there from North Africa; Japanese Americans (Nisei) came to Ritchie after performing with extraordinary heroism on the battlefields of Italy and Germany.

It was part of the program to have the new noncommissioned soldiers (noncoms) who would be entering Camp Ritchie's classes work at least for their first full week at "slave labor": in the mess hall, on cleaning duty, and, in one case, on building a pier out into Lake Royer. During this period, the men had to wear fatigues rather than the pressed uniforms required of them in the classroom. This was the notorious "Company E," a "holding company for a huge conglomeration of linguistically qualified yardbirds, many of them Ph.D's, who were fair game for every lousy detail in camp while waiting for a class to start in the Combat Intelligence School (Companies F and G)." These men received their assignments from Master Sergeant Frank Leavitt. He was known to all of them as the flamboyant former wrestler "Man Mountain Dean," and he had the power of arbitrarily deciding who would get which work assignment. "Down through the decades rings the stentorian voice of Master Sergeant ('Man-mountain') Dean," one recalled, saying, "'Alright, you guys! I don't want to see anything but elbows and asses all day!'"[18] When the Black linguist Daniel Skinner was assigned to work on the garbage truck alongside a Franco-American soldier named André, the two men "tried to overcome the stench of garbage pails by reciting lines from Villon, Hugo, and Baudelaire."[19] Technical Sergeant Max Horlick was luckier: during his month-long wait for the start of his class, his task was "picking up cigarette [butts] until mid morning . . . then hiding in the furnace room."[20]

There were odd juxtapositions in this labor company. Klaus Mann reported that he worked side by side there with the Italian sculptor Count Sforza-Galeazzo ("Sforzino") Sforza: "two promising privates, [who] did KP together and discussed world affairs."[21] David Chavchavadze described going off KP duty one evening and meeting as his night shift replacement Dr. Walter Hasenclever, his old German teacher at Andover Academy. "'My God, Dr. Hasenclever,' I mumbled. 'Considering ze zircumstances,' he replied, 'you may call me Walter.'"[22] William Sloane Coffin Jr. told about how, when he first arrived at the camp, Sergeant Leavitt took him to the mess kitchen and pointed out to him the royalty at work there. Coffin seems to have condensed a number of visits to the kitchen when he claimed that he saw "Private Bourbon," who was busily scrubbing the insides of a giant vat; a "Hapsburg," who was involved in similar work; and David Chavchavadze (a Russian prince descended from Tsar Nicholas I) and Chinghiz Guireya (a Circassian sultan-prince), who were sweeping the floors.[23] The heavier work, the "ash and trash" detail, was performed by "the brawn boys, usually groups of African Americans who weren't linguists."[24] Meanwhile, the American aristocracy—David Rockefeller, Archie Roosevelt Jr.—were exempted from these tasks, since they came to Ritchie as commissioned officers.

As in all army camps, there were educational distinctions among the Ritchie students, but the camp held unusually high numbers of men with advanced academic degrees—and high IQs. Master Sergeant Robert Sternberg reported that the Ritchie students had "extremely high IQs—minimum 110, highest 150, average 127."[25] Still, fluency in a critical foreign language trumped all other considerations. Technician Fourth Grade Earl Prebezac, for example, described himself as "an 18-year-old who dropped out of HIGH school at age 15: immature, uneducated, provincial, and semiliterate; I didn't know what the word INTELLECTUAL meant . . . nor could I spell it. I could, however, speak and understand a few SLAVIC languages."[26] This prioritizing of special linguistic skills meant that deliverymen, day laborers, and short order cooks mingled in the barracks and the classroom with men who had distinguished themselves in academia, media, and the arts. This could create odd pairings for class assignments. As Prebezac wrote about his partner in Ritchie's field exercises:

> [Master Sergeant] Dave [Seymour] was a mature, intelligent, worldly, well educated, multi-lingual, intellectual and a skilled photographer. HE DID NOT LIKE THE ARMY. . . .
>
> I LIKED THE ARMY, and I was disappointed when I was transferred from the 101st Cavalry Regiment at Ft. Devens, Mass to This School in Md. (I loathed school).
>
> How were two disparate personalities such as Dave and I selected and thrown together for this Military Adventure? By Punch Cards . . . a forerunner of the modern day computer.[27]

In Prebezac's case, the match with Seymour may have proved beneficial. Prebezac was trained in photo and aerial intelligence, and after the war, the man who'd hated school went on to college and then made a career teaching high school history.

The Ritchie men who were intellectuals rather than ardent soldiers were often an embarrassment to the men who engaged them in basic military training. First Lieutenant Archie Roosevelt, who admitted that he himself was "patently unfit" to teach military skills, found himself a platoon leader at Camp Ritchie's subcamp in Gettysburg, Pennsylvania, where he was to supervise the enlisted men in firing, bayonet practice, and close-order drill. He thought it "criminal" for the army to be sending "these barely trained, miscast intellectuals to their death."[28]

The unmilitary sensitivities of the soldiers made even the most routine assignments a challenge. As Klemens von Klemperer, a twenty-six-year-old staff sergeant from Berlin, noted in a letter to a friend, "I often fancy myself to be a soldier, but it is not so. Today I was sent out on patrol, and through my binoculars I was supposed to observe 'the enemy' on a faraway hill. But soon the binoculars turned away from the hill and focused on the cherry blossoms and meadows nearby. I was reminded of some Dürer etchings that I have seen."[29]

There were also tensions among those with differing viewpoints, ethnicities, or personal histories. George Bailey noted that the Europeans were "naturally if indulgently disdainful of most of what was native American. But it was the exuberance—the naïve enthusiasm—of the American [officers] that taxed the Ritchie men most sorely." William Sloane Coffin felt similarly, remarking that he "liked the people at Camp Wheeler more than I did the highly educated Ritchie-ites. Intellectually they intimidated me and their sophisticated cynicism about everything military made me feel uncomfortable about my own enthusiasm for army life. Besides, they were hardly a humble crowd."[30] Even the French scholar Leon Edel found that the "German writers among us [were] a bit arrogant and aggressive," although "always imaginative and intelligent." But he was "put off by a certain Germanic heaviness, an excessive use of cultural references and German philosophy."[31] Best-selling novelist and technical sergeant Stefan Heym was one of these somewhat "arrogant"

German writers. Commenting on some of the American officers serving above him, he observed:

> *It is only among the officers that there are no experts of any kind; one speaks Italian, another some German, nothing more. That creates a strange, not very healthy relationship between the officers, or at least some of them, and the men in training. The officers have evidently been ordered to go easy on the gentlemen artists; on the other hand their feeling of inferiority towards these men causes a resentment toward them of which they are perhaps not even aware.*[32]

Eric Bondy explained the cause of some of this friction by pointing out that "at the time the Army did not want German refugees or recent refugees from Germany being officers in the Army, so that the lieutenants in the office were usually German speaking or poorly German speaking from places like Milwaukee."[33] Fortunately, this situation would change later in the war.

Many of the recent European émigrés, surprised at meeting one another in a US Army camp, formed a clique not open to many of the American-born Ritchie trainees. This exclusion could only add to the Americans feeling that the Europeans were snobs. James Mims, a Texan assigned to Photo Analysis, remarked, "There are so many of Hitler's children here who have terrific accents and think America owes them a living. They figure being specialists, they shouldn't do a thing."[34] In addition, "For some reason few of them had had basic training and therefore had no soldier skills. We felt that they were selfish and goldbricks and generally found them not compatible."[35] In defense, European aristocratic, Russian-born count and technician fourth grade Igor Cassini stated that "it was drummed into us by the Army itself that we were a special baby and would have special care."[36]

Even among the émigrés there were wide discrepancies in political orientation. Some were liberals, some Communists or Communist sympathizers, some pacifists, some religious conservatives, some even nationalists. They held lively discussions about how the Allies should deal with Germany after its final defeat, such as whether there should be mass punishments of the Germans or universal re-education programs and, if the latter, who should administer them. There was also the question as to whether Germany should be governed by occupying Allied forces or be given its independence. The Americans at Ritchie were far less likely to get involved in these debates; they were simply interested in getting the job done.

Private George Bailey noted that the German-born soldiers did recognize the American army's superiority in matériel and the mechanical aptitude of the American-born students. "They acknowledged and approved of American strength, wealth, and organization while amusedly deprecating our lack of culture, our naïveté, and our psychological crudeness," he recalled. "We were the Romans, they were the Greeks."[37]

The foreign-born soldiers also took note of the racial, ethnic, and religious prejudices that were prevalent in the United States. The American soldiers took no notice of the African Americans serving in positions requiring strength and stamina, and the Blacks at the camp were housed and fed separately from the other service cadres. The Native Americans, too, had segregated quarters at Ritchie. They were more visible to the soldiers, however, because they took on the roles of enemy combatants in the trainees' various field exercises. The only African American that most soldiers ever remembered seeing at the camp was the aspiring opera singer William Warfield. He held the rank of sergeant, oversaw the camp's theater and recreational facilities, and played or sang at Sunday services in the Camp Ritchie chapel. With his knowledge of French, Italian, and German, he conversed easily with the soldiers during their off-hours. There were at least forty-eight Black soldiers assigned to classwork at the camp, several of them foreign born. One was the Haitian folk artist François Des Pres. Another was an occupation child of the First World War, who spoke German with "a pure Cologne accent."[38] Earl Prebezac remembered that there was "a Giant of a 'negro'" in his barracks:

This black man's presence was quite perplexing to many of us . . . especially those from the South. However, in time, we learned he was an immigrant from West Africa and a Muslim. . . . I do believe he was pretty much isolated from us all . . . by choice. Furthermore, he had a run-in with our immediate commander and the Mess officer . . . complaining that he was starving because the food he received was not in agreement with his faith. Most of us were not sympathetic to his problems since G.I.'s of other faiths received dispensations for eating restricted foods.[39]

Fortunately, Colonel Banfill, the Ritchie commander, was focused on the camp's mission and showed no preferences based on color or religion. Once he was made aware of the problem, he made it possible for the Muslims at the camp to eat halal.

William Warfield recalled an episode where Banfill's authority even made it possible for a Black sergeant to give an order to a white captain:

Col. Ban[fill] had a thing about making the camp beautiful, and that included seeding the lawn and planting flowers. He made it clear to me that he'd hold me responsible for the landscaping around the theater as well as for the theater itself.

I had [an] encounter of the Camp Ritchie kind, with an officer who wanted to take a short cut across our yard. . . . I literally ordered the captain (in a polite voice) to use the sidewalk.

"Who in hell are you, Sergeant, to tell a captain what to do?" he demanded. . . . "Standing orders, Captain," I told him. "Would you rather talk to Col. Ban[fill] about it?" The captain waved me off— orders were orders—and followed the signs around the grass, the way he was supposed to.[40]

Only occasionally were there actual physical confrontations at the camp that turned violent. Sergeant Klaus Mann prepared a report on one such occasion about an anti-Semitic sergeant:

[Private Albert] Wolf was alone—on the way from the main "P.X." store down to the cellar bar—when the sergeant suddenly shouted at him: "You're a Jew, one of those refugees. Whenever I see a Jew, I feel like punching his nose." Wolf, although of course considerably shocked, thought it wiser not to answer at all. But the sergeant followed him

downstairs and, in the cellar bar, attacked him physically. Other
men interfered, warning the sergeant that he might lose his rank
on account of his conduct. The aggressor, more and more infuriated,
reacted to these admonitions by tearing the stripes from his sleeves, as
a gesture of defiance and anger. Then he attacked Wolf again.[41]

Despite the welcome many Jewish refugees found in the United States, they were aware of prejudices and restrictions against Jews—such as student quotas at universities and exclusion from membership in country clubs—that existed even here.

There was even a violent confrontation between two Native Americans stationed at Ritchie. Their tribes were involved in a long-standing blood feud, and it didn't take long before one of the men was found murdered.[42] Another Native American, a Navaho, was found drowned in Lake Royer; the reason behind his death was never made known.

Such instances of violence were rare, however, and most of the Ritchie men remained firmly focused on their mission. Indeed, the feature of Camp Ritchie most remarked upon by its participants was the fluidity between officers and enlisted men in the classrooms, and between teachers and students. This led to a more relaxed, less "military" atmosphere at the camp. One soldier described the training at the camp as "hard and rigorous, especially mentally," but at the same time "without excessive discipline (everything is very informal)."[43]

Like most army camps, Camp Ritchie had separate quarters, separate mess hall, and separate recreation facilities for its officers. These included an officers' club house with a bar, dining room, and around twenty guest rooms. Lieutenant Walter Bodlander was delighted with the living situation: "A magnificent lounge, opulently furnished, faced the lake and small beach. Beautifully landscaped walkways led to the many cabanas in which we, the officers, were quartered—four to a cottage—each with our private bath and bedroom." He learned only much later that the accommodations for the enlisted men were "harsh and unpleasant" in comparison and admitted that during his time at Camp Ritchie he "was completely unconcerned and probably unaware of the injustice of it all."[44]

In the schools and classrooms, however, officers and enlisted men were integrated. "Even colonels and generals had to adjust to the sometimes upside-down hierarchies of Camp Ritchie life," William Warfield remembered. "All our students, whether wearing a single stripe or a shiny star, had to follow the directions of instructors who were often corporals and sergeants. Rank didn't carry over into the classroom."[45] If a noncommissioned officer had a special skill, he was made a class instructor. George Mandler was impressed both by the Camp Ritchie program and by its esprit de corps, remarking that there was "a degree of enthusiasm and hard work rarely seen elsewhere."[46] Lieutenant Ed Linville remembered, "We were officers and gentlemen even though the student body was mixed with noncoms and commissioned officers in class together. . . . Everyone was treated rationally and in a remarkably unmilitary manner."[47] Robert Sternberg summed up the situation, noting, "The discipline was lax—for somebody who had infantry training."[48]

A gathering of proud Texas A&M grads, all of them officers serving at Camp Ritchie. COURTESY OF KAY FULLER MITCHELL

Some of the Composite School Unit boys relaxing at Lake Royer. SOURCE: WESTERN MARYLAND REGIONAL LIBRARY, MARYLAND STATE ARCHIVES

Composite School Unit men in their Camp Ritchie barracks. SOURCE: WESTERN MARY-
LAND REGIONAL LIBRARY, MARYLAND STATE ARCHIVES

An MP gets a shave in
off-hours. SOURCE: WESTERN
MARYLAND REGIONAL LIBRARY,
MARYLAND STATE ARCHIVES

Chapter Four

The Composite School Unit

*When we had at last passed through the gate of an Army camp . . . I
thought I was dreaming. A company of uniformed SS men marched
past us. A German staff car . . . rattled past, with two German officers sitting stiffly in the back. A moment later we met three or four
Japanese soldiers. In the field on our right a whole Japanese company
was drilling, while the outlines of a German tank appeared in the
distance before us.*[1]

In addition to those servicemen who rotated in and out of
Camp Ritchie as members of the eight-week classes or those who came
for intense instruction in a specific area of study, there was a sizable
semipermanent cadre of men who provided visual instructional support
by demonstrating both Allied and Axis uniforms, weaponry, vehicles, and
battle and interrogation techniques. Known as the Composite School
Unit, or CSU, it eventually consisted of 420 enlisted men and ten to
thirteen officers. When the unit was first founded by Colonel Theodore
A. Fuller as a demonstration battalion, its one hundred members were all
designated for German army demonstrations. They were housed at first
in pyramidal tents on concrete slabs until they were moved into permanent new barracks on the mountainside above the main camp. There they
operated independently, with their own cooks, drivers, clerks, and supply
personnel. They studied German and, later, Japanese army organization,
weaponry, and tactics, in order to demonstrate all kinds of enemy army
operations effectively to the camp trainees.

Their commanding officer was Leonard McNutt, an infantry lieutenant who had spent part of his childhood growing up on a Texas ranch. He was transferred to Ritchie from the Infantry School in Fort Benning, Georgia, where he had completed its tactical course of study. His childhood experiences in Texas proved useful in his new post, since the Ritchie CSU maintained 126 horses in order to simulate German and Japanese troop movements. These horses had been brought to Ritchie from the Front Royal Remount Depot in Virginia. As the first cadre members learned, the animals had not been ridden in a long time, since the United States, unlike Germany and Japan, no longer maintained active horse cavalry units. As Bill Lewis, one of the early cadre members, recalled it, "An old cavalry sergeant tried to convince [us] that [we] had nothing to fear from the half-broken, wild-eyed mounts, but he failed in this when one of the animals kicked him in the stomach."[2] Twenty servicemen were assigned to care for the animals. During the first winter, the horses were housed at the Hagerstown racetrack, and the men exercised the horses by racing them there. Once the stables were erected at Camp Ritchie, and the horses had been retrained, Lewis and his comrades deployed their "German" unit of more than one hundred men in playing out various scenarios not only in front of the Camp Ritchie students but also before visiting audiences of various S-2 and G-2 sections. In addition to horses, the CSU maintained a variety of motorized vehicles and airplanes for their demonstrations. They also had a large collection of enemy uniforms, small arms, antiaircraft guns, and field artillery. For some of their field demonstrations, they represented units of troops on bicycles and motorcycles. They even traveled by raft on Lake Royer.

Dogs were also brought into Camp Ritchie during the early days of the Military Intelligence Training Center—not to serve as demonstration animals, but rather to be trained for guard and sentry duty. CSU member Lawrence Hartnett, a cavalry man, noted with amusement that the army sent along a single guard dog with its shipment of dog houses. "This dog was captured," he recalled. "He only understood German. You couldn't tell him to sit or anything; it had to be in German."[3] Fortunately, this was not a problem with the animals that followed him; most were American dogs that had been donated to the war effort by their owners.

They were trained at Ritchie for service on the United States' eastern and western coastlines, where they would patrol the beaches and alert their handlers to any potential landing of saboteurs. The canine initiative at Ritchie was relatively short-lived, and the program was transferred to Fort Robinson, Nebraska.

The men came to the CSU from many different venues. Thirty-seven of them were locals. Some were assigned, as McNutt was, from other camps or even from active service abroad. Others were former trainees from Ritchie, who had either received unsatisfactory grades or been declared unfit for full field duty. Still other men were selected to serve in the Composite School Unit because of special skills that were particularly useful to its program; this included people with a film or theater background who were assigned to its Visual Demonstration Section. Also, as it became clear that the main invasion into Europe would occur through France, some of the men originally being trained for maneuvers in Norway and Holland were reassigned to the teaching cadre.

Because of these reassignments, many members of the Composite School Unit had the same credentials as students in the camp. "Seventeen members [of the German unit] were European refugees, some spoke as many as 5–6 languages," McNutt later recalled. One instructor was even a former German soldier.[4] To lend reality to their actions, the men in the unit sang German songs as they marched. Master Sergeant Joseph Simon, a Jew who had emigrated from Austria, was startled to see these troops march through the camp gate "singing defiantly: 'Germany belongs to us today, tomorrow the whole world.'" This was the official song of the Hitler Youth. Simon said he also heard the "Panzerlied" (Tank Song) and other Nazi songs for the first time at Camp Ritchie.[5]

African Americans were part of the permanent cadre at Ritchie; they transported weaponry from one site to another with horse-drawn carts, and served as ammunition carriers. They did not participate actively in maneuvers, and there were not large numbers of them at the camp. Native American soldiers were part of the CSU's firearms platoons— about two hundred, as one trainee recalled it.[6] Even though they, like the Blacks, were housed in segregated barracks removed from the white men's quarters, the Ritchie trainees took far more notice of them, since these Indians—Navaho, Apache, Cherokee, Fox, and Sioux—provided support to the teaching faculty by taking on the role of enemy combatants in the camp's various field exercises, as well as by demonstrating enemy uniforms and battle tactics. They played this role in all the staged combats, as German, Italian, and Japanese soldiers.

The Composite School Unit was divided into ten demonstration platoons: Headquarters, First Rifle, Second Rifle, 30 Cal. Machine Gun, 81 Mortar, Anti-Tank, Engineer, Artillery, Mounted Infantry, and Interrogation. All platoons were trained to work in their own specialty; however, each platoon was also trained to work in rifle, machine gun, bicycle, and motorcycle units. Although all the platoons had their normal US Army weapons and equipment, their main objective was to show the Ritchie trainees "all types of enemy organization and tactics . . . and to permit students to operate in the field against Japanese and German tactics." In addition to representing practically every kind of enemy unit from a squad to a company, the demonstration troops depicted "the various elements of the combat echelons of German and Japanese Divisional and Regimental Troops."[7] They consistently employed German or Japanese tactics and equipment.

Part of their function was simply to give the Ritchie students the training necessary to visualize given enemy units in all types of war situations. Through this process, students learned the characteristics and capabilities of the weapons used in the German army. The CSU men provided complete crews, in numbers and in strength, for all their demonstrations. A German mounted infantry platoon, for example, demonstrated the strength and armaments of a reconnaissance unit. This was true of the motorcycle platoon, as a battalion of a German Panzer division, and the German bicycle platoon, as that part of a German Mountain division employed, like the mounted infantry, as an element of reconnaissance.

In addition to exercises in the demonstration of enemy weapons and unit strength, the CSU constructed a German strongpoint—"a German island of resistance with its wire entanglements, revetted emplacements, and crew-served weapons"[8]—to show German field principles currently at play.

There were also unique demonstrations of Japanese defense systems. In a heavily wooded and marshy area of the camp, intended to give the impression of jungle, actual defense positions, camouflage, perimeter of defense, spider traps, pillboxes, obstacles and entanglements, communications trenches, and bunkers were constructed for demonstrations of jungle warfare. Cross slit trenches and individual foxholes were constructed in open country to give the trainees knowledge of defensive techniques in open terrain. The most innovative addition to the CSU demonstration of Japanese war tactics was the employment of ruses introduced into all the Japanese field problems. These included dummy snipers and soldiers playing dead; faking surrender; using barking dogs and herds of cattle to draw attention; dressing in British, Dutch, and American uniforms; faking machine-gun fire; talking in loud, slang-ridden English; and raising white flags of false truce.

All the CSU platoons were involved in observation demonstrations offered at night, in daylight, and at dawn. The night demonstrations made use of all types of sights and sounds to help the trainee interpret the nature, direction, and distance of battle sights and sounds: rifle fire, ground and aerial flares, flashlights, moving motorcycles, half-tracks, wagons, horse units, and, finally, the actual firing of all types of German, Japanese, and American light and heavy weapons. The purpose of these demonstrations was to train soldiers to identify enemy action and weaponry by sound alone.

Daylight exercises focused on the students' power to estimate range, search the ground, and identify enemy units and emplacements. Here, too, the enemy activity included gun and artillery fire, motorcycle and horse-drawn artillery columns, and smoke shells, with the addition of hidden mortar positions and concealed tanks and personnel carriers. The CSU participated as American, German, or Japanese personnel, using the appropriate equipment, depending upon the type of terrain required.

Members of the CSU also portrayed prisoners of war: German, Italian, and Japanese. These men were all fluent in their languages, although the Ritchie trainees in the German section noted that some spoke German with a bad American accent. These "prisoners" dressed in German uniforms and carried the documentation normally found on

German soldiers. Other CSU men took on the roles of informants and interpreters so that students could learn how to collect information from informants by working through an interpreter.

For all these demonstrations, the camp collected large numbers of enemy weaponry and uniforms, much of it left over from the North African campaign. A closer look usually revealed that the uniforms did not always fit the men of the teaching cadre. There was a greater problem in acquiring the vehicles of war. Since it was impossible to obtain the complete gamut of tanks and motorized vehicles necessary for their demonstrations, some dummy tanks were built of plywood and mounted on jeeps and trucks. Still, when called upon, the CSU men could put on a remarkable show. Lieutenant McNutt recalled that when President Roosevelt's secretary of war, Henry L. Stimson, brought some generals from the Pentagon to Camp Ritchie in late 1942 as part of an inspection tour, Colonel Banfill asked McNutt to "show them something." McNutt "led a parade as a German General on horseback, followed by a German goose stepping platoon, German bicycle and motorcycle, cavalry, horse drawn artillery and machine gun platoons and various German vehicles." Secretary Stimson "was amazed at what he saw," and the next day orders came through from one of the generals promoting McNutt to captain. McNutt joked that Roosevelt's secretary of war had personally promoted him.[9]

In preparation for these various demonstrations in American, German, and Japanese organization, tactics, and weaponry, the CSU platoon members had to study these subjects, make plans based on them, and rehearse repeatedly. As the CSU booklet put it, "Every duty day and approximately twenty nights each month will find the Composite School Unit busy in garrison or field—studying, drilling, rehearsing, demonstrating, or instructing in Military Intelligence subjects."

Finally, in addition to the CSU's many outdoor visual demonstrations, which had either commentary or fluid tactical dialogue, the Visual Demonstration's Section 9 staged indoor mini-dramas with fixed scripts. At first Colonel Theodore Fuller wrote, produced, and directed these plays, despite initial skepticism among his "more conventional" senior officers.[10] They became accepted, however, and Fuller then turned the work over to professional theater people. These men were brought to

Camp Ritchie specifically for their work in these playlets. This was an enviable assignment, since these professionals were assigned to Ritchie for the duration of the war. Many of them were figures known from Hollywood or the Broadway stage: Joseph Anthony, Curt Conway, Owen Davis Jr., for example, as well as Larney Goodkind, story editor for Universal Pictures. Anthony Russo, a vocalist with the Xavier Cugat Band, entered Camp Ritchie with the fifth class but was then transferred into the Visual Demonstration Section.[11] Paul Stockdale Ousley was apparently assigned to this section because of his theatrical performances in high school and at Swarthmore College; his college yearbook called him the "biggest Thespian on Campus" and a "constant singer of any song with anyone," whose "store of weird accents and lines are [a] guarantee against boredom."[12] In addition to the playlets composed for them, these singer performers often entertained area guests at special performances in the camp theater.

Joseph Anthony and Owen Davis Jr. served the Visual Demonstration Section as both actors and playwrights. WAC captain Helene Stoumen Potamkin held the position of Camp Ritchie's theater officer, and she remarked, on the occasion of Owen Davis Jr.'s death, that his "writing, acting, and directing of the demonstrations was instrumental in making it one of the most famous features of Camp Ritchie and one sought after by top Army Schools for Instruction in Intelligence methods."[13] The men in Section 9 took these plays on the road and performed them regularly at Fort Leavenworth, Kansas, and at more than a dozen other military schools and bases around the country, especially in the larger camps where soldiers were preparing for departure from the United States. As of October 1945, the number of demonstration performances exceeded three hundred, and the total attendance was more than 225,000.

The playlets were performed for every class at Camp Ritchie at the completion of its eight-week course of study; they were intended to dramatize the basic lessons the students had learned in their classes. This was demonstrated by their titles: *Photo Interpretation*, *Interrogation of POWs*, *Military Intelligence Interpreters*, and *Battalion Command Post*. The plays were regularly rewritten to keep their messages up to date. Thus the skit called *Hitler's Secret Weapon*, written to demonstrate the ease with which German spies could pick up valuable information from just one casual slip of the tongue, treated this theme in a variety of settings. In one version of the script, an apparently harmless old woman overhears a soldier's conversation and unknowingly passes the information on to the enemy.[14] In another version, a soldier and his buddies go to a bar just before shipping out to Europe. There one of them casually mentions that he and his fellow soldiers are departing for Europe the next day; a German spy hears this detail, passes it on, and, as a result of this slipup, the troop transport ship is sunk by a German submarine.[15] In this version, the classically trained Black bass-baritone William Warfield took the role of bar pianist.

In addition to writing and performing demonstration pieces for the war effort, some men in the Visual Demonstration Section got involved with producing films on Interrogation, Close Combat, House of Horrors, and such for the Office of Strategic Services (OSS) at its nearby camp in the Catoctin Mountains. And one of the Ritchie soldiers, German-born actor Peter van Eyck, acted in a US Army Air Force training film, *Resisting Enemy Interrogation*, that was produced under the auspices of the Office of War Information. The film was nominated for an Academy Award as best documentary of 1945.

Along with the mini-dramas that served as a dramatic summation of all the soldiers had learned in their classes at Camp Ritchie, the staff of the Visual Demonstration Section mounted an elaborate Nazi mass rally in the camp theater every six weeks, so that members of every Ritchie class would be able to attend the spectacle. The script was written and directed by Gordon A. Ewing, who would later become the department director of RIAS (Radio in the American Sector) in Berlin; Ewing also served as English-language commentator of the action. The rallies were based on the annual Nazi rallies held in the multipurpose Sport Palace in Berlin. The Ritchie players pulled out all the stops to make this drama as realistic as possible. Nazi flags lined the walls and stage of the theater, banners hung from the galleries, a camp band played Nazi songs (the "Horst Wessel Song," "Erika," and the "Badenweiler March"), costumed German soldiers and citizens enthusiastically gave the Hitler salute, and the major Nazi leaders held speeches. At these staged rallies, the most popular soldier to play Hitler was Private Harry I. Kahn, a pantomime artist; another successful Hitler impersonator was Major Robert B. Noack, a member of the Ritchie faculty. Joseph Anthony played Joseph Goebbels, while Hermann Göring was portrayed by the professional wrestler Man Mountain Dean (Frank Simmons Leavitt). The speeches of the Nazi leaders were constantly interrupted by loud chants of "Sieg, Heil!" which echoed beyond the walls of the theater and across the quiet valley.

An even greater spectacle took place on the final day of class instruction, when the Ritchie men gathered on the grandstand by the Counterintelligence House to see a major drama played out by the members of the Composite School Unit. In this elaborate production, which represented what the men should do when securing a German command post in France, Hanuš Burger played the role of a Frenchman. He has provided a detailed description of the spectacle: The "drama" began by showing how the Germans dealt with the French villagers—"Très correct!"—followed by the panicked and somewhat hectic activities during an American attack: "The first shells hit close by, the recorded sounds of battle came closer . . . the units at the front fled 'according to plan,' and finally came the seizure of the site through an American team."

This, however, was only the beginning, since the purpose of the presentation was to show the actions that followed seizure of a French town:

In doing this, we saw . . . how one secures documents, and how one interrogates the local population. A high French liaison officer also appeared, played by a French-speaking private first class, one learned of acts of sabotage from a French collaborator who had hidden out in the cellar. German prisoners were brought in and questioned, the new intelligence was passed on through a field telephone in code, couriers were sent out, the motor park of the camp was fully involved, in short, it was a gigantic show, a three-ring circus, which peaked precisely on cue with the overhead passage of a courier plane that tossed out a message for the intelligence officer.

The viewing public applauded this grand spectacle, in full agreement that "they had experienced an enjoyable afternoon."[16]

Weapons demonstration on the Camp Ritchie rifle range. SOURCE: NATIONAL ARCHIVES AND RECORDS ADMINISTRATION

The men study a 75 mm Howitzer Motor Carriage M8 as part of their Camp Ritchie instruction. SOURCE: WESTERN MARYLAND REGIONAL LIBRARY, MARYLAND STATE ARCHIVES

Men of the Composite School Unit portray Japanese mounted troops. SOURCE: NATIONAL ARCHIVES AND RECORDS ADMINISTRATION

An instructor explains the details of an enemy uniform. SOURCE: NATIONAL ARCHIVES AND RECORDS ADMINISTRATION

A simulated battle scene, showing German soldiers and defensive post. SOURCE: NATIONAL ARCHIVES AND RECORDS ADMINISTRATION

Simulation of a Nazi rally, with Master Sergeant Frank S. Leavitt portraying Hermann Göring. SOURCE: NATIONAL ARCHIVES AND RECORDS ADMINISTRATION

A demonstration held at Camp Ritchie's cutaway house, portraying proper methods of capture and interrogation. SOURCE: CHRISTOPHER G. NASON MILITARY INTELLIGENCE LIBRARY, FORT HUACHUCA

CHAPTER FIVE

Interrogation of Prisoners of War (IPW)

They used non-violent interrogation methods tailored for individual POWs that have since been considered the gold standard of interrogation techniques.[1]

ONE OF THE MAJOR THRUSTS OF THE GERMAN SECTION AT RITCHIE was its training program IPW, or Interrogation of Prisoners of War. Most of Ritchie's German-speaking European emigrants specialized in interrogation training; more than half of them were Jews, and they formed the core of those Ritchie trainees who referred to themselves as "Ritchie Boys." The program seems to have been based, at least in part, on lectures or "discussions" originally developed in 1942 by Sanford Griffith for the Third Army IPW school held at Camp Bullis, Texas. Griffith, who worked as a British intelligence agent in the 1930s, had been a US infantry major and POW interrogator in World War I. After the war, he had studied psychology, persuasion, and marketing for the advertising industry. The principles of good marketing melded well with principles of successful interrogation. In his third lecture,[2] Griffith outlined sixteen principles for a successful interview:

1. Try to see things from the prisoner's point of view.

2. Avoid preconceived attitudes ("All Germans are Nazis"; "They can't be trusted").

3. Germans are folks, not supermen.

4. Take an individual approach: What has he suffered? What are his wants?

5. Get at them when they are shaky; despite their ordeals, they have a will to live.

6. Intimate (e.g., religious) questions may reveal some common feelings.

7. Hide your focus of attention (don't suggest the answers you're looking for).

8. Potential relations between interviewer and prisoner: one front soldier to another; pal to pal; one good Catholic (or musician) to another.

9. Make a good first impression.

10. Make close name and interest identification.

11. "Bait the hook to suit the fish."

12. Let the prisoner tell us.

13. Don't look for repentant Nazis; do not put on an air of moral superiority.

14. Listen to prisoners' complaints.

15. Use some propaganda as a softener.

16. Give them paradoxes to worry about ("If Germans are invincible, why are you losing?").

Colonel Charles R. Warndof, who had been in charge of instruction at Camp Bullis, came to Ritchie to serve as chief of Section 5 (the German section), bringing Camp Bullis staff and instructional materials with him. He quickly won the respect of the men serving under him. "He was very, very intelligent," George Frenkel recalled. "He spoke English with quite an accent, but apparently the U.S. Army had done

one masterful thing and selected this man to be in charge of an intelligence operation when our intelligence effort, in my opinion, was very inadequate."[3]

Guy Stern remembers that the interrogation program under Warndof placed a special emphasis on five components:

1. Exhibit superior knowledge (about German military organization and individuals).

2. Serve as a friend (provide cigarettes, special privileges, etc.).

3. Introduce a subject of common interest (e.g., soccer).

4. Let the POW speak on his own subject; pick a particular one to expand on.

5. Play on the POW's sense of anxiety (e.g., threat to their families).[4]

A thorough knowledge of the German Order of Battle gave the Ritchie interrogator an immediate tool for exhibiting superior knowledge to a prisoner of war; he could begin a session by asking a prisoner a military question to which he already knew the answer. When the prisoner refused to answer, the interrogator could supply the answer himself. This would ease the prisoner's mind regarding military security, and he would then respond more readily to the questions that followed, thereby giving the interrogator the information he really wanted.

Components 2 through 4 were techniques designed to relax the prisoner and make him more likely to open up to the interrogator. The trainees recognized, right away, the effectiveness of this technique, since each of them had to go through interrogations themselves, not only so that they could understand the psychology of prisoners but also in preparation for the possibility of their being captured and questioned by German interrogators after they got to Europe.

Component 5 addressed the prisoners' very real concerns about the terms of their imprisonment, the safety of their families, and the rapid advance of the Russians from the East. The German soldiers were especially fearful of the retribution the Russians were sure to take on the

German population and of being sent by the Allies to a Russian prison camp. The Ritchie Boys learned to take advantage of that fear.

Although many of the American-born participants in the program had developed fluency in German through study, prolonged residence in Germany, or family background, the German and Austrian emigrants were uniquely suited to interrogation because they had grown up in Germany, understood the German psyche, and had cultural and sports interests in common with the enemy. At Ritchie they were taught to pick up on signals given off by a prisoner. They learned that rank alone did not dictate the approach one should take with him. Although the prisoners of war were required, by the terms of the Geneva Conventions, to give only name, rank, birthdate, and identification number, it was the task of the interrogator to coax them into giving more information either by trickery or by winning their trust. To do this, they had to make a swift calculation as to what tone to take with each prisoner. This decision might depend on the prisoner's age, background, family situation, political views, or level of education. The men were strictly forbidden—again by the dictates of the Geneva Conventions—to force prisoners to give up information, to humiliate them, or to submit them to any physical harm or injury. Indeed, they were instructed not even to touch a prisoner during interrogation. This was a difficult lesson for the German Jews who would be interrogating SS officers and concentration camp guards. Still, one of the Ritchie interrogators, Lieutenant Eric Bondy, stated after the war, "Even when I interrogated a concentration guard that you wanted to rip apart with your hands, we never touched them, and I don't think any of the other interrogators ever touched German prisoners."[5] This was a sentiment echoed by Lieutenant Hans Habe, who became a particularly adept interrogator in the North African and Italian campaigns: "After the War I read several German accounts of brutal American interrogation. While I do not wish to suggest that they are all inventions, I must say that they greatly surprised me. I did not once have to raise my voice, let alone use violence, to obtain from the prisoners all the information I wanted."[6]

In their interrogation classes, a GI would be given a soldier's pay book, so that he could use the information in it to begin an interrogation. Since these pay books listed all the captive's military assignments, they provided an easy opening to the interrogation. "One of the techniques that was drummed into us consisted of not asking any false questions and giving the prisoner no time to think about the interrogation situation," Rudy Michaels stated.[7] They had plenty of opportunity to hone these skills, since "the basic method was practice, practice, practice."[8] This training took part not only in the German section but also in the French and Italian sections.

The GIs conducted the first interrogations at Ritchie with one another. They were paired off, with one playing prisoner, the other playing interrogator. They then reversed roles. These interrogations were held in front of their class members, so that they could study their technique and critique their performances.

The next step involved questioning men from the camp's Composite School Unit who had been trained in how and when to respond to the student interrogators, and what information they should—or should not—divulge. Some of these men were American GIs with knowledge of German, but not with the degree of fluency that would make them productive members of an IPW team in the European theater. Others were MIS staff recently returned from the war; now they were pretending to be the very men they had fought, from German privates to senior officers. All these men appeared in German uniforms appropriate to their pretended ranks. Some of these interrogations were also conducted in front of the class, and they could be extremely difficult since part of the intention of the exercise was to rattle the interrogator. The "prisoners" sometimes refused to give even their name to the interrogator, in order to see whether the GI lost his temper.

One example, which did indeed cause a student officer to lose his temper, involved a "prisoner" who, when questioned about a piece of German artillery called a "Kanone," responded with lots of useless information about the army field kitchen, or "Goulasch-Kanone." One of the officer's classmates remarked, "The interrogation ended very badly because this officer was fuming, and rightfully so, because the make-believe prisoner had made a fool of him."[9]

In a more comic turn, one of the GIs began his questioning of an apparent German officer. The trained "prisoner" responded that the GI was mistaken; he was not an officer, he was the division chaplain. He then asked the GI to pray with him, and the GI, now caught totally off guard, began to pray rather than continuing the interrogation. In this case the lesson was reinforced, through laughter, that one must always be on one's guard so as not to be taken in during questioning.[10]

The CSU men enjoyed these interrogations. Sergeant Walter C. Wolff, for example, wrote to his family, "What a 'job' I have for the next eleven days! . . . I play a civilian 2 times a day and I get interrogated. For this afternoon, I was assigned the role of the owner of a whore house who wants to make an arrangement with the American army. Boy, will we have fun!"[11]

The "professional" POWs were all given specific roles to play in the mock interrogations, so that the students would encounter the different types of German they might meet on the field of battle. "Some were briefed to respond only to the subtle approach," George Bailey, from the ninth class, remembered, "some to the legalistic dismantling of the significance of their military oath, others would 'spill their guts' only when browbeaten and hectored at the top of the interrogator's lungs." Some of the men were actually professional actors. The film star Peter van Eyck assisted in the practice interrogations. It must have been disconcerting for the men to "interrogate" the man they had recently seen playing the role of a Nazi in Hollywood films. Van Eyck's character as "prisoner" was similar to that he portrayed on the screen: "He always played a high-ranking Prussian staff officer, arrogant but correct; he would respond with extremely valuable information if the interrogator could find a way to appeal to his code of honor." Bailey recalled another one of the actors, "famous throughout the camp, who was allowed to play it by ear—he could react to any interrogator whichever way he chose."[12]

The men practiced their interrogation techniques on women as well as men. Rudy Michaels recalled interrogating one woman, a Ritchie WAC named Ellen Kaufmann, who was a native German. She took on the role of a telephone operator in the German army. The soldiers had learned that when a telephone operator who served in an important German army unit was taken captive, one had a real prize, since she was "a walking telephone book," with some fifteen hundred names and telephone numbers in her head. This was information that could prove useful down the road. Sergeant Kaufmann had been informed of how she was to react to the interrogators: "If one was not friendly and didn't treat her like a gentleman, she simply began to cry and did not say another word. But when one handled her well, when one held to the rules, which she knew and we didn't, then one learned something from her." Rudy Michaels was one of the lucky ones: "She spoke with me and told me everything without stopping: telephone numbers, names, units, which company, which battalion, on and on until late in the evening."[13] Still, Michaels admitted that one always learned more through mistakes than through successes, since mistakes were an important part of the learning process.

Perhaps the most difficult interrogations were with "prisoners" speaking an extreme local dialect. Ritchie Boy Hans Vogel recalled, "The school threw some German and Austrian dialects at us that almost defied comprehension. I remember one actor who assumed the role of a PW from Austria, who was supposed to have been a farm boy from some remote village. . . . His dialect was so guttural and thick, I swear he didn't utter a single German word. As far as I was concerned, he might have been speaking Outer Mongolian."[14] It was a deliberate tactic of the Ritchie instructors to give the students the assignment of trying to elicit information from people whose speech was unintelligible to them. In some cases, Native Americans even took these roles, speaking in their native tongues.[15]

During their training, the Ritchie men were learning how to extract both tactical and strategic information from prisoners. Strategic information related to broader issues of the war; tactical related to the situation at hand. As one of the Ritchie Boys put it:

> *Tactical meaning what's going on across the river, or what unit is our unit facing. When are they planning to attack, how strong are they. That's tactics. We were also interested now, at this late stage of the game in strategic information. Again, we want to know more about do the Germans have the atom bomb? What's this V1 and V2 business? Chemical bacterial warfare. All of those things we knew nothing about. That was strategic information, and we call that detailed interrogation.*[16]

He Passed through Camp Ritchie

Second Lieutenant **Peter Skala** (1924–2017) was born Peter Pollak in Austria into a well-to-do Jewish-Catholic family in Vienna. He was, in the words of his aunt, "brought up like a little prince." Rising anti-Semitism caused Skala's father to change the family name to the more Aryan-sounding maiden name of Peter's mother, actress Lilia Skala. Three weeks after the Anschluss, Peter Skala left Vienna for good, going first to England and then to New York. He was drafted into the US Army at age eighteen. After completing the tenth class at Ritchie, he went to officer's school and then was attached to the Ninety-Fifth Division of the Third Army as leader of an IPW team.

In the battle for Metz, Skala took over leadership of a field platoon. Having learned from a captured German that the commander of Metz, General Friedrich Kittel, was wounded and lying in the basement of a heavily fortified house, Skala led his men into the house and rushed up the stairs even as grenades were being thrown down at him. He cleared out the upper stories and found the wounded

Strategic information was usually gathered from officers, often in multiple sessions with a given informant. Because the Ritchie men had learned that rank was an important issue with German soldiers, they often put on an American uniform before meeting with a captured officer that was either the equal of the prisoner or one degree higher. Because tactical information could change from hour to hour, most of the IPW teams were placed at the front, rather than somewhere in safety behind the lines.

When the interrogation program was first set up at Camp Ritchie, the men conducted interrogations with the very first German prisoners of war taken in North Africa and brought to Ritchie for that purpose. The program was still in flux, and an occasional instructor decried showing any kindness to prisoners. Such views were an exception. It became a hallmark of the Camp Ritchie interrogation program to use courtesy general, who insisted that he be allowed to surrender to a man of similar rank. Skala arranged this and then continued to battle well ahead of the front lines, securing information from the enemy and forcing the surrender of four hundred enemy troops. For this action, he received a Silver Star and a promotion to first lieutenant.

Skala's regiment—the 377th—moved on later to the Siegfried line, where Skala and his platoon received orders to attack a heavily fortified bunker. Bunker attacks inevitably resulted in the loss of American lives, but Skala had learned from a recently captured prisoner on the eve of the attack that the Germans in that bunker were sick of the war and wanted to surrender. Skala, unarmed and under no white flag, accompanied the prisoner back to his bunker and persuaded the fifteen men inside to surrender to him without a single shot being fired.

Sometime later, the war ended for Skala when he was severely wounded by machine-gun fire and evacuated from the field. He returned to the United States, went to Yale University, married, and raised a family. He worked as a key manager in several large multinational firms before becoming a successful head hunter at Boyden International Limited and spending the last forty years of his life in Europe, mostly in London.

first, rather than dominance, and trickery rather than shouting to achieve one's ends. Effective interrogations depended most on a soldier's ability to read a prisoner's psyche. Whatever tricks the interrogators played, they all had to abide by one "absolute" rule: "Don't touch. You can play whatever intellectual trick you want to play on them to make them talk, but you can't touch them."[17]

The instruction at Camp Ritchie had already improved when German prisoners of war were replaced by trained Ritchie staff. Now some of these new practice interrogations involved role reversal: during night maneuvers Ritchie men might take some "Germans" captive and question them, or else they might be captured and interrogated by the Germans. This kind of give and take was important in teaching the Ritchie men how they should behave if they were ever taken prisoner in Europe. These exercises gave them practice in how to hold back information and how to defend themselves against any psychological pressure that might be exerted by a German interrogator. At the end of the eight-week course, the Ritchie men had to conduct an interrogation with one of these trained staff members as part of their final examination. Then, upon graduation, they were formed into IPW teams, consisting of two officers and three or four enlisted men. Victor Brombert described the organization of these teams: "In addition to the captain in charge, a first lieutenant, and a master sergeant, who were the chief interrogators, the table of organization provided a staff sergeant for the translation of documents, and two technical sergeants who served as combined linguists, typists, and jeep drivers." In reality, he said, the men on his team shared all these tasks. "The captain would often type the reports, we all interrogated, and I . . . interrogated French and German civilians, and was frequently at the wheel of one of our jeeps, as on the day we landed in Normandy."[18] Each six-man team had two jeeps at its disposal.

Before shipping out of the country some of these teams were sent on maneuvers, primarily to Tennessee, Louisiana, and Texas, where they were assigned to divisions so that they could further develop their soldierly skills. Some were sent to POW camps in the United States, where they could practice their skills on German POWs. Before they were sent into the European war zone, all the IPW teams received more intense training in Britain before being assigned to an army, a division, a regiment, or even an army group at the front. The soldiers found the training in Britain especially useful because "the British, unlike our fellow Americans, were either professionals or somehow had a much better intelligence background."[19] At the front they shared military intelligence duties with a Military Intelligence Interpreter team (MII) and an Aerial Photo Interpreter team (API). It would be the task of the IPW teams to interrogate the prisoners taken as those units advanced, in order to gather tactical information and study the morale of the enemy.

The army quickly recognized the value of the intelligence work of men sent from Camp Ritchie, and both general and field-grade officers from military divisions in the United States as well as from units already overseas were brought to Ritchie to get special training in interrogation, order of battle, and aerial photography. Thus quite a number of G-2 (military intelligence) officers joined the Ritchie classes.[20]

The various IPW teams were carefully put together not only to match temperaments but also to cover a variety of languages and German dialects. Master Sergeant Victor Brombert [Bromberg] recalled that the six men of his interrogation team "calculated that between the six of us we spoke fifteen languages."[21] Theirs was a team of mixed nationalities, while another team, the "Rosenberg Combat Group," consisted solely of émigrés from German-speaking Europe. Lieutenant Albert G. Rosenberg was the officer in charge of this elite group of American interrogators, who, in addition to having some familiarity with all the major European languages, represented all the German and Austrian dialects. Because all of them had either grown up or spent their childhoods in a German-speaking area of Europe, they understood the German way of thinking and could easily interpret the defensive stance taken by each of the prisoners. During the European campaign, they performed an especially wide variety of interrogation services. In their first months in England, they spent fifteen-hour days interrogating German prisoners at a secret camp in Yorkshire. They then went to France in September 1944 to interrogate French civilian populations as well as German collaborators and prisoners. Later in the war, they debriefed the enemy and made contacts with the German civilian populations. During the Battle of the Bulge, this sometimes involved going behind enemy lines to work with German collaborators, or working with German collaborators placed in the POW cages. Finally, when the Americans liberated the Buchenwald concentration camp, Rosenberg and his team received orders to prepare a detailed, comprehensive report about Buchenwald before the liberated prisoners left the camp and returned home. Rosenberg selected a team of prisoners from the camp to write the main body of the report, while he and his men interviewed all of the Buchenwald prisoners in order to verify and amplify the material produced by the prisoner team. The final report became a key resource for the prosecution of crimes committed at Buchenwald and Dachau.

Guy Stern, member of another IPW team, feels that the training at Ritchie proved adequate for nearly any situation. "The demands were heavy on us throughout the war, but I never felt we were over-extended beyond our ability and our training," said Stern. "Virtually, there was nothing we encountered that we were not prepared for thanks to our training at Camp Ritchie."[22]

One of the essential tactics of interrogation training was patience. Private Walter J. Monasch, who completed course work at Camp Ritchie in counterintelligence, put it this way:

> *You build confidence, you build communication and you talk about all sorts of things except what you really want to know until you establish a sort of rhythm of communication. Then somewhere along the line people get into this rhythm. You do, and they do. Somewhere along the line at the right moment you break that rhythm and you ask the question you want to ask and they'll give you the answer—nine times out of ten—because you've established a pattern.*[23]

Staff Sergeant Richard Schifter agreed. In November 1944, he was performing civilian interrogations in Aachen when he found himself facing an engineer who, he learned, was employed at Peenemünde, where the German V-1 and V-2 rockets were manufactured for use against England. Thanks to his training at Camp Ritchie, he did not show the excitement that he felt upon realizing this man's importance. Instead, he concentrated on simply chatting with him in a pleasant way. After some time he got the engineer to open up to him, so that he not only told him about the effects of the Allied bombing at Peenemünde but also drew for him a sketch showing locations and results of the damage. Schifter then turned him over to Air Force Intelligence headquarters and was told, "You have hit a goldmine. We are taking him back to London."[24]

Sometimes, of course, pleasantness alone could not make a prisoner talk. Nearly every Ritchie Boy has a story about how he loosened the tongues of defiant prisoners. They sometimes did this not through violence but by deliberately creating situations of physical discomfort. Rudolf Michaels's technique was not allowing a bathroom break until the prisoner had divulged the information he was seeking. "There was no brutality ever," he declared. "No physical excesses of any kind, other than not letting them go potty."[25] In order to get vital information from a German sergeant captured outside the fortified city of Metz, Lieutenant Herman Lang simply overheated the interrogation chamber until the prisoner, who was dressed in a thick woolen greatcoat, boots, and winter weight woolen trousers, was overcome by heat and gave the information Lang requested.

Erhard Dabringhaus's team played upon the prisoner's fear of torture. "We used tricks with ketchup," he recalled. "We had a sergeant dressed as a German. We'd throw ketchup into his face, and he'd run out screaming while we're interrogating the guy who wasn't talking."[26]

The Ritchie Boys became masters of trickery. It became a fairly common technique to have the interrogator threaten to turn a recalcitrant prisoner over to the Russians if he did not give the information the interrogator asked for. Typically, the interrogator would instruct one of the sergeants to hang a sign around the prisoner's neck—reading "R" for Russia—and then to lead him out to a waiting Russian officer. Some creative teams went even further and had one of their members put on Red Army insignia in order to convince a prisoner of the "reality" of this threat.[27] Ritchie Boys Fred Howard and Guy Stern developed this technique into a highly successful good cop/bad cop routine; Stern dressed up in a Russian uniform, spoke German with a Russian accent, made a show of outrageous temper, and pretended to be "Commissar Krukov." When Howard escorted defiant prisoners to the "Russian tent" to turn them over to Krukov, the ploy nearly always worked; prisoners would rather talk than be turned over to Russian hands. Howard and Stern found that this technique worked especially well with the enlisted German soldiers.

Another ploy that sometimes worked with the enlisted Germans was when the interrogator pretended that the prisoner would be killed if he did not cooperate with his captors. The interrogator made a show of having a prisoner clearly write his name down upon a piece of paper, so that his grave marker would read correctly. If the prisoner still resisted, he was taken outside and ordered to dig his own grave. And, if the prisoner preferred death to betraying his German unit, there was a third step. Leo Handel, for example, "would turn to his sergeant in disgust and say in

German, 'All right, he's almost finished. I'll get the leader of that band of partisans who's been begging us for a Kraut. They'll take over. I'll be in the interrogation room. You know I can't stomach to watch.' And he then turned on his heel to walk away." As Handel's friend Ib Melchior has noted, "Death might hold no terrors for the PW, but the prospect of death at the hands of a vengeful band of partisans was usually too much to face. Faced with the 'P' ploy—P for partisans—the PW would talk." As for the grave the prisoner had dug, "a slit trench was always in demand for other purposes."[28]

Unless there was urgency for immediate information, interrogators generally used different tactics with German officers: "We greeted them as fellow officers, offered them cigarettes and coffee (and sometimes, when necessary, even some brandy), and then settled down to discussions of their units and the action they had recently been in." Here it was a great help to know as much as possible about the German units and their officers. As Staff Sergeant George Mandler put it, "Knowing the names of the officers in those units, knowing about rivalries among them, and particularly having available snippets of gossip was most helpful. Knowing that Major X had an affair with some colonel's wife in Berlin was the kind of gossip that helped create an atmosphere that conveyed that we already knew everything anyway."[29]

Throughout the war, the Ritchie interrogators developed techniques uniquely designed for the situation at hand. One German-born Ritchie sergeant developed an unusually effective tactic for obtaining information from the enemy: he would seek out a working telephone at the local railway station of a German village just taken by the Allies and then call the unit in the village ahead of them, identify himself as "Lieutenant Schmidt" of a nearby harassed German unit, and exchange information with the German commander defending the village just ahead. In this fashion, he got highly accurate tactical information by telephone even before he went to question any Germans in the prisoners' cage.[30]

Finally, in a particularly critical case, Leo Handel interrogated a German officer captured from Axis forces preparing a battery assault on Santa Maria, Italy. The officer continually cited the Geneva Conventions and refused to supply any information until he was held in the village schoolhouse, which, he knew, was at the center of the planned assault. As the minutes ticked by, the officer finally told Handel that an attack was coming at midnight, but he still refused to release the location of the German battery. At this point, all the Americans moved out of the schoolhouse except Handel and the prisoner. Handel announced that they would wait out the attack unless the officer gave him the exact location of the German assault battery. When the German nervously protested that the Geneva Conventions dictated that a POW must be given the same protection as an American soldier, Handel replied, "*I* am an American soldier."[31] Then, to heighten the tension, Handel stopped the schoolhouse clock at 11:30 p.m. and confiscated the officer's watch. Finally the tension proved unbearable, the officer gave Handel the coordinates, and the battery was destroyed.

Clearly, the Ritchie interrogators not only were well trained for their task but also demonstrated complete mastery of prisoner psychology in dealing with the enemy.

An interrogation scene enacted by members of the Visual Demonstration Section. SOURCE: NATIONAL ARCHIVES AND RECORDS ADMINISTRATION

A later interrogation scene staged by the Composite School Unit. SOURCE: NATIONAL ARCHIVES AND RECORDS ADMINISTRATION

Special interrogation tents where various interrogation assignments were carried out. SOURCE: NATIONAL ARCHIVES AND RECORDS ADMINISTRATION

Section 5, IPW staff, preparing materials for practice interrogations. COURTESY OF ANITA BOUCHER

An exercise in interpretation. SOURCE: NATIONAL ARCHIVES AND RECORDS ADMINISTRATION

CHAPTER SIX

Aerial Intelligence and Photo Interpretation

Photo Intelligence became one of the most widely employed sources of information in military conflict and is officially credited with obtaining 90 percent of our military intelligence in World War II. No important defensive or offensive action was taken on land, sea, or in the air without the trail first being blazed by PIs. These PIs constituted in effect a corps of exceptionally efficient secret agents who covered infinitely greater areas of any enemy territory or endeavors than was ever before possible.[1]

IT HAD BEEN DETERMINED AT THE TIME THAT THE MILITARY INTELligence Training Center was set up at Camp Ritchie that a basic course in the interpretation of aerial photographs would be taught to all students, regardless of their areas of specialization, in the advanced phases of the program. The course work was rigorous, both in the basic introductory work of the eight-week course of study and in the specialized work that followed. In the basic course, all students were taught to identify ambiguous-looking features in a photograph and to "read" the landscape for signs of enemy forces.

The Composite School Unit was able to assist the aerial intelligence instructors by performing field demonstrations. Camp Ritchie had five aircraft available for training: one twin-engine, seven-passenger plane; two twin-engine, four-passenger planes; and two single-engine, two-passenger planes. These were housed in a hangar leased at the Waynesboro Municipal Airport, ten miles northwest of Camp Ritchie. In the basic "Aerial Photograph Reading" course, however, students first learned about the best method of camouflaging materials by standing at a vantage point that gave practically the same view as one would get in a low-flying aircraft. For this exercise, various vehicles and weapons moved into various backgrounds (barren ground, a green area, and a wooded area). In the meantime, both German and American pup tents were erected and camouflaged, while two pyramidal tents were set up—one with camouflage, one without. The students were required to study the vehicles moving into the area and report what they had seen to "headquarters." James Mims remembered that the observation post was "on the side of a mountain overlooking Cumberland Valley," and the exercise in the spring, when "sitting in the sun after a long cold winter wasn't conducive to staying awake."[2] After completing this exercise, students searched the area for items that had previously been camouflaged and moved them out to reveal their location. They then were set to work analyzing photographs of the terrain around Camp Ritchie. In the advanced courses, students observed the terrain from airplanes.

Only the most skilled students would be selected for specialization in photo intelligence. Here they learned to become familiar with the different types of aerial photographs: "high- and low-altitude photos; verticals and obliques, depending on the optical axis of the camera at the time of exposure; composites taken with a multi-lens camera and consisting of a vertical photo surrounded by four transformed obliques; controlled and uncontrolled mosaics, a series of overlapping verticals; and pinpoints, strips, and photomaps."[3]

The students worked with 3-D stereoscopic views of various terrains that mimicked what one might see from an airplane. The exact time of day was noted on the back of each photograph the men studied, so that they might make use of shadows in determining various factors of the terrain, such as hillsides. Analysis of these photographs was much more difficult than one might assume. It was difficult to determine the degrees of height and depth in photographs taken from an airplane. In the first class, for example, one student misidentified the shadow of trees as a "car" and an array of tents as "corn shocks." Another "found it relatively easy to raise tall objects like buildings, but much more frustrating when it came to trying to differentiate smaller objects more or less similar in profile, for example between a light tank and a medium tank. This often required using a ruler to measure the miniscule shadows cast by the vehicles . . . shown in the photos."[4] Private Henry Kolm found it "quite an art" to look at stereo pairs taken fifty miles apart that showed the difference in elevation between objects, "so that you could see a camouflage net which is not at ground level, for instance." For him, this work "was a very exciting experience."[5] Eventually students learned not only to make these distinctions but also to say whether drainage ran generally north or south in a picture, or whether a man standing at one point in a picture would be able to see a person standing at another.

In one of their more advanced demonstrations, the CSU troops organized front lines positions, road blocks, mine fields, gun positions, and camouflaged weapons and vehicles for aerial photography and for student aerial observation. The students flying over the local terrain would have the opportunity to compare actual troops and weapons with photographs of the same area. The students also made ground photographs of the area; these and the aerial photographs were then used in class. The students were taught not only to recognize camouflaged vehicles, weaponry, and troop positions in aerial photographs but also to identify the size and movement of enemy forces. It was no easy task. Master Sergeant Robert Potash remarked, "Over time, I became proficient enough to pass the class work but I never felt fully comfortable dealing with photographs, in contrast to what I had always felt in language courses or other academic subjects."[6] James Mims remarked that, by the end of the course, "we could measure the exact length of bridges or width of rivers for the engineers, or find good forward observation posts for the artillery. We could either plot all this on a map, or make our own maps when we had poor ones, as on Leyte and Mindanao. It was truly a useful and necessary skill."[7]

All the men agreed that photo intelligence played a crucial role in war operations, for it served three important functions critical to success on the battlefield:

The first is reconnaissance—to learn vital facts, both tactical and strategic, about enemy territory, positions, strength, installations, and artillery.

The second one is mapping. General Omar N. Bradley once said, "The nation with the best maps will win the war."...

The third function of PI is to record the results of actions such as bombing raids and artillery bombardments and accurately assess the damage inflicted upon the targets.[8]

Alumni of the photo interpretation classes were asked to send photos from the war zone back to Camp Ritchie for the training of students in the advanced classes. James Mims vividly recalled one particular class problem because of a coincidence in timing: "We were working one photo interpretation problem studying the coast of France mapping the various defenses. Imagine our surprise and delight when we discovered that the Invasion of D-Day was taking place at this site and at the very time we were studying it! We had the combat films from the invasion at the end of that week before any of them were released to the public." Mims, who became a staff sergeant upon completion of his course work, was sent to New Guinea and the Philippines, and his team was now asked to produce course material: "One of our pieces of equipment was a compact photo developing kit, housed in a trunk like box about three-feet square. The idea was for us to take ground shots of various things that we had detected in aerial photos and send them both back to camp Ritchie for training purposes." Unfortunately, the team now discovered a gap in their Camp Ritchie training: "[W]e had no training at all in how to develop and print pictures! Miller knew as little as did Packard and I, but not enough to do the job right." Fortunately, a master sergeant in their G-2 section was a professional photographer and was able to give the men a crash course in photography.[9]

Sergeant David E. Feller's experiences demonstrated the special skills he'd acquired in photo analysis, as well as its potential pitfalls. He had gotten into the program by asking an ophthalmologist at the camp to certify that his eyes were good enough to do photo intelligence work. By the end of the course, he was amazed at all he had learned: "I could look at a photo taken at 20 thousand feet," he said, "and, by looking at the latrines and the paths and such, could tell you what kind of division it was. I had to know the exact composition, what kind of armor it had. I learned all about the German Army. You could look at a photograph and glean all the information necessary to know what the nature of your enemy was, by the picture taken."[10] Ironically, Feller's sophisticated knowledge of the German army was not utilized; he was sent, instead, to work in the Pacific theater.

There his skills were put to the test in terrain utterly different from what he had trained for. At Bougainville Island in Papua, New Guinea, for example, everything was first-growth jungle. As he reported it, "When you take an aerial photograph [there], you can't see anything except trees. And all we had were these pictures with trees. . . . But I had to find some way to be useful." Feller already had stereoscopes at his disposal. He acquired a manual on map making and then taught the men in his unit how to draw maps from the aerial photographs. "They were rather rough maps with lots of blanks," he admitted, but they corrected the many misperceptions of the soldiers who had gone out on patrol, since "when you're making a map from just reporting where you had gone, you tend to greatly underestimate the space you've covered. In clear areas, you go fast; then you get into places that have been burned over, and you have to hack your way. You a go hundred yards, and you think you've gone three hundred." Feller's skills provided a corrective to the useless "maps" that had been created by the army patrols.

But later on Sergeant Feller made a blunder that, in his words, "probably cost the Army more money than any other enlisted man." The US Navy was planning to land two regiments at Cebu City, in the Philippines. Navy photographers dropped off photographs of the beach where they were planning to land, and Feller, after studying them, said that the navy could not land its regiments on that beach because there were pillboxes there. "So they held up the landing operation for a day, and they brought the whole Navy, and they pounded that beach. They knocked the hell out of the sand dunes because that is what they were—sand dunes. There weren't any pill boxes."[11]

At Camp Ritchie, Theodore Fuller had taught the students specializing in photo intelligence how to develop stereovision. "Experience with

He Passed through Camp Ritchie

Staff Sergeant **Peter Burland** (born 1923), the son of Greek immigrants, was studying chemical engineering at Louisiana State University when he broke off his studies in December 1942 and volunteered for military service. He was assigned to Camp Ritchie, along with 150 other Greek Americans and speakers of Greek, to form the fifth Greek guerrilla warfare class trained to secretly enter Southern Yugoslavia and Northern Greece and join the Greek battalion. On graduation day, these Greek soldiers learned that they would not be sent to Greece; instead, they were being reassigned to photo reconnaissance.

After three weeks of training by the Canadian OSS (MI5), they were sent to England, and Burland began going on two reconnaissance missions a week, flying behind the pilot in a P-38 and taking photos of German defensive positions all along the French coast to aid in identifying a safe landing site for D-Day. These missions ended as soon as new cameras were developed that could be mounted directly onto the planes. The Greek soldiers were now spread out among the United States' various fighting units, since Greek was a relatively unknown European language and these men could pass on orders and information between units in relative safety.

Burland was assigned to the Second Armored Division as part of a team consisting of six interrogators and six military reconnaissance men. He landed on Omaha Beach on D-Day plus 1 and conducted reconnaissance missions both by Piper Cub and by jeep throughout the remainder of the European war. He was hit three times, but he was wounded most seriously during the Battle of the Bulge, when he ran into a barbed wire fence buried in deep snow.

Burland was released from the service in January 1946, completed his studies at Louisiana State University, and made a career as a research chemist, developing a class of water-soluble compounds known as "telomers" that revolutionized the industrial water-treatment industry. In 1992, he founded the nonprofit Military Museum of Texas to honor Texas veterans of all American wars.

large groups of men reveals that anyone with eyes good enough to be in the Army can see stereoscopically," he declared. Also, "stereo studies properly done put no strain on the eyes."[12] Stereovision was the ability to fuse two photographs into one three-dimensional image without the convenience of a stereoscope viewer. This skill required one to diverge one's vision. Fuller offered several techniques for developing this skill. As Henry Kolm recalled in an interview,

You . . . put your thumb[s] on two photographs and then you moved them apart and let your eyes diverge, so each eye sees a different photograph, but this way you have a great stereoscopic view of the ground that distinguishes between forage and the camouflage net. But unfortunately, when you disturb the convergence ratio of your eyes, it doesn't come back to normal, and so after I got out of the Army I wound up with a year of training in a military hospital to get my vision back without getting a headache from reading.[13]

Kolm was not alone in having this problem. Ironically, those who came out of the war with double vision were able to correct the problem by working with special stereoscopic images that exercised eye divergence and restored the accommodation-convergence ratio.

But the advantages gained by photo intelligence were worth the effort. Aerial photographs could be processed and analyzed almost immediately after they were taken. This provided the most immediate tactical information possible as to the presence of fortifications, tents, camouflage netting, and the presence and number of mechanized vehicles in a given area. On the ground, the photographs could be coordinated with area maps to show troop movements in the field. But photo intelligence required not only the good eyes of photo analysts but also the skills of the pilots, photographers, and film processors who provided the analysts with the raw materials. Only the most basic training was given at Camp Ritchie to the men assigned to work as aerial photographers. Nevertheless, a goodly number of Ritchie graduates went on in this field. Prior to D-Day, these men were sent on missions to film the German defensive positions all along the Normandy coastline and east to

Peenemünde. Staff Sergeant Peter Burland, a graduate of Camp Ritchie's ninth class, described his work:

> *I was taking reconnaissance photos by sitting behind the pilot and filming through the plane's plexiglass windows. In order to prevent the plane's wings from blocking the vision, the pilot had to tip the plane, one wing at a time. During the time it took the pilot to do these figure eights, I had to change my film. The reconnaissance plane was escorted by bombers; the smoke from the German anti-aircraft guns gave the bombers their targets and they were easily taken out. The Germans soon caught on and stopped firing.*[14]

Even before D-Day, however, more sophisticated cameras were developed that could be mounted on the plane itself, and the men who had managed the cameras were now assigned to air surveillance. This was the most dangerous assignment for the men working in aerial intelligence, since their job was to fly in a small observation plane over enemy territory, look for German Panzer units, and radio in the coordinates where enemy tanks were spotted. Captain Hugh D. Jones performed this service for the Second Armored Division, which had been founded by General George Patton in 1940 and was popularly referred to as "Hell on Wheels."

Jones was paired with pilot Major Stewart Gordon in his surveillance missions, and the press took note of his success. When a large German armored column near Roncey, Normandy, was destroyed by Allied bombing on July 31, 1944, credit was given to Captain Jones. He was reported to have sighted the German tanks and motorized equipment and signaled their location to the Allied air forces while working as "an artillery spotter in a Piper Cub."[15] It was Jones's second day of service in air surveillance, and he was ecstatic. On the next day, he gave an interview to war correspondent John Thompson, in which he described his work:

> *"I've been flying for three days," said Jones, "and it's the most marvelous way to see a battle. I had read about Napoleon sitting on a hilltop watching a battle. Well, we did the master one better. We could watch*

our columns advance down parallel roads with the center out in front like a wedge. We could spot the enemy's tanks and guns and let the boys know at once. And every time the Germans took a shot at us our artillery would come down with a great crash.[16]

The job was not without peril. Shortly after giving this interview his plane returned from a mission with fifteen bullet holes. Jones, too, had been shot in the shoulder. For his actions, he was awarded the Bronze Star and a Purple Heart.

Given the danger of flying in a Piper Cub at eight hundred feet above enemy territory, it is sadly ironic that Hugh Jones was killed on the ground rather than in the air. On August 31, 1944, he accompanied Lieutenant Colonel Jesse M. Hawkins to what was believed to be the secure town of Le Fay-Saint-Quentin, in Picardie, France. There, according to the records, Jones "experienced a critical situation which resulted in loss of life."[17] The French described the situation more bluntly in the memorial plaque they erected at the spot of Jones's death: "Here two American officers, Lieutenant Colonel Jesse M. Hawkins [and] Captain Hugh D. Jones were killed in cowardly fashion [*lâchement*] by the Germans." Jones was buried in the American Cemetery in Normandy. His young widow carried on his work by serving with the American Red Cross in Italy.

Master Sergeant Billy M. Northwood uses a stereoscope to interpret aerial photos at Fifth Armored's Photo Intelligence Section, while T/3 Bill Lane orients from a map the photos to be interpreted. SOURCE: NATIONAL ARCHIVES AND RECORDS ADMINISTRATION

T/4 Joel R. Acevedo annotates aerial photo mosaics at München-Gladbach, Germany, for use by the Twenty-Ninth Infantry Division of the Ninth US Army. SOURCE: NATIONAL ARCHIVES AND RECORDS ADMINISTRATION

In an abandoned German house, Staff Sergeant Frank Di Vilio (right) makes a distribution of photo maps of the western front with a private on his photo interpretation team. SOURCE: NATIONAL ARCHIVES AND RECORDS ADMINISTRATION

CHAPTER SEVEN

Order of Battle and the Military Intelligence Research Section (MIRS)

The research mission of MIRS was primarily to extract from documents all information of value for operational or occupational intelligence and to evaluate and compile it in suitable manner for prompt dissemination.[1]

TASKS SUCH AS SORTING THROUGH HUNDREDS OF MAILBAGS, CREATING extensive card catalogs, and compiling lists, books, and intelligence reports for the Pentagon may have lacked the drama of the missions performed by the Office of Strategic Services and Counterintelligence Corps, but the Military Intelligence Research Section—MIRS—played a crucial role for military commanders and for intelligence teams at the front. Until its founding on May 1, 1943, British and American agencies held widely divergent estimates of German combat strength and deployment, and this created an urgent need to verify this information for their combined field operations in North Africa and their preparation for the invasion of France. From the start, then, MIRS was a cooperative endeavor, with offices set up in London and in Washington. The program was put into motion by Major Eric Birley, then chief of MI 14 (b) of the British War Office; American lieutenant colonel John R. Lovell, chief of the German Order of Battle Section for the Central European branch of the Military Intelligence Service (MIS); and Lieutenant (soon to be Captain) Jack William Votion of Camp Ritchie. Votion was Belgian born and raised, a World War I "boy hero" knighted by Prince Albert and, by 1943, the Hollywood producer of several Lum and Abner film comedies. Votion and Birley served as co-chiefs of the London branch. Votion served in this capacity from the MIRS founding in May 1943 until its deactivation in July 1945.

A Czech graduate of Camp Ritchie's second class, Captain Siegfried F. Gronich, also played an important role in the establishment of MIRS by serving as conference participant in March 1943; he was the War Department Order of Battle specialist recently attached to Allied Force Headquarters (AFHQ). Gronich built up the first G-2 Document Section in Algiers at the same time MIRS was founded, and he sent the first extensive collection of captured war documents to London.

Because the London branch was closest to the action, it was of higher importance than Washington and had an authorized strength of eighty-two individuals, while the Washington branch had an authorized strength of only twenty-five. The Americans clearly dominated MIRS, however, since two-thirds of the members in the London branch and all but one in the Washington branch were American military personnel; the rest were British, with a scattering of Poles. Since most of the American officers and all the American enlisted men assigned to the two MIRS branches had Camp Ritchie training, one might even consider MIRS a Camp Ritchie operation. Certainly, its courses in the Order of Battle (OB) program provided the specialized training that the MIRS operatives needed.

There was some rivalry at Camp Ritchie between those men chosen to specialize in the Order of Battle program as opposed to those in Interrogation of Prisoners of War (IPW). The IPW men claimed to have been selected because they had better instincts and finer linguistic talents; the OB men claimed the greater scholarship and higher analytical skills. The men could agree, however, that the Order of Battle unit taught to the interrogators was the most challenging part of their program, because they had to memorize detailed information on the structure of the German army, its unit designations, unit makeup and hierarchy, weaponry, transport, supply chain, and fluctuating chain of command. In an ever-evolving war setting, it was imperative for students to know not only the names of unit leaders but also their temperament and their situation within the army hierarchy. The history of each unit had to be traced: Where was the unit formed? What kind of soldiers were serving in it (e.g., professionals, Nazi party members, green recruits, older veterans)? What was their history of previous battle engagement? Stephan Lewy, who took the OB specialty with the eleventh class, recalled the reaction of a fellow student when they were given their study materials:

"Jesus, we have to memorize the history of every goddam German division, their fucking generals, their campaigns, the casualties they experienced, and even the firing power they have?" the boy in front of me asked as he turned around.

"Yeah. We have to be able to report on how much fighting experience and efficient leadership each division has."

"I feel like I'm back in school learning history."

He was right. It was a great history lesson.[2]

In addition to its thirty-one eight-week classes, Camp Ritchie offered twenty-two four-week courses to OB specialists. Fifteen of these focused on the European theater and seven on the war in the Pacific. The course work involved work with captured documents: how to interpret them and how to extract from them every bit of information critical to the war effort.

It was the task of the Ritchie men in MIRS to keep this Order of Battle information absolutely up to date. Their mission quickly evolved into one of handling and exploiting captured enemy documents. These documents were sent from the field to the London branch, circulated and processed for short-range Order of Battle Intelligence (OBI), and then promptly sent on to Washington for long-range Order of Battle studies. Captured enemy documents included everything from military newspapers to soldiers' pay books, written orders, army manuals, information flyers, and even personal letters. It was often a struggle to prevent combat personnel from destroying these documents or keeping them as souvenirs. S. F. Gronich, who, for the duration of the war, was called "Sidney" rather than "Siegfried," provided an incalculable service in setting standards for the preservation, evaluation, and organization of documents.

Initially, the work of the London MIRS office was closely tied up with intelligence planning for the invasion of western Europe. Because of its location in London and its stated mission of conducting tactical as well as strategic studies of captured enemy documents, it contributed directly to the operational intelligence of the Supreme Headquarters Allied Expeditionary Force (SHAEF). Its success is reflected by the fact that Jack Votion, who had come to MIRS as a lieutenant, was promoted to lieutenant colonel by the end of his MIRS service and was the recipient of nineteen decorations.

The Washington offices got off to a rockier start. There Colonel John Lovell served as co-chief with British junior commander Enid S. Malcolm. Working from the Pentagon, these two men set up operations at Fort Hunt, Virginia, an old Civil War camp halfway between Mount Vernon and Alexandria, Virginia, and roughly twelve miles south of the Pentagon. Throughout the war, the work at this camp was considered so secret that it was identified only as PO Box 1142. In addition to MIRS, Fort Hunt housed two other secret intelligence branches: one was MIS-Y, which interrogated mostly high-level German prisoners of war (POWs) in order to study German army morale and extract strategic military intelligence; the other was MIS-X, which sent coded letters to the American soldiers and airmen held in German POW camps, alerting them to packages of sports equipment and game supplies they were sending with hidden escape aids (maps on silk, compasses, some small weaponry) through the International Red Cross. Whereas virtually the entire American MIRS staff came from Camp Ritchie, roughly 18 percent—or 95 of the 548 men assigned to these MIS-Y and MIS-X sections of PO Box 1142's military intelligence work—also had Ritchie training.

While Colonel Lovell and his British counterpart operated out from the Pentagon, the men working under them created their own workspace at PO Box 1142. For the first five months, they moved twice in quick succession from the original, single large room maintained by the Prisoner of War Branch at the camp. In July 1943, they finally obtained accommodations "in a new and adequate building" on the base, which was soon referred to as the "Farm" or "Berlin."[3] During this period, Austrian-born Sergeant Alfred T. Newton, part of Ritchie's fourth class, served as acting (noncommissioned) chief of the Washington branch. Newton was called upon, again and again, to give lectures and demonstrations at the Pentagon in order to instruct intelligence personnel about the form and content of documents relating to German military personnel. By the end of 1943, he had become "the greatest expert in the United States Army" on this subject. In December 1943, Captain John Kluge, of Ritchie's seventh class, was named permanent Washington chief. Kluge was a native of Chemnitz, Germany. He came to MIRS from an eight-month stint of service in the Aleutian Islands—an assignment triggered by questions regarding his loyalty to the United States. By December, he had been cleared of all charges and spent the remainder of the war as Washington chief of MIRS.[4] In the meantime, Sergeant Newton wrote and published his lecture notes and demonstration materials as a manual. This work, *The Exploitation of German Documents*, proved invaluable to the Allied forces in Germany, especially after the German surrender, when German military personnel were being screened and demobilized.

During the first months of service, the Washington MIRS branch had numerous personnel problems. Some of the men brought to PO Box 1142 were found "unsuited to the work" and transferred elsewhere, while others were transferred to the London branch or were given other duties at the Pentagon. In mid-July 1943, Captain N. Horton Smith, from the British Army Staff, was attached to the Washington MIRS unit as liaison officer with the London branch. He became the general research adviser, thereby helping the Washington office establish a clearer mission and avoiding duplication of efforts in the London office. The effects of personnel turnover were now also mitigated when the more experienced MIRS personnel began training and mentoring new arrivals.

Gradually, then, the mission of the Washington branch became less ambiguous. This was a major achievement, since, in the words of the MIRS official history, "Its mission was without precedent; its method was trial and error; and its contribution to the development of intelligence on the German Army was unique."[5] MIRS occasionally sought information from MIS-Y interrogations of highly placed German POWs being held

He Passed through Camp Ritchie

Technical Sergeant **Paul Fairbrook** and his twin brother Uri were born in Berlin in August 1923, with Schoenbach as the family name. The family left Germany in 1933 and settled in Palestine, near Tel Aviv. After four years, his father went bankrupt but managed to get visas for the United States, where they arrived via freighter in 1938. His father started a retail stamp business in New York, while Paul got a number of jobs working in hotels and hotel restaurants.

After Pearl Harbor, Fairbrook tried to enlist but, as an "enemy alien," had to wait to be drafted. He graduated from the seventh class at Camp Ritchie and completed a special four-week class titled "Order of Battle Intelligence." He expected to be assigned to an infantry unit as a POW interrogator. He was sent instead to the Pentagon and assigned to the Military Intelligence Research Section at Fort Hunt, or "PO Box 1142," in Virginia. Here he joined seventeen other enlisted men and three officers in writing the "Red Book" (*Order of Battle of the German Army*). He also researched a number of

at PO Box 1142; Captain Kluge even questioned one or two of them personally. But, in general, the Washington MIRS concentrated solely on the documents delivered to them from the London office. To assist in the organization of compiling and writing reports, Colonel Lovell brought in a civilian, professor of English Philip Tucker, whom he knew from prior service in the embassy in Berlin. Tucker became indispensable to MIRS Washington. With German Ritchie trainee Dieter Kober, he revamped the whole approach to organizing materials for a new Order of Battle book. Captain Kluge reported directly to Tucker, who read every MIRS document before it was sent out. "He was a weirdo," Kluge remembered, "but he was a tremendous brain."[6] Each man assigned to the Washington studies, including "Political Indoctrination and Morale-Building in the German Army," in which he revealed that, following the failed assassination attempt on Hitler in July 1944, Nazi officers were routinely assigned to each major military unit to keep tabs on the loyalty of their commanders and their men. He received a commendation for making this discovery.

After Germany's surrender in May 1945, the men in MIRS returned to Camp Ritchie to join the German Military Document Section and organize the captured documents for future use by the Defense Department. Fairbrook's twin brother Uri Schoenbach joined him there.

After his discharge, Fairbrook went to Brown University and majored in comparative literature. During the year he worked in a private club; in his summer vacations he worked as a tour escort for the Thos. Cook Travel Agency. He got an MBA from Michigan State University while serving as food cost controller at the campus hotel's restaurant. He then went on to make a career in the food service industry as dean of the Culinary Institute of America and as director of auxiliary services at Northern Illinois University and the University of the Pacific. In 1985, he received "The Silver Plate" from the International Food Manufacturer Association, an award giving him national recognition for excellence in the college dining business. He is the author of three books addressing various aspects of college and university food services.

office was required to submit at least one weekly report, ranging from one to twenty pages in length; Tucker saw to it that in writing these reports, the men maintained "uniformity of style, neatness of presentation, and meticulous accuracy. . . . His criticisms, often severe and always detailed, were related to the men at the next meeting of the unit."[7] Many of these reports were disseminated to various agencies of the War Department; some were especially useful for the work of the Order of Battle Branch, and others to the Central European branch of the Military Intelligence Service.

The work settled into a fixed, rather pleasant routine. Technical Sergeant Paul Fairbrook, from Ritchie's seventh class, recalls his work on the MIRS "Red Book":

Life at P.O. Box 1142 was like life in a research organization. We got up at a reasonable hour, made our beds, had breakfast, and then went over to our large office barracks where each of us had a desk with card files, documents and a typewriter. Each had a specific chapter to write. To make certain that we knew how to write properly, we had the benefit of a Mr. Tucker, a civilian who went around to each of us and taught us how to organize our material.

Fairbrook had nothing but praise for Tucker: "His lessons were like a three-year private tutoring experience, and by the time I attended college, I already knew how to write and was therefore excused from all the 'bonehead English' courses."[8]

For his part, Kluge praised his charges, remarking, "you had to really be on the ball to be in charge of them because they just absorbed knowledge like sponge[s] and had a great memory." This was crucial, he said, because they were "going over thousands of documents."[9] The MIRS men showed initiative, thoroughness, and precision in their work. German-born corporal Frank Sternberg, for example, devised a form card for recording information on German Replacement (*Ersatz*) units. The file that he began would be relied on heavily in later MIRS publications.

When the documents from London reached Washington, the various research specialists took the ones relevant to their assigned areas of research and worked them up for publication and dissemination. Paul Fairbrook spent a couple of months researching German soldiers' morale. Sergeant Alfred Newton made a systematic study of personal documentation, while Private Stefan Rundt, from Ritchie's eighth class, wrote a detailed study of all aspects of the SS High Command, including individual SS personalities. Rundt had come to Ritchie—and to MIRS—with unique qualifications. Already before the war, he had conducted research on German military organizations for the NBC Listening Post and authored articles on underground anti-Nazi radio stations for the *New York Times*. Rundt was born in Germany and educated in Vienna, and his abilities led to his being transferred to the London MIRS branch to organize and supervise the study of Germany's semi-military organizations and to oversee publications about them.

In addition to writing reports and making compilations of lists crucial to the war effort, the men in the Washington office sometimes were asked to take on a special rush assignment. In August 1943, for example, Siegfried Gronich, now a major, sent a rush request for all the information available on the location of German military headquarters and installations on the Italian peninsula. The entire Washington staff spent the next twenty-four hours compiling this information from the enormous backlog of documents in their possession. They were able to identify more than fifty enemy headquarters, giving even the exact addresses for some, and to fly this list to North Africa. They learned later that the Allies had used this list for several successful bombing missions in Italy.

During the first half of 1944, the men in the Washington branch produced four books. The most important of these was the Red Book—*Order of Battle of the German Army*—which was an updated and completely revamped version of the 1942 *Order of Battle of the German Army* book that had been produced by British intelligence. Philip Tucker supervised its compilation. There was also a Yellow Book, *The German Replacement Army*, also under Tucker's supervision, and a Grey Book, *Military Headquarters and Installations in Germany*, under the supervision of Captain Geoffrey Watkins of the London MIRS branch. Sergeant Alfred Newton was sole compiler of the fourth book, *Exploitation of German Documents*. During this production period, a sizable contingent of Ritchie men was brought in to PO Box 1142 to serve as typists.

MIRS had been founded because of the need for up-to-date information on the strength of the German armed forces, and on their armaments and movements. The Red Book study on *Order of Battle of the German Army* was intended to do just that. As Ian V. Hogg, military historian, has remarked:

The depth of detail revealed in [the 1944] Order of Battle may surprise many people; but it would not be enough to know, for example, that the German infantry division contains thirty-six field howitzers, sixteen 15cm howitzers and eight 10cm guns. It is also necessary to know how these weapons are distributed and organised into units and sub-units, for only then will the counter-bombardment artillery

*know that it must locate three 10.5cm howitzer batteries, four troops
of 15cm howitzers and two troops of 10cm guns, a total of nine different targets to be bombarded and neutralised before an attack begins.
If the observations posts, aerial observers, photo interpreters and other
sources have only located six artillery positions in the divisional area,
then the attack will be surprised by three undetected groups of guns,
possibly at a critical moment.*[10]

With knowledge of the location and participation of individual German fighting units in prior encounters, one could gain a sense of a unit's
threat in future fighting. Similarly, knowledge of the unit commanders—
knowing their tactical and strategic idiosyncrasies—could give valuable
insight into their possible responses in future battle situations. One typical example from the 1944 Red Book suggests that the Fourteenth Panzer Grenadier Division might be less of a threat than one might suppose:

14 Panzer Grenadier Division

Commander: — Genmaj. FLÖRKE.
*Composition: — Pz. Abt. 114 ?; Gr. Rgt. (mot.) 11; Gr. Regt. (mot)
    53; Arty. Rgt. 14; Pi Btl. 14;*
Pz Jäg Abt. 14; Pz. Aufkl. Abt. 114; Nachr. Abt. 14.
Auxiliary unit number: 14
Home Station: — Leipzig (Wkr. IV).

*As 14 Infantry Division, a Saxon division belonging to the
peacetime army, it took part in the campaigns in Poland and France,
without winning special distinction. Motorised in the autumn of
1940. Identified in the Russian campaign in the battle for Vitebsk.
Since then, continuously in action in the Central sector. It appears to
have sustained heavy casualties in autumn, 1943.*[11]

This kind of detailed information would give battlefield commanders a
good idea of what to expect from a division that served "without winning
special distinction" and had quite recently "sustained heavy casualties."
To those in psychological warfare, it would suggest that the men were

demoralized and possibly more eager to surrender than members of the more successful fighting units.

Following the completion of these four volumes, the Washington MIRS men were assigned to desks devoted to follow-up, issuing amendments, revisions, or special studies on their subjects. Sergeant Newton, for example, was assigned to personal documentation, Sergeant Kober to important field units, Sergeant Fairbrook to minor German headquarters units and types of units, and Sergeant Sternberg to replacement army. Private Oscar Kritzer had now come to MIRS from Camp Ritchie to serve as documents editor.

After the invasion at Normandy, the situation in Washington changed. Paul Fairbrook has written:

> I recall that on June 6, 1944, when the Allies stormed the Normandy beaches, the Military Intelligence Division at the Pentagon decided to move offices, as an apparent attempt to mislead any potential spies. I recall Dieter [Kober] and I pulling up with a big Army truck and "requisitioning" a number of desks and desk chairs that were out in the hall and bringing them back to our barracks to the great jubilation of my comrades.[12]

In a similar vein, Captain Kluge remembered stealing light fixtures from the basement of the Pentagon.[13]

Paul Fairbrook continues: "About a month later a number of us were sent to London to help process German documents for the War Office. . . . That, however, lasted only a few weeks, when we were hurriedly shipped back to the States, because our officers at the Pentagon couldn't really manage without us—the experienced German speaking noncoms." Eight of the sixteen available enlisted men were assigned to this temporary duty with the London MIRS because of the flood of German documents that flowed into London after the invasion of France and the urgent need for their proper dissemination. By late September, these men had all returned to the United States, where a newly formed Captured Personnel and Material Branch at the Pentagon had proven completely inept at continuing the research work of the Washington branch.

Considerable time was lost before things went back to normal, especially since the reduced personnel numbers at the Washington branch made it difficult to pick up the various neglected research subjects. The only subjects that had been adequately dealt with were the replacement army, the SS, and military headquarters and installations.

Once it was up and running again, the Washington branch began the most productive period of its history. The unit was close to its full allotted strength, and many of them were now seasoned research/writers. The unit produced two books, part of a third, and a number of "very valuable studies and compilations." In addition to research, Washington MIRS began the systematic circulation of documents to other agencies. Late in January 1945, fifteen enlisted men from Ritchie were attached to the unit for six weeks to assist the unit in its work. "Most of them proved to be willing workers of average ability," the MIRS historians reported, "and several were exceptionally capable and were afterwards recommended for assignment to MIRS." Several others, however, "were not only unsuited to the work but were either unwilling or unable to endure the 12 to 16 hour day which had to be instituted . . . to meet the deadline on the books."[14]

One important subject taken up after D-Day was a systematic, organized study of the German High Command. Sergeant Fairbrook discovered that one could gather a good deal of information from the semimonthly General Army Orders and other captured official publications through the signatures and ink stamps on the orders appearing there, since these revealed officer responsibilities, subordination, and composition of agencies. This eventually made it possible "to piece together the entire structure of the Armed Forces High Command (OKW) and of the Army High Command (OKH), with all their offices, groups, branches, and sections and the exact functions of each."[15] A color-coded card file was developed to show which larger agencies controlled smaller ones, and a cross-reference file identified the important officers connected to these agencies. This system made it possible to extract information as to the frequent changes in organization of High Command agencies and became a valuable contribution to the 1945 *Handbook on German Military Forces*. Other MIRS projects included a second and third Red Book (*Order of Battle of the German Army*), each of which was substantially larger than the ones that preceded it, and a revised *German Replacement Army*, which appeared in February 1945.

The MIRS historians have noted that more than half of London and Washington efforts was devoted to intelligence research rather than to the mere handling of documents and the extraction of raw information from them. "The results of this research were universally acclaimed," they noted, "and their value should not be underrated."[16]

Still, there were problems with the MIRS setup. The existence of two MIRS branches in London and Washington led to inevitable duplication of tasks. And through its concentration on intelligence gathered from documents, it failed to benefit from that gathered from the interrogators of German POWs. This was true even at PO Box 1142, where high-value POWs were housed on the same base as the MIRS researchers.

An even bigger problem—in both London and Washington—was with document storage and agency access. There were no designated MIRS librarians to catalog and properly shelve the tons of documents that poured into the Washington office. Even the added space that it acquired for storage after D-Day was inadequate, and the buildings housing the MIRS section lacked any kind of fireproofing. As a result, other agencies were unable to browse the materials, and they had to request access to them in writing.

These problems were alleviated at the close of the European war when, on July 14, 1945, MIRS was deactivated, and men and documents were transferred from the London and Washington branches to Camp Ritchie, where there was now ample room—and staffing—to create a well-ordered library of captured German war documents. Here former MIRS researchers and Ritchie staff continued their work as the German Military Document Section, or GMDS. Researchers at Ritchie now had the assistance of high-level German officers with expertise in various areas of the German High Command. These prisoners worked side by side with American researchers and translators in what would become known as the Hill Project.

As a major, Eric Birley helped set up the MIRS program. After V-E Day, he moved to Camp Ritchie to serve at the German Military Document Center. SOURCE: SPECIAL COLLECTIONS & COLLEGE ARCHIVES, GETTYSBURG COLLEGE

Mark Churms's painting of the MIRS office at PO Box 1142. From left to right: Philip Tucker (standing); Paul Fairbrook and Dieter Kober (seated at desks); John Kluge (holding a file); Horton Smith (in the doorway). SOURCE: NATIONAL PARK SERVICE

Siegfried F. Gronich sent the first collection of captured war documents from Algiers to London. Later, he served as the first chief of PACMIRS and then went to Europe to collect and catalog military documents sent to the German Military Document Center at Camp Ritchie. SOURCE: SPECIAL COLLECTIONS & COLLEGE ARCHIVES, GETTYSBURG COLLEGE

The *Order of Battle of the German Army*, one of the most important documents to come out of the MIRS office at PO Box 1142. MIRS updated it constantly. SOURCE: NATIONAL ARCHIVES AND RECORDS ADMINISTRATION

CHAPTER EIGHT

Field Maneuvers and Close Combat Training

Have you hit the trail to High Rock,
Emmitsburg or Monterey,
Have you driven a jeep to Foxville,
On a freezing winter's day?

Have you made the Twenty Stations,
On the two-day problem, Nein
And deciphered Turkish road maps
When dead tired and almost blind?[1]

FIELD MANEUVERS

As was the situation with most US Army training camps, the men at Ritchie were required to participate in a number of vigorous field exercises during daylight hours in order to maintain strength and endurance, and to practice flexible battlefield skills. There was the mandatory running and long-distance marching, for example, as well as calisthenics and training at the rifle range. The men practiced throwing hand grenades and loading shells, and firing submachine guns, pistols, and small carbines. There was a trainasium available at the nearby Office of Strategic Services (OSS) camp—an elaborate construct of logs, rings, ropes, and nets designed to provide extreme training in balance and agility, in climbing and descent, in swinging, and in jumping over barriers. The men were also trained to take apart and put together M-1 rifles and machine guns. And there were mock battles, staged by the permanent cadre of the Composite School Unit. These included German tank attacks. The Ritchie trainees were taught to deal with an enemy entrenched in various defensive structures, and with detecting and destroying nests of hidden sharpshooters. A local farmer's son remembers the realism of these battle scenes:

> *The army placed a pontoon bridge across the creek. A machine gun was on the hill about 50 yards from the bridge. Once each week, the trainees would charge from the west bank across the bridge and up the hill to "attack" the machine gun position. The machine gun would be firing at them. It was blanks of course, but made a lot of noise. Some sort of smoke bombs were set off to simulate artillery shell bursts as the trainees were advancing.*
>
> *The machine gun and the soldiers firing . . . took place not far, maybe 150 yards, from my uncle's house and farm buildings. I know it affected his flock of laying hens. I am not certain if he just sold them or what.*

He also recalled:

> *On another occasion, an army truck went up the road. We saw them cut the fence and drive to the other side of the pasture by the woods. The soldiers immediately began to cut branches off trees and put them beside and on the top of the truck to hide it. Not long afterwards, a small Piper Cub airplane flew across the area several times. It was testing how well the truck had been hidden.[2]*

Even the camp commander got involved in the war exercises. As Lieutenant William Sloane Coffin recalled, Banfill had a disconcerting habit: "[T]o keep his men on their toes he would take to the air and without warning fly bombing raids in his Piper Cub, dropping five-pound flour bags on us as we raced for cover. Any man caught with flour on him was gigged" (i.e., given a demerit).[3]

Despite the realism of the daytime exercises, nearly all the Ritchie graduates recalled their night maneuvers as a particularly challenging part of their practical training. They participated in a variety of these exercises during the regular eight-week course of study. Their length varied from a few hours to eight days. One exercise tested the men's ability to identify vehicles that they could hear but not see. Another was to be driven at night up to a lookout at Pen Mar, from where one could look far down into Pennsylvania. The purpose of that exercise was "to demonstrate that one could quite clearly see when somebody two kilometers away lit a match down in the valley."[4] This kind of graphic demonstration was typical of the Camp Ritchie style, and it taught the men that, when out at night in enemy territory, they should use a match or flashlight only when it was completely hidden behind a helmet or under one's coat. A more active nocturnal exercise involved driving heavy army vehicles at high speeds on unpaved forest roads.

The men also learned how to "unload" from a truck going ten to fifteen miles an hour. As Private Baldwin T. Eckel of Camp Ritchie's sixth class explained, "We held our rifle across our waist, stepped off backward hitting the ground on our feet and then rolling into a ball letting the helmet take the brunt of the roll. After rolling head over heels for 20 to 30 yards one comes to a stop none the worse for wear."[5]

One exercise, repeated weekly, involved army azimuth training. The men were trucked out into the countryside and dropped off in pairs with nothing but a map and compass. Their assignment was to determine their location on the map and, from that, to find their way to specified coordinates, where they would be met by the Ritchie trucks for a ride back to camp. Those who failed to arrive at the site within a given time frame had to return to the camp on their own. Orders stated that they were not to follow any paved roads, nor were they to ask directions of any local residents. Furthermore, after their first nighttime experience, the men were given maps that listed all the mountains, rivers, farms, and such in a foreign language; on one such outing, Sergeant Peter Burland and his partner were given a map in what he believed was Vietnamese.

It is therefore perhaps not surprising that, especially in the one- and two-day exercises, cheating was quite common. On one occasion,

Sergeant Daniel Teeter, a native of Gettysburg, happened to lift the flap of the truck as his platoon was being transported out for a night exercise. As he peered out, the truck was passing the Lower Marsh Creek Presbyterian Church, where he had gotten married three weeks before reporting to army basic training. From this he knew they were traveling on the Fairfield Road; he also knew the location of his in-laws' home two miles distant. Teeter told the men with him not to worry; he knew exactly where they were.[6]

More often, soldiers simply disobeyed orders and stopped at a farmhouse to ask for directions. As the German author Stefan Heym put it:

One simply needs to find one's way to the next farm and knock on the door, because, you see, with the military's lack of fantasy one is asked to complete the same exercises in every course, and the local population has known all about them for a long time. The friendly farmer sticks his head out of the door, inquires as to which map one is carrying, in which language, and what the fixed coordinates are, the goal, simply. Then he shows where one is at the present time and shows the lost troop the shortest way to the camp.[7]

Sergeant Hans Tuch recalled the help given his unit by a twelve-year-old farm boy: "He asked us were we 'Italian' or 'German,' meaning were we in the program directed against the Italian or German Army? We told him 'German Army'; he told us to wait a moment, dug up a sheet of paper and told us to strike an azimuth of 35.5 degrees on our compass and follow the direction! (He obviously got the same question frequently from other 'lost' GIs.)"[8]

Another teenaged farm boy, John Fuss, lived close to the drop-off point. "At least 75% of the nights, there would be a knock on the door in about ten minutes," he recalled:

There would be four soldiers asking for help. . . . Dad would show them where they were on the Harney Road. They used the compass to determine the direction to walk. . . . My mother would always serve each a piece of pie or cake. They would eat it hurriedly because they had to be on their way. She often gave them a pack of cookies to take along and eat later.

The soldiers knew that they were cheating. "On one occasion," Fuss remembered, "a vehicle pulled into our driveway. The soldiers grabbed their map, helmets, and equipment and rushed out the back door. They knew they were not supposed to be in a house. It happened that the vehicle was just turning around."[9] Occasionally, the soldiers were found out. In such cases, the men might be denied the usual promotions given at the end of the Camp Ritchie training. Commenting on the "don't ask any farmer" rule, Private Henry Bretton remarked, "Ironically, once in Germany . . . I found German farmers most helpful when I asked them for direction."[10]

The farmers could not offer as much assistance to the men on their longer two- and eight-day maneuvers, however, since on these the men were required to locate tents set up at various sites in the surrounding forest and to perform a given task at each tent site. These exercises were carried out by larger groups of four to ten men. One man recalled the two-day maneuver with a shudder:

A group of us missed our goal in the middle of the night by a hundred yards, and tramped on for more than a mile through a rocky and hilly forest, until we came to a steep canyon and could neither move forward nor backtrack. We had to sleep on the ground as best as we could and wait until dawn. We did not even have a flashlight with us. Since many of us lacked field experience, there had been nothing in our previous training to prepare us for this contingency.[11]

The exercises were conducted in all kinds of weather and often in treacherous terrain. Even in good weather it was never an "easy or rapid hike,"[12] and rank made no distinctions. Captain John Kluge recalled how, during his night maneuvers, he "sat on a nest of snakes. . . . And, of course, they were copperheads. . . . Maryland was loaded with copperheads."[13] And Spanish Civil War veteran Lawrence Cane said, "We did about 45 miles through very rugged mountain country in two days, we had no sleep to speak of, and very little food." In addition, "it poured the first night, and we were drenched. I didn't really get dried out until . . . we got back."[14]

On November 8, 1943, a particularly ugly situation arose when a flash flood occurred in the Emmitsburg area. Six Ritchie soldiers had been out in the driving rain, following a farmer's fence across a flooded field, when the fence collapsed and they were swept by a surge of water into Tom's Creek. Five of the six men were able to cling to a tree; the sixth, Syrian-born private Peter Asaad Peters, was swept away by the current. The accident occurred at 9:30 p.m. The farm owner heard the shouts of the five men, but he was unable to reach them from his flooded field. He summoned help, and a team of fifty firemen, state troopers, and Ritchie soldiers rescued the men about five hours later when they finally managed to get seventy-five feet upriver and throw a rope that drifted downstream to them in the current. When they were finally pulled to shore, the men were suffering from shock and exposure and were taken to a nearby hospital. A hundred men from Ritchie then continued the search for Peters' body, and it was eventually found about one thousand yards farther downstream.[15]

The two-day and eight-day maneuvers set the men up for a wide range of tasks testing what they had learned in the classroom. The young John Fuss remembered, "The upper floor of our barn was used on several occasions by groups of 10 or more. Once I saw one soldier point a gun at several others. It appeared that they were 'prisoners.' At the same time three or four others on the other side of the building were asking questions. I suppose it was a practice interrogation."[16] Lieutenant Howard Bowman said of his exercises:

A covered truck would take us up in the Catoctin Mountains. . . . It was cold and it was snowy. They would dump us out of [the] truck and made us find our way to a certain point on the map. . . . There was a tent there and there was a German prisoner to be interrogated. . . . We would interrogate him and then write up the interrogation report. We then had to transmit it by Morse code or radio to some place.

Then, we would go to another point and there we would find some German Army documents which we had to interpret and analyze and so on.[17]

There were many variations in the maneuver activities. Private Henry Bretton recalls how his team of five was given no map when it was sent out at night with instructions to locate an unlit tent concealed in the forest. As part of the exercise, "enemy" cavalry was sent to intercept and punish them. These "enemies" were "American Sioux Indians on horseback, dressed in enemy uniforms—German in our case, Italian or Japanese in others—and authorized to rough us up in the event of capture."[18] Lieutenant Maximilian Lerner confirmed this story. "At times," he wrote, "we were captured by soldiers from the permanent cadre wearing German uniforms. They put us through long periods of interrogation without damaging us too much. At times, we did the interrogating. We played games wearing different uniforms and practiced hiding out behind enemy lines."[19]

Staff Sergeant Stephan Lewy found the eight-day maneuvers stressful. He, too, remembers being attacked "by 200 hooting and hollering Native Americans dressed in German and Italian uniform." He provided a different take on the "attack," however. "To say we were startled and terrified is to put it mildly, but our job was to identify the 'enemies' insignias." Part of their assignment was to figure out which division they belonged to, what guns they were firing, and what the "casualty" count was.[20]

These strenuous field maneuvers prepared the Ritchie soldiers for all sorts of battlefield situations. They learned to find their way around unknown territory with only a compass and a map. They learned to evade an attack, secure an enemy site, acquire and interpret enemy documents, and pass on the information to Headquarters by Morse code. And, perhaps most important, they learned to take prisoners in a battlefield setting and interrogate them for tactical and strategic information. Lieutenant Bowman said the program was "intensive and strenuous. I never worked so hard. I went to two tough colleges, but I never studied as hard as I did there."[21]

CLOSE COMBAT TRAINING

In 1943, a new degree of realism was introduced to the fields of combat and counterintelligence when Major Rex Applegate joined the instruction staff at Camp Ritchie. A former military policeman, he had been recruited the year before to help Colonel William "Wild Bill" Donovan build a nearby OSS training camp for intelligence officers in the Catoctin Mountains. At this camp, popularly known as "The School for Spies and Assassins," Applegate had coordinated instruction in hand-to-hand combat, knife fighting, and pistol firing for the camp while perfecting methods for effective unarmed combat in collaboration with William Fairbairn, a British operative who had worked for the Shanghai Municipal Police and developed techniques that relied heavily on Chinese martial arts. Late in 1942, Applegate had also gone to Britain to train with British commandos and had participated in reconnaissance missions into German-occupied Europe. A lung ailment prevented his return to active service, but, together with William Fairbairn, he was given free rein at Ritchie to duplicate and expand upon his OSS training methods, and to design realistic training aids at the camp.

Major Applegate was a formidable man. He was six feet three inches tall, weighed 230 pounds, and was an expert marksman. He was also a collector of weaponry. "His office was an arsenal," one Ritchie man recalled. "In addition he had covered the walls with signs praising the Colt pistol, *the great equalizer.* 'You can be as weak as you want—with a Colt in your pocket you are as strong as a giant.'"[22] He was also an enthusiastic teacher of the art of killing. The Europeans in the class had difficulty dealing with this excitement; for them, American exuberance was a sign of appalling naïveté, and they found it difficult to get enthusiastic about learning killing techniques. On one occasion, when Applegate was teaching the men how to garrote a sentry, he remarked, "Now, when you have thrown the piano wire over the sentry's head and pulled it tight around his neck—like so. Now! Is he going to like that?" There was a long pause, and then Technician Third Grade Benno Frank, an overweight German opera director, replied, "No, he is not going to like it!" Applegate responded, "You are absolutely right—he will not like it!" "By this time," a friend of Frank's recalled, "Frank and the instructor were staring at each other."[23] It was difficult enough to drill these intellectuals in close marching and calisthenics; knifing and garroting were subjects totally foreign to them. Yet Applegate was thoroughly committed to giving the men the benefit of his experience.

He had developed and refined a system for "point shooting" or "instinctive firing" of pistols. Whereas most combat soldiers, like law enforcement officers, were trained in marksmanship with hand guns, Applegate rejected the idea of using pistol sights and aiming at fixed targets. He found four conditions on the battlefield that required the development of new techniques:

1. In most cases, the *time* to take an aimed shot will not be available, and the hand gun ordinarily will be used a distance of 50 feet or less.

2. The light necessary to see and use the sights (if the time were available) is not always sufficient.

3. The grip on the weapon is a *convulsive* one, because of combat tension.

4. The instinctive position assumed by a hand gun user in a fire fight will usually be an aggressive forward *crouch*.[24]

He taught men that speed was more essential than accuracy. "You hit where you look," he instructed. Instead of raising one's pistol to eye level, one should swiftly whip it up to the hip and extend one's arm as though pointing a finger at the enemy. Then one should immediately fire off two shots, followed by another two if necessary.[25] Firing two shots increased the likelihood of hitting one's target.

The Ritchie soldiers had several hours of training in point shooting at an indoor pistol range before being sent to the grounds of the nearby OSS camp and what the Ritchie soldiers—and Applegate himself—referred to as a "House of Horrors." This dimly lit indoor combat firing course had uneven flooring, tilting floor boards, winding stairways, and unexpected turns. The soldiers entered, individually, armed with a pistol, twenty-four rounds of ammunition, and a knife. An instructor, or coach, followed closely behind each soldier, maintaining contact with him at all times and offering an on-the-spot critique of each of the soldier's actions. It was he who tripped all the targets at the appropriate time. Some targets were bobbing silhouettes, some were stationary silhouettes, and some were dummies. Some of these targets even fired at the trainee. At one point, each soldier had to crawl through a tunnel, stabbing four dummies hidden there among mock-up dead bodies in fatigue suits simulated by inflated inner tubes. At one point, entering a room to encounter the enemy, the soldier found, instead, a soldier clearly wearing an American uniform. "If he fires at it," Applegate said, "he is reprimanded for shooting one of his own men, when recognition was easily possible." About 10 percent of the soldiers who passed through the House of Horrors made this mistake. Ritchie soldier Hanuš Burger, who assisted in filming the House of Horrors for the OSS, said that it was "a labyrinth, an authentic one, a kind of ghost house. Everyone had to go through it once. . . . The labyrinth was draped in black and unlit. But every once in a while a horrifying, life-sized figure, harshly lit, jumped out of the darkness and moved towards the visitor. He had to shoot it away immediately from the hip. The hits were recorded electronically, and the grinning major stood at the exit and presented him with the list of shots."[26] A good score was the successful "killing" of ten of the house's twelve targets. The experience was made particularly stressful through sound effects: music (Stravinsky!), sounds of torture, moans of dying men, barking of dogs, sounds of a woman being raped, German men at leisure in a pub. Applegate noted, "All the elements involving the use of the handgun . . . have taken place while the shooter was making his way through the course. He was subjected to physical and mental tension, to the element of surprise, and to the unknown. Realistic and difficult shooting and reloading conditions were caused by poor lighting, unsteady footing, and sound effects; and the loss of sense of direction, because of his irregular progress, was emphasized." It was, he said "as close to the real thing as possible."[27] The "House of Horrors" experience served two purposes. First, it prepared the men, in a controlled environment, for the stressful situations they might encounter on the battlefield. Second, and equally important, it identified those shooters "who were psychologically unsuited for combat or who had the wrong kind of temperament."[28] These men would be reassigned to other duties.

Another training building, a "Counterintelligence House" on the Camp Ritchie grounds, was simply an old farmhouse with one side cut away from it so that students could sit on a grandstand and watch as the Composite School Unit cadre demonstrated various techniques of search and seizure and their class members performed various exercises. The house had multiple purposes: it was used to demonstrate the right and wrong ways to conduct raids and searches and how to sneak into a building and steal German maps without getting caught. Each student then had to participate in the planning, reconnaissance, and conduct of a raid and search. A particularly difficult part of these exercises involved the recognition and defusing of booby traps and anti-personnel devices that were placed throughout the house. Sergeant Peter Burland recalls that seventeen booby traps were placed there, and each member of his class had to go through all the rooms of the house to find and defuse them. They were told that anything that could be opened or picked up could be booby trapped: a door, a military helmet, a book, a picture slightly askew upon the wall. All that was needed to booby trap an object was to attach a nearly invisible fuse to an explosive. "Fuses set the booby traps off like firecrackers," Burland recalled. "Only one of my class made it all the way through. I was 'killed' by the seventh booby trap there."[29]

Booby traps and hidden land mines were, in fact, scattered at various sites around the camp to tweak the soldiers' skill in detecting and defusing them: in a field, in the forest, even in an airplane fuselage. Although they were designed to frighten—but not injure—the trainees, Staff Sergeant Sandor Sigmond, from the eleventh class, recalls how one soldier was killed when he entered the booby-trapped house. "Realistic conditions were an important component of our training," he remarked, "and we had to be on alert every second."[30]

Veterans of the camp testified that the experience the men gleaned from these exercises proved critical in the European theater. Captain Arthur Jaffe, for example, recalled how he and Ritchie sergeant Bert Anger were patrolling a field in France when Anger suddenly threw him to the ground. Anger's sharp eyes had seen that Jaffe had been about to step on a land mine. Jaffe noted, gratefully, that "Bert Anger saved my life."[31] In another close call, Lieutenant Ed Holton, who came ashore several days after D-Day, was ordered to raid the vacated Gestapo headquarters. "The only thing the Gestapo left behind as they fled was booby-trapped toilet seats," he remembered. "I could tell by the elevation of the seat." His sharp eyes saved the lives of his men. "We had to do our business on the floor of their headquarters," he remarked. It was an "interesting way to start out."[32]

A "German village" was also constructed at the camp. Built of plywood and burlap, the "village" consisted of a town square flanked by a variety of official, business, and private structures, built in a variety of styles. The Ritchie soldiers were trained here in conducting door-to-door searches, flushing out enemy soldiers, and engaging in both street and close hand-to-hand combat. British major William Fairbairn came from the OSS camp to teach the secrets of the latter. "Never hold the knife pointed down," he instructed the men, "you may gut yourself." Some of the men regarded the lessons as preparations for glorified bar fights. They were told to use broken bottles where they could for self-defense and that below-the-belt kicks were quite acceptable. This form of fighting, the Ritchie men discovered, "was intended more to disable German guards than [to fight] enemy soldiers."[33] The men also learned how to kill a man silently by coming up behind him and grabbing his face to cover his mouth and nose while simultaneously plunging a knife deep into his kidneys and then swiftly pulling it out to cut the man's throat. The men were given rubber knives to use in these exercises.[34]

Although the knives were rubber, the men also worked with all sorts of live ammunition since they, like all infantrymen, had to learn "how to throw grenades, fire the bazooka, launch rifle-grenades and wallow through the infiltration course" under live fire.[35] Many of the trainees were not particularly adept at these skills. One soldier, Albert Guerard, was told that he had passed his rifle range test with an "astonishingly good score." Only later did he learn that he had, in reality, hit the wrong target.[36] Sometimes the ineptness of the trainees had more serious consequences. William Aalto, a veteran of the Abraham Lincoln Battalion during the Spanish Civil War, was training the Ritchie soldiers in demolition work when he saw someone drop a live grenade. He made a lunge for it, but, before he could throw it away, the bomb exploded, severing his arm at the wrist.[37]

To remind the men of the consequences of inattentiveness, Colonel Banfill had a mock cemetery constructed that the Ritchie men had to pass every day of instruction. It served as a constant reminder that war was a serious business, requiring constant vigilance in the battle zone. If this wasn't sobering enough, the gravestones provided moral lessons. One declared, "Under this sod / lies Mortimer Todd. / He put his trust / in a rusty rod"; another, for "J. E. Draper," read, "Fools may come & / Fools may go. / This one went: / He drew too slow." Perhaps the bluntest of them all simply stated, "Billy Mize / He didn't practice. / Here he lies."

Two men try to solve a night compass problem by orienting their map to the terrain. SOURCE: NATIONAL ARCHIVES AND RECORDS ADMINISTRATION

During their field exercises, the Ritchie men were frequently "attacked" by "enemy" soldiers. SOURCE: NATIONAL ARCHIVES AND RECORDS ADMINISTRATION

Ritchie men perform tasks assigned to them as part of their final eight-day field exercise. SOURCE: NATIONAL ARCHIVES AND RECORDS ADMINISTRATION

Major Rex Applegate designed a "House of Horrors" in which Ritchie men were tested for their ability to function in a war setting. SOURCE: FORT RITCHIE

A German village was constructed on the Ritchie grounds. Here men were taught how to take and secure a German town. SOURCE: NATIONAL ARCHIVES AND RECORDS ADMINISTRATION

The men learned how to find and defuse booby traps. Here a soldier defuses a booby trap in the fuselage of a downed plane. SOURCE: NATIONAL ARCHIVES AND RECORDS ADMINISTRATION

The men practiced with all types of weaponry, including hand grenades. SOURCE: NATIONAL ARCHIVES AND RECORDS ADMINISTRATION

CHAPTER NINE

Instructional Units

Growing old and gray at Ritchie,
Have you looked back at your prime,
Shook your head and told your children,
"I was a soldier in my time"?

Fully trained in G-2 tactics,
And past master of Z-5
Schulterklappen, Battle Order,
Pigeons, maps and Vogue-Room jive.[1]

THE INSTRUCTION AT CAMP RITCHIE FOCUSED ON THREE AREAS OF
specialization: Interrogation of Prisoners of War, Photo Intelligence,
and Order of Battle. Nevertheless, a great many other aspects of military
intelligence were packed into the basic program. In all these cases, fieldwork supplemented classroom lectures and work with manuals created by
the US War Department and by the Camp Ritchie instructors. In their
work—whether detecting and defusing bombs, occupying and securing
a town, or rounding up prisoners—the students learned the value of
understanding enemy psychology. The Visual Division of the Composite
School Unit stressed this in its mini-dramas and its Hitler rallies, but
German and US Department of War documentaries were also valuable
teaching tools. For a time, Leni Riefenstahl's monumental documentary
Triumph of the Will was the only German documentary available to the
armed forces, and it was shown weekly to all the Camp Ritchie students.

It captured, with frightening artistic intensity, the pageantry, grandeur, and fanaticism of the seven hundred thousand Nazi supporters who attended the 1934 Nazi Party Congress in Nuremberg. From this film, the students could study the rise of National Socialism and the characteristics and personalities of high-ranking Nazis. Second Lieutenant John Dolibois, a native of Luxembourg, noted that by viewing this film the students "became thoroughly familiar with the Nazi personalities. We observed their manners of speech, their walk—or strut—their posturing and, especially, their fawning behavior toward Hitler. We identified uniforms and rank insignia of the leaders of the military and paramilitary organizations in this Nazi Rally." As an instructor in the German section at Camp Ritchie, he showed that film every Thursday afternoon for eight months. "I could," he remarked, "almost recite all the speeches myself."[2]

The camp also took advantage of the expertise of the men enrolled in its classes for special presentations. Second Lieutenant Lawrence Cane, for example, had fought with the International Brigades in the Spanish Civil War, and he was asked to give a lecture titled "Military Geography of Spain." In preparation for this lecture, Cane noted with some pride that "highly confidential information [was] placed in my hands—stuff that the British Admiralty has been compiling."[3] Later Cane would go on to win the Silver Star in the European theater.

Language classes were also a part of the Camp Ritchie curriculum. Although the students who entered the program were selected for their language ability, most did not know the specialized military terms necessary for functioning as interrogators, interpreters, translators, or counterintelligence agents in the field. Staff Sergeant Peter Burland was already fluent in Greek when he was assigned to the fifth Greek guerrilla warfare class at Camp Ritchie, but he and all the 150 Greeks assembled for this class were required to study Greek military language. "All languages were taught there," Burland recalled, "including the five Arabic languages."[4]

In addition to its special class offerings, there was instruction in a variety of intelligence areas that was required of all participants in the eight-week program. The most important of these was *Army Organization*. Before any of the Camp Ritchie soldiers could function adequately at the front, they needed to know the organization of the armies they would encounter: British, French, Italian, Japanese, and, especially, German. This involved both a good deal of attention to detail and lots of memorization. Lawrence Cane was certainly not the only student to be surprised when he looked at one of the textbooks issued to him for this course. As he wrote to his wife, "Imagine when I opened the Field Manual on the organization of the German Army and found it to be in German! A reprint of the latest field manual issued by the German Army itself. I was half-afraid to open the manual on the Japanese Army. I thought the damn thing might be in Japanese. But it wasn't." Still, he wrote, "I sure see why they want us to know foreign languages."[5]

From this manual, the students learned the structure of the German fighting units, their weaponry, and German military ranks, uniforms, uniform insignia, and other markings, and they were asked to commit it all to memory. As Sergeant Ib Melchior, from the tenth class, put it, they were asked to learn about any and all units one might encounter in the war:

> *The future IPWs learned German army organization directly from the training manuals of the German army itself, until they knew by heart the exact breakdown of every type of unit, including the number and types of weapons and all other equipment carried. Even such outlandish units as a Nachrichtenhelferinneneinsatzabteilung (female signal operations battalion), an Astronomischer Messzug (astronomical survey platoon), and a Kraftfahrzeuginstandsetzungabteilung (motor vehicle repair battalion) were studied and remembered.*
>
> *They learned German army identification, from the colors of all the various services and arms and the insignia of all the ranks, to the individual emblems of specialized jobs in the German army, right down to the special insignia of the apprentice to the noncommissioned officer in charge of shoeing horses.*[6]

After successful completion of the eight-week program, those students who excelled in Army Organization would be assigned to additional training in German Order of Battle.

In addition to mastering German or Japanese army organization, the students learned to evaluate *Army Documents*. These raw materials contributed greatly to reliable military intelligence. One of the most valuable documents available to the Allied soldiers was a German soldier's pay book, or *Soldbuch*. All German military personnel were required to carry this twenty-four-page document with them at all times. It contained a great deal of information besides the soldier's pay grade. It provided the name and address of the soldier's next of kin; a list of the clothing, equipment, and weaponry issued to the soldier; his medical information; and awards. Most important for intelligence gathering was the book's listing of the soldier's current and past assigned units. All previous replacement units were crossed out, but always in such a manner as to remain legible. Thus an interrogator could, by looking at a prisoner's pay book, determine all the places where the soldier had served prior to his capture.

The Camp Ritchie students were thoroughly trained in reading German pay books. But there were other documents to be studied as well. Technical Sergeant Hanuš Burger of Ritchie's sixth class remembered that a special barrack at Camp Ritchie "housed tons of captured documents, letters, maps, and pieces of equipment. Here one learned how to interpret, evaluate, and archive such a windfall from a battlefield."[7]

Once in the field Technical Sergeant Leo Handel became a master at using documents to his advantage. As his friend Ib Melchior recalled it:

> *It was Handel's wont, when entering a bivouac area previously occupied by the opposing forces, to gather all the papers he could find, including old hometown newspapers left behind by the troops. . . . From a previous PW, Handel had learned the name of the CO of the 6th Company, a Lieutenant Kaiser, and in a local paper from a small town in the area from which the personnel of the 6th Company of the 1044th Regiment were recruited, he had read an article about a hometown boy, a lieutenant of the same name, congratulating him on the birth of a son, Karl Otto, born in January.*

When men from this company were taken captive, Handel sought out the lieutenant, walked up to him, addressed him by name, and congratulated him and his wife Liselotte on the birth of Karl Otto. The lieutenant, now convinced that the Americans must know everything about him and his company, gave Handel the location of the three 88 mm self-propelled guns that had been harassing the American forces.[8]

Terrain Intelligence—map making and map interpretation—was another essential part of the instruction at Camp Ritchie and was constantly reinforced with exercises in the field. The students' first assignment was to learn and reproduce all symbols that might appear on American, British, and German maps. In addition to learning basic symbols for roads, streams, and railway lines, students learned to differentiate between symbols for different kinds of buildings (churches, hospitals, factories, radio stations); landscape features (trees, rocks, shrubs, swamps); and man-made changes to the landscape (dikes, quarries, vineyards, mines). They learned the finer distinctions in these symbols as well: evergreen versus broadleaf forests, for example, or Christian versus non-Christian cemeteries, or stone walls versus wood fences versus barbed wire barriers. They had to know the German abbreviations of the various landscape features that might appear on a hand-drawn map: "Brn." for distillery (*Brennerei*), for example, or "E.F." for railroad ferry (*Eisenbahnfähre*), "S.W." for sawmill (*Sägewerk*), and "Schp." for shed (*Schuppen*). Students in the earlier classes were even taught symbols applicable to Iranian and Iraqi maps, such as those used for camel trade routes, mosques, and palm trees. Each nationality had variations in its symbols and in the abbreviations of terms, and the students were required to recognize and reproduce them all.

In addition to these standardized symbols, the men were taught symbols for marking specific military units on a field map; these included symbols for individual armored regiments, infantry regiments, coast artillery, medical battalions, cavalry regiments, tank destroyer battalions, and prisoner of war enclosures. These skills were essential for interrogators seeking tactical intelligence from German prisoners.

The instructors used the local topography for their class exercises in map creation and interpretation. There was a certain irony to this situation, since it meant that the Ritchie Boys were studying the terrain from Antietam to Gettysburg, sites of some of the bloodiest fighting of the

American Civil War, while imagining that the landscape was threatened by enemy soldiers of the Third Reich. The important thing was for the Ritchie Boys to learn and understand the local terrain, so that they could carry out nocturnal field exercises with some knowledge of the land around them. The skills they acquired for these exercises could be applied to any setting, but actual battle situations could be simulated only locally. In one of their first classes, for example, students were asked to determine the military grid coordinates to the nearest ten yards of small, specific sites in the area, such as the isolated Eyler's Valley Chapel northeast of Flint and the Roddy Road Covered Bridge near Thurmont. This exercise tied in neatly with the students' two-day field exercises.

Soon they were being taken into the countryside for daytime field exercises and given incomplete maps showing only roads, stream lines, and critical elevations. They were taught how to use the compass in order to determine the magnetic azimuths of various points: a hilltop, for example, or the Buena Vista Hotel, a highway underpass, and so on. They were then taken on a daytime field exercise to an observation point familiar to them and asked to orient a map by using terrain features that could be clearly recognized on the ground. Technical Sergeant Leon Edel marveled at the effect this training had on his appreciation of his surroundings:

> *Suddenly the nature of the land, the contours of the roads along which we marched, the softness or hardness beneath our shoes, the vegetation, the birds fluttering away from us when we disturbed them, represented an environment. . . . All this was a particular revelation to the city-bred, and even to someone like myself, long removed from the Canadian prairies.*[9]

The course work culminated in an observation post exercise. Here students, using field glasses, learned to fill out ground observer's reports. The Composite School Unit provided "enemy" activity consisting of a half-track vehicle moving along a road; a platoon squad reconnoitering the area; a column of trucks; camouflaged guns and prime-movers, including camouflaged heavy machine guns firing live ammunition; and smoke screens represented by smoke pots. The students had to observe the activity of the enemy, identify and record it, take azimuths, estimate ranges, and plot all of the enemy activity on an overlay.[10]

In addition to studying the terrain, the Ritchie Boys were instructed in *Weather* terminology. Because this knowledge was necessary for men engaged in airplane and glider activity, it was an essential part of the training for those intelligence officers who would be engaged in aerial photography and in paratroop work. The students were required to master a glossary of weather terms and then study the military aspects of various climatic elements for their favorable and unfavorable effects on ground and aerial activities. For "snow," for example, favorable aspects included "Fast ski patrols possible. Aerial observation and photography facilitated," while unfavorable aspects were that "Chains [are] needed for motor vehicles, tracks made visible from air. Slows rail transport. Ski-landing."[11] An "Intelligence Officer's Weather Check List" named the particular weather elements that would hamper air operations. These were important not only for the flights of Allied planes but also for predicting enemy action. The students were required to report on all aspects of the weather, such as cloud types and amounts, ceiling height, hindrances to and distance of visibility, wind, fronts, and so on, and then remark how each affected piloting a plane, navigation, observation, and bombardment capabilities.

Although many of the Camp Ritchie alums would serve as paratroopers, most of them got this training elsewhere. Many, in fact, were recruited in England shortly before D-Day and received their training there. Still, limited *Parachute* instruction was given at Ritchie. The men did not jump from aircraft there, but they did take practice leaps from a stationary tower.

Another unit of instruction involved *Writing Reports*. In order to transmit the information the men gathered in the field—from observation or interrogation—they had to be trained how to prepare and send messages and reports to the appropriate command officers. Just as with the exercises in maps and terrain intelligence, report assignments dealt with the local terrain. In one class situation, for example, German forces were reported to have landed on the East Coast and pushed forward

He Passed through Camp Ritchie

 Private First Class **Richard Topus** (1924–2008) was born in Brooklyn, New York, the son of Russian Jewish immigrants. Brooklyn was well known for pigeon racing, and Topus was eager to participate in the sport. Although his parents forbade him to have his own pigeons, Topus befriended neighbors who had pigeon lofts on their roofs and spent most of his boyhood learning how to handle the birds and train them for racing. Two of these mentors had served as pigeoneers in World War I. Thus, by the time Topus enlisted in the army, at age eighteen, he was an expert pigeon trainer.

He was assigned to the Army Signal Corps, which included the Pigeon Service. Eventually, he was brought to Camp Ritchie to train pigeons and soldiers for military service. The pigeons were bred and trained for service in a combat situation; the men were taught how to handle the pigeons in a war setting.

After the war, Topus went to Hofstra University, where he earned a bachelor's degree and master's degree in business. While a student, he sold chicken eggs door to door; afterward, he started a wholesale egg business. He became the first salesman at Friendship Food Products and retired from this firm as executive vice president for sales and marketing. He also taught marketing and, at State University of New York–Farmingdale, started a management training program for supermarket professionals. In retirement, Topus moved to Scottsdale, Arizona, where he taught part-time at Arizona State University and served as a securities arbitrator and volunteer with the Scottsdale Police Department. His passion for pigeons continued; he trained and raced pigeons throughout his lifetime. Topus combined his passion for pigeons with his marketing skills when, in the early 1960s, he oversaw the design for the Friendship Food logo: a bird in flight. Even though "Friendship Food Products" changed its name to "Friendship Dairy," it has, to this day, kept this logo—a tribute to Topus's lifelong passion.

from Philadelphia to Hanover, Pennsylvania, while German planes were active in the Gettysburg, Chambersburg, and Emmitsburg area, and German patrols were seen west of Gettysburg along the Gettysburg-Fairfield road. With this information, the Ritchie Boys were sent into the countryside in order to report on numerous conditions found within the area—and staged by the ever-present Composite School Unit. This included enemy motorized or mechanized movements, enemy identifications, road conditions, and so on. After creating a detailed report covering these aspects, the students were told to identify those items in their report that should be passed on to one's superiors and to isolate those that should be reported immediately. Finally, they were asked to identify the method of sending each item of immediate importance.

In another assignment, students were given a number of individual observations that were gleaned from a full report and asked to identify the value of each piece of information. Did it refer to terrain, to morale, to division histories, to tactical movement, to evidence of gas? And to whom should these pieces of information be sent? To regimental commanders? To an army or marine regiment intelligence officer?

The *Communication* of intelligence could not always occur by means of a written report. The Camp Ritchie students were told that, in a war setting, matters of urgency had to be reported by the fastest means available, to be followed, if necessary, by more detailed information as soon as it could be obtained. Ideally, students could pass this information on by radio, and they had ample practice doing this in their field exercises. This included working with different types of radio sets under a variety of war situations. Morse code was another means of passing on crucial information rapidly, and all the Ritchie Boys were required to learn the code and be tested in their ability to transmit messages. They were deemed successful in this if they were able to send and receive twenty words a minute.[12] Some of those students specializing in prisoner interrogation questioned the necessity of learning Morse telegraphy, when radio transmission was so efficient. As Staff Sergeant George Mandler put it, "The most extreme case of apparent irrelevance was the insistence by one of the senior officers in charge of communication that we all take and pass a course in Morse code. I also still have a short manual on *Pigeon Communication*—another leftover from World War I."[13]

Whereas all the Ritchie Boys were required to learn how to transmit and receive messages by radio and by Morse code, work with carrier pigeons was not part of the basic course work; it was one of Camp Ritchie's specialized offerings to a small number of trainees. Here the pigeons themselves were the students, along with the handful of men assigned to work with them. After a program of intense training at Ritchie, the pigeons and their handlers were sent into the war zones in Europe and Asia.

It appears that Sergeant Mandler was wrong to regard pigeoneering as irrelevant. Although the idea of using pigeons to carry crucial information across war zones had gained preponderance during World War I, pigeoneering peaked during World War II, when 54,000 pigeons, 150 officers, and 3,000 enlisted men were trained for pigeon service in the US Army.[14] Although the breeding and training program was headquartered at Camp Crowder, Missouri, Ritchie was one of several American army camps at which this training also occurred.

The pigeons were a special variety of domestic bird with an innate ability to find their way home over distances of up to one thousand miles. The advantages in warfare were obvious: pigeons could fly behind enemy lines and cover rough terrain inaccessible to humans; they could carry messages from battlefields and resistance cells on the European continent all the way to London; they could communicate between centers of battle; and they were especially valued wherever army units feared that the enemy could intercept radio broadcasts. As a result, pigeons would be heavily involved in the invasion of Normandy and in Operation Market Garden.

Unlike the static trench warfare of World War I, the World War II battle lines were fluid. This situation called for a specialized army training program for the pigeons: they now had to be taught to return to a loft or roost that might have moved some distance from its original site. It became a major task of the Camp Ritchie pigeoneers to train the pigeons to return to combat lofts that were moved around the grounds and surrounding area of the camp. The Pigeon Service also ran a small breeding program at the camp, designed to increase the speed and endurance of the birds.[15]

In this service, the Ritchie men worked side by side with the pigeons. The training of a war pigeon took eight weeks from its hatching. At four weeks, the chick was placed in a mobile loft, and, for the next three to four weeks, the loft was moved daily. This part of the training was critical if the birds were to be employed in active war zones. By the eighth week, the birds had built up enough stamina to make hour-long flights. At this point, they were trained to fly fifty to sixty miles, and then even farther; only at that point would they be considered ready to serve in combat.

While the pigeons were being trained at Ritchie, those dozen or so soldiers who were assigned to work with them learned how to handle and care for the birds, how to house and transport them, and how to insert and retrieve from a capsule tiny maps or encoded messages that they wrote on lightweight paper and tied to the pigeon's leg. The men learned how to drop the pigeons from airplanes or carry them on their chests or backs in special "pigeon vests" manufactured by the Maidenform brassiere company.

Despite the contempt for pigeons shown by many army men, the Pigeon Service proved to be a remarkable success. Roughly thirty thousand messages were sent from war zones and retrieved successfully, and, although the pigeons had to contend with enemy fire, power lines, and falcons, they successfully completed more than 90 percent of their missions.[16] Thirty-two pigeons even received medals of valor from the British Dickin Society for meritorious achievements in the field. Indeed, the men in the Pigeon Service regarded these hardworking birds as comrades in battle and gave many of them names, such as "Princess," "Commando," and "Navy Blue." Veterinarians supervised the birds' health; they received good medical treatment when they were wounded and a proper burial when they died. Unfortunately, the pigeons didn't always fare so well among the very people they were trained to help. Ritchie lieutenant colonel Seymour Steinberg tried gathering intelligence by dropping pigeons into France. But, he reported, "it didn't work well—the hungry French ate the pigeons."[17]

During the first five weeks of their training, Colonel Banfill carefully monitored the men's progress, in order to discover the particular strengths of each student and to place him in an appropriate area of specialization during the last weeks of class. Even then, a rapidly changing war situation could cause a sudden change of assignment. This led to some suspense during the graduation ceremony; as Peter Burland told it, "The graduates gathered in the camp theater, and the camp commander, Banfill, had a pile of envelopes in front of him, which were given to each of the commanders of the various missions. The mission commander would then call out the names of the participants in his group, and they would disappear."[18]

For the Ritchie soldiers, this uncertainty made graduation as much an occasion for stress as for joy. Some would be immediately sent abroad, where they might receive additional intelligence training in Britain before being sent on to France. Some might be sent to other US Army camps as instructors. Banfill selected a few lucky graduates for assignment to Officer Candidate School at Fort Benning, Georgia, where they, as "90-Day Wonders," could be commissioned as second lieutenants. Other graduates would be sent on maneuvers to camps in Tennessee, Louisiana, Kentucky, or Texas, where they would go through rigorous field training. Here they might spend several months training in live ammunition situations while also conducting interrogations of actual German POWs. Some might be sent to Ritchie's subcamp in Gettysburg, Pennsylvania, for intensive training in psychological warfare. And some would remain at Ritchie, filling various small assignments while waiting to be called to wartime action. A few unfortunates were even sent back to service under Master Sergeant Leavitt in the dreaded Company E, working in the mess halls or picking up cigarette butts.

Sand table models were another form of visual display in the Ritchie classes.
SOURCE: NATIONAL ARCHIVES AND RECORDS ADMINISTRATION

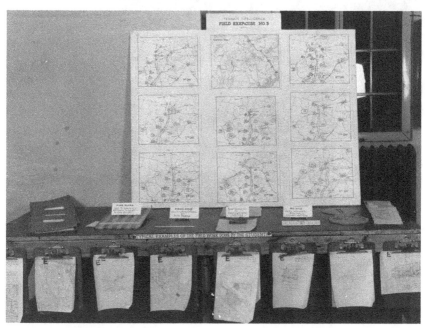

Student work in terrain intelligence was put up for display to visiting dignitaries.
SOURCE: NATIONAL ARCHIVES AND RECORDS ADMINISTRATION

A sample class handout for studying war tactics. SOURCE: NATIONAL ARCHIVES AND RECORDS ADMINISTRATION

A signal intelligence class listens to and interprets Morse code messages. SOURCE: NATIONAL ARCHIVES AND RECORDS ADMINISTRATION

Pigeon lofts at Ritchie. A mobile loft can be seen to the left. SOURCE: NATIONAL ARCHIVES AND RECORDS ADMINISTRATION

CHAPTER TEN

The Camp Ritchie WACs

The country is filled with WAVES and WACS;
Women in overalls, shorts and slacks.
Nobody now bakes bread or pie.
Grandma's at the airport, learning to fly,
Mom's at the plant, making ammunition,
And Dad is suffering from malnutrition.[1]

THE WAR DRASTICALLY CHANGED THE LIVES OF MANY AMERICAN women, as they entered the workforce to serve in office and factory positions formerly held by servicemen. Others were eager to play a more active part in the military. Prior to the attack on Pearl Harbor, Congress had been adamant in its refusal to allow women entry into the armed services. Battlefield nurses were acceptable because nursing was generally considered a "womanly" profession. But there was public opposition to the idea of women joining the military, fueled in part by false imaginings of women bearing firearms and by a slander campaign portraying army women as little more than promiscuous camp followers.[2] Finally, however, the women prevailed, and the Women's Army Auxiliary Corps (WAAC) was authorized in May 1942. The WAAC mission was to take over many of the administrative duties of the army men and thereby free them up for active service at the front. Since not all men were eager to exchange their office desks for the rigors of the battlefield, there was some resistance to the women's corps even among the GIs, who challenged the idea that women were up to the task. But the program proved so successful, as its members demonstrated their ability to work well beyond the confines of secretarial offices, that its mission expanded, and, with that expansion, a full-fledged Women's Army Corps, or WAC, was created in July 1943. The new corps members could now truly say that they were "in the army now."

And they were needed, as the war effort expanded exponentially and there was an ever greater demand for qualified personnel to fill the army's administrative offices both at home and behind the front lines in Europe and in the Pacific. WAC recruitment soon became a priority in the United States. Unfortunately, the WAC never met its goal of 150,000 recruits, but the nearly one hundred thousand women who did join proved the value of the program to even its harshest critics.

The requirements for WACs were relatively high. In order to become a WAAC or WAC, a woman had to be a high school graduate, between twenty-one and forty-five years of age, "of good health and character," and "stand between five and six feet tall, and weigh between 105 and 200 pounds."[3] The average woman filling the position of officer or enlisted personnel had a bachelor's degree. Many who joined did so out of patriotic enthusiasm and because they saw it as an opportunity both for career advancement and for overseas travel. Once the word *auxiliary* was dropped from their title, the members of the Women's Army Corps received the same pay, ranks, and privileges as their male counterparts.[4]

There had been discussion of bringing a WAAC contingent to Ritchie for training and office deployment as early as December 1942. On September 14, 1943, the first contingent of redesignated Women's Army Corps women arrived at Ritchie from the WAC Training School at Fort Des Moines, Iowa. This group included twelve enlisted women and two officers, Captain Ruth Mills Bradley and Lieutenant Natalie H. Tufts. Captain Bradley, a former trust company employee, served as the first commander of the Camp Ritchie WACs; Lieutenant Tufts, an actress, was the post's executive officer.

Nine new buildings were built for the women on the far side of Lake Royer, including a WAC administration building and the women's barracks. The two-story wooden barracks offered some amenities denied the Ritchie men: there were separate rooms for noncoms, window shades, a well-equipped laundry (with ironing boards), a latrine with six showers (and shower curtains!), and—to the delight of all of them—two enclosed bathtubs. "This," Captain Bradley exclaimed, "was almost too good to be true. We put on fatigue outfits, started to clean, and unpacked and in almost no time it began to look like home."[5]

On their second day at Ritchie, the women fixed up the administration building. This building included not only the WAC's administrative offices but also orderly and supply rooms; a room planned as a beauty parlor; a large day room for company meetings, parties, and relaxation; a library/writing room; and a branch post exchange store. During their first days at Ritchie, all the women worked together staining woodwork, scrubbing and waxing floors, and hanging curtains. Smaller groups of women arrived in the weeks that followed: in the second week, Lieutenant Harryette Hunter Emmerson, a renowned cooking instructor, came from Fort Oglethorpe, Georgia, with about eight women; she was the first WAC mess and supply officer at Ritchie. By March 20, 1944, thirty-five WAC officers arrived at camp to take over operational jobs. They were housed in a large frame building across the street from the administration building. There were now 107 women stationed at the post; all in all, about two hundred WACs came to serve at Ritchie. More than one-quarter of these women were officers.

Some, like Colonel Banfill's daughter Sergeant Margaret Manley, were married, although few were as fortunate as she in having their husbands stationed for a time at Camp Ritchie. Others were widows, although the majority of women were single. A few WACs got married during their service; this was not against WAC regulations. Getting pregnant was, however. In line with a government directive that no army woman could be discharged for a reason not equally applicable to an army man, pregnancy was declared a medical problem.[6] One Ritchie WAC, Corporal Patricia Crane, became pregnant during her service at the camp and received an honorable discharge as a "disabled" veteran; she then went on to work in the war industry.

The WACs at Ritchie came from all walks of life. Most were former teachers, stenographers, and typists, but their numbers also included waitresses, dressmakers, librarians, telephone operators, bookkeepers, writers, store clerks, beauticians, window dressers, language interpreters, and housewives. As with the Ritchie men, many of the Ritchie WACs had special language skills; there were also some rather exotic figures among them.

There was, for example, Lieutenant Jere Knight, a Quaker activist, poet, and editor. She had been one of the women who had lobbied most actively for the establishment of the WAAC. And there was Lieutenant Eleanor Moffett, a former Rockette at New York City's Radio City Music Hall, who was fluent in French and an ardent horsewoman. Before coming to Ritchie, she had taught infantry drill regulations at Fort Des Moines, Iowa—in French!—and had given riding lessons to the women on weekends. And there was Second Lieutenant Barbara Rode, who had attended English and Belgian schools, pursued graduate study in Italy and at Columbia, and danced before the king and queen of Belgium.

One WAC, Corporal Gregor Armstrong, was photographed at Ritchie in her WAC uniform for *Vogue* magazine; she was the socialite daughter of Mrs. Walter Lippmann and the American diplomat Hamilton Fish Armstrong and had just completed her studies at Bryn Mawr.

Those Ritchie women with strong language skills often had a foreign background to back them up. Private Larissa Patrekeyeva, for example, was the daughter of a Russian naval officer and had served as an interpreter for the Soviet government prior to her immigration to the United States. Private Altagrazie Rizk had a particularly colorful background: She was born in the Dominican Republic to parents who had emigrated to the United States from Lebanon. As a student, Rizk had gone to Lebanon to study French and then on to Tripoli to study French, Italian, and Arabic. By the end of her studies, she had mastered three of the five major dialects of Arabic. She also spoke Haitian Creole, having returned to live in Port-au-Prince before applying to become a WAC.

The Ritchie WACs were given tasks appropriate to their special skills. Most were given administrative and clerical positions. They quickly took over the duties of the enlisted men, working as typists, clerks, mimeograph operators, librarians, and truck drivers. They worked as projectionists, photo lab assistants, and radio and code operators. Many of the women who knew more than one language were assigned to service in the French, German, and Japanese sections of the school headquarters. Twelve of them took courses with the Ritchie men: "Order of Battle," "Special Photo Interpretation," and "Special Japanese Subjects." At least fifty were assigned to the faculty. WAC officers understudied the army officers in the various school sections as instructors; in personnel, classifications, the finance department, the theater office, and special services; and as assistant adjutant. Eleanor Moffett served as a French instructor at Ritchie; then she joined Section 7 in British Military Intelligence. Barbara Rode joined MIRS (the army's Military Intelligence Research Section) after completing Ritchie's "Order of Battle" course; she also served as the camp's theater manager. Larissa Patrekeyeva served as a Russian typist for Section 7 and then stayed on to serve in PACMIRS (the Pacific branch of MIRS). Lieutenant Dorothy Fischer took a special course in photo interpretation and subsequently became one of the course instructors. Corporal Frances S. Nichols, who'd been raised in Japan as the daughter of an Episcopal bishop, became an instructor in Section 7 (Enemy Armies—Japanese). And Lieutenant Carmen B. Knox, who had been born in France, taught the men at Ritchie how to act as Frenchmen so that they could serve as spies in occupied France.

In addition, WACs took on special tasks when needed—for example, acting as informants in the Ritchie men's practice interrogations with French and German subjects and performing the women's roles in skits and demonstrations staged by the Visual Demonstration Section.

The WACs enjoyed their time at Ritchie. Their only complaint seems to have been about the camp's remote setting and the food served in the WAC mess. As Ruth Mills Bradley noted, the WACs received the same food as the Ritchie men, even though they had their own mess hall. "The girls would like salads and lighter entrees," she wrote, "but all are treated alike. In spite of all the marching, waist lines increase."[7] Still, the contingent was small and congenial—and proud of its contributions to the camp.

The Ritchie WACs' day began at 5:45 a.m. when they rose, dressed, and put the barracks and the rooms in the administration building in order. The 6:30 a.m. breakfast was obligatory, as was the noon mess from 11:30 a.m. to 12:30 p.m. At 7:00 a.m., the women fell out for work formation. They were organized in platoons and, in their march to the main camp, often were called upon to drill flank and oblique movements. They marched back to the WAC mess hall for lunch and then returned to work in march formation.

Training in the WAC camp included military drill, training films, lectures on current events, instruction in topics of special concern and interest to WACs, and lectures on overseas experiences. It was considered critical that the women have "a clear understanding of the army, its equipment, its work in the different theaters of war."[8]

The actual working day ended with the women's retreat to their quarters. They were then free to attend to their own work: writing letters, washing and ironing clothes, going to the occasional noncom party or the weekly dances ("GI Nights") organized by the Ritchie United Service Organizations (USO). Two pet dogs, named "Hush" and "GI Joe," contributed to making the WAC quarters a home.

Many sports were provided for the WAC recreation: softball, volleyball, bowling, skating, tennis, and badminton, as well as boating and swimming in Lake Royer during the summer. The women formed a choir for weekly music in the chapel and for performance on special occasions at the camp. And they put together several programs for the patients in the Camp Ritchie hospital.[9]

In addition, the Ritchie WACs actively cooperated with the local recruitment office in Hagerstown. During a WAC week, which was held in area movie theaters in an effort to enroll new recruits, the Ritchie women put on a WAC fashion show at the Maryland Theater and modeled fifteen different uniforms worn by WACs serving throughout the world.[10] They joined the members of the local recruitment station in mounting a WAC display-mobile for several consecutive evenings and then moving with it to other area towns. In return, WAC applicants took their physical exams at Ritchie. When a local Hagerstown woman enlisted in the WAC, she was invited to the WAC headquarters at Ritchie, where the Ritchie WAC commander administered the oath before inviting her to a luncheon and tour of the barracks and administration building.[11]

The Ritchie WACs were also invited to various social activities in neighboring towns, such as a progressive party held in their honor by

She Passed through Camp Ritchie

Lieutenant **Jere Knight** (1907–1996) was born Ruth Frances Brylawski in Philadelphia, Pennsylvania. She learned fluent French as a girl and, after graduating from high school at age fifteen, spent a year in Paris. Afterward, she earned her bachelor's degree in psychology and languages, as well as a master's degree in political science from the University of Pennsylvania; during this time, she competed in and won state and college championships as an Olympic-caliber fencer.

After completing her studies, Knight took a job as secretary for the Pennsylvania chapter of the League of Nations Association, holding that job until she met and married Eric Knight, who, she said, taught her humor. While he struggled as a screenwriter in California, she served as assistant story editor with Selznick International Pictures, where she oversaw the development of such films as *Gone with the Wind.* In 1940, she edited her husband's book *Lassie Come Home.* She also edited his war novel *This Above All*, which was made into a popular motion picture.

After her husband entered the war and was killed in a 1943 plane crash, Knight became an aide to Oveta Culp Hobby, founding director of the WAAC. She became a WAC and, as a specialist in well-being and intelligence, wrote a speech on logistics for General Eisenhower. She served at SHAEF (Supreme Headquarters Allied Expeditionary Force) in the European theater, where she directed a team of cryptographers and reported directly to Ike. She was awarded a Bronze Star and retired from the WACs as a major.

After the war, she taught, continued her research and editorial work, wrote an opera libretto, and translated poetry written by Central American women. She continued to promote her husband's *Lassie* by writing two children's versions of the book and visiting school classes with her collie. Later in life she became an active ecologist and helped preserve four thousand acres of the Cooks Creek Watershed in Bucks County.

the members of the Hagerstown service sorority Beta Sigma Phi. They attended social events at the local USO headquarters in Cascade and were bussed to more distant parties and dances. And there were accidents. On one occasion, some of the Ritchie women, under the command of Captain Jane A. Miller, were involved in a serious bus accident when they and some Ritchie soldiers were returning late at night from a Hagerstown party. The bus hit a telephone pole and overturned, badly injuring sixteen of the forty passengers. Nine WACs required hospital treatment of head lacerations and fractured ribs.

The Hagerstown Zonta Club, an international women's service organization, was interested in learning from the WACs with foreign experience. Larissa Patrekeyeva gave a talk about the severe Russian famine of 1921–1922 and the difficulties she and her family faced in getting enough food to sustain themselves, and she described in vivid detail her family's flight to Leningrad in the back of a covered truck.[12] Frances Nichols also appeared at the Zonta Club to give a talk about the beauties of Japan and the customs of its people. She gave this presentation the day after Germany's surrender. Immediately after this event, more Japanese American soldiers and WACs were brought to serve at Camp Ritchie, and their WAC numbers increased even more significantly after V-J Day.

Some WACs spent their entire period of service at Camp Ritchie as instructors and office staff. Technician Fourth Grade Ellen Kaufmann, for example, took on a variety of jobs. In addition to assisting with interrogation instruction, she drove trucks and jeeps through rugged terrain in order to take training materials out into the field. After V-E Day, she worked at the Pacific Military Intelligence Research Section (PACMIRS) stationed at Ritchie and for the camp's Hill Project, where she worked with German prisoners who had fought at Anzio, Italy, by translating their experiences into English for the military history portion of the project.

Many of the Ritchie WACs were sent on to various offices in the United States or into service overseas. Captain Gladys Rachel Clark was assigned to Fort Benning, Georgia, as an aviation cadet; she was one of 140 WACs assigned to its Parachute (or Airborne) School to work as parachute riggers and packers and to inspect those used by members of the US Army Airborne. Corporal Lucille Potter was sent as an instructor to Camp Riley, Kansas. After graduating from the "Order of Battle" course 6, Lieutenant Agnes Thiemann went to serve at the Pentagon for the duration of the war, and she rose to the rank of major. At least five of Ritchie's WAC officers were stationed for a time at PO Box 1142, in Northern Virginia. Captain Emilie Berkley and Lieutenant Elizabeth Stewart served there with MIS-X, a section of the US War Department that provided aid both to American prisoners of war and to downed airmen at risk of capture. This section furnished airmen with silk maps and with uniform buttons containing hidden compasses. In prisoner of war (POW) aid packages to the camps, they managed to hide radios in cribbage boards, baseballs, and other harmless-looking objects, so that MIS-X could maintain contact with American POWs held in sixty-four German prison camps.[13]

Ritchie's former mess and supply officer Harryette Emmerson went on to command the WAC detachment at Los Alamos, where she was awarded a meritorious unit plaque for contributing—as a hospital dietician—to the Atomic Bomb Project.

Meanwhile, more than eight thousand American WACs were sent to the European theater of operations for service in England, France, and Germany, and more than five thousand served in the Pacific. The Ritchie WACs were part of both groups. Many took up assignments in Britain, where the majority worked as telephone switchboard operators, clerks, typists, secretaries, and motor pool drivers, while WAC officers served as executive secretaries, cryptographers, and photo interpreters.[14] Service in London was not without its dangers. Most of the Purple Hearts awarded to WACs stationed in Europe went to women wounded in the German V-1 and V-2 rocket attacks on London.

In late September 1943, Ritchie private Erika Kaul, a former beautician from Cleveland, was pictured in the army newspaper *Stars and Stripes* as well as in newspapers throughout the United States, showing her as representative of three hundred WACs who had recently arrived for service in London; her contingent of WACs was assigned to serve with the Supreme Headquarters Allied Expeditionary Force (SHAEF). These women were thoroughly involved in the planning for D-Day as stenographers, typists, translators, legal secretaries, cryptographers, tele-graph and teletype operations, radiographers, and general clerks. After D-Day, they were sent to France and, eventually, on into Germany, where they continued to handle these operations until V-E Day.[15] They were often working with highly classified material, decoding reports from the French underground, for example, or tracing the activities of German officers. Captain Lillian Tombacher served as Eisenhower's Polish inter-preter and was rewarded with an American Bronze Star and the Polish Cross of Merit for her services.

Ruth Mills Bradley was assigned to the Southwest Pacific Area with nine hundred WACs under her command. Helene Novak was one of several Ritchie WACs who went with her, first to Hollandia and Oro Bay in New Guinea, then to Leyte and Manila in the Philippines. Although these women were doing crucial office work well behind the front lines, conditions were primitive. It had been decided that, to protect the WACs from the large number of male troops in the area, who, in many cases, had not laid eyes on an American woman in more than a year, the WACs should be locked inside barbed-wire compounds at all times except when escorted to and from work by armed guards. Their military attire represented a major problem. They arrived in New Guinea in win-ter uniforms and heavy twill coveralls issued while en route. Both were highly inappropriate for the climate, and many of the women developed skin diseases, since the heat and humidity kept the clothing wet from perspiration. They had tents for shelter and had to cover their cots with heavy nets at night to ward off rats. Salt water showers and latrines were in the open, and, on some days, "only a helmet full of water was available for drinking, washing, everything." They had to wear leggings at night to protect themselves from insects and take daily doses of anti-malaria medication. Despite these efforts, illness ran rampant, and the number of WACs evacuated because of illness was disproportionately high com-pared to that of the men, who had been issued lighter protective clothing. Captain Bradley used music to raise the morale of the women under her, and, at Oro Bay, she organized a choir of men and women to sing in the services held in a thatch-roofed chapel. As she wrote to her sisters, there was "much work to be done here, and it is a satisfaction to realize that we are contributing something important to the war effort."[16]

The situation in the Philippines was not much better. There the women witnessed the damage from the heavy bombing of Manila, and they had only candlelight in their tents. For a few months after their arrival in Manila, the Japanese were still shelling and firing on the city.[17] Nevertheless, the women persevered until after the Japanese surrender in September 1945, and their spirits rose as they watched columns of Japanese war prisoners pass through the city.

After V-J Day, WACs were given the opportunity to reenlist for continued service in Germany or in Japan. Many of the Ritchie WACs elected to stay in service. Polish-born Helen Kulikowska was stationed at Pearl Harbor and the Pentagon in this postwar period, and she was one of the first to join the Women in the Air Force when it was organized in 1948. She then served in England and in Germany. Carmen Knox, now a captain, became the first WAC officer to serve in Japan after its surrender. Georgia Fay Hunt continued in service and was stationed with the air force in Tokyo. Helene Novak, who rose to the rank of lieutenant colonel, also served in occupied Japan. Elaine Homan remained with the Military Intelligence Division in Frankfurt, Germany, while Nelly Singer served in Dachau as interpreter at the trial of war criminals from the Dora concentration camp and its subsidiaries in Thuringia. After a short hiatus, Alice A. Parrish and Ruth Mills Bradley rejoined the WAC and served until retirement with the rank of lieutenant colonel.

WACs at work with documents produced at Camp Ritchie.
COURTESY OF ANITA BOUCHER

Captain Lillian Tombacher with General Eisenhower upon receipt of her Bronze Star. SOURCE: NARA

Corporal Nelly Singer serving as interpreter at the Nordhausen Concentration Camp military trial held at Dachau. SOURCE: NATIONAL ARCHIVES AND RECORDS ADMINISTRATION

Ruth Mills Bradley, first commander of WAC forces at Camp Ritchie, served in New Guinea and the Philippines with more than nine hundred WACs under her command. COURTESY OF PATRICIA S. AUDLEY

CHAPTER ELEVEN

Interactions with Civilians

Even though they were hundreds of miles from their home states, a large number of soldiers who are stationed at a nearby Army camp spent a very merry Christmas here in Hagerstown yesterday afternoon and evening as the guests of local residents. . . .

A Herald *representative telephoned at the home of one of the local families that was entertaining five of the soldiers last night. . . . One was from Boston, three from New York and one from North Dakota.*

All were unanimous in their thanks for the good time that was shown them by the people of Hagerstown.[1]

DURING THE FOUR YEARS THAT MEN CAME TO CAMP RITCHIE TO TRAIN in military intelligence there were many different levels of interaction with civilians living in the area. Farmers were the first to take notice. From the very beginning, the army's intent was to incorporate large swatches of land around the camp into a training area for the many field exercises that were being planned. John Fuss, who was eleven years old at the time, remembers how, on July 20, 1942, an army vehicle pulled up to his parents' farmhouse outside Emmitsburg, Maryland, as they were eating their noon meal. An officer got out and told Fuss's father that the army would be using his farm for some of its intelligence training. He handed his father a short agreement to sign, stating that the government would pay any reasonable claims for damage to the property. The army would be using the property in any case, he was told, but if he did not sign the agreement, he would not be paid for damages. The officer explained that he was in somewhat of a hurry since he had "to cover all the other farms between here and Harney."[2] Emmitsburg was eleven miles east of the camp; Harney was eighteen miles.

Soon men and vehicles from Camp Ritchie appeared regularly near the area farms. It was an exciting time for the farm children. On Sunday afternoons, John Fuss and his friends rode their bicycles to the site where mock battles had taken place during the week. "The big prize was to find the copper cartridges left behind from the shooting. Boys in the area had dozens or more of them." The old Waynesboro Road became a frequent setting for movements by army jeeps, motorcycles, and men on foot. One Fountain Dale resident, Howard Kline, had strong memories of columns of tanks, which tore up the road with their tracks.[3] Not all of these were genuine tanks; several were trucks disguised to look like specific tank models not available at the camp.

At first area civilians were startled to see men in German or Japanese uniforms combing the countryside, but they adjusted quickly. It was a heady time for children to see lines of troops pass by their homes, to see soldiers practice driving jeeps at full throttle up and down hillsides, and to hear the firing of machine guns and field artillery in their local woodlands. Fuss remembers that "damage did occur. We would see damage to the crop of wheat or corn trampled down where [the soldiers] had walked. There were a number of times that a fence was cut. This meant that the cows or sheep might get out on the road. My father would repair the damage. As far as I know, he never filed a claim for damages." More serious damage occurred when a ten-year-old boy, David Glass, found a smoke bomb that had been left behind by the soldiers. He piled stones around it and lit the fuse. It went off immediately, injuring him so seriously that he spent two weeks in the hospital. The army refused to pay the medical bill because the accident was not the result of army action but had been caused by the boy's own mischief.[4]

The small businesses in the immediate area of Camp Ritchie enjoyed the first economic benefits caused by the influx of thousands of soldiers. Eating and drinking establishments located just outside the entrance to the Ritchie grounds were immediate attractions: the Fox Hole Steak

House, owned by "a tall, well-groomed Frenchman with a mustache"; a restaurant next door to it that offered sandwiches and sundaes; and the more casual Chocolate Park Tavern. A large United Service Organizations (USO) center opened up across from the tavern, adjacent to the Lake Royer dam; it boasted a guest house, cafeteria, dance hall, music room, and library, and it offered the GIs a place to go for entertainment and recreation during their off-hours. One local, who was a boy at the time, remarked, "Apparently, the GIs who shot pool at the USO either hit the balls hard enough to send them out the window or threw them out because we kids found pool balls near the Cascade Creek just below the dam."[5] The army built a train station; here the Western Maryland Railway delivered and picked up mail and passengers. There was a local store across from the train station, operated by Sylvia Wastler, daughter of the man who had constructed the artificial lakes at the camp; along with selling groceries there, she and her daughter did laundry for the soldiers. "They used part of the large store room for ironing," Richard Happel recalled. "There were always large amounts of uniforms in that room." In addition, a laundry was built right outside Ritchie's main gate; it offered dry cleaning and catered mainly to GIs. Because Merle Wise's grandparents lived just outside the fence surrounding the Ritchie complex, soldiers sometimes came to the fence and asked his grandmother to patch their pants when they tore them on field maneuvers. "She charged 25 cents!" Wise remembers. "She did it to help them, not for the money."[6]

Although all noncommissioned officers were housed at the camp, quite a few of the commissioned officers brought their wives with them and looked for housing in Ritchie's nearby towns. Blue Ridge Summit, Pennsylvania, was an especially desirable location, since it had many sizable inns and guest houses that had been built earlier in the century. Those officers assigned to shorter or uncertain periods of time at Ritchie could not afford the luxury of renting a large home and rented smaller guest houses instead. Lieutenant Ed Linville found lodging in a summer guest house that belonged to the widow of General Walter Reed. Like many of the old summer residences, it was now a fading home in a posh area, and the Linvilles ultimately moved to a more modern home in Sabillasville, Maryland. There was heavy competition for rooms at the finer boarding houses. Captain John Dolibois had brought his pregnant wife with him when he was assigned to Camp Ritchie. He had trouble finding housing until Nora Hoffmaster, who owned a number of guest houses on her Blue Ridge Summit "Locust Inn" property, permitted the young couple to sleep in the parlor of the main house until a larger, more private space opened up for them. Five newlywed lieutenants—Rex Applegate, Kirk Collart, Harry Dow, Smith Harris, and Office of Strategic Services executive officer James Johnson—rented a big old house with five private bedrooms, and their wives took turns cooking for all of them. One advantage to Blue Ridge Summit at a time of gasoline shortages was that it was only two and a half miles from the camp, making it possible for most of the officers to walk there and back each day. Applegate and his friends had it easier: they drove home together each night in an army truck and returned in it each morning. Colonel Theodore Fuller borrowed one of the twelve German motorcycles from the Composite School Unit and used it for travel to and from camp for about three or four months. Ironically, Captain David Rockefeller, whose grandfather had founded the Standard Oil Company, chose to cover the hilly terrain each day by bicycle.

Wives and sweethearts of noncommissioned soldiers also came to the area, for shorter as well as longer stays. The common arrangement for them was to move into a small room near the camp in a rental house full of other soldiers' wives. Technical Sergeant Max Horlick's wife, Ruth, found just such a room in a boarding house in nearby Highfield. The women shared a kitchen, which created a pleasantly communal atmosphere. They also socialized with other wives at the USO center next to the camp. There Ruth was able to do some sewing, since the center had placed a sewing machine at the women's disposal. Her boarding house had a good-sized dining room, and the resident couples were treated to special meals there on holidays. Ruth lived in Highfield for the duration of her husband Max's four-month stay at Ritchie. Max recalled how he and a Ritchie buddy broke curfew in order to visit their wives at night:

Ernie Low and I sneaked out every night to be with our wives. Sneaking out without leave was easy, but getting back into camp was

*not. In the morning Ruth would drive us, at 5:30 A.M., to a steep
hillside corner of the camp. She turned out the car lights and coasted
down the mountain. We lifted some pipes which were meant to plug
a hole under the fence. We wormed in under the fence and sneaked to
the bunks until awakened for reveille and breakfast.*[7]

Because Camp Ritchie was a "secret" site engaged in training soldiers
for specialized intelligence operations, local newspapers were barred from
mentioning the camp by name. For the duration of the war, newspaper-
men conscientiously averted their eyes and referred to Camp Ritchie
simply as a "nearby camp." It was a poorly kept secret among the civilians
living in the area, since they had a good deal of contact with the men
stationed at Camp Ritchie. Soldiers attended the local churches, participated in various patriotic celebrations, and got involved in numerous civic
organizations. In most cases, they were welcome additions, since many
of the local men had been drafted and the towns were partially emptied.

Still, there was serious concern that the influx of large numbers
of soldiers into Camp Ritchie might cause a rise in prostitution and
in female juvenile delinquency and that this might lead to a rampant
spread of venereal disease. It was said among the military that "a diseased
prostitute can do far more damage than a 500-pound bomb dropped
squarely in the middle of an army camp."[8] During their basic training,
army recruits were warned about the dangers of syphilis, both in lectures
and in disturbingly graphic films. Camp Ritchie addressed this problem
early on. On July 23, 1942, at the City Hall Courtroom of Hagerstown,
Maryland, twenty-five officials from Washington and Frederick Counties
gathered to hear lectures from four Camp Ritchie officers, the deputy
State Health officer, and a state's attorney, who spoke about the state laws
affecting prostitution and the loss of manpower that would result from
syphilitic infection. The local paper reported, "Whether the conference
held last night would result in a concerted effort to close local houses
of prostitution, if any, was not discussed. There have been no reports of
commercialized vice in this area."[9]

By January 1943, city and county officials acknowledged the problem, and they held a second meeting in Hagerstown with military officers

at Ritchie. The Ritchie officers now declared that local teenaged girls had been responsible for the infection of several soldiers at the camp. Arguing that "the health of the fighting man must be safeguarded," the officers made three recommendations to Hagerstown authorities: first, to require all hotel and rooming house proprietors to take down the serial number of every soldier using their facilities, so that any infection could be better traced; next, to bar teenaged girls from all taverns and bars in the county; and, finally, to round up women suspected of being infected and to detain them pending physical examinations.[10] The city-county health officer, Dr. W. R. Willard, protested, saying that syphilis could best be contained not by legislation but by education. He argued for more public health nurses and social workers, as well as more teachers qualified to offer instruction in sex education. He felt that legal action should be taken only against prostitution and vice, since laws regarding enforced treatment for syphilis might well discourage parties from seeking help.[11]

No direct action was taken, however, and in April 1943 Colonel Carlton Starks, medical officer at Camp Ritchie, addressed the Hagerstown Business and Professional Women's Club, reporting that there had, in fact, been an increase in sexually transmitted diseases at the camp since January. In March, nine servicemen had been affected, with eight of those cases resulting from association with "amateurs." The colonel had three concerns: Hagerstown had, at present, twenty-five houses of ill repute; "many young girls" roamed the streets and frequented taverns; and the city had "at least three solicitors for the purpose of inducing soldiers to have relations with women."[12]

As a major railway center, Hagerstown, like other railroad towns, had always attracted prostitutes. The Hagerstown police, however, vehemently denied Colonel Starks's statistics. "If there's 25 houses of ill-fame here, I'll eat them," one protested. Others said they could not understand "why such derogatory publicity as given Hagerstown . . . should be tolerated." After all, "it usually takes two to make a party and . . . the soldier-boy is equally responsible." In fact, they added, "time after time they [had] seen soldiers coax and plead mere children to accompany them." Perhaps, they concluded, the camp should consider exerting discipline among its soldiers and offering other diversions, rather than expecting the citizens of Hagerstown to deal with the camp's own problems.[13]

In reality, Hagerstown itself already offered a good deal of diversion to the Ritchie soldiers, since it had founded a local unit of the USO in July 1942. Ironically, the Hagerstown chapter was organized the day before state officials and Ritchie officers first gathered to discuss the problems of prostitution. Since this USO chapter was situated in the area's largest town, it often worked in tandem with USO groups in other towns in Maryland (Cascade, Emmitsburg, Sabillasville, and Thurmont) and in Pennsylvania (Blue Ridge Summit, Greencastle, Waynesboro, Chambersburg, Gettysburg, and Hanover).[14]

The USO was a brainchild of the federal government, which had foreseen the need to provide wholesome entertainment to soldiers on leave, and in February 1942 Mary Ingraham had established the program at the request of President Roosevelt. Ingraham was a Vassar College graduate and president of the National Board of the YWCA; she had a strong interest in promoting war work and interracial understanding. One purpose of the program, which originally brought together the Salvation Army, YMCA, YWCA, the National Catholic Community Service, National Travelers Aid Association, and the National Jewish Welfare Board, was to offer soldiers a "home away from home." Through its activities it was hoped that soldiers would be discouraged from seeking less savory entertainments in their off-hours. The Hagerstown USO was particularly active in organizing dances for the servicemen. In July 1942, Hagerstown citizens came together to plan a first Saturday night dance, to be held on July 25 of that same year. Hosts and hostesses were drawn from various Hagerstown organizations: The Zonta Club and the Women's Club were responsible for refreshments, the Business and Professional Women's Club organized music, and the American Legion Auxiliary and the Auxiliary to the Veterans of Foreign Wars took charge of decorations. Girls interested in attending the dance as hostesses and dancing partners were asked to register at the YMCA beforehand. The Hagerstown USO also put out a call to other service organizations, since "with additional help, the dances may become a weekly affair."[15]

Because more than one hundred servicemen had already expressed interest in attending the first dance, the Hagerstown women had to change the venue from the Hagerstown Alsatia Club to the YMCA. Soon weekly dances at the Y became the norm, with different groups taking on the duties of providing entertainment and refreshments. Although most of the men came for the dancing, entertainments were always part of the USO program: these included everything from performances by pupils from the local school of dance to songs and musical entertainments by Hagerstown citizens to readings and performances by area drama clubs. The weekly dances were open to all GIs; in addition, 150 officers from Ritchie were invited in April 1943 to a dance held in the ballroom of the Hotel Alexander, where they danced with a "selected group of local young ladies," including college girls home on spring break. That experience, too, proved popular enough to encourage repeats. The most spectacular dances were the debutante balls held each January in Hagerstown, with Ritchie officers serving as escorts. Thirty to forty Hagerstown weddings resulted from these balls as well as from the weekly USO dances.

The next USO initiative came in August 1942, when the Hagerstown chapter organized the first home visits for Ritchie men. The fifty families who signed up to host soldiers unanimously declared the weekend a success, and quite a few of them enjoyed the experience enough to invite the soldiers to "drop in anytime you happen to be in town." The USO could point out that for many of the soldiers, it was the first time in many months that they had been inside a family home and enjoyed a home-cooked meal, and it called for more volunteers to host soldiers the very next weekend.[16] In the meantime, the Elks Club donated all the proceeds from its annual horse show toward USO entertainments at the Y. The Y let the Ritchie soldiers use its swimming pool, its billiard room, and a small writing/reading room. It even had scores of cots, blankets, and pillows available to soldiers who wanted to spend the night in town.

Other civic and religious groups offered programs for the Ritchie soldiers. St. Rita Catholic Church in Blue Ridge Summit offered a wiener roast and dance, and the church showed Hollywood films to the soldiers; the National Jewish Welfare Board catered seders at the camp. Waynesboro offered the benefit of being six miles closer to the camp than

Hagerstown, and many interactions occurred between its citizens and the Ritchie soldiers. Paul Fairbrook dated a Waynesboro girl and recalls being invited to dinner every Sunday at her family's home. Gyorgy Sandor, a concert pianist, made a number of friends in Waynesboro, and they put a grand piano at his disposal so that he could practice there regularly.

Individuals and groups were especially generous in making donations to the camp as new spaces were constructed there. The Women's Democratic Club of Clear Spring made donations of ashtrays, games, and magazine subscriptions to the Ritchie men. When the camp asked for two pianos for its recreation center, it received them within three days. Books were donated to the camp library, and chairs, tables, lamps, and a sofa were donated when the camp received a grant to purchase, remodel, and equip two frame buildings adjacent to the Buena Vista railway station as recreation areas offering entertainment and overnight lodgings for the soldiers' relatives and friends. When a hospital was built at the camp, citizens and civic groups donated all the furnishings for its sun and day rooms as well as pictures to brighten the patient rooms. And, of course, they contributed Christmas lights and decorations for the numerous Christmas trees erected at the camp each year.

Although it was underreported in the press, Ritchie servicemen offered programs and entertainments that greatly enriched the area's cultural offerings. Lectures and concerts were the most common offering to churches, service clubs, and area schools. Oddly enough, newspapers were banned from covering performances by Camp Ritchie's classical musicians.[17] Weddings were the one exception. The Black bass singer William Warfield and concert violinist Henry Liscio were both mentioned in the newspaper coverage of local weddings. Still, although he performed with some frequency in the area, Warfield was not mentioned again in the Hagerstown press until after Japan's unconditional surrender. Warfield explained the progression that led to camp musicians finding appropriate outside venues for their performances:

Sometimes, when Col. [Banfill] decided to show off the talents of his cadre, we'd have guests in from nearby towns. If they heard me sing, I'd sometimes get an invitation to perform for them off-base. I did several recitals at nearby colleges as a result. In that way I came to the attention of a New York City socialite, Mary Schlesinger, who had a summer place in the Blue Ridge Mountains not far from Camp Ritchie and who hosted soirees there from time to time.[18]

Pianist and master sergeant Leslie (Laszlo) Bartal became well known as a local performer. William Warfield recalled a Richard Strauss concert that he and Bartal gave at Wilson College in Chambersburg, Pennsylvania, and the Hagerstown reporter Libbie Powell reported that Bartal "was in demand by well-known hostesses of this town."[19] One can assume that the other classically trained musicians in camp—Nathan Chaikin (cello), Werner Isler, Henry Clay and Fred Barton (piano), Mark Kondratieff (violin), and Claude Monteux (flute)—received similar invitations. Banfill was proud of his musicians, and he gave them special privileges. For example, pianist Henry Clay reported to his hometown newspaper in Texas:

Many musicians entering the armed forces lose their touch, the nimbleness of fingers so necessary to a good pianist . . . because they have to dig ditches and peel potatoes and [do] other routine army jobs.

Henry is fortunate in being stationed at a Maryland base where the men like music, and he entertains with concerts. And his officers, who also like music, let him practice.[20]

Colonel Banfill opened up the entertainment programs and classical concerts held in the Camp Ritchie Theater to invited guests from the neighboring towns. An unusual string quartet was a particular hit. Its string players were all actors and performers in the Visual Demonstration Section 9 of Ritchie's Composite School Unit: Vaughn Taylor, Joseph Anthony, Don Haggerty, and Owen Davis Jr. William Warfield remarked that their "every performance was sold out!" The same held true for the piano concerts by Gyorgy Sandor.[21]

There was less constraint put upon newspaper coverage of the non-musicians who interacted with the community. Women's Army

Corps (WAC) speakers were regularly named and featured in the press. Officers from Ritchie were always named and coverage given to the content of their lectures. Noncoms got occasional named coverage, provided that the topic was of general public interest. Newspapers reported that Sergeant Arestidis Parousis, who was a Ritchie MP and a World War I veteran, spoke to the Army Mothers of Washington County about how they should treat their sons when they came home on furlough, while also stressing the importance of sending them daily letters after they left.

Good coverage was also given when Private John Finder spoke to a local boys' club about the life of young boys in various European countries. And when it was announced in the Hagerstown papers that the young sculptor Hans Pawlak would be speaking at the Washington County Museum in Hagerstown's City Park about the army's attitudes toward art, the paper gushed in anticipation of the lecture: "Most interesting and stirring . . . is Sergeant Pawlak's personality. Vitally alive himself, he has the ability of a true leader to infuse into his audience that same vitality and zest for living—and for the living form, on which basis his craft rests. Without seeking to be controversial, the speaker arouses in the listener a desire to know more and more about any subject under discussion."[22]

The papers even gave detailed coverage of a presentation that Major Rex Applegate gave to the Hagerstown Kiwanis Club on some of the techniques used in the army (and Camp Ritchie) to train soldiers for close combat fighting. Applegate said the US Army had little to fear from the Japanese soldiers' jujitsu training, since a soldier trained in this form of fighting "fights mechanically and does not react quickly to the unexpected." He "has not been trained to fight using blows and does not know how to react to an opponent who 'comes in swinging.'"[23]

In their spare time, soldiers from Ritchie participated in numerous social activities, from sports to music and the arts. The camp fielded its own "fast-stepping Army team" to compete against others in the area.[24] In the two years he spent stationed at Camp Ritchie, Corporal Raoul LaPointe became an especially well-known sports figure. He joined the local sports scene as a part-time shortstop for the Hagerstown Owls of the Interstate League, with the understanding that he would be available only for home games. "I'll never forget when I signed my first contract with the Owls," LaPointe recalled. "The Army frowned on its men participating in outside activities, so I decided to play here under an assumed name. . . . I signed the contract 'Joe Moss.'"[25] LaPointe would also play basketball with the Ludwig Treaders under this new name. After being discharged from the army, LaPointe—as Ralph LaPointe—became a professional baseball player.

LaPointe was not the only man to get involved in "outside activities." Ritchie captain George Green and WAC lieutenant Eleanor Moffett both took home prizes from a regional horse show, and several camp musicians played in local orchestras and bands. There was a surge in attendance at meetings of the Acacia Lodge No. 155 of the Order of Ancient Free and Accepted Masons in Thurmont, Maryland, during World War II, because of Ritchie servicemen coming to its meetings and taking Masonic degrees.[26]

Hagerstown served as a surrogate "city" for the men unable to travel to Washington or Baltimore on their days off. The Vogue Room in the Colonial Hotel was a major attraction, with its large circular bar and evening entertainments. When twenty-five Ritchie men were invited to attend a dance put on by the Phi Gamma Pi sorority, one of them penned a poetic reply, offering thanks

> *To all you gals from Gamma Pi*
> *Who listened to our lonely cry,*
> *Who came to us with open arms*
> *And offered us your lovely charms.*[27]

Casual entertainment could be found close to the camp at the Chocolate Park Bar and at the USO building located by the Lake Royer dam. A summer overnight camp for Jewish girls called Camp Louise also adjoined the Ritchie grounds. The men were forbidden any interaction with the camp, and it was surrounded by protective fencing, but that apparently did not prevent some men from getting onto the grounds for trysts with the older girls. As one Ritchie poet put it:

There was Hagerstown, the Vogue Room,
Becks and Baldwins where we danced,
And when spring came with its blossom
Camp Louise brought us romance.[28]

But the Ritchie men also stepped forward when disaster threatened the area. Ritchie firemen and support staff assisted local officials in dealing with fires and floods. When a manpower shortage threatened the timely packing of two hundred tons of ripe peas grown around Smithsburg, Maryland, Camp Ritchie released some fifty soldiers to help save the crop.

The Ritchie soldiers were allowed much free creative expression, even in producing works critical of aspects of the American armed forces. While at Ritchie, Technical Sergeant Stefan Heym worked on *Of Smiling Peace*, a novel set in Algiers that featured a military intelligence officer as one of its two main protagonists; in this work, Heym critiqued American policy toward its defeated armies. And, in an exhibition of Cumberland Valley artists, Sergeant Jirayr Zorthian took second place with a work titled *Enduration*. The papers reported that this work "caused more discussion than any other feature" at the Washington County Museum. It was intended to suggest "the adjustments and hardships, mental and physical, which must be endured by a sensitive person in the armed forces." It was, the paper declared, "the best constructed composition ever to appear in Hagerstown" and was inspired by the techniques of Albrecht Dürer and Michelangelo.[29]

Given the fact that thousands of soldiers passed through Camp Ritchie, it was inevitable that there would be incidents requiring police intervention. Nearly all the offenses were minor ones: theft was the most common crime reported by the Ritchie soldiers. Traffic accidents were relatively frequent and often resulted in severe lacerations and broken bones. Only one proved fatal, when a Gettysburg man driving a gravel truck crashed into a motorcycle ridden by Ritchie MP Cecil Oakley.

In one bizarre case, a drunken Native American soldier, Private Alex Ree, tried to break into four parked cars before entering a private home and chasing a fifteen-year-old girl to the second floor, thereby causing much distress both to the girl and to her older sister. The police came, and when he was being handcuffed, Ree struck the detective and broke his dental plate. Ree had frequently been arrested for drunkenness; after this episode, he was confined to the camp.[30] Although this incident never made it into the newspapers, one local remembered another occasion when a group of drunken Native Americans missed the last bus back to Ritchie and stole a Hagerstown city bus to make the return trip. They, too, spent the rest of their service at the camp confined to base.[31]

To keep order, three military policemen from Ritchie regularly patrolled in Hagerstown, supplemented by two additional MPs with no attachment to the camp. In one particularly abhorrent case, one of the Ritchie MPs, an unnamed sergeant, was sitting in a car with several other soldiers in front of the YMCA, enjoying an evening off, when he saw two young girls walking home from work. He leapt from the vehicle, dragged the older one down to the rear of the building, and attempted to rape her. Her younger sister begged the other soldiers to intervene, but they refused, since the MP was a sergeant and they were only buck privates. Eventually the girl was able to escape her attacker, and the sergeant was chased down and arrested about half an hour later. The newspapers reported that the local police were "somewhat incensed over the attack," calling it "one of the boldest assaults on local records." Ritchie Camp officials assured the Hagerstown police that they would act on the matter.[32]

The police also stepped in to make an arrest when a technical corporal from Ritchie was arrested with a younger, married woman in a Hagerstown hotel for being drunk and disorderly. The papers made a point of noting that the corporal was a German and that he had registered himself and his companion into the hotel as husband and wife. The police stated, with some satisfaction, that "the case is just another example of the soldier being more to blame than the woman, since his training should have been such that he would have been afraid to do the things he did."[33] Both the man and the woman were required to pay a fine, but, since adultery was considered a military crime, the corporal suffered more serious consequences when he returned to camp.

The only other crime tied to a Camp Ritchie soldier occurred just a month before the closing of the camp, when Thomas Treeharne, a support soldier at Ritchie, tired of being asked repeatedly by the Hagerstown police to show them his papers. After going to police headquarters to complain, Treeharne apparently went to another part of the City Hall building and started a fire in the stairwell. He was sentenced to thirty days in the county jail.

One of the most important aspects of interaction between the town of Hagerstown and Camp Ritchie's foreign-born GIs was the soldiers' naturalization. This was a necessary step for the camp's noncitizen soldiers, since they could safely perform their duties at the front only if they were American citizens. This was especially true of those who had emigrated from Germany and Austria; they would be executed as traitors to the homeland if they were taken prisoner by Nazi forces. Fortunately, the US Congress had foreseen that problem by providing for the expedited naturalization of noncitizens serving honorably in the US armed forces. Under Title 8 of the Second War Powers Act of 1942, US servicemen applying for citizenship were exempted from requirements as to age, race, residence, educational tests, fees, filing a declaration of intention, and enemy alien status. As a consequence, most of the Ritchie noncitizen soldiers received citizenship upon successful completion of the Ritchie course of study. At first, many went to Baltimore for the ceremony. Later, the process at Ritchie became streamlined in that smaller groups of student candidates were bussed in to Hagerstown, where they received assistance from a representative of the US Naturalization Bureau in filling out their application papers. All the men then returned to Hagerstown several days later to take their oath of allegiance from Judge Joseph D. Mish of the circuit court for Washington County. These candidates came from many nations. A Hagerstown newspaper reported that the 120–25 Ritchie men naturalized on March 10, 1943, included "Turks, Cubans, Armenians, South Americans, Greeks, a citizen of China of Russian parentage, Swedes and Norwegians and several Germans."[34]

On May 20, 1945, Judge Mish noted at an "I Am an American Day" celebration in Hagerstown that he was proud to have given American citizenship to more than a thousand Ritchie men, since "men willing to fight and die, if necessary, should have the right to become citizens . . .

in accordance with a decree of Congress."[35] This was the same statement that he made to all the new American citizens from Camp Ritchie.

Usually the naturalization ceremony was a brief one, with an opening statement from Judge Mish in which he explained how the naturalization law applied to men in the military. The court's deputy clerk Harry Shafer then administered the oath of allegiance, in which the candidates renounced all fealty "to foreign princes and potentates,"[36] and the ceremony concluded with Judge Mish issuing the oath of citizenship while emphasizing the seriousness of the moment and the fact that now "130 million Americans 'extend to you the hand of fellowship.'"[37] One soldier was disappointed by the procedure: "It was not the kind of ceremony I had expected. A clerk rattled off some phrases, and I lifted my right hand for the obligatory oath of allegiance. And that was that: no handshake, no little flag, and a most perfunctory performance on the part of that anonymous clerk of a ritual that meant a great deal to me."[38] Still, not all the Ritchie soldiers took the ceremony seriously. When the presiding judge asked one group of soldiers whether they were willing to "take up arms" in defense of their new country, one young soldier in the back of the room shouted, "No." The judge ostensibly banged his gavel and said, "Shut up you wise guy. Raise your right hand and repeat after me the Pledge of Allegiance."[39]

In addition to acquiring American citizenship, Colonel Banfill urged the European soldiers to Americanize their names in order to avoid being detected as European-born citizens subject to German law. Many of the recent immigrants had already done so as a gesture to their new homeland. Still, there were others who had not. And for those facing European deployment, it seemed advisable for those with obviously German or Jewish names to hide their national or "racial" origins. One Ritchie private, Hans-Heinz Bismark, recalled being called in to the Ritchie commander's office at the close of his training. "Are you comfortable with your name?" Colonel Banfill asked him. "'Is there a problem, sir?' I asked. He explained, 'You may serve behind enemy lines.'" When Bismark asked how long he had to come up with a new last name, he was told that he had twenty-four hours. "You can count on our full assistance, making your choice legal," the commander added. Bismark chose the name Henry Bretton, to honor the Bretton Woods Agreement that had just created the International Monetary Fund and the International Bank for Reconstruction and Development. He chose this name, he said, because of schoolboy memories of "how [badly] the victorious allies had treated my country, especially economically" at the end of the last war.[40]

Bretton had already acquired citizenship before coming to Maryland. Those who were naturalized upon graduation from Camp Ritchie simply changed their names when they filled out their citizenship application forms in Hagerstown. Some of the soldiers were caught off guard. Technician Fifth Grade Charles M. Natowitz, for example, complained because "in the morning they didn't tell us that 'at ten o'clock you're going to change your name.'" Nevertheless, he came up with a creative solution: Newton, first because he was an admirer of Isaac Newton, and second because it contained three letters—"n," "w," and "t"—from his birth name. It became a common practice for emigrant soldiers to retain the initial letter of their original last name: Werner Cohen became Werner Chilton, for example, and Anthony Duschnitz became Anthony Dunning, while Chester Chrzanowski became Chester Carlow. Luckier ones were able simply to replace their old names with their English translations: Paul Schönbach became Paul Fairbrook; Bernard Zehngut became Bernard Tengood; William Fuchs became William Fox, and Alois Sturm became Louis Storm.

Some, however, chose names that had no resemblance to their former names at all: Karl Leff became Roland Carroll; Ulrich Schwerdtfeger became Ulrich Vodin. Others chose names based on places associated with their past lives. Nick Hadjikypris changed his last name to Cyprus, to honor the land of his birth. Michel Rothschild became Michel D'Etampes, in honor of happy times spent living in that Parisian commune.

During the war years, Ritchie soldiers who changed their names in Hagerstown averaged five to six petitions a week, with 1944 being the peak year, when "petitions were filed in court here by the score and in practically every case the petitioner was a soldier stationed at Ritchie." In the first half of 1946, however, when the war was long over, the court received a single name change petition.[41] The soldiers were gone, and life had begun to return to normal.

An officers' social, held at Camp Ritchie. SOURCE: SPECIAL COLLECTIONS & COLLEGE ARCHIVES, GETTYSBURG COLLEGE

Area guests are given a demonstration of CSU capabilities in the Camp Ritchie theater. SOURCE: NATIONAL ARCHIVES AND RECORDS ADMINISTRATION

Classical pianist Gyorgy Sandor's concerts were a big hit among guests to the camp. SOURCE: AUTHOR'S COLLECTION

CHAPTER TWELVE

The First Mobile Radio Broadcasting Company

Since this was the first attempt in the history of the United States Army to put such an organization into the field there was little information or experience of a practical nature which could constitute a basis of precedent. Consequently, the activation of this unit was a combination of logical needs and illogical experimentation.[1]

IN MARCH 1943, CAMP RITCHIE INITIATED SPECIALIZED TRAINING IN war propaganda services. The men in this program were referred to as a "Mobile Radio Broadcasting Company," or MRBC. Although early MRBC units had served with the Military Intelligence Service, and then been briefly transferred to the Office of Strategic Services (OSS), the army regained control over them and established a "First Mobile Radio Broadcasting Company" at Camp Ritchie under the command of Lieutenant Colonel John Oren Weaver, a former CBS radio man from Chicago. Major Edward A. Caskey, a former advertising man, served as the company's "cheerful blustery Executive and practical Commander."[2] Two lieutenants served under them: Martin F. Herz (in charge of the German platoon) and Alfred de Grazia (Italian).

The First MRB Company was its own closed unit within the camp, with its own barracks, mess, driving pool, printing section, and broadcasting section with three-kilowatt transmitters. The full company numbered around three hundred soldiers, most of them taken from the Signal

Corps or recruited directly from civilian life. Because these men were training for the invasion of Europe, many of the forty men in the propaganda section were European refugees who were chosen chiefly for their linguistic abilities and communication skills. As a consequence, many of these men already knew one another. The Hungarian Jewish journalist Hans Habe described his arrival at Ritchie:

> *At the "German" hut I was welcomed with much laughter and cheers. My dormitory neighbor on one side was Private Hans Wallenberg, son of the former Editor-in-chief of the [newspaper] B.Z. am Mittag. My neighbor on the other side was Private Klaus Mann, son of Thomas Mann and himself an author of considerable standing. A nephew of the French General de Lattre de Tassigny, a Stuttgart merchant by name of Hans Lehmann, an Italian university lecturer by name of [Alfred] Grigis, and the Hungarian reporter [Eugen] Fodor—this was the crowd among which I suddenly found myself.*[3]

Klaus Mann echoed Habe's surprise at meeting up with "so many familiar faces! This place is teeming with old friends from Berlin, Vienna, Paris, Budapest; it feels as if one were in a club or one's regular coffeehouse."[4] Despite its title, and the fact that the First MRBC did, indeed, include radio broadcasting as a major component, it was being asked to perform all kinds of propaganda services. This work would include the production of printed propaganda material and direct appeals to the enemy. Civilian and prisoner of war interrogation and analysis of Axis publications were also important to the company's mission, in order to gauge enemy morale and respond to it.

The core of the Mobile Radio Broadcasting Company was the forty men selected for its specialized propaganda section: these were the men who bore responsibility for the analysis of enemy morale and the production of propaganda texts and their dissemination by radio, print, and microphone. A major criterion for their selection was knowledge of the language, life, and culture of Germany and Italy. Even here, though, there were occasional slipups. Alfred de Grazia, head of the Italian platoon, was far from a fluent speaker of Italian; when he arrived at Camp Ritchie, he had just completed the fourth lesson in Italian on commercial Lingua-phone phonograph records that he had purchased as soon as he learned of his new assignment.

Otherwise, de Grazia was well chosen for the task. As a student at the University of Chicago, he had written an honors thesis on the Italian aggression in Ethiopia and made a study of the Spanish Civil War. He had spent a year studying law at Columbia University and then became a researcher and teacher at Indiana University. As a soldier, he worked his way up through the ranks from private to second lieutenant, with a specialty in mechanized warfare. His fellow platoon leader, Martin Herz, made it clear that he "was delighted with finding a genuine soldier who was an officer and more than that, an intellectual, and even versed in the field of public opinion,"[5] since de Grazia's background complemented his own.

Herz had been born in the United States but had lived in Vienna from age five to nineteen, during the rise in Austria of the conflicting movements of Pan-Germanism and Austrian nationalism. When he returned to the United States in 1936, he was not only completely fluent in German but also fully cognizant of the political forces then raging in Germany and Austria. Before being drafted, Herz had occasionally worked as a translator and propaganda analyst for NBC and CBS; as an army private, he had written one of the first American studies about the possibilities of "tactical psychological warfare."[6]

Major Darrell T. Rathbun noted in his history of the First MRBC that "the activation of this unit was a combination of logical needs and illogical experimentation." Certainly, the instruction at Ritchie was spotty at best. It was a simple matter to train men in setting up and taking down radio transmitters or in acquiring mastery of a portable offset printing press. But there were no materials for teaching men the art of producing propaganda in a war setting. The commander of the company, Lieutenant Colonel Oren Weaver, was no help. He "appeared in jump shoes, paratroop uniform, and beret, out of the skies, so to speak

He Passed through Camp Ritchie

Private **Mohammad Siblini** (1910–2002) was born in Beirut, Lebanon, into a prominent Sunni Muslim family claiming descent from the Prophet Muhammad. He studied classic Arabic and Islam, and he became a skilled reader of the Koran. He was also fluent in French and English. In the 1930s, he moved to New York, where he started a fur-importing business. He became a US citizen, was drafted into the US Army, and graduated from the second class at Camp Ritchie with an Arabic course specialty. He was then sent to North Africa to aid in Operation Torch, which aimed to liberate French North Africa from Axis control.

From the moment he landed, Siblini was an indispensable intermediary between the Americans and Moroccans. He became the only American soldier to be invited by Sultan Mohammad V to read from the Koran at his private mosque, and soon he was doing regular readings on the air, in which he was careful to read passages that showed a contrast between Nazi ideals and the principles of Islam. He was sent from Morocco to Algeria to continue making propaganda for the United States as a nation that offered refuge and equality to members of all races and creeds.

The popularity of Siblini's radio broadcasts and his frequent meetings with Arab nationalists, tribal chieftains, Muslim religious figures, and Tunisian royalty aroused the ire of Hitler's propaganda minister Joseph Goebbels, who made serious but fruitless attempts to discredit him. He also was a great annoyance to the French, who felt that he was undermining France's position as a colonial power in North Africa. When influential Arab leaders questioned why a man of Siblini's breeding and background was only an army private, he was quickly promoted to second lieutenant and, soon after that, to first lieutenant.

After the war, Siblini returned to the United States with his Moroccan wife, and he resumed his career as a successful business-man in New York.

. . . exuding confidence, smiling, teaching nobody anything."[7] De Grazia remarked, as he looked back on their training,

> *There was no manual, no routine, no training program, no tests, nothing but serious talk and good fellowship . . . for the forty intellectuals of the Company. We should have been, but were not, being trained in the interviewing of prisoners of war, of politicians, of ordinary civilians, in the production of certain kinds of reports on the political situation as known to or believed in by respondent and informants, in map-reading, and in propaganda analysis and propaganda policies.*

Only "snippets of all these things" came their way. "Russian Front leaflets were passed around, cleverly written, well designed and illustrated," but "not a single leaflet was written and printed at Camp Ritchie as a sample of what would be effective for dissemination among civilians or enemies at the front." De Grazia found that two major operations were completely lacking in terms of both equipment and training: "loudspeakers for delivering messages to audiences across the lines, and the system for distributing leaflets by artillery. They would have to be developed in the field."[8]

After a few weeks at Camp Ritchie, the Europeans in the MRBC were transported to nearby Hagerstown and made American citizens. The company, consisting of 16 officers and 112 enlisted men, was then shipped off to Oran before going on to Algiers and Tunis, where, during their wait for the invasion of Sicily, they had more opportunity to develop their skills. This was necessary, since, according to the company's historian, "practical application brought to light the fallacy of [their previous] experimentation."[9] Here, the men learned that their combat propaganda unit (the MRBC) was "overly ambitiously organized" and "too unwieldy"; as a consequence, it was broken up into small task forces and its members often integrated with British intelligence officers, with members of the OSS, and with the Psychological Warfare Branch (PWB).[10] Their interrogations of prisoners were not aimed, as were those of Ritchie's IPW (Interrogation of Prisoners of War) students, at eliciting strategic or tactical information regarding troop strength and troop movement. "We front-line propaganda specialists were not out to extract military secrets from the prisoners," Sergeant Hans Habe noted, "but were trying to sound the morale of the enemy, its weak spots, and the mood of the German population back home." With this information, they were better able to develop effective propaganda, not only in their pamphlets but also in their oral appeals. The war was over in Africa, but there were more than one hundred thousand men of the Afrika Korps still in Africa, and the MRB men spent many hours in the prisoner of war (POW) cages questioning them.[11]

The MRBC also got busy with radio propaganda. Its radio engineers and technicians, linguists and programming experts, administrative personnel, and propaganda specialists came to North Africa equipped with their three one-kilowatt mobile transmitters, one instrument van containing radio receivers and recording and monitoring equipment, and sufficient personnel of all categories to constitute a fairly complete radio propaganda team for use in the combat field. They augmented the radio dissemination of propaganda that had begun with the rehabilitation of the powerful one-hundred-kilowatt transmitter at Tunis.

With the invasion of Sicily and the Italian peninsula, the MRBC men were immediately put to the test in creating propaganda appropriate to the current state of morale among the German soldiers. Habe's first attempt at speaking directly to German troops by loudspeaker, "one of our less enviable duties," failed in its attempts to persuade a surrounded German company to surrender: "We came under lively fire, but took no prisoner."[12] In Italy, the MRB men produced their first leaflets that were fired by artillery shell into the enemy lines. This was a new technique, and de Grazia perfected the firing tables for the 105 mm howitzer, allowing for the difference in weight between smoke canisters and the leaflets that replaced them. Still, the men first met with failure in this area as well until they learned to adjust the content of the leaflets to appeal more effectively to the German soldiers. Reporting on a leaflet that described the good treatment awaiting the men held in Allied POW camps, Captain Martin Herz wrote:

Experiments with POW's showed conclusively that the facts, although true, seemed so fantastic that they considered them the crassest "propaganda." The leaflet was consequently discarded. The rule was adopted that "propaganda must not only be true, but also credible: if truth seems exaggerated, we must deliberately understate it." For instance, although some prisoners got eggs for breakfast, we did not mention it in leaflets after it was found out that the balance of the leaflet was disbelieved because our assertion seemed too incredible.[13]

Herz would go on to become one of the army's most successful authors of leaflets, both in the field and later in work with the Psychological Warfare Division in London. Habe would also excel in leaflet writing and become one of the company's best interrogators.

Looking back on his time in the United States, Alfred de Grazia wrote that his long training period had been an expensive waste of time: "I had done about 300 hours of learning and training; the rest of 3000 working hours had been wasted. And of these 300 hours, only perhaps a hundred represented skills and knowledge that would be used." His conclusion:

I might have been sent overseas ten days after I was inducted, a day for clothing and shots, a couple of days to explain a batch of equipment and arms that were to be draped upon me and carried overseas, and several days of military intelligence about the front to which I was being sent. All the rest could have been learned, and a lot more, especially concerning the environmental factor, in and near the action, or behind the action getting acquainted with the people I'd be working with.[14]

In summer 1943, the army responded by seeing to it that a new, highly structured program would be introduced for the four remaining MRB companies to be trained under Camp Ritchie auspices. This program would be led by someone already trained at the front and would cover all contingencies the men were likely to encounter in the field.

Sergeant Klaus Mann composes propaganda leaflets for use on the Italian front. SOURCE: MÜNCHNER STADTBIBLIOTHEK / MONACENSIA

Lieutenant Martin Herz loads leaflets into an empty artillery shell for firing into enemy territory. SOURCE: AUTHOR'S COLLECTION

Some of the finished printed matter, together with the English translations, written and printed by the First MRB men in Florence, Italy. SOURCE: NATIONAL ARCHIVES AND RECORDS ADMINISTRATION

CHAPTER THIRTEEN

The Counterintelligence Corps and the Office of Strategic Services

Definite weapons, slicker than wounds, surround them,
they camouflage, they bristle with arms to the teeth,
they implement with knives their patient wonder
and wander like children the iron techniques of death.[1]

TWO EXTERNAL ORGANIZATIONS RAN OPERATIONS CLOSELY INVOLVED with the Camp Ritchie program in military intelligence: the Counterintelligence Corps (CIC) and the Office of Strategic Services (OSS). While these two agencies provided intense training in the intelligence field, they differed in focus and in makeup. The goal of the CIC was to foil the espionage attempts of the enemy. It did this by capturing enemy spies and documents while preventing the army's military secrets from being leaked to the enemy. It was the job of the OSS not only to collect strategic intelligence but also to operate espionage activities behind enemy lines, arm and train guerrilla forces, and use black operations, or deceptive tactics, in pursuit of their aims. Another main difference: the OSS was an agency of the US government, and, as a consequence, its personnel was 35 percent female and 25 percent civilian, while the CIC was an organization of the US Army, with all-male infantry personnel.

COUNTERINTELLIGENCE CORPS (CIC)

The Counterintelligence Corps could trace its roots back to World War I, when, as the Corps of Intelligence Police, it had served as an attachment to the American Expeditionary Force in Europe. Virtually disbanded at the end of the war, the corps was officially resurrected as the Counter-intelligence Corps on January 1, 1942, and began recruiting men into its ranks with a minimum IQ score of 120, with legal or investigative backgrounds, and with foreign language skills, especially in French and German. The IQ requirements were even higher than for the Ritchie Boys, so it is not surprising that their ranks included many well-known names. Perhaps the most famous of the CIC agents trained at Camp Ritchie was J. D. Salinger, who worked on his novel *Catcher in the Rye* during his off-duty hours of service.

The CIC training program went through major changes from its inception in January 1942 to its relocation at Camp Ritchie in 1944. In 1942, the CIC recruits were first sent to preliminary training schools scattered at nine US locations; afterward, they attended the CIC's Advanced Training School in Chicago. It was here that the training shifted from generalized counterintelligence work in the United States (surveillance, interrogation, lock-picking, etc.) to specialized techniques more appropriate for work in a war setting. Indeed, an agreement was reached at this time with the FBI that the CIC would handle all security matters pertaining to the US Army exclusively. Because much of the CIC training was taking place in the classroom, the army began on July 5, 1943, to provide a month-long crash course of combat training for the recruits about to be posted overseas. This training began at the CIC staging area at Camp Holabird in Baltimore, where recruits learned marksmanship, map reading, and handling a tent. At the end of a week, they went on to Fort Hunt in Virginia to learn how to handle prisoners of war (POWs) and enemy soldiers resistant to interrogation. After four days of instruction there, the men came to Camp Ritchie for a special-ized two-week course that included instruction in scouting, patrolling, and enemy identification, with special two-day close combat instruction given to small groups of CIC officers and enlisted men. From Ritchie, the CIC men went on to Fort Belvoir, Virginia, to learn the art of camouflage, how to detect and evade mines and booby traps, and how to discover and dispose of explosives.[2]

Camp Ritchie had actually become involved in CIC training even before this time, when, in November 1942, it offered its first specialized course in counterintelligence. It graduated one hundred students, including some who had previously graduated from the Advanced Training School in Chicago. Then, late in 1943, plans were made to concentrate the full specialized CIC training at Ritchie and to close the training programs at the Advanced Training School in Chicago, as well as at Camp Holabird, Fort Hunt, and Fort Belvoir. From August 1944 to May 1945, all Counterintelligence Corps training of agents for overseas service was conducted at Camp Ritchie, where they enrolled in the standard eight-week classes before taking their more specialized training. Close to twenty-five hundred CIC agents enrolled in Ritchie's twenty-two special classes (two-week and two-day courses) and in four redeployment classes. After V-E Day, CIC agents, while continuing to take the standard eight-week program at Ritchie, were sent to a new Counterintelligence Center at Fort Meade for their advanced training.

Technician Third Grade Thomas O. Schlesinger noted that the Composite School Unit at Camp Ritchie provided a unique environment for the CIC's immersive study of the paraphernalia and tactics of war in the European and Pacific theaters:

> On a typical day one could see a complete battery of German horse-drawn artillery clatter across the parade ground. Walking by a classroom building one might see a class form into ranks and practice German short-order drill. On night field exercises in the Blue Ridge Mountains, men staggering into an exercise station half dead with fatigue had to get an "abandoned" Japanese radio functioning to learn the compass azimuth to the next station.[3]

Another CIC operative, Arthur Hurlburt, commented, "At Ritchie we fired a familiarization course with just about every weapon known to man, mostly enemy types. We worked with hand grenades, concussion grenades, explosives, crawled under live gun fire, examined all sorts of captured enemy uniforms and insignia."[4]

Still, he said, the main emphasis was on map reading. The men took the same one-night field exercise as all Ritchie Boys, in which they were dropped off in pairs with the assignment to find their way back to the camp on a course "up over the top of the mountain, through thick woods and briar patches, in the pitch black night." The next day they learned the differences between Grid North, Magnetic North, and True North and between azimuth and back azimuth before being sent out at night again, in groups of twos or threes, with a compass, flashlight, and map. The next day, after studying "contours, elevations, signs and symbols," they were given a map for their night exercise with an eight-inch circle completely blanked out: "We were to meet the truck at 11 at the center of the circle."[5] And, on another night, after having learned the symbols unique to French and German armies, they would be sent out with French or German maps of the area.

Although the eight-week CIC classes contained many of the same elements as those offered men in training for intelligence work, there were slightly different emphases placed on them. IPW (Interrogation of Prisoners of War) trainees, for example, were learning how to extract strategic and tactical information from POWs, while CIC recruits were concentrating on how to detect saboteurs and spies. They needed to learn how to trick enemy agents into revealing themselves by making a trivial error and to read the tell-tale signs of a liar by studying "his Adam's apple, his eyes, his nostrils, his lips, the little arteries in his temples—all the places where a man might involuntarily betray himself." And they had to learn to trust their instincts and to deepen their investigation when something did not feel quite right.[6] Second Lieutenant Jack Hunter remarked that former German military personnel at Ritchie taught him how to pass for a German military man, while his instructor in Documents Interpretation stated that the goal of the course was to train operatives how to function like a "Dick von Tracy"—a spy who could work in enemy territory. "I study Wehrmacht order of battle, Nazi paramilitary organization; I learn to espy military significance in captured trivia, from matchbook covers to booze tabs. I learn how to pick locks, open safes, make surreptitious entries, the opening and re-sealing of mail. I learn infiltration techniques, how to kill with my hands," Hunter said.[7]

Following their training, counterintelligence operatives were stationed around the globe. CIC agents were sent to Alaska, Panama, Newfoundland, and Iceland. Detachments were formed in every theater of operations, and "at every stepping stone along the attenuated air transportation routes—in the Caribbean, British Guiana and Brazil, remote Atlantic islands like Ascension, bases in black Africa like Liberia, Gold Coast and Sudan, North African cities like Cairo and Marrakech." They were also active in the United States. "Wherever an American soldier shouldered a gun, wherever an American plane took off on a mission, wherever an American Navy ship tied up or merchant ship set out with troops and supplies, there the clever young men of the Corps . . . waited and watched, ferreted and sleuthed, totally committed to their task of protecting the American war effort."[8] They played a pivotal role in the United States' atomic energy program, or Manhattan Project, not only in guarding its centers against sabotage and espionage but also in transporting highly classified documents and dangerous radioactive materials across country by train.

In the European and Pacific theaters of operations, the services of CIC detachments were available to army, corps, and division commanders. A CIC detachment was composed of four officers and thirteen enlisted men with the transportation necessary to form teams of two individuals to accompany each regiment and work in cooperation with the regimental intelligence officer (S-2). Five other teams worked with the division at large or, where necessary, supplemented the regimental teams. Nearly all of them held only noncommissioned officer rank and operated either in civilian clothing or in a Class "A" officer's uniform without any display of ranking. Although irked by their noncommissioned status, they were given the authority to require the unquestioned assistance of troops "from any officer up to and including full colonel." Whenever one of these officers questioned the agent's authority and inquired about his rank, he was instructed to reply firmly, "My rank is confidential, but at this moment I am not outranked."[9] These operatives had many duties in the field: providing security for military staging areas, locating enemy documents, carrying out interrogations, and uncovering enemy agents. They also provided training to combat units in security, censorship, the seizure of documents, and the dangers of booby traps.

In his wartime memoirs, Ib Melchior repeatedly emphasized the importance of finding simple solutions to complex questions. When, for example, US troops needed to ford the Kyll River near Bitburg, Germany, the river was badly swollen from rain and melting snow, and photo intelligence could not provide the detailed information the corps needed regarding the consistency of the river bottom, the condition of the river banks, and the strength of the current along a twenty-five-mile stretch of the river. Melchior got the information he needed by going to a fishermen's club in Luxembourg City, since "who would know more about the river than the sports fishermen who had walked along its banks and stood in the middle of the stream, searching for the places richest with trout?"[10]

Like his colleagues in IPW, Melchior also found that bluffing was an effective tool. When he was returning through enemy lines with a defecting German physicist, for example, he avoided having to show the physicist's nonexistent papers by shouting at the border guard that the scientist was Heinrich Himmler's nephew and that the much-feared head of the SS would be furious if "Colonel Himmler" was held up on his journey to the front. The intimidated German sergeant allowed the jeep to pass.

Although frequently put in danger, death rates among CIC agents were relatively low. One agent who willingly put his life on the line was Staff Sergeant Robert Ebaugh, a thirty-year-old operative from Westminster, Maryland. After the CIC learned that German agents had parachuted into the area around Tehran in December 1943 with plans to assassinate President Roosevelt on his way to the Soviet embassy for meetings with Stalin and Churchill, Ebaugh served as a decoy. He rode in the president's car during the five-mile trip from the airport to the Soviet embassy, wearing Roosevelt's hat and cape and holding Roosevelt's trademark cigarette holder in his mouth. Fortunately, nothing happened.[11]

CIC work in Europe took on new urgency as the war wound down and thousands of Germans were on the road: "deserters and DPs [displaced persons], discharged soldiers and German civilians fleeing the Russians, politicians and party members." The CIC agents searched for saboteurs and "mandatory arrestees"—top tier Nazi officials, SS officers, and Gestapo leaders accused of war crimes.[12] In one of these actions, "Operation Nursery," the CIC successfully infiltrated and destroyed an underground Nazi movement aiming to establish a Fourth Reich in postwar Germany by arresting more than one thousand Nazis in a single night. As the operative in charge of this program, Jack Hunter adopted the persona of Hans Jaeger—which was a direct translation of his name into German. As Jaeger, he convincingly played the role of a Lithuanian displaced person now working as a black marketeer.

CIC operatives were heavily involved in secret missions to find the German scientists, nuclear materials, and equipment involved in Germany's program in developing atomic weapons (the Alsos Mission, from the Greek word for "groves"); to bring German rocket scientists, like Werner von Braun, to the United States to work in advancing the United States' rocket and space programs (Operation Paperclip); and to capture personnel and materials relating to cryptography and spying before these materials could be destroyed ("Target Intelligence Committee," or TICOM). In these operations, the CIC frequently made use of former Nazis, because they had both inside knowledge of German and Russian intelligence and the credibility that made it possible for them to infiltrate various subversive circles.

CIC agents were also intensely involved in the Pacific theater of operations. There they were more tightly integrated into activities at the front. In Burma, CIC operatives made jungle safaris to secure enemy documents, to identify security threats and suspected spies, and to arrest collaborators—especially those who had been responsible for the deaths of any Allied personnel. Ritchie trainee Edmund Fong, for example, went to great lengths to capture the headman of Kansi, a remote village in northern Burma, because he had been responsible for capturing fifteen Burmese soldiers and one US airman and turning them over to the Japanese for execution. To get to him, Fong traveled for two weeks through the Burmese jungle. Then, to get the man turned over to him, Fong deceived his Chinese counterpart into believing that he wanted him only for the information he could get from him regarding the Japanese. Fong picked up three more collaborators on his return trip to headquarters.[13]

Another Ritchie-trained agent, Woodrow G. Hunter, became the first CIC operative to be killed in the Pacific theater. A Cincinnati lawyer, Hunter was a member of the 5227th CIC detachment, supporting a task force from the Sixth Army. He was part of the assault wave on Insoemoar Island just off the coast of Dutch New Guinea. Japanese forces harassed the troops as they unloaded, and Hunter was shot and killed by a sniper's bullet on May 18, 1944. His sacrifice was not forgotten. Fort Holabird, Maryland, honored Hunter's service with a portrait and a named building in May 1952; Fort Huachuca, Arizona, named a street in his honor in March 1977.

The CIC was also in the thick of things on Okinawa. There they were chiefly engaged in combat intelligence and so effective that, by the end of the campaign, the CIC had taken more Japanese prisoners than any single infantry regiment. These prisoners included almost the entire Japanese secret police organization active on the island—the Kempei Tai. After the war, the CIC had offices in all the major Japanese cities, where they worked to detect and prevent subversive activities by ultranationalists and Japanese Communists.[14]

For his part, Arthur Hurlburt and his team had been stationed in the Philippines during part of the war, where, with the aid of guerrillas, he had rounded up and arrested Filipinos collaborating with the Japanese. Later he was sent to New Guinea to check oceangoing merchant vessels. He expressed deep appreciation for his Ritchie training "since we knew we would be traveling in a strange place in small groups or alone—not like Infantry soldiers, where the Captain tells people where to go." He recalled that "most of the time I was away from even my own people, from ten to over a hundred miles, sometimes without any Americans at all around." He got hurt in the Philippines, "some 108 miles away from Detachment HQ," and although "most infantrymen would shudder to be that far away from the rest of their men," he was able to make it back to his unit. "Ritchie was a good training ground for what we faced," he stated. "It was physically toughening as well as mentally sharpening, so that overseas weather, distance, aloneness and strange terrain were never insurmountable."[15]

Office of Strategic Services (OSS)

Whereas the CIC was a deliberately low-key operation, many actions undertaken by the Office of Strategic Services were more conspicuously adventurous. This office also outlasted the Counterintelligence Corps by morphing into the Central Intelligence Agency, or CIA, in July 1947. At its peak, the OSS employed almost thirteen thousand people, with nearly seventy-five hundred of them serving overseas.

It was the brainchild of General William J. "Fighting Bill" Donovan, a World War I hero who, to this day, remains the only person to have received the United States' four highest awards: the Medal of Honor, the Distinguished Service Cross, the Distinguished Service Medal, and the National Security Medal, in addition to the Silver Star and the Purple Heart. Donovan had the foresight to realize that the United States' intelligence operations were deficient to nonexistent. At the start of World War II, the collection of American intelligence was scattered randomly among the State Department, the US Army, the US Navy, and the FBI, with no real direction or coordination. To counteract this problem, President Franklin D. Roosevelt created the Office of the Coordinator of Information, or COI, to streamline the process of collection and dissemination of intelligence. It was also to conduct unconventional warfare. General Donovan was appointed head of the organization. Some months after the United States' entry into the war, Donovan moved the COI under the Joint Chiefs of Staff to ensure the support of the military. At this time, Roosevelt moved half the staff of the COI to the Office of War Information, giving it the responsibility of producing white (that is, admittedly Allied-inspired) propaganda. Donovan expanded his operations in black propaganda while soliciting a broad network of spy-informants and saboteurs, thereby building the OSS into the nation's first wartime espionage service.

OSS tasks included research and analysis, communications, and morale operations. The most glamorous missions by far were performed by its Special Operations branch (SO) and country-specific Operational

Groups (OGs). Although the OGs would operate as larger teams than the three-to-four-man SOs, their missions were similar. They were assigned to infiltrate enemy lines, link up with native resistance forces, and perform acts of sabotage. It was the daring actions of these groups that captured the imagination of the public. Three Hollywood films were made in 1946 featuring breathtaking OSS missions: *O.S.S.* (1946), with Alan Ladd; *13 Rue Madeleine* (1947), with James Cagney; and *Cloak and Dagger* (1946), with Gary Cooper. All three films had former OSS operatives as technical advisers.

From late April 1942 until June 1944, the men in Special Operations were trained in Catoctin Mountain Park, Maryland, at Camp B-2, an area known to the locals as Camp Greentop. Until it was leased to the OSS, Camp Greentop had served as a handicap-accessible summer camp for children crippled by polio. This camp was located just eight miles south of Camp Ritchie in the most rugged part of the Catoctin Mountains—and a little over a mile from President Roosevelt's wartime retreat of Shangri La. After the Special Operations branch was well established at Greentop, in 1943 and 1944, new nation-specific Operation Groups were also sent there for advanced training. As at Ritchie, the camp's main focus was on the war in Europe, and it trained operatives for action in France, Italy, Greece, Yugoslavia, Norway, and Germany.

Training at Camp B-2 was intense and both mentally and physically exacting. Whereas the Ritchie men were primarily focused on developing their interrogation and intelligence skills, the SO and OG operatives underwent a punishing physical program to prepare them for interactions with guerrilla forces and dangerous acts of subterfuge behind enemy lines. As soon as they reported for training, they were given false names. OSS recruit Ib Melchior, son of the Wagnerian tenor Lauritz Melchior, has provided what is arguably the most detailed personal description of the SO training program: "Our group consisted of thirty-six men ranging in age from eighteen to fifty-one and chorusing a Babel of accents." Arriving almost at midnight, "we were at once plunked down for a lengthy examination, which consisted of a standard IQ test and what was called a confidential psychological evaluation."[16] Some of the OSS training—the night map exercises, the driving of military vehicles, the firing of a wide range of weaponry, mastery of the Morse code—was similar to that offered at Ritchie but carried out at a more advanced level: their Morse code instruction, for example, included classes in coded telegraphy. New courses involved the mastery of explosives, creating disguises, dealing with poisons, picking locks, and working with miniature cameras and the X-35 (a compact radio receiver and transmitter built into a case the size and shape of a portable Underwood typewriter).

The men were sent on physically grueling missions while carrying a backpack filled with rocks. These exercises culminated in a long and much-dreaded obstacle course. Here the candidate had to carry a forty-pound backpack containing a mock radio set (rocks) and mock vacuum tubes (an empty Mason jar) on a harrowing, cross-country obstacle course that took him up and down steep hillsides, over walls and under fences, and across bridgeless streams while under constant attack from machine-gun fire, booby traps, and explosives. Through all of this, he was forbidden to remove the Mason jar from the backpack. The task was to end the course with the jar still intact. Those who passed this test were sent to intensive, two-day training in parachute jumping at Quantico Marine Base. By now, the number of men left in Ib Melchior's class had been reduced from thirty-six to six.

As a final assignment, the SO students were required to conduct an actual night raid on a dam, railway bridge, or industrial facility as a practical exercise in reconnaissance and sabotage, all the while evading the unknowing police, FBI agents, or military guards who might be policing the site. They were then to relay material back to Camp Greentop on an X-35 radio receiver/transmitter. Melchior's assignment was slightly different: He was to gather information on how to "paralyze" the entire town of Hagerstown through sabotage and to ascertain how the local Fairchild Aircraft plant could be taken over "by a company of paratroopers with the object of holding it for forty-eight hours." He was to report his progress back to home base four times a day on his compact radio receiver/transmitter without being detected.[17]

The assignments required a good deal of creative thinking. Melchior decided that he could best get the information he needed by assuming the role of a journalist eager to write a magazine article about the town of Hagerstown. This, he said, made the assignment ridiculously easy, since the people of Hagerstown were "cooperative to a fault." He was given full access to records and plans by the town's Building and Safety Department, Public Works Department, and Water and Power Department. Everybody he encountered was "most accommodating and willing to help out a struggling young magazine writer who might say something nice about their town." The public relations department at Fairchild Aircraft was equally accommodating in giving Melchior a tour of the plant. At the end of the exercise, he knew not only exactly how to paralyze the town but also how to destroy the entire Fairchild Aircraft plant and the railroad serving it. He found the exercise "a little frightening. This was, after all, a time of war, and there *could* be the real McCoy out there."[18]

Upon completion of his course work, Ib Melchior was offered a choice of participating in missions with Britain's Special Operations Executive (SOE) or entering the US armed forces. Although the SOE had served as the British prototype of the OSS and its training and missions were similar, a transfer would mean coming under British authority. However, if Melchior remained under American authority, he would become an American citizen. Melchior chose the latter, and he was sent to Camp Ritchie for training in interrogation.

Generally the men in Special Operations were trained to work alone or in teams of two or three, and to focus on specific tasks of sabotage or subversion behind enemy lines, while those in OGs, or Operational Group units, were organized into sections of thirty-four men or smaller half sections of two officers and thirteen NCOs. They functioned as a free-standing unit, and their numbers included weapons and demolition specialists, a shortwave radio operator, and a medic.[19] Their task was to organize, supply, and train indigenous guerrilla bands that they then led on hit-and-run missions in the Axis-occupied countries.

A good number of Ritchie-trained OSS men served in Special Operations. Staff Sergeant Alfred Andrew "Fred" Eden (né Ehrenfreund) is a good example of one who functioned independently behind enemy lines as a CO operative. Prior to D-Day, he parachuted into German-occupied France with orders to establish an underground railroad for downed American pilots. He carried with him papers validating three separate false identities: one as a resident intern at Central Hospital in Paris, one as a Roman Catholic priest, and one as a French fisherman. He received considerable help from members of the French resistance, who gave him valuable information that he was able to radio back to London. Many of the pilots who were rescued through Eden's efforts went on to serve as pilots in the invasion of Normandy.

Eden, too, participated in the invasion; under assignment to V Corps, Second Armored Division, he landed on Omaha Beach on D-Day and immediately began work as an interrogator of captured Germans before returning to German-occupied France to serve as liaison between Allied operatives and French resistance cells active in sabotage and guerrilla warfare. For his service, he earned a Purple Heart, a Bronze Star, Belgian and French Fourragères, and a Russian Guard Medal.[20]

After they arrived in Britain, a goodly number of Ritchie Boy interrogators were approached and asked whether they were interested in working for the OSS. Most of the men selected for this service were excited by the prospect of contributing so importantly to missions behind enemy lines. In cases such as these, the men were trained by British Special Services. Since the SO school at Camp Greentop had been modeled on the British SOE, the two-month training program in Britain was similar to the American one. Second Lieutenant Robert Fulton Cutting II had been assigned to Field Artillery after graduating from Ritchie's seventh class, but he was then recruited by the OSS and trained by the SOE. He was parachuted into France on a special assignment to take still photographs and film footage of the French resistance movement and of American officers and men in the field. To do this, he accompanied the Operational Group "Percy Red" and the Jedburgh Team "Lee" on their missions.

"Jedburgh" teams were part of a cooperative effort between the OSS and the British SOE.[21] The first Jedburgh team parachuted into France the day before D-Day in what was the first cooperative mission between the SOE and OSS in Europe. In reality, the main motive for the British SOE to work cooperatively with the OSS was a shortage of British aircraft to ferry its operatives and supplies in and out of Nazi-occupied France, Belgium, and the Netherlands. The Jedburgh teams usually had three to four members, always including an American officer, a British officer, and a radio operator. They might include a Free French officer or enlisted man, or a Belgian, Dutch, or Canadian soldier. Their purpose was "to coordinate airdrops of arms and supplies, guide local partisans on hit-and-run attacks and sabotage, and assist the advancing Allied armies to defeat the Third Reich."[22] While he was attached to the Jedburgh "Lee" team, Cutting actively participated in a number of hit-and-run guerrilla attacks in southwest-central France around Limoges.

Like Cutting, French-born René Défourneaux went through OSS training in England before parachuting into France and linking up with the French resistance forces, or Maquis, in the wine area of Sancerre and Pouilly. He supervised the retrieval of weapons and explosives that were parachuted into the area on an almost weekly basis, trained the Maquis in their use, and directed them in placing explosives and blowing up bridges across the Loire River.

OSS Ritchie Boys were also active in Italy. One of these was Major Felix Pasqualino, an Italian-born World War I veteran who followed up his training at Ritchie with OSS training at Camp Greentop. Pasqualino was involved in the training of resistance fighters and the gathering of intelligence information. He used charitable work as a smoke screen for his work, and by seeing to it that food rations were distributed to fifteen convents and two orphanages in Rome, he endeared himself to the pope and various high-ranking church officials. In part because of these good relations with the Vatican, he was able to procure documents essential to the Allied mission. He received two awards for his World War II service: the Legion of Merit Medal for having "procured intelligence of a most important nature" and the Papal Cross of the Order of Saint Sylvester for his charitable work in Rome.

By late 1942, the OSS was particularly eager to recruit Greek Americans into its service. First Lieutenant Costa Couvaras, a graduate of Camp Ritchie's fourth class, proved to be one of its most successful recruits; in spring 1944, he parachuted into the mountains of occupied Greece as head of Operation Pericles. With his team, he was the only operative to reach the headquarters of the National Liberation Front (Ethnikó Apeleftherotikó Métopo, or EAM). He remained with the EAM until liberation, supporting them in their successful efforts at liberating a large area of Greece from German, Italian, and Bulgarian occupation forces. After liberation, as tensions between former EAM fighters and the British-supported Greek government army escalated into civil war, Couvaras crossed the lines of fire at least fifteen times to maintain the flow of information. He also protested actively when, in response to Britain's withdrawal of assistance to the Greek government army, President Truman asked Congress to step in and support the forces fighting the Greek Communists.

Couvaras had promised the Greek guerrillas that the United States would stand by them after liberation. That promise could not be kept. In many ways, this was typical of the problematic situations that arose in the United States' postwar politics since many of the resistance fighters in Axis-occupied countries had been Communists. Cutting anticipated this problem in a report he submitted after his SO mission in France:

> *In Region 5 around Limoges the F.F.I. [French Forces of the Interior] is mainly made up from the forces F.T.P.—Franc Tireur et Partisans. All these men are openly communistic. . . . I must say that we were all rather annoyed when the F.T.P.s paraded in front of our HQ in Limoges with such banners as "Sans Stalingrad pas de Debarquement (in Normandy)" [Without Stalingrad no landing in Normandy]. Personally I think we were right in arming these groups as they fought the Germans keenly. But now that the fighting is over you have the embarrassing set-up of large communistic restless groups in France all armed by British or American container droppings.[23]*

It was American policy during the war to side with any group actively fighting the Nazis. This position created any number of sticky situations for OSS operatives once the Truman Doctrine took effect and the United States got actively involved in countering Soviet expansion on the European continent. Captain Thomas E. Stefan, son of Albanian immigrants, was one of these whose reputation was damaged by the United States' changing policies.

Stefan had been smuggled into Albania, where, under his field name "Art," he served as chief of the OSS mission in Tirana. He became intimate with Albania's Communist partisan leader Enver Hoxha during the most critical period of the partisan war against the German occupation. At the time it seemed to be a win-win situation: Stefan supplied the partisans with weaponry, and Hoxha supplied him with valuable intelligence. For his services, Stefan received the Bronze Star and the Legion of Merit from the US Army and the Partisan Star from the Albanian foreign minister Omer Nishani. After the war, however, Hoxha ridiculed all British and American assistance to the partisans as naive and ineffective. Now thoroughly dependent on Stalin's good will, Hoxha claimed that Stefan had never provided any worthwhile assistance to his troops.

René Défourneaux already had qualms about his mission when he was sent to Indochina to supply and train the Viet Minh guerrillas in repelling the Japanese occupation forces. The Viet Minh organization's primary aim was to win Vietnamese independence from French rule as soon as the Japanese had been defeated, and while Défourneaux was training its forces in the use of American arms and explosives against the Japanese, he was fully aware of the paradox of arming and training forces for war against an American ally. "The elimination of the Japanese control of the area may have been their immediate and pressing goal," he commented, "but there was no doubt in my mind that Van's [Vo Nguyen Giap's] true aim and that of Mr. Ho [Ho Chi Minh] was to establish a new political order in the region, along the lines of Communism. We were there to instruct this select group in the use of the weapons we were providing and to train them in the fine art of guerrilla warfare!"[24] He did not dream that, ten years later, the United States would get involved in a long and futile war against these seasoned leaders.

Défourneaux had trained for the Asian war on the American west coast; OSS training at Camp Greentop was shut down after D-Day, and all operations were moved west in order to concentrate on the war against Japan. At this time, the OSS military training areas in the Catoctin Mountains were turned over to Camp Ritchie. This included the feared "trainasium" and the "House of Horrors."

Even before D-Day, however, the ties between camps Ritchie and Greentop had been close. They shared instructors, such as William Fairbairn and Rex Applegate, as well as firing ranges, and they conducted some of their training activities in the same forested terrain. Early on, OSS had placed two officers and nineteen enlisted men from the First Special Service Force into Camp Ritchie's fourth class, mainly to specialize in counterintelligence and photo interpretation. By the end of the war, more than 270 Ritchie-trained servicemen or instructors had served with the OSS. And when, after several name changes and temporary dismantling, the OSS was reconstituted as the Central Intelligence Agency in 1947, many of the Ritchie Boys who had served in the OSS joined this new agency and made a career in its service.

CIC men evaluate documents found in an office abandoned by the Germans.
SOURCE: NATIONAL ARCHIVES AND RECORDS ADMINISTRATION

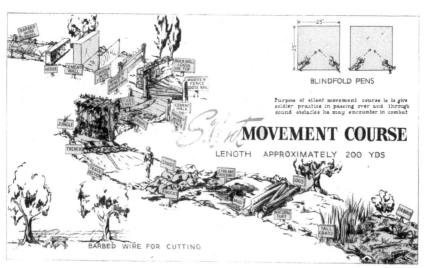

A silent movement course was designed to train OSS soldiers. SOURCE: NATIONAL
ARCHIVES AND RECORDS ADMINISTRATION

Jack Hunter is awarded the Bronze Star by General Edwin Sibert (1946). SOURCE: AUTHOR'S COLLECTION

Robert F. Cutting took this photo of the OSS Mission Germinal. It shows the Jedburgh team and Maquis members with whom he conducted hit-and-run attacks in France. SOURCE: NATIONAL ARCHIVES AND RECORDS ADMINISTRATION

Ho Chi Minh (in shorts) and General Vo Nguyen Giap (in white suit) gave a farewell party for the Deer Team. René Défourneaux is standing to Ho Chi Minh's right. SOURCE: NATIONAL ARCHIVES AND RECORDS ADMINISTRATION

CHAPTER FOURTEEN

Camp Sharpe

*Camp Sharpe was important to me. It was a way stop to victory in
World War 2.*

Fortunately, I survived.

*Unfortunately, many of the people I served with did not. I
remember them.*[1]

ON NOVEMBER 9, 1943, ABOUT SIXTY MEN WHO HAD COMPLETED THEIR
military intelligence training at Camp Ritchie were ordered to pack
their basic equipment, take their weapons, and prepare for a twenty-mile
march. They were the first of nearly nine hundred soldiers who would
pass through Camp Sharpe in Gettysburg, Pennsylvania, over the next
nine months. Lieutenant Maximilian Lerner blamed Colonel Banfill for
this move, saying that, because he "apparently, desperately, wanted to be
a general," he "kept bringing in more and more soldiers for training" at
a time when the army was not calling the camp's "highly trained graduates" into active service. This situation, he said, had created a bottleneck
at the camp.[2] Certainly overcrowding at Camp Ritchie was a problem;
the Gettysburg newspapers confirmed this situation by reporting on the
commander's need for an "expansion of the regular camp site [i.e., Camp
Ritchie]." They added another reason to the mix, when they stated that
this expansion was made in response to some "extensive training activities
instituted by the main encampment."[3]

The creation of an ancillary camp was not unique to Camp Ritchie.
The Office of Strategic Services (OSS) camp at Catoctin Mountain

Park expanded onto the adjacent grounds of an abandoned Conservation Construction Corps (CCC) camp known as Area B-5, while PO Box 1142 created an ancillary camp some 120 miles to the north at an old CCC camp in Pine Grove Furnace State Park, Pennsylvania. In this remote setting, military intelligence officers could conduct initial interviews with captured German (and, later, Japanese) officers and determine who had valuable intelligence. Those who did were sent on to PO Box 1142 for more in-depth interrogation; those who did not were sent to other prisoner of war (POW) camps. Camp Ritchie alumni were among the interrogators at both camps.

Camp Sharpe, too, was located at a former Conservation Construction Corps camp, which had previously been known only as "CCC Gettysburg 2." It was located at the edge of the Confederate line on the Gettysburg Battlefield, at the bottom of a steep dirt road in what is known as MacMillan Woods. It had originally housed an all-Black unit of corps members who were brought in to clear the Gettysburg Battlefield of brush and to build bridges, roads, and outbuildings prior to the 1938 Civil War Veterans' reunion and the dedication of the Peace Light monument north of town. After the reunion, the corps remained behind to engage in further projects to beautify the battlefield; however, after Pearl Harbor the CCC camps all lost their funding, and, in March 1942, the camp was abandoned. As a Camp Ritchie subcamp, the site was named Camp George H. Sharpe after General Meade's intelligence officer at the Battle of Gettysburg, and it became a new training ground for military intelligence. It served two functions. The first was as the site for advanced infantry training, since Colonel Banfill was determined that no Camp Ritchie graduates should be sent behind enemy lines without first undergoing intense Ranger (commando) training. Then, in January 1944, the camp began training men for psychological warfare.

The Gettysburg CCC camp had stood empty for twenty months when the Rangers in training arrived to claim it. The buildings were dirty and drafty, and they had been taken over by rodents and spiders. Because the barracks had been built only for summer usage, they had no insulation, but wood stoves had been set up at the ends of each building to provide warmth. Unfortunately, the winter of 1943–1944 was exceptionally cold. Master Sergeant Harry Jacobs arrived in Gettysburg with frozen feet; after a few days' stay at the Gettysburg Hospital, he was transferred back to the hospital at Fort Ritchie, and then into counterintelligence training.

Meanwhile, at Camp Sharpe, the Ritchie men pursued their infantry training in full force. Gunter Kosse, a German Jew from Berlin, recalled night marches when the men had to travel at a pace of seven miles an hour across snowy fields while laden with heavy field equipment. He found the moonlit marches "eerily beautiful" as they marched past nineteenth-century cannons and out among the statues of Civil War soldiers. The men practiced "extended ordered drill" over and over again: storming hills, for example, and jumping in and out of foxholes. They also learned how to take frozen machine guns apart and put them back together.[4] "I do not believe I was ever as cold, as walking a tour of duty in the snow there," Lieutenant Lerner said, "not even during the Battle of the Bulge a year later. . . . Camp Sharpe was one of my least pleasant experiences."[5]

Even as most of these men were being moved out and sent to Northern Ireland for further training, men enrolling in four Mobile Radio Broadcasting Companies (MRBCs) started coming to Camp Sharpe to receive intensive training in psychological warfare. Camp Ritchie's First MRBC had, after a rocky start, already demonstrated the value of propaganda as a tool of war in the African and Italian campaigns. Its commander, Major Edward A. Caskey, declared that it was "one of the most important supporting weapons of modern warfare" and cited, as an example, the surrender of an entire German regiment in Tunisia, following a drop of leaflets that described the hopelessness of its position and the promise of good treatment in Allied POW camps.[6] Lieutenant Hans Habe, one of the ablest young officers in the First MRBC, had been recalled to Washington and put in charge of training Camp Sharpe's four psychological warfare detachments for the landing in France. The first two were requested for February, a third for May, and a fourth for June. "I was furnished with full powers that many a general might have envied," Habe remembered. "I was allowed to pick from the superbly organized card indexes of the War Department those men whom I considered suitable for the task in hand, and within forty-eight hours the people thus chosen would arrive at Gettysburg."[7] He made a stellar selection, particularly of men destined for working in propaganda. Twenty-two of them were assigned to the Second MRB Company directly from Camp Ritchie; others were transferred to Camp Sharpe from other wartime assignments. Many of the future propagandists came from academia; many others were salespersons, artists, and journalists. Among the members of the Second MRBC—143 enlisted men and 21 officers—thirty-three languages were spoken, dominated, of course, by speakers of German and French. A preponderance of the men were Jewish. Indeed, the percentage of Jews at Camp Sharpe was so high that some of the soldiers began referring to it as "Camp Shapiro."

The men of the Second MRBC arrived at a camp that consisted of four barracks for enlisted men (sleeping quarters and classrooms) and one for officers; company and battalion headquarters; housing for the battalion commanding officer; a sparsely furnished recreation hall; a supply building; mess hall; poorly functioning showers; a latrine; and an extensive motor pool area with garages, two workshops, and dispatch office. Somewhat later, a training platoon of army engineers, mostly Mohawk Indians, erected an eighty-foot antenna tower on the grounds.

New arrivals to the camp were dismayed by its condition. German novelist Stefan Heym found the barracks more like hovels (*Schuppen*) than dwellings "in different stages of scantily painted-over decay."[8] Lieutenant Arthur Jaffe, who was destined to become captain and commander of the Second MRB Company, agreed: The barracks were "surrounded by a sea of mud," and the wind "whistled through gaps in the walls."[9] For men used to the relative luxury at the Maryland camp, life at Camp Sharpe was "rugged and barren." In order to preserve the secrecy of their mission, the enlisted men were forbidden to go to any of the bars in town. No officer wives were allowed to visit the camp, and it was not even connected to the outside world by telephone. No one, not even at Camp Ritchie, was to be informed of what was going on in Gettysburg.

Major John T. Jarecki was the camp commander. A Chicago lawyer by trade, he had graduated from Camp Ritchie's fifth class with a specialization in photo interpretation. He was, Lieutenant Jaffe remembered, a "good detail man."[10] The camp was organized into five sections: headquarters, radio, propaganda, printing, and motor pool.

All were designed to deliver propaganda to the front lines of the war, whether by leaflet, radio, or direct appeal to the enemy combatants by microphone. The men in the propaganda section would be composing the leaflets produced by the print section; they would be creating the radio broadcasts transmitted by the radio section; and they would be driven to the front lines by the men in the motor pool to make direct appeals to the enemy. While at Camp Sharpe, the men in radio and in printing would get used to broadcasting and printing under all types of war situations, with all types of equipment. Trucks were brought in to the camp to be outfitted as mobile rigs devoted solely to broadcasting or to printing. However, while the radio section at the camp ordered four four-hundred-watt mobile transmitters, and tested them in code broadcasts from one to the other as well as to Camp Ritchie, the men in printing were handicapped by a late arrival of equipment. As a result, several were sent to a lithographic school in New York City for a refresher course and detailed training in varitype printing. The men in the motor pool were trained to drive and make repairs to a full variety of motorized vehicles; this included waterproofing them for the invasion of France. They, like the men in propaganda services, were fluent in at least two languages.

Habe trained the men in the propaganda section for a variety of assignments. Some might be sent to film or take photographs in the battle zones both for purposes of military intelligence and for propaganda; some would broadcast in different languages, to local populations as well as to the German army; some would serve as translators of captured and local news and war documents and as interpreters between captured war leaders and Allied commanders; some would monitor German and civilian radio and newspapers in order to gauge morale; some would produce propaganda pamphlets, posters, and leaflets in record time for the changing war conditions; some would interrogate POWs in order to gauge enemy morale. And some would have the most dangerous task of "hog calling." This involved driving out to the front of the Allied lines to speak directly to the German solders by microphone and to urge them to surrender. In all these areas of training, Lieutenant Habe was sole instructor.

On the first day of class, the men in the propaganda section were somewhat taken aback when Habe sailed to the front of the classroom, hesitated briefly, and then swung around to face the class and introduce himself as "Hans Habe de Bekessy, returned from Africa."[11] Habe had a colorful history. A Hungarian Jew by birth and a newspaperman by trade, he had served in Vienna as the youngest chief editor of any major European newspaper. After war broke out in Europe, he fought the Nazis as a member of the French Foreign Legion. He had been captured but, with the help of friends, escaped from the Dieuze Dulag, or transit prison camp, in Lorraine, France. He had emigrated to the United States, quickly become an American citizen, lectured at West Point, and written a best-selling novel about his prison camp experiences. He had married Eleanor Post Hutton (heiress of General Foods) and become a prominent figure in the Washington social scene. When his wife gave birth to a son, Anthony Niklas Habe, Eleanor Roosevelt served as his godmother.

Habe was also something of a fop. Contrary to army regulations, he dyed his hair chestnut brown with blond tints, causing some of his fellow officers to call him "Goldilocks" behind his back. When he was not dressed in riding boots, jodhpurs, and a leather vest, he accessorized his uniform with a white silk handkerchief in his breast pocket and a bejeweled tiepin in his regulation necktie. As German-born Peter Wyden (né Weidenreich) put it, "It was like perpetually being at a show, at a circus just to see this guy perform. I would have paid money for it."[12]

Despite his vanity and strongly French-tinted English, the men soon realized that Habe was an extraordinary instructor: "He was by turns German teacher, journalist, radio director, political lecturer, copy editor, language teacher, voice trainer, psychology professor—whatever the course material required," Hanuš Burger enthused. He found this all the more remarkable in that "in those moldy, cold . . . barracks we were, even in political respects, a motley bunch of people—Communists, Sympathizers, Anti-Communists. Habe managed to bind us together for our assigned task."[13] Stefan Heym, whose socialist views could not have been further from those of Habe, agreed: "I . . . know of no one whose individual contribution to the development of psychological warfare in this army contributed so much to its victory. Beneath all the flickering and all the glitz stood a man of industry, great knowledge, and, occasionally, heart."[14]

In his training, Habe stuck to policies that had been worked out with British military intelligence. Technician Third Grade Joseph Eaton, a native of Nuremberg, Germany, described the companies' mission as twofold. First, they were "to get the Germans . . . to believe in what they were being told by the U.S. and by the British, and second, to get the Germans to question their regime. . . . We had to focus on inconsistencies in German policies from the point of view of the German public."[15]

Because of their specialization in psychological warfare, the men at Camp Sharpe were freed from instruction in terrain intelligence, map making, and azimuth exercises. They were required, however, to participate in military training. Already before breakfast "they slipped and stumbled around the icy square in drill formation and at odd times during the day took hikes, engaged in mock battles or spent time familiarizing themselves with company weapons."[16] They learned interrogation techniques as well, but with a somewhat different focus than at Camp Ritchie, since the primary purpose of their questioning was to gauge enemy morale. These interrogations would be crucial if the men were to figure out how to "turn" the Germans by radio, pamphlet, and hog calling. "No prisoner is uninteresting," Habe stated. "We must know the attitude of the average German soldier. Moreover, the dullest prisoner may reveal a choice item of information at the end of a long interview."[17] Since they had no Composite School Unit members to take on the roles of captured Germans, the men at Camp Sharpe practiced only on one another.

Habe taught that another method of acquiring valuable insights into the German mentality was by anonymously polling the caged prisoners on a monthly basis. In these polls, they would give prisoners a number of questions to which they would simply check off "yes" or "no." These included questions such as the following:

"Do you think it is still possible to eject the Allies from Italy?"

"Do you believe that Germany possesses 'secret weapons' which can decide the war?"

"Do you believe that revenge will be taken against the German people in case Germany loses the war?"[18]

To aid them in their work, the men learned not only German army commands but also German army slang. Some of this slang was sardonic in nature: bullets were called "blue beans," "SOS" meant "sleep without sirens," and the "Frozen Flesh Order" was the ribbon given for service at the Russian front.[19]

Habe also taught a basic course in contemporary history. Hanuš Burger recalled:

> We honed up on the names of politicians and military men that were mentioned in the news, we memorized what parties they belonged to, which organizations they represented, and the abbreviations by which these organizations were known. We had to be able to name immediately the participants in important conferences, and also, of course, the results of these conferences. We learned which newspapers represented whose interests, who financed them, which important men wrote for them.[20]

The men were given descriptive lists of leading personalities in Europe, including important prewar figures, historical figures, collaborators, resisters, and governments in exile. They received handouts on all the important news agencies in Europe and Japan, as well as the important newspapers and publications of the Allied, Axis, and neutral countries, with their political slant listed: "fascist minded," "sensational," "rightist, popular," for example. These lists included underground papers being produced in Belgium, the Netherlands, Denmark, France, Czechoslovakia, and Poland. Another handout listed the important journalists and commentators in the United States, Great Britain, France, the Soviet Union, Italy, and Germany, together with their affiliations and areas of expertise. All this was important for the men monitoring reports in the radio and in the press. Monitoring the various media outlets was essential to creating propaganda that was both timely and accurate.

Habe placed special emphasis on teaching his men how to monitor and record radio reports. "The monitor is a news reporter," he told them. "It is his job to listen to news broadcasts and to report them as faithfully as possible."[21] The men were taught not to editorialize in writing up their monitored news reports and not to eliminate any news story they heard, no matter how inconsequential it might seem. The all-important word in radio monitoring was accuracy. For the men who did not know shorthand, Habe taught them a "cue word system" to use in its place. Cue words were simply abbreviations of words that could be quickly reconstructed after the broadcast. Thus the statement "Allied headquarters announced today that 5th army troops had captured Lanuvio, Nemi, and Mount Castellaccio" could be abbreviated to "AL HQ 5 AR CAP LAN NEMI MT CAST." The men would be monitoring both Allied and Axis broadcasts.

After completing the initial monitoring, the man designated as the team's "chief monitor" arranged the reports by classifying them as "Allied," "Enemy," or "Neutral" news stories; he would then index them and write a page of "Personalities in the News" and another of "Highlights in the News." These reports would be mimeographed and distributed to all the writers on the team. The men at Camp Sharpe took several turns monitoring and then preparing reports on radio programming available to them in Gettysburg.

In Europe, these reports would provide the information for the propaganda the Camp Sharpe men prepared for radio broadcasts and for the single-sheet flyers and newsletters fired into enemy lines. Habe was a hard taskmaster in his critiques of these texts. He taught the radio script writers who rewrote the monitored reports for fifteen-minute broadcast news segments to keep their sentences short, use adjectives sparingly, and keep the language simple.

The composers of broadsheets—calls to surrender and one-sheet newspapers—had similar constraints. Habe emphasized, again and again, that one main idea should carry through the calls to surrender. This made an indelible impression on Private Konrad Kellen, whose prewar employment had been as private secretary to the Nobel Prize–winning novelist Thomas Mann. Many years later he would recall Habe asking, when he sought permission to print a propaganda leaflet, "Where is the red thread?"[22] Habe said that the messages on the leaflets should be "sober and terrifying" and yet "simple but striking enough to have souvenir value." These "striking" pages were, as a rule, tactical in nature and written to address a specific combat situation.[23] The men were encouraged to emphasize the Allies' superiority in equipment and weaponry but never to criticize the German soldier. Instead, they were to speak to them as comrades. The same rules applied to the statements made by microphone at the front. The written calls to surrender demanded brevity because they had to fit into shells on five-by-eight-inch sheets of paper for firing into enemy lines; the microphone broadcasts (hog calling) could not exceed ninety seconds, lest the enemy direct gunfire and artillery shells at the speaker.

Even though the men would be assigned to a specialty, Habe insisted that they be instructed in all techniques of propaganda. Habe himself determined each man's specialty. He appeared to have his own hidden reasons for some of his assignments. He assigned both American- and German-born speakers to radio broadcasting, in the knowledge that they would be involved in both "white" and "black" radio work. The white broadcasts were those admittedly made by Americans, and here an American accent might even be desired. The black broadcasts were supposedly made by Germans loyal to the Führer, and here Habe tended to choose men who spoke perfect "Prussian" German. Although Si Lewen (Lewin), a Polish-born Jew, was an art student in New York when the United States entered the war, he was not chosen (as he had expected) for designing and illustrating propaganda flyers; he was made a hog caller instead. Lewen believed that Habe made this decision because of his height. Tall hog callers made good targets, but Lewen was only five foot three.

Habe was right to have all the men study all aspects of psychological warfare because the war situation required flexibility. And he trained his men well. They were flexible, they were resourceful, and they often took the initiative in adapting to the war situation.

Si Lewen, for example, persuaded his superiors to publish a pamphlet that taught the Axis soldiers how to surrender. "Don't mention politics, or allude to their 'loved ones at home,'" he told them; "even patriotism becomes lost on a battlefield. Just convey definite, simple instructions on 'how to surrender.'"

> *[I] then devised a simple phonetic way to teach enemy soldiers a few simple steps: "Ei ssorenda" would become the basic message of every leaflet and every loudspeaker appeal directed into enemy lines, together with a few simple steps on "how to surrender." Repeated over and over, this tactic proved increasingly effective. Eventually, I learned, from some just captured prisoners, that long before surrendering, they had practiced among themselves the "correct" pronunciation. "Ei ssorenda" became an insidious challenge, intruding into enemy minds and eventually the trigger for surrender. Subtly and obliquely, the strategy—call it brainwashing—worked.[24]*

Lewen's commanding officer, Captain Arthur Jaffe, agreed. "About 20 different leaflets were prepared," he said, "all written by T/3 Lewin; and more than a million copies were produced. . . . The concern of the German command over their effect was evident in reports of captives telling of the strict punishment meted out to those caught with Allied leaflets in their possession." Indeed, their concern was so great that the enemy unit commanders and propaganda agencies attempted to counteract them through nightly air drops of literature to their own forces.[25]

Ironically, one of the most provably effective flyers created by an MRB man broke with some of Habe's rules by using no words at all. Colonel Clifford R. Powell, commanding officer of the Twelfth Army Group's Psychological Warfare Service Battalion, asked Technical Sergeant Stefan Heym to come up with an appeal to an entrenched group of Axis soldiers on the island of Cézembre. It was crucial, he was told, that the Allies clear this island because it blocked the entrance to the major harbor of St. Malo, which made it nearly impossible for the Allies to get the reinforcements needed for their advance on Paris. During the summer of 1944, the Allies had bombarded the island with land artillery, naval artillery, and air strikes, and, in mid-August, they had even dropped some of the first napalm bombs on it, but the garrison had held. Now, on

September 1, Heym was given free hand as to what to write. He decided that, instead of writing, he would appeal to the Axis soldiers graphically, by simply showing a picture of the island as a target with an extra-large bomb coming in to land there. The leaflets were quickly printed up and scattered over the island, and, within hours, the first white flags appeared at the openings in the battlements, and the first soldiers came out with their hands raised. It turned out that many of these soldiers were Poles, and they would not have been able to read a propaganda leaflet written in German. Now they came out and surrendered despite the opposition of their German officers. The official surrender came the following day. Heym said, with some pride, "This was the only leaflet of the Second World War whose effectiveness could be observed immediately and in full measure."[26]

The Camp Sharpe broadcasters were equally creative in their appeals to the enemy. Two were particularly effective in getting troops to listen—and surrender—from Lorient and the adjoining German submarine base at Keroman. One was Technical Sergeant Fred Lorenz, an Austrian Jewish actor with the birth name Manfred Inger. The other was the Rhineland German Jewish opera director Benno Frank, who had made occasional radio broadcasts to Palestine after his 1938 emigration to the United States. Both men worked closely with David Hertz, an OSS man and Hollywood screenwriter in charge of their nine-man team.

Lorenz quickly put his rich acting background in Viennese cabaret and theater to use by broadcasting a regular segment titled *Overheard in Lorient* [*Erlauschtes aus Lorient*]. This segment presented possible conversations with actual German officers. To prepare these segments, Lorenz worked closely with the POWs. When a deserter mentioned a particular officer within the garrison, Lorenz went to him to learn all he could about the officer's vocal patterns. As Hertz told it,

> *Our best actor, Corporal Fred Lorenz, would work at the difficult job of mimicking a voice he had never heard by trying various nuances of tone until the deserter would say that Fred had hit the correct one. Next we would write dialogue we believed to be characteristic of the individual selected. After that, both the dialogue and Fred's*

mimicking were tried in rehearsal and on dozens of deserters before
we actually produced an approximation of the man on the air.

Lorenz eventually developed six or seven characterizations that were featured regularly on the broadcasts. These, Hertz said, "constituted the most popular feature on our program."[27] One of these figures, named Schimak, was fanatically devoted to Hitler. Lorenz would have him make statements such as "Today it seems apparent we will soon be rid of Italy as an ally. This is just the beginning of successful shake-offs. One victory after another for der Fuehrer." On another day: "The Russians are fleeing from Russia—to Hungary, to Finland, to Germany. They don't like it in Russia. Well, who does?"[28]

Hertz's team tried out various programming devices that later became a staple of the wartime broadcasting. They read lists of German soldiers who had been captured or killed. They read undelivered German letters taken from abandoned mailbags. They were casual in their approach. Hertz said they were so successful because "[o]ur existence as a functioning tactical weapon depended on intelligence from prisoners. We ate, slept, and drank with prisoners. . . . We were so constantly in the company of prisoners that the French were suspicious of us until they learned what we were doing."[29]

Benno Frank was the most successful at getting the Germans to surrender. "Benno," Hertz said, "was dynamically original in his attack on the enemy. He could sell anyone anything." It was Frank who persuaded his G-2 to let his team take prisoners out of the cage in order to interrogate them under relaxed conditions. And it was he who created a successful persona as "Captain Angers," a former German soldier now fighting in the American army. Many of the German deserters specifically asked to surrender to "Captain Angers," especially when he made an on-air promise that, if they were not happy after a "30-hour free trial" in captivity, they would be allowed to return to the German garrison. Only one ever did. But Frank made the most of the occasion, loading the man down with chocolate, cigarettes, and canned goods to take back to the German lines and then citing him on the air as proof that "Captain Angers" kept his promises.[30]

The team stayed at Lorient for just over two months. In a postwar report to his superiors, Major Ray K. Craft noted, "An average of 20 German soldiers each day deserted to the Americans during the period of this program, and after discontinuance of the program—when the radio team was called for another mission—almost no prisoners were taken."[31]

The hog callers from Camp Sharpe were equally effective. One of the most successful of these, Technical Sergeant Hans Curt Deppisch, had the personal history that lent authenticity to his appeals. Deppisch, a native of Hamburg, Germany, had fought with the Germans in World War I and been wounded and captured by American forces. The fact that he had been treated decently as an American POW lent his appeals credibility, especially since he could say that he had chosen to return to the United States, become a naturalized citizen, and make a good life as an insurance salesman. American newspapers reported that Deppisch was credited with "several thousand prisoners" taken on his combat-speaker missions. These included successful missions at Brest, Aachen, Koblenz, and the Siegfried Line. He was photographed and filmed during his Koblenz mission, wearing a mouth microphone in order to eliminate extraneous sounds and provide a clearer appeal over great distances. He was one of only three MRB enlisted men—and the only hog caller—to receive both the American Bronze Star and the French Croix de Guerre avec Bronze Star. After the war, he was awarded the New York State Conspicuous Service Cross for "exceptionally meritorious service while serving in the psychological warfare branch of the armed forces."[32]

Another MRB man, Arthur Hadley, brought a new dimension to his work as a hog caller. As he told it:

Loudspeaker missions were not popular, as the Germans most often tried to shut them up with heavy fire. Initially, we'd place our speakers near the front lines and then run cables to the relative safety of the foxhole from which we'd broadcast.

Having trained as a "tanker," I hoped to get loudspeakers off the ground and mounted on tanks, where they would be mobile and infinitely more effective during an attack. It was a wish that would not be fulfilled overnight: I was a young lieutenant in the position of having to persuade a tank general to give up a fighting vehicle for a loudspeaker.

Eventually, and somewhat to my surprise, I succeeded.

A loudspeaker was mounted on a light tank of the Second Armored Division. The broadcasters lived in the turret, and the tank driver and the electrician who maintained the loudspeaker sat in the driver's compartment and the assistant driver's seat. As a rule, Hadley's tank was number three in an attack column, where it could broadcast without interfering with the two point tanks. Hadley was proud of his success: "In three weeks fighting beyond the Rhine in 1945, the Second Armored Division credited the talking tank for the surrender of 5,000 prisoners." The willingness of the other tankers to hold their fire made this possible. "Germans had time to weigh the alternatives: an attack from our tanks versus imprisonment under the Geneva Conventions. In this way, American and German lives were saved."[33]

Camp Sharpe's radio men were also active on the Continent throughout the war. There were the "fixed broadcast" men, who repaired the transmitters destroyed by the retreating Germans and reestablished fixed broadcasting capabilities for the Allies. And there were the "mobile broadcast" men, who traveled with two trailer trucks, one of which was outfitted with a big broadcast transmitter, the other with a studio "doghouse." Brooklyn native Phil Pines (Pinkofsky) was with the mobile unit, and after landing at Normandy, he made the first broadcast back to England and from there to the United States under the call letters JESQ ("Jig Easy Sugar Queen"). He remained with the mobile unit throughout the war, accompanying the troops across Europe while broadcasting to the French, to Britain, and to the United States. He worked with French leaders General Marie-Pierre Koenig and General Charles de Gaulle and with war correspondents such as Howard K. Smith and Stanley Maxted.

The Camp Sharpe printers followed the same pattern as the radio men. There were those who repaired damaged printing equipment and set up business in fixed locations, and there were printers in mobile units at the front who hastily printed leaflets as they were needed. Both the printers and the radio men took over newspapers and radio stations as the Allies advanced through Germany, replacing the German press and radio with "white" Allied reporting.

Early in the war, when a reporter visited these units in France, he gave a good picture of the kind of work going on just behind the front lines:

> *Authors, psychologists, newspaper men and college professors [prepare] scripts and messages. They confer in shot-up houses and in tents, and when they are not conferring they are absorbed in reading heavy literature. Among them are Germans, Czechs, Poles, Hungarians, French and serious-looking Englishmen.*
>
> *With them are large vans which have been converted into printing offices, radio stations and photographic dark rooms. Pamphlets are being printed which, encased in shells, are hurled against the Germans. There are also passenger cars with loud speakers on their roofs, patrolling nearby villages and spreading the gospel of good will. In one town not far back of the lines a printing press has been salvaged which turns out a paper that is showered down on unretrieved, nearby France.*[34]

Whether as writers, broadcasters, hog callers, radio men, printers, or drivers, the Camp Sharpe graduates worked interactively—and effectively—in all aspects of psychological warfare in the European theater.

A page from the *History of the 2nd Mobile Radio Broadcasting Company* written by its commander, Arthur Jaffe.
SOURCE: AUTHOR'S COLLECTION

The team of Fred Lorenz (Manfred Inger), David Hertz, and Benno Frank achieved unusual success in their broadcasts at Lorient and in Luxembourg. SOURCE: NATIONAL ARCHIVES AND RECORDS ADMINISTRATION

Using a mouth microphone and portable loudspeaker, "hog caller" Hans Deppisch calls on German troops to surrender. Lieutenant Colonel Gordon Eyler stands behind him. SOURCE: NATIONAL ARCHIVES AND RECORDS ADMINISTRATION

Lieutenant Arthur T. Hadley sits in the turret of a "talking tank" of the Second Armored Division. SOURCE: NATIONAL ARCHIVES AND RECORDS ADMINISTRATION

CHAPTER FIFTEEN

The Nisei (PACMIRS and MITUs)

*I feel that I belong here. . . . I feel that I'm American, [and] I feel that
I'm just as much American as any white person . . . I felt good that I
was doing my little part in serving the country.*[1]

FOR THOSE FIRST-GENERATION JAPANESE BORN IN THE UNITED
States—Nisei—the American declaration of war against Japan made
many of them subjects of suspicion and hostility. They considered themselves as American as their Caucasian neighbors, and many were eager
to prove it by enlisting for military service. Already on the day after the
Pearl Harbor attack, however, they found that nearly all armed forces
induction centers refused to enlist them; meanwhile, those already in
service were consolidated at bases in the Southern United States and
given service support roles. After President Roosevelt signed Executive
Order 9066 on February 19, 1942, which allowed the secretary of war
to declare parts of the West Coast military zones, the Japanese families
living in those areas were removed from their homes and interned in ten
large camps located in remote areas around the country.

Only small groups of Hawaiian Nisei were interned. Japanese Americans constituted more than 35 percent of the Hawaiian population,
making mass internment unfeasible. Also, no mass hysteria prevented
the Hawaiian Nisei from showing their patriotism. In May 1942, two
Hawaiian Nisei National Guard regiments were organized into a single battalion and sent to Camp McCoy in Wisconsin, where they were
designated as the 100th Infantry Battalion (Separate) of the US Army.[2]

The US Army then made an about-face on its induction policies and began to recruit mainland Nisei. Many of its interviews were conducted through the barbed wire that surrounded the internment camps where the West Coast Nisei were housed. Victor Masao Matsui, one of the Nisei who would eventually be stationed at Camp Ritchie, said that the recruiters at the internment camps asked two questions: First, were the young Nisei loyal to the United States, and second, were they willing to serve their country? Matsui found the question of loyalty grotesque. What they were being asked, he said, was "Are you loyal to Uncle Sam who has slapped you in this horrible, dire situation?" As to the second question, he was tempted to answer, "I do not agree to serve my country when my country has me in the slammer."[3] Still, he and many others, with encouragement from their parents, answered in the affirmative and joined up. The new Nisei infantrymen were placed in the 442nd Regimental Combat Team; this was a four-thousand-man unit that included a mix of island Nisei and Nisei from the mainland.

The army set down rigid restrictions for Nisei service: these soldiers could not be commissioned as officers, nor could they fight in the Pacific theater. Those Nisei soldiers selected for combat intelligence as linguists, however, were being prepared precisely for the battlefields of Southeast Asia and would play a prominent role there. As Colonel Gaspare Blunda, commanding officer of the Southeast Asia Translation and Interrogation Center, put it, "Each one was as valuable as an infantry company, despite the fact they were not combat troops. Many Allied soldiers returned safely to their homes because the Nisei lighted the darkness in front of them by interrogating prisoners and translating documents."[4]

The first Nisei linguists had been trained in the Military Intelligence Service Language School (MISLS) in California; after the relocation and internment of West Coast Japanese Americans, the school was moved to Camp Savage in Minnesota. There students learned the terminology used by the Imperial Japanese Army and Navy, as well as words and phrases used to describe the nuances of military organization and weapons systems. They were also taught about "the probable attitude of Japanese soldiers if [or] when they're captured. And how to talk to them, how to interrogate them."[5] The expansion of the school required it to remove from Camp Savage to Fort Snelling, Minnesota, in August 1944.

That same month, because the Allies had collected too many Japanese war documents to operate out of the Pentagon, and because of the need to keep work with them a secret, a plan was developed by the Military Intelligence Service to set up the Pacific Military Intelligence Research Section (PACMIRS) at Camp Ritchie. There it would serve as a centralized agency to coordinate the research of all document services in the Pacific theater. In September, graduates of Camp Savage were brought to Ritchie, along with graduates of the Canadian Army Japanese Language School. Officers and staff came from the United States, Great Britain, Australia, New Zealand, and Canada, and PACMIRS grew from eighty-two officers and enlisted men in September 1944 to a total of 168 in September 1945.

Colonel Siegfried F. Gronich was the first chief of PACMIRS. A native Czech, he had been a member of the second class of Camp Ritchie and a Ritchie instructor. He had served in North Africa, been wounded in Algiers, and parachuted into Italy. As one of the Ritchie Nisei put it, Gronich was "a rough and tough regular army guy."[6] More important, he had been head of the G-2 Document Section in Algiers during the North African offensive, and he had helped establish the Military Intelligence Research Section (MIRS) in London, where the British and American Allies had operated a joint translation center for German-language materials. Gronich arrived at Camp Ritchie on September 6, 1944, with a small contingent that included four Nisei from the Pentagon's Order of Battle team. At the time, PACMIRS' mission was still unclear; it seems that it was initially envisioned primarily as an organization for producing Order of Battle information. By late October, however, Major General Clayton Bissell made it clear that PACMIRS was to focus solely on translation.

During its first weeks at Camp Ritchie, the confused relationship between the army post and PACMIRS made it difficult for PACMIRS to obtain funds and facilities. As a consequence, its staff suffered from an absence of suitable office space. It was given a former warehouse at the post, which had most recently housed Italian prisoners of war. The official history of PACMIRS describes the condition of the building: "At this time it was completely uninhabitable and the extensive renovations of floors, ceilings, wallboards, etc. had to be carried out with largely improvised materials because of the shortage of funds."[7]

Many of the Nisei assigned to PACMIRS were dissatisfied both with their stateside assignment and with an army structure that made it impossible for them to advance into the officer ranks. Colonel Gronich was well aware of this problem and even sympathized with their position. At their first meeting, he addressed the latter issue: "A great deal is going to be expected of you. You'll be asked to work far beyond your rank. Some of you certainly deserve commissions, all of you higher rankings. I wish I could give you what you deserve. I cannot. I'm in no position to do so. But this isn't going to keep me from asking you to do what I feel each of you is capable of doing."[8]

It was during these first tumultuous weeks at Camp Ritchie that one Nisei sergeant, Kazuo Yamane, made what turned out to be the most significant discovery of the PACMIRS mission. The Ritchie commandant, Brigadier General Charles Banfill, had passed on to PACMIRS fifteen crates of Japanese documents that had been captured by the US Navy on Saipan. The navy had deemed them to have "no military significance" and had shipped them on to Ritchie for training purposes. In an effort to check that no classified material was included in the crates, Colonel Gronich had Yamane go through the materials one last time. By the second or third crate, going through documents that were "all battered up [by] some shrapnel, torn off and all that," Yamane came across a book that was badly water-stained. As Yamane opened it up to the table of contents, Gronich commented that it looked like a textbook. Yamane saw at once, however, that it was far more than that: it was a "listing of very top secret information. It listed the manufacturers of [Japanese] weapons, it listed the munitions plants, it gave you the address. It listed an inventory of what they had and . . . whether they had spare parts, how many they had, every weapon that the Japanese army had was listed from what I [could] see in the table [of contents]." Yamane examined the book for about half an hour, flipping through the pages and seeing that it listed all the military equipment of the Japanese army. "I knew this was a very hot document," Yamane said, and he called to Gronich to tell him about it. Gronich took the book to his office, where he had the three other Nisei on Yamane's team look through it and confirm its significance.[9] He alerted the War Department and then took immediate action, canceling all furloughs and putting his entire translation staff to work on it. Each day a staff car delivered the day's translations directly to the Pentagon. The final text was four hundred pages long, full of obscure technical subject matter; it was, according to the history of PACMIRS, "an excellent test for PACMIRS' tentative system."[10] Ichiro "Joe" Nishida, a West Coast Nisei who had taught the course "Japanese Language and Military Terminology" at Camp Savage before coming to Ritchie, reportedly translated the technical and mechanical terms in the document. The full translation was published as *Pacific MIRS Special Report No. 1: Proceedings of Conference, Japanese Chiefs of Ordnance, Tokyo, May 1944.* This document provided aerial targeting information to the Allies and information to the occupation forces regarding the location of Japanese arms caches. For their work on this document, the Nisei PACMIRS translators were awarded a commendation ribbon with pendant. And in 1997, Yamane was awarded the Legion of Merit in recognition of "exceptionally meritorious conduct in the performance of duties which profoundly influenced the successful outcome of the war against Japan."[11]

By the end of 1944, PACMIRS had produced fifty-seven published reports under oversight of the Pentagon. Documents continued to be received at the Washington Document Center and redirected to PACMIRS or to Naval Intelligence. Once PACMIRS was fully staffed, positions were equally divided between Japanese-language specialists and non-linguists, and it even included a few American and Canadian WACs. About forty of the men were Nisei.

By April 1945, the PACMIRS translators had been organized into seven teams grouped around the various liaison officers, with linguist officers as team leaders. Teams consisted of two to five Nisei, depending on the requirements of the task at hand.

Despite their bitterness at seeing soldiers of other nationalities given the officer status denied to them, the Nisei appreciated the international nature of PACMIRS. Masaru J. "Mas" Jinbo, a California Nisei, stated that one of his most significant military experiences was "working with non-American military personnel ... at Camp Ritchie, Maryland. We got along very well socially and professionally."[12] Yoshiaki Fujitani seconded that statement: "We had British, Canadian, American, New Zealand, Australian linguists, officers, and non-coms. And ... from the American group, there was a major who was a former missionary in Japan. So he knew Japanese very well. . . . There was an Englishman who was *hapa* [half Japanese, half Caucasian]. . . . He was ... in the ... British air corps."[13] When Nisei WACs were brought to Ritchie, they were equally positive about the international setup of PACMIRS. Haruko Sugi found that "meeting people from other countries was a broadening experience. I would not have had the opportunity to know and meet so many soldiers of other nations, had I not been in this situation."[14]

Chinese American soldiers were also a small part of the PACMIRS personnel. Unlike the Nisei, these men were eligible for promotion to higher rank. The most notable Chinese American at the camp, Major Won-Loy "Charlie" Chan, had served in G-2 intelligence in the China-Burma-India theater and was a member of General Joseph Stilwell's staff. He became the research control officer for PACMIRS and coordinated PACMIRS' activities with about twenty other War Department agencies.[15]

Because Japanese fighters were expected to commit hara-kiri rather than submit to the shame of capture and interrogation, the examination, evaluation, and translation of vital Japanese documents was especially critical to the war in the Pacific. The number of documents was daunting. PACMIRS developed a system whereby all incoming documents were sorted and scanned as to their relative importance for the war effort. Of these, about 10 percent were considered valuable enough to be translated. The Document Group created brief English summaries of these items and then passed them on to a panel that determined the priority level for each document. The assigned priorities were published as a PACMIRS Bulletin, and the documents were sent on to the Translator Group. There the documents were translated and edited before being passed on to the Production Section for the addition of drawings and for layout and publication. These publications then went straight to the Pentagon for distribution.

By the end of August 1945, nearly eight million pages had been given to the Document Group for initial evaluation; PACMIRS translated 22,985 of them. About one-third of these related to the Japanese air force, one-tenth to tactics and strategy, and about 4 percent to chemical warfare. By the end of August, PACMIRS had published 1,068,901 pages.[16]

Colonel Gronich was sent to Europe in July 1945 to collect and catalog the German military documents that would be sent to Camp Ritchie for placement in a new German Military Document Section. These would serve as resources for the study of the German military machine. Lieutenant Colonel E. A. Wright became acting chief of PAC-MIRS until Colonel Sidney P. Marland assumed the title of chief on September 1.

There had been fewer than fifty Nisei working at Camp Ritchie while Gronich was chief of PACMIRS, but that all changed once victory had been achieved in Europe. Now all eyes in the United States turned to the war with Japan. The US War Department responded to this situation by changing the focus at Camp Ritchie from training for the war in Europe to intensive training for action in the Pacific. In June 1945, large numbers of Nisei poured into Camp Ritchie, coming both from training camps throughout the United States and from the European theater of operations, where they had distinguished themselves for their exceptional heroism in the struggle for Allied control of Italy and in the Battle of the Bulge. At Ritchie, these men were assigned to sixteen Mobile Intelligence Training Units, or MITUs. Because the Nisei soldiers—even the heroes who had fought in Italy and Germany—were not allowed to become officers, these units were composed almost entirely of noncommissioned Nisei soldiers, most of them privates.[17]

To prepare the Maryland citizenry for this influx of Nisei soldiers, Major Glen Moorhouse spoke to the Girls Service Organization of the Hagerstown USO (United Service Organizations) about how they should be treated. Moorhouse had served with the renowned Nisei 100th Battalion and the 442nd Infantry Regiment in Italy and France, and he made a point of telling the young women about their heroism: "These troops were the first to land on the beaches at Anzio; they were the first to enter Cassino; and were the first to dig in on the beaches in southern

France. . . . Over 20 of the Nisei have been awarded the Distinguished Service Cross, over 1000 have received the Purple Heart, many have received the Congressional Medal of Honor, and innumerable Nisei have been awarded silver stars."[18] For this reason alone, "It would be a grave injustice to men who have given so liberally of their best for their country to be kicked around." Certain rules of courtesy should apply: "They should not be called 'Japs.' Call them Americans, Nisei, or just don't mention their race at all. Above all, if you don't want to have anything to do with them just let them alone. They have earned the right to be treated like loyal American citizens."[19] Ritchie officers repeated this talk to most of the local service clubs in the area.

Hagerstown rose to the occasion, and the Nisei soldiers appreciated the fact that they did not meet up with the racial hostility that lingered on the West Coast. Mamoru "John" Fujioka, a gay Nisei, remarked that "we were treated extremely well by the locals. . . . It was good to know that most Americans were not racists."[20] The *Daily Mail* in Hagerstown reported in August that "the Nisei soldiers . . . have been a familiar sight on local streets for several months. Modest, unassuming and well-behaved, the 'glory boys' are popular at USO doings, often obliging the hostesses by singing selections from their repertoire of Hawaiian songs. On Sundays they escort local girls to the band concert, treat them to pop and hot dogs, and surprise hearers by the purity of their English."[21] About a dozen of them showed up weekly at the city park and performed informal concerts to ukulele accompaniment. There, the newspaper reported, they "sit along the lake and nibble Cracker Jack and sip cokes while they sing hauntingly beautiful songs in the Hawaiian tongue, native to many of them. Occasionally breaking into rousing theme songs of their Army divisions, which made it plenty hot for the Jerries in the ETO, the boys are always surrounded by a crowd of delighted and appreciative listeners."[22]

The Nisei were also pleased with the living situation at Camp Ritchie. "I felt as if we were in a resort camp rather than an army camp," one reported. "The living conditions were excellent. All menial duties were performed by German POWs. The food was tasty and well prepared. . . . The camp also had a lake where we could go swimming or boating."[23]

At Camp Ritchie, the new arrivals moved into the quarters of the former Composite School Unit. Ralph Yoohachi Nishime recalled their training:

The purpose of the training unit was to familiarize us with Japanese infantry unit tactics and . . . the psychology of the Japanese soldiers. To accomplish this end, the training consisted of two sections. In the first section a Japanese infantry unit was formed, including uniforms and weapons and the unit was trained in Japanese maneuvers. In the other section, we took part in a stage play depicting . . . the behavior of . . . Japanese soldiers while in the armed forces.[24]

The first Mobile Intelligence Training Units had been set up in Britain to prepare Allied infantrymen for battle in the European theater. Long before D-Day, MITUs had instructed the Allied soldiers in Axis uniforms, weaponry, and transport. In cooperation with the Americans, the British army had collected enemy war materials to be used for instructional purposes. In North Africa and Italy, commanders had been the first to realize the importance of studying Axis weaponry, citing instances when Allied troops had not been able to use enemy ammunition and weapons when their own supplies were exhausted "because they had received no training in the use of enemy weapons."[25]

Now Camp Ritchie would provide this critical instruction to troops heading to war in the Pacific. Sixteen Japanese MITUs were created at the camp in May and June 1945. The Composite School Unit had already created a jungle demonstration area filled with defense positions, camouflage, bunkers, and entanglements. And it had already introduced training in the Japanese war tactic of ruses, fake dead soldiers, fake uniforms, fake machine-gun fire, and fake surrender. In this respect, Camp Ritchie was well prepared to convert seamlessly into a camp training exclusively for the war in the Pacific.

Now, however, it was Nisei soldiers and not Native Americans or Caucasians who were ordered to dress in enemy uniforms and participate in war games. One of PACMIRS' Nisei translators, Technician Fourth

Grade Yoshiaki Fujitani, recorded this fact as the "most vivid memory of [his] military experience":

> *One day I was surprised to see a bunch of Japanese soldiers in full combat gear, including rifles, running through the trees. We were informed later that those were Nisei boys, selected for their short stature, who were dressed in the enemy's clothing to simulate for the benefit of the non-oriental what the Japanese soldier looks like in the battlefield. The unit was known as the "Military Intelligence Training Unit" [sic] and I have no idea what else it was assigned to do, but my reaction at that time was one of embarrassment for the boys being ordered to do such a demeaning task. I certainly can't picture myself dressing up as a Japanese soldier.*[26]

Some of the Nisei who had not yet seen battle may have found it demeaning to put on the uniforms of Japanese soldiers, but for wounded Nisei veterans of the battlefield the assignment was simply unacceptable. The veterans of the 442nd Regimental Combat Team had fought in Italy and France, not in the Pacific; now they were being asked to demonstrate tactics foreign to them simply because they *looked* like the enemy. One of these soldiers, Norman Ikari, was a Seattle native who had seen his parents and siblings evicted from their home and placed in an internment camp in Arizona. He had been drafted shortly before their internment; he had fought in the Italian campaign and had both his legs shattered by enemy gunfire. After four months in a Naples hospital, he was released and classified for PLA—Permanent Limited Assignment. Now he and sixty-four other PLA veterans of the 442nd Infantry Regiment were assigned to Camp Ritchie and given the order to dress as Japanese soldiers and demonstrate Japanese infantry tactics to American GIs. "[We] were shocked and dismayed and disgusted," Ikari stated, "and we all refused. A different officer tried asking us again, in a less offensive way. We refused again."[27] One of the other war veterans, Jesse M. Hirata, remembered that, after their refusal, their commanding officer "put us on KP, but we refused to work. I guess we felt we did our part in the war. MPs came, and we were ready to fight them, so they did not touch us."

She Passed through Camp Ritchie

 **Tamie Tsuchiyama** (1915–1984) was born in Hawaii to Japanese immigrant parents. She discovered a passion for anthropology while studying at the University of Hawaii and went on to complete her BA (with honors) at the University of California, Berkeley. As a doctoral student, she became the only Japanese American woman to work full-time for the Japanese American Evacuation and Resettlement Study (JERS). She went undercover and was voluntarily incarcerated in the Poston Relocation Center in southwestern Arizona. Here she kept a wide-ranging sociological journal in which she recorded the effects of long-term incarceration on the detainees at the camp. To avoid being suspected of being a government spy, she kept her research a secret.

After a year in the camp, Tsuchiyama began to experience stress from the pressure for secrecy and getting access to inside information. Eventually the situation became too much for her, and she left Poston in July 1944 and joined the WACs. She was sent to Fort Snelling, Minnesota, for intensive training in written Japanese and military language; later she was assigned to Camp Ritchie to translate captured war documents for the Pacific Military Intelligence Research Section.

After her release from the army, Tsuchiyama returned to Berkeley to complete her doctorate in anthropology, becoming the first Asian American to do so. She then spent three years in occupied Japan working as a researcher for a government program run by the Supreme Commander for the Allied Powers. Here she engaged in extensive fieldwork on the transition of the Japanese village.

Still, when Tsuchiyama came back to the United States late in 1951, she was unable to find a job in academe. She returned to Berkeley and earned a master's degree in library science. She worked at a number of jobs as a university librarian before moving to Texas, where she was hired by the University of Texas at Austin to oversee the campus's large Asian language collection. She spent the remainder of her working career in this position.

This situation left the rebellious Nisei "in limbo" at Camp Ritchie. "There was nothing to do except go to the movies and rent rowboats in the camp lake," Hirata said.[28] A few weeks later, the United States dropped the atomic bomb on Hiroshima and Nagasaki, and the war came to an end. Soon after that, Ikari and Hirata were discharged.

Not all the Nisei soldiers found their assignment to an MITU that outrageous. Many, especially those coming to Ritchie straight from basic training, not only saw value in their Camp Ritchie assignment but also took pride in training white Americans for war in the Pacific. At the conclusion of their training, the army planned on sending the sixteen MITUs to all the American replacement centers for the Pacific theater of operations to help train those replacements for the war ahead. "The object of the training unit was to provide those replacements that were to fight in the Pacific knowledge of the enemy, the Japanese," Hiroshi Sakai said. He continued:

> The [units were] organized to display how the enemy appeared, how they were taught as soldiers, how they operated as a combat unit, their firearms, rifles, bayonets, machine guns, bombs, and grenades. Our soldiers were taught to recognize enemy arms visually and by their sound as compared to U.S. arms. They had information on Japanese aircraft and the different types of troops so U.S. soldiers could recognize such aircraft. . . . The unit also trained soldiers for combat action against Japanese soldiers as they fought in close quarters, on island and jungle terrain in the South Pacific. . . . Viewing troops would get some feel from the simulated battle conditions.[29]

As Japanese Americans, these soldiers could not be sent to the Asian front as combatants. But, by participating in these demonstrations and war games, they would be not only training the Caucasian soldiers but also learning for themselves the Japanese war organization, with its uniforms, weapons, and battlefield tactics. As long as the war continued, they would play a critical role in training Caucasian soldiers for an Asian war.

Because, until V-E Day, the Composite School Unit's Visual Demonstration Section 9 had been almost exclusively devoted to performing skits that related to the situation on European battlefields, its members now had reason to fear for their future. William Warfield described the situation: "If we had no military intelligence function in the Pacific war (which we all figured could continue for years to come) . . . every one of us could expect to be shipped out to the South Pacific as part of the invasion of Japan. It would be an oriental version of the Normandy landings, and nobody had any illusions about how fierce that fight would be." To prevent becoming part of those forces, playwright Joseph Anthony was instructed to come up with a new training play directed exclusively toward the Japanese situation. It was "the commission of his life."[30] He consulted with the new cadre of Nisei soldiers, as well as experts on the Far East, and then sat down and wrote an entirely new script titled *A Scrap of Paper*. The lead character in the first act of the play was a "Japanese general lamenting over his problems while he was commanding his troops in Taiwan."[31] After giving final orders, the general commits harakiri. The play further depicted the behavior of captured Japanese soldiers and how US soldiers, with their Nisei interpreters, collected important information regarding the battle ahead. At first all roles in the play were taken by Caucasians. They soon realized, however, that "Broadway actors did not resemble Japanese soldiers," and Anthony looked for members of each Military Intelligence Unit to take these roles. Private Ralph Yoohachi Nishime, a recent arrival at the camp, now assumed the role of the general. "The play was produced like a Broadway production," Hiroshi Sakai remembered, "with lights, drama and action":

> *The [second] act showed two Japanese soldiers pursuing their task of carrying the final battle orders to the front line and [the] subsequent capture of [these] Japanese soldiers, stripping [them] down to their "fundoshi" (shorts) and how the Nisei interpreters and U.S. soldiers treated the messengers with water and cigarettes and reassurances that they would not be killed. It was intended to show that with some kindness and reasonable treatment, U.S. soldiers would be able to gain important information on the pending battle.*[32]

William Warfield noted that this new script "differed significantly from the European version. . . . For example, the best interrogation techniques now called for extreme politeness rather than bullying threats for maximum effectiveness."[33] All aspects of the play were designed "to demonstrate, teach, act the part of the Japanese soldiers"; that was the mission of the Mobile Intelligence Training Unit.[34] And now only the roles of the US soldiers were played by American actors.

The MITU members completed their Ritchie training in August 1945 and prepared to go on tour; however, the war ended, and the MITUs were disbanded. In September, many of them were sent to Fort Meade, southwest of Baltimore, and attached to the Counterintelligence Corps (CIC). From there they went on to Japan to observe and report on the activities of Japanese ultranationalists, Communists, socialists, and labor unions.[35]

The PACMIRS Nisei also vacated the camp at this time; they were sent on temporary duty to Tokyo to collect more war documents, diaries, and other materials that were deemed worthy of further study. These men were replaced at Ritchie by Nisei WACs. Some of these women, like their male counterparts, had been recruited directly from the American internment camps. Because these women came from the Military Intelligence Language Training Center at Fort Snelling and had the same rigorous linguistic training as the men they replaced, there was no time lost in picking up the men's workload. Most of them appear to have worked conscientiously on their tasks of translating captured Japanese war documents while showing little enthusiasm for their content. Haruko Sugi remarked that translating "technical stuff" was "very uninteresting." "It would have been fun if we were translating novels, or some mystery story, or something like that," she said. In fact, her most notable memory of her time at Ritchie was the fact that "we had to walk in the snow. [Ritchie] was on the top of the mountain. . . . It snows a lot." For their twice-daily walks from their barracks to their PACMIRS work space, the Nisei WACs were issued Arctics. "They were things that went up to here," she said, pointing just below her knee, "buckled up to here. You walked in through the snow from your barracks."[36] Still, the women made the best of the situation. "There was a Japanese document center and a German document center," one recalled. "I met some of the fellas that were doing German transcribing." Hisako Yamashita understood the need for her services at Ritchie. "I remember that the Japanese were building airplanes," she said. "They weren't getting resources, so they were using wood.... The things were wood instead of metal, the way American [planes] were, because we had all of the iron needed to build planes; they didn't. And so these manuscripts were telling about these things.... These were important things for Americans to find out."[37]

The Nisei WACs remained at Ritchie until the Japanese war documents were moved to the Washington Document Center in April 1946. The Nisei WACs moved with them, and they continued working on documents that aided in the prosecution of Japanese war crimes and in the Allies' postwar occupation of Japan.

Although the last Nisei would not vacate Camp Ritchie until April 1946, a special candlelight service held in Hagerstown's St. John's Lutheran Church on Christmas Eve 1945 best demonstrates the harmonious relations that existed between the diverse members of the Ritchie community and the citizens of Hagerstown. At this service, Technical Sergeant Trooda Oda, a mainland Nisei WAC from Grand Junction, Colorado, became the bride of Corporal Henry Hirokawa of Honolulu. Oda was stationed at Ritchie to work with PACMIRS; Hirokawa was a veteran of the 442nd Regimental Combat Team who had fought in Italy, France, and Germany before being reassigned to the United States. Ritchie sergeant Edna Higgins of Saskatchewan, wearing the uniform of a Canadian WAC, served as matron of honor. The bride was given away by a Hagerstown citizen, Dennis Byers, and the wedding reception was held in his home, attended by "friends from Camp Ritchie and Hagerstown."[38] It was a fitting way for Hagerstown—and Camp Ritchie—to celebrate the end of hostilities with Japan.

Paul Y. Hosoda (left) and Jack K. Foroya (right) help select music for the evening's dance at the Nisei USO club in Washington, DC. Nisei often came here on weekends from Camp Ritchie, Camp Lee (Virginia), the Pentagon, and Walter Reed Hospital. SOURCE: NATIONAL ARCHIVES AND RECORDS ADMINISTRATION

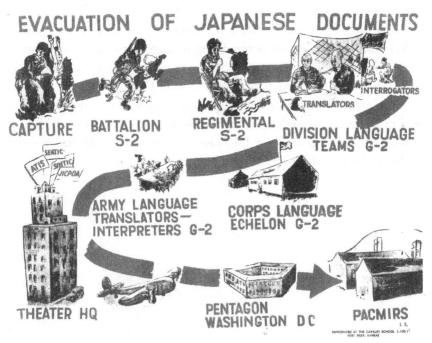

The PACMIRS documents had a long, tortured journey to Camp Ritchie. SOURCE: NATIONAL ARCHIVES AND RECORDS ADMINISTRATION

Kazuo Yamane made the most important discovery of the PACMIRS mission and was awarded the Legion of Merit for his services. COURTESY OF THE YAMANE FAMILY

A wounded war hero, Norman Ikari refused to put on a Japanese uniform for the MITU demonstrations at Camp Ritchie. COURTESY OF CAROLYN IKARI MCCARTHY

Trooda Oda and Henry Hirokawa met at Camp Ritchie and were married in Hagerstown. SOURCE: STEPHEN H. HART RESEARCH CENTER AT HISTORY COLORADO

Chapter Sixteen

The German "Hillbillies"

Paperwork was once frowned upon,
But one has accustomed
Oneself so much to it
That one can no longer
Part from it.
Let's get to work![1]

ON SEPTEMBER 25, 1945, TWENTY-SEVEN GERMAN OFFICERS AND eleven German enlisted men embarked from Le Havre on a voyage that would bring them to Camp Ritchie and make them "Hillbillies." They were part of an initiative that would eventually grow to two hundred German prisoners of war (POWs) directly involved in what the US government referred to as the "Hill Project." In addition, hundreds more German POWs would be transferred to Ritchie; although these men would not be directly involved in work on the project, they would be needed to work in the POW enclosure and to serve as support staff.

Of the first group of officers to arrive at Ritchie, Lieutenant General Walther Buhle was the acknowledged leader. A former World War I infantry officer, he had served as chief of staff of the Armed Forces High Command (Oberkommando der Wehrmacht, or OKW); as chief of its organizations section, he had come under the direct command of Count Claus von Stauffenberg. He had had the distinction of being awarded two wound badges: one, in 1918, for serious wounds sustained on the battlefield, and another, on July 20, 1944, for injuries sustained during von Stauffenberg's failed assassination attempt on Hitler. In the last days of the war, Hitler had named Buhle chief of armaments for the German army. Three other generals were part of the initial group at Ritchie: Brigadier General Hellmuth Laegeler, who had taught tactics at the German War Academy and become chief of staff for the Replacement Army in Berlin in the last four months of the war; Major General Franz Kleberger, director of the Army High Command (Oberkommando des Heeres, or OKH) and chief quartermaster and finance officer for the German Field Army; and Major General Rolf Menneking, who had served in the Wehrmacht personnel office and on the staff of the Army High Command. These were all "second-tier" officers, unlikely to be involved in the early war crimes trials being held in Germany, but they were also extremely knowledgeable about German recruitment, staffing, and the conduct of the war.[2]

The Hill Project arose from an informal agreement between Major General Clayton Bissell of the US War Department and Major General John Alexander Sinclair, the director of military intelligence in the British War Office. They created the project as "a skeleton German General Staff organization formed for the purpose of conducting such research for the War Department General Staff and the British General Staff as may be directed." This agreement was formalized in late May 1945 with a fifteen-point agenda of "Subjects for Research of German Documents."[3] The French and the Soviets were kept in the dark about this arrangement, as they had been about PACMIRS, and only officers from Great Britain and Canada joined their American counterparts to work in the German Military Document Section (GMDS) operations at Camp Ritchie.

The project evolved during the months that followed. Originally it was intended to pursue research that would aid in the war against Japan, but the first German generals did not arrive at Camp Ritchie until after the Japanese surrender. The American and British governments were also interested in studying the German war against Russia, in order to be better prepared in the event of a Soviet Union invasion of western Europe. However, the bulk of that research was carried on at the equally secret PO Box 1142. German spymaster Reinhard Gehlen, former chief of the German army's military intelligence unit on the eastern front, was taken there. He had preserved his organization's intelligence records and delivered them to the American army, and, as a consequence, intelligence into all aspects of the war between Germany and the Red Army became the focus of study at this location.

The research at Ritchie was directed instead on "improving intelligence organization and techniques and . . . other . . . matters on which important lessons can be gained from studying German methods in detail." Because the Allies were intensely interested in understanding the efficiency and efficacy of the German military, they wanted "complete studies of combat under all types of circumstances and conditions."[4] Still, the reasons for pursuing these studies remained rather ambiguous. The Sinclair-Bissell Agreement merely stated that it was to "aid in preserving military security in Europe."[5]

The German military documents that formed the basis for this study had been collected and cataloged in Oberursel, near Frankfurt am Main, under the command of Siegfried Gronich, who, in 1942, had been a student and then an instructor at Camp Ritchie before going overseas to head the G-2 Document Section in Algiers. Until July 1945, he had been serving at Camp Ritchie as the first chief of PACMIRS. The Oberursel documents were first divided between London and Washington, DC, but the Allies soon realized that it would be much more efficient to have them in one place. Before the arrival of the German POWs, an initial staff of nineteen American officers and fifty-three enlisted men labored to set up the library at Ritchie, using the German filing system with some American adaptations. Nearly all these initial holdings consisted of previously captured documents. For most of September, the American, British, and Canadian personnel conducted practice searches for material on specific subjects in order to test their filing and indexing systems and to prepare for training the personnel that would be joining the project. In the months that followed, one American, one British, and one Canadian officer worked with two of the German prisoners in listing individual files for the final catalog of the German Army Archives (*Heeresarchive*). Special projects continued there as well. One, for example, involved sorting items in the German Army Archives in such a way that they had on file "one situation map of each theatre of war, for each week, throughout the course of the war, providing a complete picture of the movements of the German army." While one of the German prisoners worked on this task, the British junior commander Liesel D. Goetze, of the women's branch of the British army, worked on flow charts of the German army units to create a complete index of "*all* German units, date of formation, composition, and Ersatzgestellung [replacements]."[6] Similar work was carried on in the library of documents from the German Armed Forces Supreme Command and the German Army Supreme Command (OKW/OKH Library). This would prove useful not only for the studies to be carried out at Camp Ritchie but also for other agencies that needed speedy access to crucial war information, such as, for example, the team prosecuting war criminals at the Nuremberg trials.

Material continued to pour into the libraries. At the end of September, five rail cars filled with captured enemy documents were delivered to the camp to be integrated into the Ritchie libraries. The project's research agenda expanded accordingly, requiring additional Allied and German POW personnel. To accommodate this expansion, the project was reorganized and given a more disciplined structure. All activities were now grouped under three headings: Library, Research, and Production. There were ten areas of research that went into reports on everything from "The German Training System" and "Organization and Functioning of German High Command" to "Transportation System of the German Army."[7] Colonel George (Gaspare) F. Blunda was transferred from the Southeast Asia Translation and Interrogation Center (SEATIC) in New Delhi to assume command over both PACMIRS and the German Military Document Center.

Whereas the PACMIRS program focused solely on processing and translating Japanese war documents, the GMDS' emphasis was on the creation of comprehensive reports covering all aspects of the German military machine. These were created by teams of German and Allied officers. Since all these reports were written in German and then had to be translated into English, as did the supporting manuals and documents that accompanied them, the Hill Project, like PACMIRS, required a large pool of translators fluent in both German and English. As originally conceived, different translating teams would be assigned to the ten different areas of research; by December, however, these men were organized into a translation pool headed by British major Horton Smith. Through his office, all translators were assigned to projects according to the priorities of the time. The translation pool consisted originally of eight German officers and nine enlisted men transferred into Camp Ritchie from the Pikesville Maryland POW camp; it soon expanded to include another eleven German officers and thirteen enlisted men from the prison camp at Camp Forrest, Tennessee. In addition, dozens of American and German subordinate officers and enlisted men already stationed at Ritchie worked as translators.[8] The pool of prisoner support staff expanded accordingly. By spring 1946, the number of German prisoners housed at Camp Ritchie had risen from 646 in January to 1,572 by the end of March.

Remarkably, the German officer POWs worked extremely well with their American, British, and Canadian counterparts and willingly shared their expertise with them. There was some self-interest involved in this cooperation. Not only were the Germans being held in a well-furnished American camp with all the amenities promised by the Geneva Conventions, but they were also given assurances that their families would come under Allied protection in Germany. The German generals were especially nervous that, at the end of their captivity, they would be turned over to tribunals and tried as war criminals, and General Buhle expressed this concern by letter and in person to Colonel John Lovell, who was on assignment to the War Department's Military Intelligence Division as overall chief of the GMDS operation in Washington, DC.[9]

There was, in fact, some initial tension at Camp Ritchie in the first weeks of the project. Ritchie's post commander, Colonel Mercer Walter, regarded the German officers simply as prisoners of war and, at first, treated them accordingly. However, the American colonel in charge of intelligence operations, George F. Blunda, viewed them as project partners, much to the annoyance of many of the German and Austrian Jews involved in the GMDS, who resented the fact that Blunda was "fraterniz[ing] with Nazi officers."[10] Blunda, whom one serviceman described as "an impatient and flamboyant type,"[11] wrote a long letter to the War Department, detailing his problems with Walter and asking that he

He Passed through Camp Ritchie

Wolfgang Thomale (1900–1978) was born into a German military family. After attending the Main Military Academy in Berlin, he fought in World War I as an ensign and earned the Iron Cross, Second Class. At the end of the war, he was promoted to lieutenant and assigned to the German army's motorized division.

He was transferred in 1935 to the Fifth Tank Regiment and, from 1938 to 1941, served on the staff of the German High Command as inspector of tank troops. He continued to win promotions and served with great distinction as a tank commander on the eastern front. He earned the Knight's Cross of the Iron Cross in February 1942; a year later, he was promoted to lieutenant general and became chief of staff to Colonel General Heinz Guderian, general inspector of the Armored Division. Here he oversaw the construction of heavy tanks and tank destroyers that were employed during the Battle of the Bulge. On the evening of the attempted assassination of Hitler on July 20, 1944, Thomale was in Berlin and gave the command for tanks to put down the insurrection.

Thomale was captured in May 1945 and, in March 1946, was brought to the United States on the navy transport USS *General Anderson* under the code name *Karamel* ("caramel" in English). Ironically, he was, at that time, on an Allied "watch" list as one harboring Nazi sympathies. He was the last of the generals to join the Hill Project at Camp Ritchie, where his knowledge of tanks contributed substantially to the project's research on armored warfare and tank training. When the Hill Project was closed down, and most of the imprisoned officers were sent back to Germany, Thomale was sent to Fort Hunt and the Gehlen Group instead, where he was appreciated as "without doubt one of the ablest young generals in the German Army." Here he prepared four papers; two on Panzer warfare in the East provided valuable material for the United States' possible armed conflict with the Soviet Union.

Following his discharge in 1947, Thomale returned to Germany, where he used his expertise in motorized vehicles to become president of the German Automobile Industry Association.

be pulled from his Ritchie assignment. He cited the inconvenience of requiring that the German officers be accompanied by an armed guard when moving from the POW compound to the GMDS offices. This practice was causing disruption to the project since the Allied officers had to serve as escorts when no camp guards were available. Furthermore, he claimed that Walter was breaking the conditions of the Geneva Conventions by denying the German officers the butter and marmalade that was served to American personnel in their shared mess. In addition to this blatant favoritism of Americans over Germans, Blunda reported that one of the German officers had been "manhandled by the guard," creating "an adverse effect on all members of the Hill."[12] Blunda's letter seems to have been at least partially successful; soon afterward, Colonel Walter sent a memo to him saying that, effective immediately, mutually agreed-upon German prisoners would be given parole privilege, while the German generals would be given special quarters outside the POW compound.[13] Colonel Walter continued to serve as post commander, and there appears to have been no more conflict between him and Blunda.

Otherwise, life at the camp was agreeable for the prisoners. Reading materials were readily available; language classes were offered four times a week for all levels of English proficiency; weekly lectures covered aspects of English literature. These interactions could only help increase respectful and effective interaction between the prisoners and the Allied staff.

Every month each prisoner was allowed to send four letters and four postcards to family and friends in Germany. This practice was likewise intended to boost prisoner morale. Because of the secrecy of the Hill Project, the prisoners' friends and relatives were instructed to address their return letters to a post office in Frankfurt am Main, from which point the US Army forwarded them to the United States. They were further instructed not to identify the rank of the prisoner on their envelopes. When the letters arrived at Ritchie, they were read and, in some cases, censored. Captain Homer Schweppe served as the Camp Ritchie censor between September 1945 and March 1946, and he withheld those letters that he felt held "discouraging contents" that might affect the prisoners' morale. These letters commented on the desperate situation that their loved ones were facing at home.[14] In one of these censored letters from

Berlin, for example, Annemarie Kluge wrote to Major General Franz Kleberger:

> *Your apartment is completely burned out inside, especially the cellar—allegedly by flame throwers. What was left "grew legs" [i.e., disappeared]. At first we weren't allowed in, then we didn't dare, then one had no transportation, Russians were living there, too! . . . At the very beginning our cottage became a Russian news station—I didn't dare show my face there for 8–12 days. For 4 or 5 weeks we were eight, sometimes 10 women and three children living in our neighbors' cellar!!!*

And in a letter to a prisoner she called "Edi," "Gretel," who had escaped to a town near Heidelberg, wrote about her attempts to learn the fate of her family, whom she'd had to leave behind in what was now part of Poland:

> *All the people on the Volkslisten I are in a concentration camp. They immediately killed many men, [a friend] thinks that my father was one of them. They took the children away from the women, that must be horrible for my Milli. The Poles took her home. . . . For days I have not been able to rest, I see them all dying in my dreams. I hope that's not true, for that would be intolerable to me. . . . I can't wait any longer and have to go there. I leave it up to fate as to whether I come back or not.*

Finally, Inge Bauer wrote to Colonel Kurt Rittmann from Bayreuth, site of the Wagner music festivals:

> *The last attacks on Bayreuth caused horrible devastation. . . . We were lucky that we weren't killed. Our old home in Bürgerreuther Street . . . was completely leveled. In general the area around the festival building and the railway station looks awful. Didn't you know the Buchners? They are all dead. Anne, Otti and their parents.*

She wrote that she now regretted the fact that, in happier times, she had resisted Rittmann's advances: "Oh, how happy we used to be. We took much too little advantage of it. I often think about how you wanted to take me with you on a skiing vacation. I was really a very stupid girl. Why weren't you more forceful with me?" She added, "Well, it is all in the past, everything is gone."

The German prisoners were also filled with longing for happier times. At Christmas time, they were allowed to put out their own Camp Ritchie newsletter. There, in verse, play form, articles, and sketches, they described their journey into captivity and across the ocean to the United States. There were many nostalgic items, as well as humorous pieces. They joked, for example, that one should "drink what is given you in the mess" since "he who doesn't drink Coca-Cola will never become an American!"[15] They provided brief verse sketches of each of the prisoners, in which they made in-jokes about their interests and habits. But the overwhelming mood of the prisoners was one of homesickness. As one camp poet put it:

> *The days which drain from his eyes*
> *The joyful sheen of good times past*
> *Serve him now only for standing still,*
> *For walking, for weary waiting, and for longing.*

His eyes scarcely notice the gentle hills that surround the camp:

> *They hurry past blue mountains' rim*
> *across broad oceans, across the land they skim*
> *to where all those he loves are dwelling.*[16]

By early April 1946, most of the Hill Project studies had been completed, and on April 15 the project was officially closed and the POW enclosure shut down. The libraries of German military documents were sent to Washington, DC, and most of the German POWs were escorted back to Germany. Only eleven of the Ritchie prisoners were retained in the United States. They were sent to PO Box 1142 to contribute to the study of Germany's war on the eastern front. At the end of June, on orders from the US State Department, all German POWs remaining in the United States were returned to Germany.

During their time at Camp Ritchie, the British, Canadian, and American officers, working in collaboration with their German counterparts, had produced twenty-five reports and special studies for their respective governments, totaling more than thirty-six hundred pages of text. However, despite the spirit of respect and good will that had developed between the Allies and the German officers, there were real concerns about the Germans' repatriation. The fears of the Germans were twofold: On the one hand, news of their work at Camp Ritchie could get them branded as traitors in the minds of many of the German citizens. On the other hand, they were still fearful of being held in denazification camps or tried as war criminals. Fortunately, neither of these fears were realized. The Allies themselves were fearful that the work of the project would become known to the Russians if any of the German officers came to trial, and, as a consequence, the US military governor in Germany, General Lucius Clay, granted amnesty to the Ritchie Germans for "service in the interests of [their] own people."[17]

But they were still not completely free of Allied control. As long as the Allied occupation of Germany was in force, from 1946 to 1949, British and American military intelligence kept Ritchie's German officers under close surveillance as "a potential security menace."[18] The Allies' fears were groundless; instead of posing a threat, the officers kept their work on the Hill Project a secret as they all reintegrated seamlessly into German society.

Colonel George (Gaspare) Blunda assumed command over PACMIRS and the GMDS. SOURCE: SPECIAL COLLECTIONS & COLLEGE ARCHIVES, GETTYSBURG COLLEGE

In this photo of the translation group of the Hill Project, T/5 Edgar Danciger (left) translates while Lieutenant A. H. Fast (standing) discusses a term with Captain W. G. Penfield. On the right, Master Sergeant S. M. Leiter advises T/3 H. E. Weinberger. SOURCE: SPECIAL COLLECTIONS & COLLEGE ARCHIVES, GETTYSBURG COLLEGE

The German documents library lent out documents to various Allied agencies. SOURCE: US ARMY WAR COLLEGE LIBRARY, PAUL FAIR-BROOK COLLECTION

German war diaries were among the items filed in the German army archives. SOURCE: US ARMY WAR COLLEGE LIBRARY, PAUL FAIRBROOK COLLECTION

This sketch was made by a homesick German prisoner at Camp Ritchie.
SOURCE: SPECIAL COLLECTIONS & COLLEGE ARCHIVES, GETTYSBURG COLLEGE

CHAPTER SEVENTEEN

Ritchie Boys in Europe

On we sweep—the tanks and half-tracks, the trucks, the jeeps careen-
ing wildly, yet orderly, in clouds of choking blinking dust. Five miles,
ten miles, fifteen miles, twenty miles behind the enemy lines.
  To hell with the enemy!
  Keep pushing. Smash through his hasty defenses, annihilate his
once proud infantry, push on—nothing can stop us. Encircle him, cut
his communications, sweep by his strong points—do it the Russian
way.
  And we keep rolling![1]

THE CAMP RITCHIE MEN WERE ACTIVE IN THE NORTH AFRICAN CAM-
paign and in all phases of the European war. They interrogated and
broadcast, wrote propaganda pamphlets and newsletters, secured maps
and documents, and performed intelligence surveillance by land and air.
They entered fighting zones by truck, jeep, tank, parachute, and glider.
They addressed enemy and civilian populations by microphone and went
behind the enemy lines to gather information on enemy movements. On
many occasions, they led combat patrols. Many were wounded, and many
earned Bronze Stars. And too many gave their lives for their country.

  Because of the ever-changing war conditions, the Ritchie Boys were
frequently moved between the various intelligence agencies operating in
Britain and on the Continent, such as the Counterintelligence Corps,
the OSS, and the Psychological Warfare Division of SHAEF (Supreme
Headquarters Allied Expeditionary Force). Ritchie Boys were also

frequently assigned to assault units, where the expectations were that they would perform alongside men with more vigorous physical combat training than they had.

One might assume that the sixty-three men who had been assigned to the four-week "Order of Battle" course at Camp Ritchie would be the safest soldiers in Europe, since the three-man teams—each composed of one lieutenant and two sergeants—were to be attached to an army group "a hundred miles from the front." This position, said Sergeant Hugh Nibley, "was as high and as safe as you could get." Nibley's three-man team had helped compile information in Britain on German generals for the June 1944 edition of the *Order of Battle* book that would assist in the invasion of Normandy. The men were then told that they were the exception to the rules of safety for the Order of Battle (OB) specialists in Britain: they were going to be attached to the 101st Airborne Division— the Screaming Eagles—and be among the first to land inside Normandy. Nibley was ordered to instruct the officers and enlisted men in the 101st Airborne Division on German Order of Battle, including instruction in strategy and tactics, German army organization, insignia, and weaponry. General Maxwell Taylor introduced Nibley to these classes by assuring the airmen that "Sergeant Nibley will be going in among the very first, so he's not going to just give you cold comfort."[2]

Nibley was scheduled to land in Normandy by glider, but, shortly before the invasion took place, he was required to yield his seat to Brigadier General Donald F. Pratt and was ordered, instead, to drive a jeep ashore on the Utah Beach. Nibley was fortunate: General Pratt was the highest-ranking Allied officer to be killed on D-Day when the glider he was riding in skidded and crashed upon landing. Nibley landed with the first wave at Utah Beach. Here he had his first encounter with the horror of war when German forces had the men pinned down and he leapt into a foxhole: "I was about to eat a chocolate bar . . . and I jumped into the foxhole and it was full of—ah—spattered with brains, a helmet full of brains. . . . [I]t was just a bloody mess there, and I immediately lost my appetite; and then after a few minutes I got hungry and ate the chocolate bar just as unconcerned as anything. I never thought I could do a thing like that. . . . But apparently you can shut off certain parts of the brain."[3] He went to work studying documents confiscated from dead soldiers and from German prisoners of war, gleaning valuable information as to troop positions, minefields, and gun emplacements from pay books, correspondence, maps, and personal items. His knowledge of the Order of Battle enabled him to quickly scan the unedited reports of prisoner of war interrogations for news on changes in the overall German war operations and to send them on for incorporation in the updated OB files.

In September 1944, he was transported by a glider called *Wambling Wabbit* into Eindhoven, Holland, for Operation Market Garden. Nibley remembers, "I became very sick, as I always did in a glider. There was an old piece of armor plate lying on the floor, and out of curiosity I wondered how it would be to sit on. Just as I slipped it on my little chair . . . it absorbed three machine-gun bullets, while another went between my feet. This particular escape became proverbial in headquarters company."[4] With few controls and no weaponry, gliders were, in the words of one soldier, "like clay pigeons at a trap range."[5] As the first glider to land in Eindhoven, the *Wambling Wabbit* was particularly vulnerable. It was all shot up, but Nibley had again escaped death.

In Holland, Nibley served as an interpreter while also gathering information through documents and through personal interrogation of prisoners of war. He quickly brushed up on his Dutch and was able to make valuable contacts with civilians and with the Dutch underground. He had new teammates now since he had lost the previous two in the battle for Normandy. After seventy-two days in fruitless combat, most of them spent in muddy foxholes, he and the 101st Airborne were trucked to France for rest and recuperation. By this time, one of his new teammates was dead, and the other was seriously injured. Nibley's fellow soldiers took notice and began to say of him, "Everything happens to Nibley, and nothing ever happens to him."[6] His next "safe but quite melodramatic" counterintelligence mission took him back to the Ardennes in time for the Battle of the Bulge. This time it was to ferret out German soldiers who, as part of *Operation Greif* (Gryphon), had entered Allied territory in an effort to hamper the Allied efforts. These men all spoke fluent English and wore Allied uniforms or civilian dress.

By this point, the two replacements for Nibley's Dutch teammates were also dead. Nibley, a devout Mormon, was the sole survivor of his OB #5 team.

Another man who landed on D-Day was twenty-six-year-old Captain Harvey James Cook, an avid baseball player from Philadelphia who met his wife while studying for a degree in business administration at Michigan State College. He was commissioned a second lieutenant and entered active duty two months before Pearl Harbor. He graduated from the ninth class at Camp Ritchie with a specialty in terrain intelligence. During his time there, he also served as an instructor in hand-to-hand combat. When the Second Ranger Battalion came to the Camp Ritchie area to practice cliff climbing at High Rock in Pen Mar, Cook was recruited to be its intelligence officer.

Cook and the battalion's commanding officer, Colonel James Earl Rudder, were the only men who were briefed on their mission prior to D-Day: they were to land and seize Pointe du Hoc. This was a triangular point of land that jutted out into the English Channel, where the surf was rough and there was only a narrow pebble beach for landing. Once ashore, the Rangers would be required to scale the one-hundred-foot-high sandstone cliffs. Once on top of the cliffs, they would be on the highest point between Omaha and Utah beaches, where it was thought that six 155 mm coastal artillery guns were located. The guns had, in fact, been removed, but the Germans had four bunkers under construction there and their troops were well armed. When the Rangers landed, they fired ropes and grapples, but many of them were water laden and fell back onto the beach. Despite withering mortar and machine-gun fire, some of the Rangers tried climbing the cliffs by creating footholds in the sandstone with their daggers. Others managed to secure ropes, but the Germans cut many of them before the Rangers could reach the summit. Still, once they had reached the top of the cliff, they managed to take it, despite fierce German resistance, and to hold it for two days until reinforcements arrived. Of the 225 Rangers who had set out on the mission, only 90 survived. Harvey Cook was one of these men. He was awarded the Silver Star for gallantry in action and went on to make a career in army intelligence.

Frank Brandstetter was another Ritchie man involved in the D-Day invasion. Brandstetter was born in Transylvania in 1912 and given the birth name Maryan Franciscus Otto Josephus Wladyslaw Brandstetter Drag-Sas Hubicki. His father was a Hungarian cavalry officer and his mother of Polish-Austrian nobility. Brandstetter had come to New York in 1928 as a penniless teenager but managed to get a toehold in the hotel industry and work his way up through its ranks. When World War II broke out, he volunteered for the US Army. He stood out among his fellow soldiers because he was older, had a thick foreign accent, and was fluent in Hungarian, Romanian, German, and Czech. Upon graduation from Officer Candidate School, he applied for parachute training but was rejected because, at thirty, he was considered too old. He graduated from Camp Ritchie's sixth class and briefly taught German tactics before being sent to England, where, following up on his desire to enter the war zone by parachute, he persuaded the commanding general of the 101st Airborne, Major General William Lee, of the necessity for Ritchie-trained interrogators to be integrated into the infantry airborne divisions. Lee agreed, and Brandstetter became the first US Army officer in charge of the first jump-qualified IPW (Interrogation of Prisoners of War) team. On D-Day, he parachuted with his men into Normandy as part of the 506th Infantry Parachute Regiment, 101st Airborne Division. By June 9, 1944, he and his men were interrogating prisoners and learning the coordinates for mobile antiaircraft guns and for German ammunition and fuel dumps. These were passed on through the appropriate Allied radio channels, and, as a result of this information, American naval guns successfully destroyed them. Brandstetter—known to his men as "Brandy"—served as General Matthew Ridgway's trusted aide with the Seventeenth Airborne Corps until the end of the war. During this time, the general sent him behind German lines to deliver a surrender demand to Field Marshall Walther Model, a major architect of the Battle of the Bulge. Model rejected it but committed suicide shortly afterward. After the war, Brandstetter served with the original, five-nation United Nations Organization. He was the recipient of a Silver Star.

Lieutenant Lawrence Cane (originally Cohen) performed a variety of tasks in the European theater. Short and slight of build, he was born in New York City to Jewish working-class parents and adopted their commitment to activism. A graduate of Ritchie's sixth class, he had fought—and been wounded—in the Spanish Civil War and boasted that he was the sole veteran of that war to land on the beaches of Normandy on D-Day. Prior to that, he commanded a supply company of Black troops of the 582nd Engineer Dump Truck Company. Eight of these men joined him at the assault landing on Utah Beach. Although officially with his old company, Cane was attached to an engineer combat group, where his task was to help clear mines, destroy fortifications, and open roads for the Allied forces. Later he provided machine-gun fire as paratroops from the 101st Airborne were ferried over the Douve River, east of Carentan. He then returned to his supply company, "running a fairly unexciting front-line trucking service.—Hauling mines, explosives, bridges, wounded, ammunition, rations, and any damn thing else they have a notion to use us for—even Nazi prisoners of war."[7] His role in the war changed when, on July 5, 1944, he was attached to the 238th Engineer Combat Battalion as a combat platoon leader. He earned a Silver Star when he volunteered, under heavy machine-gun and mortar fire, to find an escape route for some seventy army vehicles, including thirty tanks, that were in danger of encirclement and destruction by the German army.

On November 28, 1944, Cane was transferred from combat to the 238th Battalion staff, first as assistant S-2, later as acting S-2. He served as an intelligence officer for the remainder of the war. His attention was now focused on clearing mines and booby traps, improving and maintaining roads, and building bridges. In a letter to his wife during the Battle of the Bulge, he described one of his assignments. He had been sent out to scout a site for building a heavy-duty bridge across the Amblève River near Stoumont, Belgium, even though the Allies had not yet advanced to that point: "So out I go and mount my trusty jeep, and take off for the area to be reconnoitered. Pretty soon there are the unmistakable signs of the front—wrecked and burning vehicles, dead men in all the shattered and grotesque attitudes of violent death, littered equipment . . . and the marrow-chilling symphony of small-arms fire, high-velocity artillery and the roar of planes." Leaving his driver with the jeep, Cane went down the hillside toward the river, "feeling like a damn duck in a shooting gallery." He proceeded with his mission:

> *I look at the abutments. Measure the approaches. Look at the stream, sound it, gauge its speed. Tied a stone to a string and throw it across so I can measure the width.*
>
> *"Crack." A rifle shot.*
>
> *Some sonofabitch of a Krauthead is shooting at me from the woods across the river. I must look silly as hell to him, fooling around up there with a damn tape measure.*
>
> *I dive for some cover. Take out my notebook and jot down my findings methodical as an Englishman and his tea. I take another peek to check on some detail. Another shot, this time it throws dirt on me. Close.*

When Cane made it safely back to his jeep, an infantryman said, wonderingly, "Helluva job you got there, Sir."[8]

Ritchie Boy Victor Brombert felt that he was given a "helluva job" by his commander when, "by fiat," he transformed Brombert's military intelligence team into a combat psychological warfare unit. The men were now ordered not to gather intelligence but to serve as hog callers in the Cerisy forest:

> *The Signal Corps people were ordered to hang loudspeakers in trees near the German lines during the night. A signal corps GI was killed in the process. Only two members of our "French" team spoke fluent German—Sergeant Andrew and myself. It thus fell principally to us to get down to regiment headquarters, from there to battalion and company headquarters, and from there, on foot, moving forward cautiously and bent over, near the outposts, to a point beyond which we had to crawl along a sunken road, past helmets lying on the ground with ominous holes in them. Three times a day on two successive days we went on this expedition to deliver our message to the Germans, cajolingly. Three times a day we crawled along the sunken road, past the pierced helmets. Always with the same response from the other*

*side: mortar shells whistling down on us. Not a single German sur-
rendered.*[9]

Although others could appreciate the courage of the Ritchie Boys,
they often failed to comprehend the gravity of their missions. This was
particularly true of intelligence gathering. Late in the war, for example,
Richard Schifter's IPW team was sent to target offices in the German
cities that had fallen to the Allies in order to retrieve documents of
special concern to the United States. Schifter remembered, in particular,
doing this in Koblenz:

> *We were to search a Secret Police office close to the Rhine River. The
> German Army was still on the other side and its artillery was still
> firing across the river. There were three of us who were assigned to the
> task of searching the Gestapo office, two Ritchie boys, and another sol-
> dier who had been an FBI agent. As we Ritchie boys started to crawl
> along the road that led to the Gestapo office, our FBI colleague said: "I
> am willing to die for my country, but not on this stupid mission." So
> the two of us, Morrie Parloff . . . and I, made it to the Gestapo office,
> searched the papers, and made it back.*[10]

Because so many of the Ritchie interrogators were on the front
lines, they risked capture by the enemy forces. Philip Glaessner is unique
among these POWs, because he was interned twice during the war—
once by the Germans, once by the British. He was a Jew, and, although
born in Lausanne, Switzerland, he had grown up and was living in
Vienna when Hitler came to power. His parents sent him to boarding
school in England to keep him safe from Nazi persecution. Instead, after
the British declared war on Germany, he became one of the twenty-eight
thousand men and women of German or Austrian background living
in Britain who were rounded up and imprisoned in 1940, first outside
London and then on the Isle of Man. Eventually he was sent to Canada
aboard a cargo ship and was able to enter the United States via Cuba in
1942. After graduating from Ritchie as a technician fifth grade, he landed
in France a few days after D-Day and, during the Ardennes offensive,

was captured once again—this time by the Germans. "I was in a cellar with a couple of civilians and a couple of other soldiers," he recalled. "The Germans came down, we raised our hands and said 'Don't shoot, comrade!' What else could we do? I had destroyed all my papers. They mustn't discover, who I was." He could be thankful that he had had the foresight to substitute a "C" ("Catholic") for "J" (Jew) on his dog tags, because that move probably saved his life.[11]

According to stipulations of the Geneva Conventions, noncommissioned officers were put in separate "A" camps. Accordingly, Glaessner joined the GIs who were transferred from Limburg an der Lahn to Stalag IX-A, in Trutzhain, near Kassel. This camp had held French prisoners for more than four years, and although the men were underfed, this camp of more than forty-seven thousand prisoners was well ordered. The various nationalities were housed in separate sections of the camp, but Glaessner managed to speak with members of the other armies. From the Frenchmen who worked outside the camp, Glaessner was able to pick up war news and pass it on to the Americans. He also spoke regularly with some Australian prisoners who had smuggled a radio into the camp and could sometimes hear the BBC. Glaessner said that he functioned "as an agent" for the Americans, since "the most important thing for me was to strengthen the morale of my comrades by keeping them as well informed as possible." When it became clear that the Americans had come and were approaching the camp, Glaessner persuaded the camp commander to hoist a Red Cross flag and to send him out to the Americans as emissary. He then climbed the prison fence and was running toward the approaching American tanks when a jeep drove up, and one of the men in the jeep called out, "My God, Phil, what are you doing here?" It was one of his Ritchie classmates.[12]

Not all prisoners of war fared as well as the prisoners in Stalag IX-A. Ritchie Boy Henry C. Nathan was a German Jew from Frankfurt am Main who, like Glaessner, had the good fortune not to register his religion on his dog tags. When he was wounded and taken prisoner in the Battle of the Bulge on December 19, 1944, he was held in Bad Orb at Stalag IX-B, where conditions were nowhere near up to the level of those Glaessner experienced. Furthermore, of the roughly four thousand

American GIs imprisoned there, the Germans were seeking a quota of 300–350 Jews for transfer to Berga to serve as slave laborers in the construction of an underground armaments factory. They asked all Jewish prisoners to step forward, threatening them with death if they did not. About 130 eventually did, and the Germans then filled their quota by adding known troublemakers, or those who simply looked Jewish, to this "special detail." Nathan was able to elude selection. By the time the war was over, eighty of the Americans transferred to the slave labor camp had died.

Still, according to a report in *Stars and Stripes*, the prisoners held in Bad Orb had only minimally better living conditions; they "had been living at a subhuman level for months, penned up in cramped, filthy quarters while being underfed and brutalized." As Allied forces approached the camp, the Nazis tried to flee, taking the American prisoners with them. Fifteen hundred men were loaded onto boxcars, but US planes stalled the train, and the Nazis then forced the prisoners from the train and continued their flight to the east. Two hundred seventy-seven prisoners were unable to walk, and they were left behind in the boxcars. Nathan was one of these. According to a reconstructed regimental history, three "haggard, dirty, hollow-eyed men" managed after some time to leave the boxcars, stumble across a field, and meet up with a patrol of the 393rd Infantry Regiment.[13] The infantrymen found that all the men who had been deserted by the retreating Germans suffered from malnutrition and bore "large festering sores from the filth and lice they were forced to live with."[14] "The 393rd Regiment liberated us and I don't believe there was a dry eye in the whole camp," Nathan wrote.[15] The severest cases were evacuated immediately by the Regimental Medical Sections, while others waited in army care until transportation was available to take them from the battle zone. In the meantime, the regimental chaplain held a service of thanksgiving for the liberated prisoners.[16]

Like all men serving in the war, the Ritchie Boys formed attachments to their teammates and their fellow soldiers. A lifelong friendship developed at Camp Ritchie between Austrian-born Leo Handel and Danish-born Ib Melchior. After graduation, Handel was sent to Italy as an interrogator of prisoners of war and Melchior to Germany as a counterintelligence agent, but they developed an elaborate code to evade the censors and to keep in touch:

> *It was based on the beginning and end of the letter, how we greeted each other and how we signed off. For example, "Dear Leo" meant—I am in Germany; "Hi Leo" meant—I am in Italy; "Hi Buddy" meant—I am in Africa; and "Hi Good Buddy" meant—I am stuck in England. And in signing off, "Your Buddy" meant—I am in CIC, working in a rear echelon HQ, while "Your Good Buddy" meant—I work as a CIC agent with the front line troops. "Best regards" meant—I am an IPW with the front line troops. "So Long" meant—I am working in the war zone, and if there were a PS of any kind it meant—I was wounded but am OK. That way, we had a good idea of what we were doing—but nobody else did![17]*

Handel and Melchior wanted to make movies in Hollywood, and after the war, both men did. Melchior even wrote an "unproduced screenplay" based on his friend's wartime exploits.

Although death rates among the Ritchie men were relatively low, the causes of death varied greatly. Some were clearly heroic. Staff Sergeant Stephen Mosbacher ("Moose"), a German Jew from Nuremberg, Germany, was one of these. He served as an interrogator assigned to IPW Team 145 attached to Combat Command B of the Eighth Tank Division and interviewed hundreds of POWs during his division's move through Holland, to the Ruhr and the Rhine rivers, and in its push onward toward the Elbe River. He also served as part of a small advance force that entered towns not yet fully emptied of enemy forces and secured quarters for his division. In Lippstadt, his party found and was disarming a garrison of about eighty German soldiers when an SS unit of tanks entered the town. Mosbacher stayed behind to help cover the withdrawal of the rest of his party. When most were in safety, he started to leave and then turned his jeep back to rescue one of his comrades. He was able to get the man into his jeep, shoot his way out, and bring the man to safety. Then, seeing a wounded man in the wreck of a light truck, he tried to save him as well. This time Mosbacher's luck ran out. His jeep was struck by a tank shell, and he was killed instantly. His commanding officer said that, when he died, he was smiling, and he still had a firm grip on his submachine gun. Mosbacher, who was twenty-one years old at his death, was awarded the Silver Star posthumously.[18]

Some deaths were simply sad. Second Lieutenant Raymond Paul Raux was a Frenchman who had emigrated to the United States in 1933 and founded the Barbizon School of Languages in New York City. Raux was trained at Ritchie as an interrogator of both French and Italian prisoners. On Valentine's Day 1943, while studying at the camp, he married Doris Strobridge, a young French-born secretary from New York. Within the month, he shipped out to North Africa and was sent to serve at the front during the closing weeks of the Tunisian campaign. He was not prepared for the horrors of war, and his hair turned white during his service there. He found comfort in adopting a wire-haired terrier that was suffering from shell shock and nursing it back to health. When the dog disappeared in early June, Raux put a notice in the Algiers edition of *Stars and Stripes*, asking for help in locating it.

The war intervened. In early July, he joined the combat team of the 505th Parachute Infantry Regiment just days before the invasion of Sicily. On the night of July 9, 1943, he entered Sicily in the Allied Forces' first mass parachute drop at night. The next day, at a crossroad near Vittoria, Sicily, Raux approached a pillbox in an attempt to talk the occupying forces into surrender. As he stepped into the passageway, he was shot and fell. When he did not move or respond to his teammates' calls, they assumed he was dead. They watched as he was dragged inside the pillbox and the door closed behind him. Eventually, the pillbox was reduced to rubble and its occupying forces killed. In the confusion and haste of burials that followed, Raux was first interred in the enemy portion of a temporary Sicilian cemetery before being moved to the proper American section. Then, in 1947, he was moved to a grave site outside Rome before his mother had him reinterred in a private plot near her home in France. Raux was thirty-two years old when he died. He may have been the first Ritchie Boy to be killed in action in World War II.[19]

Back in Maryland the society women in Hagerstown mourned the death of Sergeant Leslie Bartal, a Hungarian-born Jew whom they had called "Laszlo." While stationed at Camp Ritchie, he had enraptured audiences with his piano performances. He continued to play a morale-boosting role when he served in military intelligence with the First Infantry Division in France. After its landing in Normandy, he wrote the musical arrangement for the song of the First Infantry Division, the "fightingest infantry division in the United States Army." And when its troops reached the village of Balleroy, France, the thirty-four-year-old sergeant gave a piano recital to the liberated townspeople on the tiny stage of the Balleroy town hall. The French were so gratified by this return to civilized entertainment that, the following week, the children of the town gave their own, return concert to the Allied soldiers. Twenty-four days later, Bartal was killed during the Division's St. Lo-Marigny breakthrough in Operation Cobra. He was buried in Normandy.

Some deaths were outright executions. Two interrogators, Technician Fifth Grade Murray Zappler (twenty) and Staff Sergeant Kurt Jacobs (thirty-four), were part of the Ritchie IPW Team 154, attached to the 106th Infantry Division; three members of the team, including Zappler and Jacobs, were sent to the 423rd Regiment. Both men were German Jews; both had been born in Berlin. Zappler had left as a child, but Jacobs had earned a law degree there. During the worst of the opening foray of the Battle of the Bulge, the American infantrymen had fought fiercely against overwhelming German forces, but on December 16, 1944, they momentarily got the upper hand and took thirty German prisoners. Zappler and Jacobs questioned them for more than nine hours. A second, even fiercer German attack began the following morning and continued until December 20, when the Americans were forced to surrender. As they laid down their arms and joined the line of three hundred captured Americans being led to Bleialf and eventual imprisonment in Stalag IX-B, two of the prisoners whom Zappler and Jacobs had interrogated called them out to Wehrmacht captain Curt Bruns as "Jews from Berlin." Bruns had them removed from the line, remarking that "Jews have no right to live in Germany." When the line of American prisoners was out of sight, he had the two men taken into a field and shot. Their four Ritchie comrades were taken to Stalag IX-B; they all survived the war, including Staff Sergeant David Epstein, who, like Henry Nathan, managed to conceal the fact that he was a Jew. In February 1945, the bodies of Zappler and Jacobs were discovered. Captain Bruns was arrested and put on trial, and on June 14, 1945, he was executed by firing squad.[20]

In an interesting twist to the stories of POW deaths, Ritchie Boy Maxwell Papurt was killed in an Allied bombing. Prior to entering the service the bespectacled, prematurely graying Maxwell Papurt, onetime chief psychologist of the New York State Department of Corrections, had made a hobby of psychoanalyzing the official war communiqués of all the warring nations and making predictions based on his analyses. Small wonder, then, that he came to Ritchie and trained in counterintelligence before being sent to Europe as head of the CIC in Italy and member of the OSS X-2 Counter Espionage Branch that had been created to provide liaison and assistance to the British in its exploitation of the Ultra program's intelligence. This program was centered in England, at Bletchley Park, and its efforts focused on decrypting enemy communications. For security reasons, any personnel with knowledge of Ultra were forbidden to place themselves in a situation where they could easily be captured. But this is just what happened on September 26, 1944, when Major Papurt and his driver drove to Patton's Luxembourg headquarters with two other passengers, OSS officer Robert Jennings and Gertrude Legendre (a Charleston, South Carolina, socialite currently in charge of the OSS/Paris message center). The jeep came under machine-gun fire, and a sniper hit Papurt in both ankles before capturing him and his fellow passengers. They were questioned, but they revealed nothing about their OSS ties and apparently aroused no real suspicion. Papurt was transferred to the hospital of Stalag XII-A, a POW camp just outside Limburg. Of the four prisoners, he was, by far, the most knowledgeable about the Ultra program. The OSS and British MI6 were confident that Papurt could not be broken, but they grew concerned nonetheless when the Germans suddenly changed their cypher settings; was this, they wondered, a routine security measure, or did it come about as a result of their interrogations of Papurt? On November 29, 1944, the US Ninth Air Force made a direct hit on the camp hospital, and Major Papurt was killed. Although it appears to have been a tragic accident, a few historians are unsure: Could they have hit that site with the intent of killing

Papurt before he could be tortured into giving up vital information? In any case, at the time of the air raid, Papurt proved his mettle by refusing shelter.[21] The "hardboiled" Papurt, whom his comrades called "Jerry," was thirty-seven years old.

Like Papurt, Major Melvin C. Helfers, an Illinois native and graduate of the Citadel, was closely involved in the intelligence that originated in the Ultra encryption program. He had first been stationed in Hawaii when the Japanese attacked Pearl Harbor and then transferred to Camp Ritchie, where he completed the eleventh class in German. He was sent to Britain as a signals intelligence officer and went to Bletchley Park for a two-week course in the Ultra encryption program before joining General Patton's Third Army as Ultra intercept officer on Patton's staff. It was his task to deliver the Ultra intelligence to the staff each day. Helfers was much impressed with the way that Patton used this intelligence. "General Patton fully appreciated the value of Ultra," Helfers said, "but he did not lose all perspective concerning it as did General Hodges and his staff at First U.S. Army and as did General Bradley and his staff at Twelfth U.S. Army group." Since Colonel Oscar Koch, Patton's head of G-2 intelligence, was ailing, he told Helfers "to give the Ultra briefing directly to the Army Commander." Helfers regarded this as a real break. "I was the only Special Intelligence Officer in all the U.S. armies who daily briefed the Army Commander directly," he declared proudly. Patton personally told Helfers that the intelligence he brought to him had "saved him the services of two divisions in the Third Army drive across France toward Germany in August and September 1944."[22]

Herman Lang, a native from Meiningen, Germany, and a graduate of Camp Ritchie's ninth class, also worked directly with General Patton. Assigned to duty as Patton's translator, he soon distinguished himself by going on a solitary mission behind German lines to gather information on troop movement on the main road to Metz, a heavily fortified city in northeast France that was close to the borders of Germany and Luxembourg. And, after V-E Day, Lang further endeared himself to the general when he learned of two exceptionally fine French race horses that had been abandoned by a German officer and helped Patton acquire them for his personal use.

Meanwhile, the Camp Sharpe men whom Hans Habe had trained in propaganda broadcasting were finally given the opportunity to practice their craft before large European audiences. The Grand Duchy of Luxembourg had the most powerful radio transmitter in Europe, and, because of its central location in western Europe, its programming could reach German, Italian, French, and British audiences. Once Luxembourg was taken by the Allies in September 1944, the nine-man operational broadcast team active in Lorient, France, was called to Radio Luxembourg. Control of the station was given to SHAEF, and Hans Habe was given the task of restoring programming to the German-speaking population of Europe. Many of the men who had trained at Camp Sharpe now came to Luxembourg to work as writers and broadcasters: Stefan Heym, Hanuš Burger, Peter Wyden, Robert Addis, Roger Brett, Walter Kohner, Joseph Eaton, and Fred Perutz, to name just a few. Their task was to give German audiences a true and sobering picture of the progress of the war. News broadcasts alternated with skits and plays. One popular series of war skits featured two speakers: "Corporal Tom Jones," a rather naive all-American GI who spoke German with a strong American accent, and "Colonel Thompson," whose accent was not so strong but who possessed a deep, authoritarian voice. These skits were addressed both to the enlisted German soldiers and to the German officers. Colonel Thompson spoke to the officers about failed German strategy. Corporal Jones, by contrast, told human-interest anecdotes to the enlisted men, always ending with an anti-Nazi joke. These jokes became a popular feature among the station's German listeners.

The Luxembourg broadcasters also used two of the same ploys as in Lorient: reading undelivered German letters on the air and lists of recently captured German soldiers. Both helped guarantee an audience. As for music, they tended to choose musical selections by "degenerate" German composers.

In October 1944, Habe began planning special programming for Christmas. One of the Camp Sharpe boys, the German Jewish soldier Joseph Eaton, suggested not broadcasting any news programs on that day but, instead, interviewing POWs and allowing one thousand of them to speak personally to their families. The men took broadcast trucks to numerous prisoner cages at the front lines and recorded each of the selected prisoners, who had a little less than a minute to speak about his treatment and his health and to send greetings to family members. The program was transmitted on Christmas Day 1944, even though the Luxembourg station was then under threat of German attack during the last major German offensive against the Allied forces—the Battle of the Bulge.

The Lorient team of David Hertz, Fred Lorenz, and Benno Frank also broadcast from Luxembourg, but, instead of participating in the daytime "white" programming, they joined General Robert McClure's Psychological Warfare Division in broadcasting four and a half hours each night as part of a "black" programming initiative known as 1212, or "Operation Annie." They pretended to be a German station, playing German folk songs and Viennese waltzes as musical interludes and giving war news from a German perspective. With Hertz as writer, Lorenz as its main actor, and Frank as the authoritative voice of the operation, they managed to deceive Germans into believing that they were a group of SS dissidents determined to defend the Führer from his corrupt subordinates. Frank now assumed the role of a German officer retired from active service because of wounds. With his full, rasping voice and his Rhine-Hessen accent, he gave credible accounts of news from the war and the home front, some of it accurate, some lies intended to make its listeners question the war—and change tactics. He and his 1212 team employed numerous deceits to achieve these ends. One was to appeal for help to rescue surrounded party leaders—thereby luring German infantrymen into capture. *Time* reported that one of "Operation Annie's" biggest successes came soon after the Allies took the Remagen Bridge: Another Allied force had secured a bridgehead near Andernach, and, between these two points, Nazi troops in the Eifel mountains had plenty of room for retreat. Yet, because Frank told his German radio listeners that there was only one way out, most of the remaining Wehrmacht marched right into an Allied ambush.[23]

Later in the war, Camp Ritchie graduates made a wide range of intelligence discoveries. One of these men was young New York film student and blue-blood Thomas Quinn Curtiss, who graduated from the ninth class with specialized training in photo interpretation. He secured the German Luftwaffe's hidden film cache, and, for this action, he was personally awarded the French Legion of Honor by Charles de Gaulle.

Another was Hans Jacob Meier, a native of Marne, Germany, who'd been running a New York deli when the war broke out. He graduated from the twenty-first class at Camp Ritchie with specialized training as an interrogator of German prisoners. He and five other Ritchie Boys were assigned in Europe to the HOUGHTEAM, a group of nineteen Americans under the command of Major Floyd W. Hough. Their mission was to seize critical German geographic data that could be used not only to shorten the war but also to aid in any global conflict to come. As "the team's ace German interrogator," Hans Meier obtained the information that led to the HOUGHTEAM's greatest finds. This included the seizure of the central map and geodetic data repository for the German army, in Saalfeld, Germany. There they found records that extended into eastern Europe and the Soviet Union. Since Saalfeld lay well within the planned Soviet occupation zone, the team acted quickly, moving 250 tons of captured material out of the area to the American zone. Hough paid tribute to Meier's work, declaring, "It is known through German sources that much of this work was done at considerable risk to his life, both at the time and in the future."[24]

Often Ritchie Boy interrogations led to more than strictly tactical information. Swiss-born Ritchie Boy Ferdinand Sperl received a Silver Star because, according to the official citation,

Captain Sperl having received information of a German Staff Group with highly valuable documents located within the enemy lines, volunteered to secure the capture of the Staff and documents. Using a prisoner as a guide, Captain Sperl[,] under the gravest personal danger, passed through the outpost lines of fanatic SS troops, contacted the German Staff commander and convinced him of the advisability of surrendering the documents undamaged to a task force. Captain Sperl then returned to his own lines again subjecting himself to the danger of capture or death and led a task force through the German lines and successfully captured the desired staff and documents.

The heroism of his act is admirable but does not tell the full story. The German Staff Group was made up of high-ranking Luftwaffe officials who were part of an espionage group fleeing Berlin with photographs and maps identifying the location of Russian airfields and military industrial centers. Captain Sperl had volunteered to enter enemy territory and attempt to reach the men, but, as he was preparing to leave, one of these officials—a Luftwaffe colonel—came to him with an odd request. It turned out that the colonel was a lover of fine horses, and a herd of four hundred thoroughbreds, many of them royal Lipizzaner horses from Vienna, were housed at a Nazi stud farm in Hostau, eighteen miles inside Czechoslovakia. The Russians were approaching, and the colonel feared that the animals would be killed for their meat if they fell into Russian hands. Sperl's commanding officer, Colonel Charles H. Reed, was himself a horse fancier, and he agreed to do all he could to rescue the horses, provided that the twenty officers surrendered and handed over all their hidden documents. To get to the officers, Sperl and the German colonel did indeed have to pass through various sentry points that night before reaching the hunting lodge where the German intelligence officers were housed. These officers accepted the Americans' conditions and agreed to surrender provided that Sperl could promise them a mock battle beforehand. Sperl went back to the American headquarters and then returned through enemy lines with a task force that staged a "battle" and burned the hunting lodge. In the days that followed, the prized horses were safely brought out of Czechoslovakia and into American hands. Captain Sperl may have been officially recognized for getting the Luftwaffe's intelligence documents, but for horse lovers, his role in the cooperative German/American action of rescuing the purebred Lipizzaners was the more significant achievement.

As the war wound down in Germany, the American forces took on a new task: tracking down and capturing the leaders responsible for carrying out Hitler's program of world conquest. One of the men assigned to this task was William Brickman, an Orthodox Jew born and raised in Manhattan, who "could read 20 European languages, in addition to Latin and ancient Greek, three Asian and two African languages."[25] A graduate of Ritchie's twenty-sixth class, he was drafted into the OSS and given the mission of capturing senior SS officers trying to escape and evade capture in the chaos of the closing days of the war. His team developed an effective method for doing this. Some of the agents went behind the enemy lines wearing German uniforms. There they visited bars, pretended to get drunk, and started bragging that they could help anyone leave the country if he had the money to do so. The agents asked for a substantial payment because they were fairly certain that only senior officers in the SS and Wehrmacht would have both the means and the desire to get out of Germany. Whenever someone asked for this help, he was directed to a cabin where, he was told, he would find a Nazi officer able to get him out of the country. Brickman posed as this Nazi officer, usually wearing a uniform one rank higher than that of the visiting German. He would question the German as to where he had served and what he had done in the war; then, after agreeing on a payment, Brickman would tell him to go to a rendezvous point on the Czech border on a certain date where he would join other German officers for transport to South America. When the SS officers showed up at this site, they were immediately taken captive by other OSS officers and transferred to Allied prisons—or to Nuremberg. Here, too, the Ritchie men would play a substantive role.

As intelligence officer with the Second Ranger Battalion, Harvey Cook was awarded the Silver Star and two Bronze Stars. SOURCE: AUTHOR'S COLLECTION

Lawrence Cane on reconnaissance during the Battle of the Bulge (December 1944–January 1945). COURTESY OF DAVID CANE

The 393rd Infantry Regiment rescued American POWs from Stalag IX-B who were too ill to travel and had been abandoned on a train. SOURCE: US ARMY, *THE 393RD INFANTRY IN REVIEW: A PICTORIAL ACCOUNT OF THE 393RD INFANTRY REGIMENT IN COMBAT, 1944–1945*, EDITED BY ERNEST W. FRITZ

German prisoners in Belgium record messages to be aired over Radio Luxembourg on December 25, 1944. SOURCE: NATIONAL ARCHIVES AND RECORDS ADMINISTRATION

Major Melvin C. Helfers (standing) briefs Lieutenant General George S. Patton (center) and Major General Hugh Gaffey on operations of German forces opposing the Third US Army in the Seine River area of France. SOURCE: NATIONAL ARCHIVES AND RECORDS ADMINISTRATION

CHAPTER EIGHTEEN

Ritchie Boys in the Pacific

This is the grimmest, and surely the holiest, task we have faced since D-day. Here before us lie the bodies of comrades and friends. Men who until yesterday or last week laughed with us, joked with us, trained with us. Men who were on the same ships with us, and went over the side with us as we prepared to hit the beaches of this island. Men who fought with us and feared with us. Somewhere in this plot of ground there may lie the man who could have discovered the cure for cancer. Under one of these Christian crosses, or beneath a Jewish Star of David, there may rest now a man who was destined to be a great prophet to find the way, perhaps, for all to live in plenty, with poverty and hardship for none. Now they lie silently in this sacred soil, and we gather to consecrate this earth to their memory.[1]

SOME OF THE RITCHIE MEN WHO FOUGHT AND DIED IN THE PACIFIC were US Marines. From its second class onward, Camp Ritchie had included Marines in its training program. Three hundred fifty-one availed themselves of this training, with more than 80 percent specializing in terrain intelligence and about 15 percent studying photo interpretation (PI). These Ritchie-trained Marines served with the First, Second, Third, Fourth, Fifth, and Sixth Marine Divisions in the Pacific, performing so well that, in early November 1944, the commandant of the Marine Corps requested that the quota of Marines to be sent into training at Camp Ritchie be doubled. It was not unusual, in fact, for Marines to be sent back to the United States from the Pacific theater for this purpose.

One Native American, for example, Wilbur H. Shongo, of the Seneca Tribe's bear clan, had enlisted in the Marines right after Pearl Harbor and had been sent to Guadalcanal to serve as a technician with an antiaircraft unit. He then fought in New Georgia and on Guam before returning to the United States for a thirty-four-day furlough, during which time he was hospitalized for malaria before being reassigned to Camp Ritchie for its final two classes (the thirtieth and thirty-first). There he specialized in terrain intelligence and Japanese Order of Battle (OB) before going on to Quantico, Virginia, and receiving an honorable discharge. He would, however, make good use of his Camp Ritchie training in the Korean War, in which he not only served as a crack sniper in the Korean Central front but also undertook numerous missions behind enemy lines to scout out supply lines, troop movements, and gun emplacements.

Marine private John Chafee, who would go on to a distinguished career as Rhode Island governor, US secretary of the navy, and US senator, followed a somewhat similar track. Born to privilege, he cut short his undergraduate studies at Yale University in order to enlist in the Marines immediately after the attack on Pearl Harbor. He, too, landed on the beach of Guadalcanal with the first wave of American Marines. His unit fought there for four months in one of the United States' bloodiest battles before being pulled out to Australia for rest and refit. He came back to the United States in November 1943, was sent to Officer Candidate School, and received his commission as a second lieutenant. He then entered the twenty-third class at Camp Ritchie, specializing in photo intelligence, before returning as a US army captain to the Pacific, where he landed on Okinawa and fought as an intelligence officer with the Sixth Marine Division.

Like Shongo, Chafee was recalled to serve in the Korean War. There, as commander of Dog Company, Second Battalion, Seventh Marines, he participated in the bloody fighting for North Korean ridge lines. Writer and columnist James Brady, who served under him as a replacement second lieutenant, recalls that "[t]he men of Dog Company idolized Chafee. He was good, he was tough, he was fair, he was cool. And though we lived in filth and never washed or changed clothes, he was almost elegant. That, too, impresses Marines."[2] Chafee was the inspiration for the main hero in Brady's Korean War novel *The Marines of Autumn*.

Both US Army and Marine graduates of Camp Ritchie died in the Pacific theater: on Iwo Jima, on Okinawa, in the Philippines, in the Marshall and Mariana Islands, and in China. One Ritchie Boy, Captain James Dorst of the sixth class, was assigned to the Fifth Observation Squadron attached to the Tenth Air Force. He died when the plane he was on as an observer was shot down while on a bomb-strike mission over Burma.

One three-man OB team from Camp Ritchie's sixteenth class lost two of its members in service in the Philippines. First Lieutenant Robert Nancolas had trained at Ritchie in photo interpretation; Master Sergeant Louis Fier and Staff Sergeant Arthur T. Nelson Jr. studied Japanese Order of Battle. Nelson was the first of these to fall. He was killed in action on May 2, 1945, while fighting with the Sixth Army on Luzon. He was twenty-three years old. His heartbroken father, a prominent Boston real estate investor, honored his son by bequeathing his entire estate to the establishment of the "Arthur T. Nelson Jr. Memorial Trust Fund," which was to provide loans to students "without regard to race, sex, color, or religion."

Four days later, the team lost its second member. Lieutenant Robert Nancolas's PI training prepared him to set off on a mission aboard an Army Air Force B25 in order to determine whether the rumors were true that large numbers of Japanese forces were assembling south of the Umiray River. The ten men on this mission successfully located the bivouac area, determined the size of the Japanese force, and identified its weaponry, but before they could break radio silence to report their findings—or even to issue a call for help—the plane came under heavy machine-gun fire from the ground, crashed into a hillside, and exploded in flames. All ten men were killed. Because recovery could not differentiate Nancolas's body from that of six others on the plane, the remains of all seven were brought back to the United States and interred in a grave in the Zachary Taylor National Cemetery in Louisville, Kentucky. Nancolas was twenty-four years old.

Private Leonard C. Brostrom, from the tenth Ritchie class, specialized in counterintelligence; his death was a particularly heroic one. Like many of the men assigned to the Pacific theater of operations, he had already distinguished himself in battle prior to his assignment to Camp Ritchie. An Idaho farm boy and son of Swedish immigrants, Brostrom planned to be a carpenter like his father. He had graduated from high school and completed a three-year mission in California for the Mormon Church when he was drafted into the army in March 1942. He was assigned to the Seventh Motorized Division and began training in the Mojave Desert in preparation for deployment to North Africa. In January 1943, his division was renamed the Seventh Infantry Division, and the men began rigorous Marine training in amphibious assault. Instead of deployment to Africa, for which they had originally trained, the men were now sent to the Arctic tundra to make an amphibious landing on Attu Island, Alaska's largest and westernmost island. Although the men had neither the training nor the equipment for Arctic warfare, they fought against strong Japanese resistance with rifles, bayonets, and hand grenades. Finally, after eighteen days of battle, and after facing a suicidal bayonet charge in the battle at Chichagof Harbor, they managed to destroy all Japanese resistance. Brostrom's regiment was awarded a Distinguished Unit Citation for its actions.

Brostrom was now called to Camp Ritchie to enter its tenth class and be trained in counterintelligence. He then rejoined his old outfit, which trained for four months in Hawaii before making an amphibious assault on Kwajalein Atoll as the first phase of Operation Flintlock in the Marshall Islands. This was followed, in October 1944, by the invasion of Leyte, in the Philippines. His platoon of Company F, Seventeenth Infantry Regiment, Seventh Infantry Division, came upon powerful resistance near Dagami. Here Brostrom died a hero's death. His posthumous Medal of Honor citation tells the story:

From pillboxes, trenches, and spider holes, so well camouflaged that they could be detected at no more than 20 yards, the enemy poured machinegun and rifle fire, causing severe casualties in the platoon. Realizing that a key pillbox in the center of the strong point would have to be knocked out if the company were to advance, Private First Class Brostrom, without orders and completely ignoring his own safety, ran forward to attack the pillbox with grenades. He immediately became the prime target for all the riflemen in the area, as he rushed to the rear of the pillbox and tossed grenades through the entrance. Six enemy soldiers left a trench in a bayonet charge against the heroic American, but he killed one and drove the others off with rifle fire. As he threw more grenades from his completely exposed position he was wounded several times in the abdomen and knocked to the ground. Although suffering intense pain and rapidly weakening from loss of blood, he slowly rose to his feet and once more hurled his deadly missiles at the pillbox. As he collapsed, the enemy began fleeing from the fortification and were killed by riflemen of his platoon. Private First Class Brostrom died while being carried from the battlefield, but his intrepidity and unhesitating willingness to sacrifice himself in a one-man attack against overwhelming odds enabled his company to reorganize against attack, and annihilate the entire enemy position.[3]

Private Brostrom was twenty-seven years old. A naval cargo ship, the USNS *Private Leonard C. Brostrom*, was named in his honor.

Captain Henry C. Whittlesey, a graduate of Camp Ritchie's third class, was killed in China. In July 1944, he had been sent to Yenan, Shensi, as one of nine members of the first of two contingents of the US Army Observer Section, or "Dixie Mission." Because Yenan was the headquarters of the Chinese Communist Armies, part of the group's secret mission was to evaluate both the potential for US cooperation with the Chinese Communists and the desirability of providing these armies with American aid and assistance. It was a delicate assignment, since the Chinese Nationalist leader Chiang Kai-shek was adamantly opposed to the Americans establishing any close relationship with the Communists. The American observers were to work in tandem with the Air-Ground Aid Section (AGAS) of the US Army Forces in China in helping rescue downed pilots in north China.

Whittlesey was admirably suited to this assignment. Born in Chungking, the son of an English mother and American father, he had also lived for four years in Chefoo before moving to the United States when he was eleven.

Lieutenant Colonel A. R. Wichtrich, the head of the Air-Ground Aid Section in Kunming, was impressed by Whittlesey's credentials, noting that he and Master Sergeant Bob Clarke were "two excellent individuals who not only spoke several dialects of the Chinese language, but who were familiar with the customs of the Chinese in north China."[4] Wichtrich picked the two men to meet with Mao Tse-tung and convince him that the United States' interests were solely to rescue downed airmen and to drive the Japanese out of China. Accordingly, the two men met with Mao and got his cooperation in setting up safe routes and formal radio communication with the AGAS. A report on the rescue and safe return of a downed American airman was penned by Whittlesey; in it he emphasized that, for the eighty-five days it took to return the airman to safety, the Communists led him safely around Japanese army patrols, and the local peasants provided him with food, clothing, and shelter without once asking for compensation.

In February 1945, Whittlesey joined the Communists in going out to stop a strong Japanese patrol from reaching a Yenan outpost. They successfully routed the Japanese and seized a Japanese general. From him Whittlesey gathered a great deal of intelligence, including details of all the Japanese emplacements in north China. This was an incredible windfall for the Allies, but before Whittlesey could transmit the information back to the AGAS headquarters in Kunming, the Japanese staged a counterattack and Whittlesey was killed. Fortunately, the Communists passed his intelligence, which included microfilm and maps taken from the Japanese general, on to Colonel Wichtrich, who cabled the information to the Pentagon. Whittlesey was buried in Yenan, where a meeting hall was named after him. Later he was reinterred in Chengdu. He was awarded the Distinguished Service Cross posthumously, for "extraordinary heroism," through "intrepid actions, personal bravery and zealous devotion to duty at the cost of his life."

Naturally the Ritchie Boys, like all men in the armed forces, were deeply affected by the deaths of comrades. During his service in Asia, Baldwin Eckel devised a strategy for protecting himself from becoming too intimate with his fellow soldiers. As he reported it, he was not upset by the enemy dying, and he learned to deal with the deaths of strangers. "That's nothing," he said. "It's your buddies. And it leaves scars that you just can't talk about." After one close friend, a lieutenant, was killed, "I never called anybody by their name. It was always by their rank, Colonel, Captain, General, Soldier, Private, Sergeant. That was my way of protecting myself. I [knew] nobody's name."[5]

Despite its location on the East Coast, Camp Ritchie had trained significant numbers of army men in Japanese Order of Battle. Lieutenant Frank Church was one of these. He graduated from the fifteenth class and became officer in charge of his three-man team. The team was stationed in Kunming, China, headquarters for the Chinese Combat Command, and its mission was to trace the movements of enemy units and to make new identifications and estimations of enemy strength. The daily presentations to the Combined Staff sections that Church gave were so well received that the commanding general, Major General Robert B. McClure, recommended him for a Bronze Star. The citation lauded Church for studies that "were so well prepared that intelligence agencies made requests for additional copies and language personnel in the field used the special studies as chief guides in interrogations."[6] After the war, Church made a name for himself as a US senator from Idaho.

Ritchie men also served in the OSS (Office of Strategic Services) and CIC (Counterintelligence Corps) in the Pacific. Robert Ettinger, a young news photographer, was one of these. Ettinger was born in Germany to White Russian parents but grew up in France. He completed the seventh class at Camp Ritchie and then was recruited by the OSS. As operations officer for the OSS's Secret Intelligence Branch in the China theater, he volunteered to parachute alone into French Indochina in order to determine existing conditions in the area. He made a blind drop into Songla province in the northwest part of the country in March 1945 and immediately began reporting on Japanese troop movements in the area. He then attached himself to the French forces under General Gabriel Sabattier and, for the next five weeks, sent back information both on Japanese activity and on the French defense plans. For this he was awarded a Bronze Star. But Ettinger was also a bit of a renegade. He

He Passed through Camp Ritchie

Major **Carl J. Gilbert** (1906–1983) was born in Bloomfield, New Jersey. He attended the University of Virginia, obtained a law degree from Harvard in 1931, and joined a Boston law firm. He was a well-established lawyer in his thirties when his work was interrupted by the war. He graduated with the last (thirty-first) class at Camp Ritchie and then joined the Thirty-Seventh Infantry Division in the Pacific theater as a major. There, at a forward observation post near Baguio, in the Philippines, he guided a flight of aircraft on a bombing and strafing mission in support of the infantry advance against enemy mortar and twenty-millimeter fire. Gilbert exposed himself continuously to enemy fire as he directed the aircraft, making it possible for their air strikes to cause 90 percent casualties among the Japanese first line of defense. For this action, he was awarded the Silver Star and promotion to lieutenant colonel.

After the war, Gilbert returned to his old law firm in Boston, but he left the firm in 1948 to join the Gillette Razor Company as vice president and treasurer. He quickly rose in the corporation to president, chairman, and chief executive officer.

Gilbert was a long-time advocate of liberal trade policies, and in 1961 he became president of the Committee for a National Trade Policy; this was a group of businessmen formed to lobby against import quotas and other restrictions on international commerce.

In 1969, President Nixon named Gilbert US special representative for trade negotiations, a position that carried the rank of ambassador. Because of his free trade stance, Gilbert was confirmed only after he had promised protectionist elements in Congress that he would protect American industries by taking a firmer approach in trade negotiations.

Gilbert resigned this position after two years. From 1973 until his death, he served as president of the Association of Independent Colleges and Universities in Massachusetts, lobbying on behalf of the fifty-nine schools and advising students on admissions and financial aid.

was one of the few OSS officers to support the Free French forces and to challenge the American view that the only effective resistance to the Japanese occupation was that of Ho Chi Minh's Viet Minh coalition. The French rewarded him by making him the only American officer to be awarded the Croix de Guerre in the field.

In August 1945, Ettinger apparently disobeyed orders to remain at the OSS base at Bakhoi and set sail instead for Vachay and Hongay on a French vessel with a French captain and crew. They received permission from the Viet Minh to take wounded or sick personnel to the French civilian hospital of Hongay, but, when the ship reached Hongay, it was boarded by the Viet Minh and Ettinger was taken prisoner. He was released only after prolonged negotiations on September 11, 1945. His captors claimed that they had not known that Ettinger was an American officer. His older sister remarked that he had been tortured during his week-long captivity and was unable to shake off the trauma of this experience. "He had a dreadful war," she said, and "he never completely recovered."[7]

The situation in the Pacific differed from that in Europe in a number of ways. Whereas OSS members in Europe dealt with underground groups that differed in politics rather than ethnicity, the men in the Pacific had to interact with remote tribesmen and try to secure their assistance. Burma, for example, was the site of what is now regarded as the most successful guerrilla operation ever carried out by US forces. Constantinos Christos Brelis was one of the Ritchie Boys involved in these operations. A graduate of the fifth class, Brelis—who would later adopt "Dean" as his first name—was the son of Greek immigrant parents. He was sent to Burma as a member of OSS Detachment 101, which killed or wounded more than fifteen thousand Japanese jungle troops and successfully destroyed their outposts and bridges while suffering the loss of only twenty-three of their number. As Brelis made clear in the history he cowrote with his commanding officer, William Peers, as well as in his novel *The Mission*, this success would never have been possible without the considerable assistance of Kachin tribesmen, who provided Detachment 101 with fighting troops, guides, and transport assistance.

Brelis's novel depicts the close relationship that an American soldier forms with his Kachin assistant, one that develops over time from suspicion to admiration to genuine, deep affection. The novel was closely based on his own experiences. During the Burma campaign, Brelis joined forces with radio operator Saw Judson and, with the considerable help of Kachin rangers, effectively ambushed Japanese forces and provided the coordinates for Allied bombing missions. As Colonel Peers wrote of the two officers, "Their activities, both operationally and intelligencewise, were a model of efficiency. They seemed to know the location of every Jap in the railway corridor. When the Air Corps hit a target designated by Dean and Saw, they knew everything about the target and got excellent results. Their raids and ambushes were carried out with comparable efficiency."[8] Brelis said this would not have been possible without the knowledge and assistance of the Kachin rangers.

Similar cooperation occurred in the Philippines, where Sergeant Estil Petty, a former policeman from Kentucky, negotiated with the Igorot tribesmen living in the mountains of northern Luzon. Sergeant Petty and Sergeant James Lindquist, a fellow CIC member of the Thirty-Third Infantry Division, went out with four of these tribesmen to survey the trails around Baguio and to make recommendations for the safe evacuation of the twelve thousand civilians who had been displaced by the incessant bombing of the city. Baguio was the summer capital of the Philippines, and many of the civilians were American and Allied nationals.

The two men came back with the recommendation that the Igorots take over the rescue operation because, despite their primitive lifestyle, the tribesmen were familiar with the territory and had the strength and endurance to make the trip as many times as necessary in order to rescue all the civilians. The Igorots carried out this assignment with admirable effectiveness. Movement on the "Refugee Trail" was slow-going and normally took seven to eight days. Because many of the civilians were greatly weakened from the poor diet they had endured in the wild, many had to be carried by their Igorot guides. Others died by the wayside. Most of them, however, were safely brought to the American lines, where they were met by personnel of the CIC and escorted to safety.

Alfred Cocumelli also served in the Philippines. The son of Italian immigrants, he was a popular campus band leader when he was a student at Ohio University. He was classified as chief photo interpreter when he graduated from the thirteenth class at Camp Ritchie. Cocumelli attributed part of his success to his work with the native Filipinos. The university alumni magazine described his exploits:

> Capt. Alfred R. Cocumelli, '44x, . . . was in charge of a photo inter-preting team attached to the 25th Infantry in the Philippines. His regiment broke all records—13+ days—for continuous fighting with-out a rest period. Early in the Luzon campaign Captain Cocumelli commanded a group of Philippine Scouts, some of them veterans of the Bataan "Death March," who aided in locating enemy positions and troop concentrations.[9]

In addition to gathering tactical information, Cocumelli organized the Filipino scouts so that they could continue to resist the Japanese after the Americans left. "That's when I met General Douglas MacArthur," Cocumelli said. "He sent me a rare autographed photo from our meeting signed, 'To Capt. Coke, Many thanks for a superior job—well done.'"[10]

It proved difficult to coordinate communications between ground troops and support aircraft, especially in the early fighting in the Pacific. It was rare for the air liaison parties attached to the infantry to call successfully upon the orbiting aircraft pilots overhead and to identify specific ground targets for bombing and strafing. Ritchie Boy Robert F. Goheen proved that it could be done. A graduate of the fifth class, with a specialization in photo interpretation, Goheen had been born and raised in India as the son of missionaries and had come to Camp Ritchie with fluency in French and Marathi, the third most commonly spoken language in India. Although he was a natural candidate for service in India, Goheen respectfully declined the assignment, giving as his reason "I knew that was going to be a British operation, basically, and I wanted to get much more involved on the American side of things."[11] After working in the War Department G-2 under Dean Rusk on the South-west Pacific, he was given the opportunity to go there as a lieutenant colonel. As G-2 of the First Cavalry Division in the Admiralty Islands, on Leyte, and on Luzon, he met up with his old Princeton classics professor, Marine captain Francis R. B. Godolphin, and the two formed a highly successful collaboration between ground troops and Marine aviators. Their work—in which the aviators successfully supported the dash of First Cavalry Division troops into Manila—is considered the biggest American success story of collaboration between ground troops and air liaison in the Pacific. For his services, Goheen was decorated with the Bronze Star with two oak leaf clusters, the Combat Infantryman's badge, and the Legion of Merit. Both Goheen and Godolphin returned to Princeton after the war. In 1957, Goheen became its president and then served as US ambassador to India under President Jimmy Carter.

James Mims was also part of a photo interpretation team that was sent first to New Guinea and then to the Philippines. It was a "typical" PI team in that it was made up of six men—two officers and four enlisted men—and outfitted with a jeep, a small trailer, and a truck. These vehicles were shipped in wooden crates. When the team members landed in New Guinea, they had to uncrate them, put the wheels on, and add side boards to the trailer. Their gear included a small kit for developing and printing photos. Although Staff Sergeant Mims was not involved in active combat, he was stationed close to the front with his team. Their task was to get and study the newest area photographs for tactical information and to pass it on to the Marines. Mims described a typical mission:

> There was a small dirt strip near Talomo called Libby Drome, and they would fly in there and come to us to get targets. Once we identified what we thought was some sort of Jap supply and dump and command post. We showed the photos to the pilots, who took off, but soon returned unable to find the site. We picked out a field that was shaped like a hand pointing directly toward the target. They took off again, quickly found the field and then the target. As we lazily swam in Davao Gulf in front of our command post, we watched as they dive bombed and strafed! Later we heard that we had been right, and that the Japs lost some high-ranking officers in that air attack.[12]

Some of the unsung heroes of the war were the technical experts who served on Enemy Equipment Intelligence Service (EEIS) teams in North Africa, Europe, and the Pacific. These men were drawn from the ninth and tenth classes at Camp Ritchie and had specialized in signal intelligence. The wartime mission of the EEIS was to go in and operate immediately in the rear of the front battle lines. Then, "whenever an enemy object—be it a tank, a mine, a microscope, or a haversack—came into American hands, it was pounced upon, given a battlefield examination and, if new or embodying improved features, tagged and sent to the rear for more careful examination and report: then shipped to the United States for detailed analysis and possible use in improving our own equipment."[13] The EEIS men had to act quickly, since the GIs were eager to seize Japanese "souvenirs." If it turned out that an object needed no detailed intelligence analysis in the United States, the equipment was sent to training areas such as Camp Ritchie, or else the captured weaponry was turned and used against the enemy, either to create tactical confusion or simply out of the need for more weaponry and ammunition. In these cases, the EEIS personnel instructed the GIs in the use of the Japanese equipment.

Although the men on these EEIS teams were sometimes called upon as interrogators, it was their technical ability rather than their linguistic skills that placed them in the field. Lieutenant Kurt Gustav Happe, for example, was German born but was sent to the Pacific without specialized training in Chinese or Japanese. The important qualification for his assignment was his electrical engineering background at Drexel University. Following his enlistment, he was sent to Harvard and MIT for specialized training in radar before joining an Observer Mission with Chinese Communist forces in Yenan, China, in 1945. Similarly, Captain Roger Merrill, who operated at the India-Burma border, had a BS degree in electrical engineering from Ohio State University.

While the EEIS teams in the European theater worked with large armies in relatively small land areas where equipment and communications services were abundant, those in the Pacific had few forces and little equipment and were dispersed over vast distances. As a consequence, they had to bring everything with them, both for headquarters and for field use. In the jungles of New Guinea and on the India-China border, they were even required to construct facilities from the ground up. One of the oldest of the Ritchie Boys, forty-five-year-old Lieutenant Colonel Robert E. Meeds, was sent to the wilderness roadway over the Himalayan "Hump" between India and China, and he recalled one especially frightening experience in the Naga Hills. His team had gone out to look for the electronic equipment of a wrecked Japanese airplane. During this mission, the men spent a night near a Naga village, where the Naga tribesmen placed a guard over them and then performed frightening torch rituals that caused the men to fear for their lives. Only in the morning did they learn that the Naga tribesmen had placed the guard and performed the torch ceremony in order to protect the team from evil spirits.[14]

When the Americans dropped an atomic bomb on Hiroshima, the Ritchie-trained forty-first OB team was serving with the Tenth Army on Okinawa. One of its team members, Sergeant Robert Potash, managed to see aerial photographs that were taken immediately after the bombing. He recalled that "[w]ith the stereoscope that was still part of my equipment and with my PI training, I was able to obtain a three-dimensional view of the devastation and show this to my colleagues. . . . We only had the photographs to look at for a short time, however, for somehow word got back to General Stilwell, and they were sent for and marked top secret." Even with these photos, he said, "Neither I nor any of my colleagues appreciated the full significance" of the bomb, "knowing nothing of the radiation damage that it caused." Since his OB team was now part of the Tenth Army's G-2 section, the men anticipated that a second bomb would be dropped, because of "two secret cables that we had seen, one before and the other just after the Hiroshima bombing. Each named several Japanese cities and warned allied aircraft to keep away from them." The Japanese surrender that followed upon the dropping of the second bomb on Nagasaki came as a huge relief to all of them: "It was like having a potential death sentence or physical disability removed from our future."[15]

But even with the September 2, 1945, signing of the Japanese surrender, it was necessary to reach isolated groups of Japanese soldiers scattered all over the Pacific and persuade them that the war was over and that they should lay down their arms. Captain Leonard Vader, the Dutch-born head of Potash's OB team, formed a small group that went to Kume Shima, an island that lay west of Okinawa in the East China Sea. He took along Nisei translator Jiro Arakaki and four Japanese prisoners whom he planned to have serve as mediators in securing the surrender of the Japanese forces on the island. Robert Potash went along as their guard. After locating the Japanese leader, negotiating meetings with him, and allowing him to bluster about his role as "protector" of the women from the African American troops stationed on the island, he and his troops handed over their weapons and signed the surrender document.

Meanwhile, intelligence officer Captain John Chafee was shipped off to Tsingtao in north China with the Sixth Marine Division in order both to accept the surrender of the last Japanese troops and to restore some kind of order to a country where Chiang Kai-shek and his Nationalists were gearing up to fight Mao and his Chinese Communist army. Back at home Americans jubilantly celebrated V-J Day, but, to the intelligence men in the field, it was clear that new wars were brewing in Asia.

Leonard Brostrom was the only Ritchie Boy to be awarded the Medal of Honor. COURTESY OF SHERMAN FLEEK

Captain Henry C. Whittlesey served with distinction on the "Dixie Mission" to China. SOURCE: SPECIAL COLLECTIONS & COLLEGE ARCHIVES, SKILLMAN LIBRARY, LAFAYETTE COLLEGE

Two American officers of the 101st Detachment with Japanese prisoners, each of whom is chained to a Kachin fighter. SOURCE: NATIONAL ARCHIVES AND RECORDS ADMINISTRATION

CHAPTER NINETEEN

Postwar Activities in Europe

I think that we're . . . beginning to realize that Peace, as well as war, must be organized and waged.

Without an alert and wise organization, without a constant sensitivity and reaction to threats whatsoever the source, Peace will remain a mere subject for babbling at cocktail parties, or brave but ineffectual struggle by small groups of people. It will remain what it has always been—a desperate and futile wish in the hearts of men.[1]

THE DOCUMENT OF GERMANY'S UNCONDITIONAL SURRENDER WAS negotiated and signed twice by all parties. It was first signed on May 7, 1945, at the SHAEF (Supreme Headquarters Allied Expeditionary Force) headquarters—a red brick schoolhouse in Reims, France—by representatives of the four Allied powers as well as by the Germans, who were represented by Colonel General Alfred Jodl at the behest of Hitler's designated successor, Admiral Karl Dönitz. The signing of this surrender proved unacceptable to the Russians, in part because they wanted amended terms regarding the laying down of German arms, and because they wanted its signatories to include representatives of all three branches of the German armed services as well as the German High Command. Their prime argument, however, was that the ceremony should not be performed on liberated French soil, but rather in Berlin, the seat of the government that had been responsible for the war; a Berlin signing would better recognize the major role the Soviets had played in defeating Hitler on the eastern front. This signing occurred on May 8. A Ritchie

Boy played a major role in both signings. As a fluent speaker of both German and Russian, Private George Bailey had been assigned to serve as Jodl's escort and interpreter at Reims. When not occupied with these duties, he was shuttled between the American and Russian offices to help coordinate terms of surrender. The next day he was asked to translate the May 7 document into Russian; this served as a basis for negotiating the amended, final document that was signed in Berlin.

One immediate concern on the American home front was finding and retrieving the bodies of loved ones lost in battle. Livio Vagnini, a graduate of Ritchie's fourth class and the first forensic chemist in the US Army's Criminal Investigation Division (CID), took on the task of running identification laboratories for the American Graves Registration Command. His work of finding and identifying the remains of American military men was centered in Liège, Belgium; the choice was no small coincidence, since many of the unknown dead had perished in this area during the Battle of the Bulge. Afterward, in 1948, Vagnini was invited to return to the CID as its chief forensic chemist, serving this time as a civilian. The division was now housed in a stately villa in Frankfurt am Main, and it provided the laboratory work needed in investigating felony crimes and serious violations of military law by US Army men. As chief forensic chemist, Vagnini was charged with analyzing anything from blood to food, narcotics, liquids, paint, glass, and poison.

The caseload of the Frankfurt laboratory increased exponentially in postwar Germany, rising from 453 criminal investigations of US soldiers in 1947 to 2,294 in 1954. Vagnini and his cohorts did not get involved in the conviction of suspects. Rather, it was their task simply to collect and analyze evidence and to report their findings to the proper military authorities. In most cases, that concluded their work on a particular case. Still, during his service at CID, Vagnini testified in more than 250 cases as an expert witness. He returned to the United States to serve as a forensic scientist and senior chemist in the CIA's Technical Services Division.

While Vagnini was working on investigating the felony crimes of US Army men, most of the Ritchie graduates were trying to identify the Germans who had willingly cooperated with the Nazi regime.

With the German surrender, many Nazi officers and government officials were trying to blend in with the civilian population and flee to the American zone, where they thought they would receive the best treatment by the Allied governments. Suddenly the Camp Ritchie interrogators had to shift their focus from information gathering and the study of enemy morale to ferreting out the Nazis hiding among the German civilians already in, or trying to enter, the American zone. They were also put in charge of interrogating Germans trying to get reinstated in their old civil service jobs: in law, education, and government. Here, too, it was necessary to determine whether an individual had been complicit in Nazism. For those who had been working in counterintelligence, this new focus in interrogation was not a difficult switch; now they were simply detecting old members of the Nazi party rather than Nazi spies. But the numbers of interrogations matched the most critical days of the war: each interrogator was required to interrogate several hundred Germans a day. Colonel Werner Michel, for example, was given the task of deciding which of the one hundred thousand German prisoners in his zone were major Nazi officials wanted for trial at Nuremberg. His team was involved in the arrests of hundreds of Nazis, many of them German generals.

Colonel Michel had been "dropped" from his Camp Ritchie class in order to fill the immediate postwar need for German-speaking servicemen. Like Colonel Michel, Lieutenant Hans Schmitt, of Camp Ritchie's twenty-sixth class, also arrived in Germany when the war was over. He was stationed in Bad Ems, one of the few towns left untouched by Allied bombs, and served there for fifteen months, interrogating displaced Germans. He had three missions: collecting military intelligence, screening prisoners for their political affiliations and segregating those who could not be released, and trying to identify participants in war crimes. In addition, he was to investigate black market activities among the prisoners. "My training had only prepared me for the first of these chores," Schmitt stated. "The rest I learned by doing, since the course of history proved too swift for the curriculum planners of the War Department." On his first working day he and his team began screening "tens of thousands of Germans of all ages and ranks":

This unkempt swarm of defeated enemy, confined to an open field surrounded by barbed wire—between the town of Ingelheim on the Rhine and the village of Sprendlingen—had been put to digging their latrine trenches, which, apart from a gaggle of soup kitchens, constituted the only "camp facilities." Here we toiled day and night to separate the innocent sheep from the Nazi wolves. Our goal was not only to keep the predators entrapped but to reduce as speedily as possible the number of mouths to be fed. It was especially urgent to return as many of this pathetic multitude to their former homes in what was to become the Russian zone of occupation.

This was more difficult than he had thought, since the Germans hoped to stay in the American zone. "Most men who passed my desk claimed Bavaria as home," Schmitt said, "making that southern state easily the most populous in Germany." Still, his team managed to shrink the numbers of interred:

Two-and-a-half-ton army trucks carted load after load of Germans to discharge centers or, if their rank and background placed them in one of the automatic arrest categories, to more permanent and, we hoped, secure detention camps. Those under arrest included officers of all services and paramilitary party formations above the rank of lieutenant colonel, party officials, and all ranks of the SS, as well as individuals whom we had reason to suspect of subversive intentions. Given the speed at which we had to work, this last became an extremely flexible category, including everyone we suspected of lying but could not grill long enough to determine the truth.[2]

But the interrogators soon discovered that their commanders were quite willing to look the other way in regard to many of those Germans who had contributed to—and benefited from—Hitler's tyranny. This was especially disturbing to the Ritchie Boys who had fled Nazi Germany. Many of them had lost close family members in the Nazis' work and death camps. Master Sergeant Victor Brombert (né Bromberg) discovered this betrayal early on:

I was assigned to work with a task force in charge of "de-Nazification" of the Saarland. . . . We were instructed to arrest—if we could find them—the likes of Kreisleiter (heads of a region) and lesser Nazi officials. It was an endeavor into which I threw myself with some zeal. . . . The only trouble was that within at most 48 hours, not only were [these detainees] set free again, they were put in charge of various town and city administrations. The U.S. military government insisted that the former Nazi officials were indispensable to run things. It was a comedy. We made arrests while our commanders, more concerned with maintaining law and order and nightly curfews than with the misdeeds of Nazi ideologues, reinstated these "able Germans," and indeed thanked us for having found them in their hiding places. They were needed to ensure that the streets were clean, to restore public utilities, and to maintain order. De-Nazification turned out to be [a] joke, as were the rules against fraternization with the German civilians. The black market flourished, and so did more intimate forms of commerce.[3]

In 1948, Brombert and most of his Ritchie colleagues would have been utterly appalled to learn that the "Butcher of Lyon," Klaus Barbie, was protected by the Americans because they considered his inside knowledge of French, German, and Russian intelligence more important than his horrific torture and murder of hundreds of French Jews and resistance fighters. Lieutenant Erhard Dabringhaus, a graduate of Ritchie's eighth class, was the first, and Captain Eugene Kolb of Ritchie's sixteenth class one of the last, who was ordered to protect Barbie and serve as liaison between him and US intelligence. During the summer and winter of 1948, Dabringhaus supervised Barbie while Barbie's network of spies gathered intelligence not only about Soviet activities in the Russian zone and in eastern Europe but also about Communist activity in France. Dabringhaus met three times a week with Barbie, took his reports, interpreted them, and sent them on to intelligence headquarters. "I put him in a nice house in Augsburg," he wrote. "Normally, I would arrest this guy." When at the end of the first month he was told to deliver an envelope to Barbie as the first monthly payment for his team of spies, Dabringhaus asked at headquarters, "You know you're working with a real war criminal?" "Yes, we know all about it," he was told. "But he's still valuable. In due time, we'll turn him over to the French."[4] "We had to pay this son of a bitch to get information from him," Dabringhaus grumbled.[5]

In 1948, French intelligence came to Dabringhaus on more than one occasion to ask about Barbie, but Dabringhaus was ordered to tell them nothing. "I felt very nauseated," he said. "Since he was a killer of French-men, I saw the urgency these people had in trying to get him. But orders are orders. . . . They had to go home empty-handed."[6] Once they had gathered all the intelligence that Barbie had to offer, the Americans facil-itated his escape to Bolivia instead of handing him over to the French. It was not until 1983 that Barbie was finally extradited to France and sen-tenced to life imprisonment. By then Dabringhaus had become a vocal critic of the United States' use of former SS officers as spies against one's former allies. Captain Kolb, however, declared that he hadn't known that Barbie was a war criminal. His only regret, Kolb said, was that the Barbie affair had "caused embarrassment to the Army intelligence community."[7]

Klaus Barbie was an extreme, but not isolated, case of the Americans putting nationalist and Cold War interests ahead of their own denazifica-tion policies. Reinhard Gehlen, who had been the head of Nazi military intelligence gathering on the eastern front, offered the US military him-self, his spy network, and his hidden intelligence archives in return for their freedom; these men were brought to the United States to become spies for the US government.

Americans as well as Russians raced to collect the thousands of Ger-man scientists and engineers who had served Hitler in building up his war machine. Both were especially eager to acquire the services of some three hundred scientists and technicians who had worked on guided missiles and rocket development at Peenemünde, on the Baltic island of Usedom. It was here that the world's first long-range guided ballistic missile had been developed. Called the V-2 ("Vergeltungswaffe 2," or "Retribution Weapon 2"), it was used to attack London, Antwerp, and Liège in retaliation for Allied bombing raids on German cities. These V-2 attacks caused the deaths of about nine thousand civilians and military personnel. In addition, thousands of forced laborers and concentration camp prisoners had been used as slave labor in Peenemünde, and thousands of them had died. Both the Russians and the Americans were eager to use the Peenemünde scientists in building up their defense systems. The Allies quite literally swept these scientists away from under the noses of their Russian counterparts. Men from Ritchie were involved in the secret transport of these and other scientists and technicians to the United States. Their mission was called "Operation Paperclip."

It was carried out by a twenty-five-man team of American enlisted men from PO Box 1142, of whom nineteen were Camp Ritchie graduates. All but three of the men were native-born Germans or Austrians. An officer, First Lieutenant Alois Schneider, was assigned to the team; not only was he a graduate of the third class at Camp Ritchie, but he also had served as a Ritchie instructor of enemy armies. Seven of the Ritchie men were sent to prepare a minimally fortified coastal defense fort called Fort Strong as a temporary holding base for what would eventually house several hundred German scientists and engineers. The fort was located on Long Island in the Boston harbor. The operation had to be kept secret, since American law forbade the entrance of enemy aliens into the United States. These scientists would have to be smuggled into the country.

Private Henry H. Kolm, a Viennese Jew, was one of the seven Ritchie men sent to Fort Strong to make the initial arrangements for housing and transport. Kolm and several of his classmates had begun the twenty-ninth class at Camp Ritchie but had been placed on alert and assigned to PO Box 1142 prior to graduation. Kolm's team arrived at Fort Strong on August 2, 1945; the first group of German scientists would arrive six and a half weeks later. Kolm recalled that his detachment faced an enormous task: "It was obvious that a large work force was required to divide the old barrack into individual rooms, restore the kitchen and mess hall into useable condition, repair the dock, mow the weeds, and tend to several hundred scientists, a few dozen at a time. The only crew we could count on to maintain secrecy was a crew of prisoners."[8] Forty to fifty German prisoners were brought in to work in construction, in the mess hall, and in offices at the camp. By pretending that they were a hospital operation, Kolm's team managed to get equipment, medical support, and rations for several hundred people. More important, they gained the services of an old mariner with a motorized whaler. He could meet the scientists at sea and transfer them to his sturdy craft before the harbor pilot met their transport.

On September 20, 1945, Werner von Braun and his brother Magnus were part of the first contingent to arrive at the Boston harbor. As they entered the harbor, a severe storm arose and lasted five days. It was a challenging transfer: "First we had to board the Corkum at our wobbly dock, and then we had to transfer a dozen seasick landlubbers and a lot of luggage from the fantail of a liberty ship to the much lower Corkum deck via a bosun's chair. The rough ride in the fish-smelling hold of a whaler and the rough debarkation at our dock is not what they had expected for their welcome to America."[9]

The pampered scientists—all of them illegal aliens—were interrogated and then assigned to centers around the country, where they contributed substantially to the United States' defense and space programs.

In the meantime, Ritchie men remained active in Europe, not only interrogating Germans but also reestablishing newspapers and radio stations. The Camp Sharpe Mobile Radio Broadcasting Companies (MRBCs) were dissolved and the men transferred from the control of the Psychological Warfare Division to service in the Information Control Division, or ICD, where their duties shifted from wartime propaganda to denazification and reeducation in the American democratic tradition. Many of the Camp Ritchie intellectuals relished the change. Hans Habe used his best writers to edit the regional newspapers being reintroduced into the conquered territories. Those who had not yet completed their term of service by the conclusion of the war then stayed on to work with Habe on *Die Neue Zeitung* [The New Newspaper], a paper directed to German readers throughout the US occupied military zone. It was initially published twice weekly but later expanded to six issues a week.

Habe, who had now been promoted to major, had his first and last meeting with General Eisenhower regarding the establishment of this paper. It was not a happy occasion. Habe was eager to reeducate the Germans by printing exemplary articles by the "good" Germans who had rejected Nazism throughout its twelve-year reign of terror, whereas

Eisenhower placed his emphasis on collective German guilt. "We don't want to entertain the Germans," the general stated, "but to instruct them. You've got to keep that in mind all the time." When Habe protested that the Americans could not force the Germans to buy the newspaper if it didn't make some concessions to its readers, Eisenhower simply stated, "We aren't here to make concessions."[10] He then dictated a statement to be printed on the front page of the first issue. In it, he decreed:

> *Denazification must be pursued with all means at our disposal. This applies not only to Party members, but to all who have, in one way or another, profited from National Socialism. There are no indispensable National Socialists anywhere. National Socialism must be destroyed, and all members of the N.S.D.A.P. and its affiliated organizations must be removed from their posts.*[11]

This issue appeared on October 18, 1945. General Eisenhower's directive was largely ignored by OMGUS (the Office of Military Government, United States), as were a number of his other directives, such as his strict rules against American fraternization with Germans.

It seemed, in fact, as if there were no consistent policy regarding the military government's policies in Germany. One ICD directive, understandable perhaps in light of the newspaper's German readership, directly contradicted the politics in Washington, DC, when it ordered Habe not to publish anything critical of the Soviet Union. Habe received this order even as the House Un-American Activities Committee was made a permanent standing committee in Washington and began focusing its investigations on the activities of real and suspected Communists in the United States. This conflict of American interests resulted in an absurd situation in the offices of *Die Neue Zeitung*. Ritchie Boy Stefan Heym, whom Habe had put in charge of reporting foreign affairs, was recalled to Washington at the end of 1945 and discharged from the army because of pro-Communist leanings, while in Germany Habe and his colleague Hans Wallenberg were severely reprimanded by the ICD for publishing an article critical of actions taken by the Russians in Silesia and the Sudetenland.

Another conflict arose over the cultural pieces in the newspaper. In truth, the ICD was not interested in cultural politics, whereas it was the heart of Habe's reeducation program. It was Habe's complaint that the Americans equated "reeducation" with "Americanization" and that they defined culture as "popular culture" instead of in the European sense of "higher culture." Nevertheless, the newspaper published occasional booklets to teach the Germans American ways, such as *Jeder lernt Englisch* [English for Everyone] and *Kleiner Kursus im Baseball-Spiel* [A Short Course in Baseball]. When Habe left the newspaper in 1949 in order to try new ventures in Germany and the United States, *Die Neue Zeitung* was considered the most important newspaper in postwar Germany. "I had served America, my new home, to the best of my belief," Habe remarked. "I had made a modest contribution to Germany's intellectual, moral, and economic rebirth."[12]

Ritchie Boys were active in all avenues of media and entertainment in the American zone of occupation. From 1945 to 1948, Benno Frank served as chief of theater and music for the US military government in Germany, reestablishing theaters throughout the American occupied zone and navigating the rocky path of what OMGUS considered acceptable and unacceptable theater fare. Actor and Ritchie graduate Peter van Eyck served for three years as a control officer for film. He, too, grew frustrated with the American military government's arbitrary censoring of "questionable content" and quit at the same time Frank did, remarking, "The situation in Berlin became more and more untenable— all our old mistakes had their revenge."[13] Ironically, when the military government's taboo on fraternization was dropped as subject matter for films, van Eyck starred in *Hallo, Fräulein!* (1949), a musical in which van Eyck played the role of an American soldier. Until that time, van Eyck had appeared only in American films, and always as a German. In the publicity for this 1949 German film, however, he was promoted as an "American" film star.

Radio was restored almost immediately in Germany. At first reinstatement of programming was totally under army control. The task was a twofold one: first restoring radio capabilities, and then gradually transforming what had been German state radio to private regional stations. The Americans in psychological warfare worked primarily with three stations in the American zone: Radio Munich, Radio Stuttgart, and Radio Frankfurt. To make their task as seamless as possible, they all received programming from Radio Luxembourg during the first months of operation, and many of the men who had worked in Luxembourg were sent to work with opening the three new stations.

In the months that followed, each of these stations took on more independent programming. Radio Frankfurt is a good example. David Berger, of the Fourth and Fifth MRB companies, and Curt Jellin of the Second, both German-born Jews, worked at getting the station reestablished. Soon Curt Jellin was airing his own program, while Bulgarian-born composer Boris Kremenliev presented on-air concerts as Radio Frankfurt's first music director. Then, when the station was granted a charter as an independent German station, it remained under Ritchie Boy control, since actor Fred Lorenz took on the role of station director.

Radio Bremen was something of an anomaly. The north German city of Bremen and its port town of Bremerhaven were a small American enclave within the British zone, and they were greatly overshadowed by the city of Hamburg. Edward E. Harriman, a graduate of Camp Ritchie's twenty-second class, had been assigned to the Seventh Army and was one of the liberators of the Dachau concentration camp. He was then named "chief of operations" to Bremen with the task of reopening the Bremen radio station. Harriman felt personally responsible not only for restoring the radio station in Bremen but also for ensuring its continued existence. The old station had been demolished by Allied bombs, and Harriman had to start from scratch. He requisitioned a villa in the residential section of the city, refitted and transformed it into a broadcasting studio, and, at 3:00 p.m. on Christmas Eve 1945, made the first broadcast from the balcony of the Bremen town hall to startled shoppers in the city square. The Bremen town mayor, Wilhelm Kaisen, then took over the microphone and gave a Christmas speech. After being discharged from the army in 1946, and enjoying a brief trip to the United States to get married and to honeymoon on Nantucket Island, Harriman returned with his wife to Bremen to continue working with the studio. He left Bremen and returned to the United States only when the future of Radio

Bremen as an independent public radio station—Germany's smallest—had been assured.

Just as Harriman is remembered with admiration in Bremen, David Berger is admired by broadcasters throughout the German Allied zones. After getting Radio Frankfurt on strong footing, he worked for Voice of America from 1946 to 1955 as editor and commentator on political and cultural matters. More important, when he came to WQXR New York as writer-producer in 1955, the Association of German Broadcasters asked him to be its representative in the United States. He did this by creating two programs that, for twenty-nine years, brought the best in German music and performance to this country. The first, *Music from Germany*, broadcast weekly on more than seventy American radio stations, and it was instrumental in introducing an American public to contemporary German composers such as Boris Blacher, Hans Werner Henze, and Karlheinz Stockhausen; it also provided German singers and instrumentalists with their first airings in the United States. The second, *Germany Today*, was broadcast over one hundred radio stations on college and university campuses, and it presented interviews with German cultural icons such as singers Lotte Lenya and Edda Moser, conductors Rafael Kubelík and Kurt Masur, and novelist Günter Grass. Berger even interviewed Harlem-born Dean Dixon, an African American classical musician who spent thirteen years conducting Radio Frankfurt's symphony orchestra. Berger's broadcasts became an important cultural bridge between Germany and the United States and served to reconcile the two countries.

Although Germany—and the city of Berlin—were almost immediately divided into four sectors (French, British, American, and Russian), the four occupying powers came together one last time for a trial of the major German war criminals at an International Military Tribunal (IMT) that was held in Nuremberg, Germany, from November 20, 1945, to October 1, 1946. Twelve more trials would be held at Nuremberg under the sole auspices of the Americans.

During preparations for the International Military Tribunal, eighty-six leading Nazi politicians, generals, and SS officers were housed in the spa town of Mondorf-les-Bains, Luxembourg, in what had formerly been a luxury hotel. Here the prisoners were to be processed and interrogated prior to their removal to Nuremberg. Eventually fifteen of them were sent to Nuremberg for trial before the IMT; the others were prosecuted in later trials. Luxembourg native John Dolibois, a graduate of Ritchie's eighteenth class, served on the five-man interrogation team assigned to Mondorf-les-Bains. Under the guise of "welfare officer," he played the role of sympathetic liaison officer between the prisoners and his fellow interrogators. Ironically, Hermann Göring unwittingly suggested this ploy when he visited Dolibois's room and asked whether this was Dolibois's function. The scheme worked remarkably well:

> *Gradually, a pattern evolved. An interrogator would work with a prisoner. Later I might drop in on the prisoner to inquire about his health or to check if he needed anything. With the interrogation fresh in his mind, the internee often felt compelled to talk about it, to set the record straight. He might recall something he had wanted to tell his interrogator. Or he would complain that the facts had been distorted by someone else, a colleague or fellow officer.*[14]

The prisoners were held at "Camp Ashcan" for four months; then those to be tried by the IMT were transferred to holding cells in the Nuremberg Palace of Justice for further questioning. During the trial, Dolibois would serve as liaison between the documents collections of the Military Intelligence Service Center in Oberursel and the Nuremberg prosecutors.

More than one hundred former Ritchie students now were assigned to the US military trials held in Nuremberg and at Dachau. Those whose terms of service were ending were encouraged to apply for these assignments.

Staff Sergeant George Sakheim, for example, was in Paris, waiting to return to the United States, when he saw a US Army sign recruiting German-speaking interpreters for the Nuremberg trials. He signed up, flew to Nuremberg, and became one of thirty language specialists on the US prosecution team of the International Military Tribunal. There were even more Camp Ritchie interpreters/translators used during the interrogations leading up to the trial; they assisted in questioning both defendants and potential witnesses. Sergeant Gunter Kosse was one of these. He recalled how his Camp Ritchie training, together with his German background, assisted the prosecuting attorneys. He sometimes advised the attorneys on the type of questions they should ask and even on how to phrase them in order to get the correct answer. In effect, he was not just an interpreter but also a co-interrogator of top Nazi officials. He even spent several hours a day carrying on ad hoc conversations with Hermann Göring.

George Sakheim worked as an interpreter during the actual trial. He described his duties this way: "During the trial sessions, we interpreted various languages into English, French and Russian, and we also interpreted the various languages into German, primarily for the defendants and their attorneys. All present—including journalists and other observers—were given headphones and could 'dial up' whichever of the four interpretation languages they preferred." The trial was the first to employ simultaneous interpretation during its proceedings.

The courtroom questioning was conducted by a prosecutor, who was usually both an attorney and a military officer. Like Kosse, Sakheim emphasized the knowledge required for a prosecutor to do a good job, and the important role the interpreter played in providing it:

> *The interpreter had to be fully multilingual and also possess knowledge of the organization of the German state and military, the Nazi Party, the SS and the Gestapo. Also present was a court reporter, who utilized a stenotype machine to prepare complete transcripts in English. Each transcript was checked for accuracy by the interrogator, the interpreter, and the defendant or witness, who was then directed to sign it. Security was provided by two white-helmeted military policemen bearing side arms.* [15]

First Lieutenant Gustave Gilbert, an American-born Jew, was somewhat older than most of his Ritchie classmates and already had a PhD in psychology when he entered its twenty-first class. He served throughout the first Nuremberg trial as prison psychiatrist, with complete freedom of access to the prisoners. Gilbert was able both to observe and to converse with all of them. As the only American officer on the prison staff who could speak German, Gilbert found them willing and eager to talk. And as the American military's chief psychologist, he provided testimony during the trial in which he attested to the sanity of Hitler's deputy Führer Rudolf Hess. Gilbert kept a diary of his daily findings and published part of them in 1947 as *Nuremberg Diary*. This diary was republished just before the Adolf Eichmann trial in 1961, and Gilbert testified at his trial in Jerusalem.

There were many other trials of war criminals held by the US military, and the Ritchie Boys were active throughout. Alfred M. Wolleyhan, from the sixth Ritchie class, served as assistant counsel at the third Nuremberg trial. Known as the "Justice Case," it tried sixteen German jurists for war crimes and crimes against humanity by "judicial murder and other atrocities . . . committed by destroying law and justice in Germany."[16] More specifically, the jurists were charged with implementing the eugenics laws of the Third Reich in order to further the Nazi plan for racial purity. It was, as one scholar has put it, "a remarkable constellation in which lawyers debated with other lawyers over a cast of defendants who were also lawyers, and all of them awaited the final judgment by yet another panel of lawyers."[17] Ten were found guilty and sentenced to prison terms ranging from five years to life.

Even as the Nuremberg trials proceeded, American military court tribunals were going on at Dachau, where its trials were held from November 1945 until December 1947 within the walls of the former German concentration camp. These trials focused on crimes committed at the German camps (Dachau, Buchenwald, Flossenburg, Mauthausen, Nordhausen, and Mühldorf) and their subsidiaries, as well as crimes against downed fliers and prisoners of war. By the time this military court adjourned, it had tried 1,672 alleged war criminals in 489 cases at Dachau. According to a senior researcher for the Simon Wiesenthal Center for Holocaust Studies in Los Angeles, 260 received death sentences (although some were later commuted), and 498 were given prison terms.[18]

One of Ritchie's older graduates, Lieutenant William R. Perl, from the sixth class, received the dubious distinction of serving as chief interrogator at the trial of seventy-three Waffen-SS members accused of the Malmedy massacre of eighty-four American prisoners of war and nearly one hundred Belgian civilians during the Battle of the Bulge. Until 1938, Perl had practiced law in Vienna; he was a passionate Zionist who had organized large-scale Jewish emigration from Europe to Palestine in violation of British law. Now he was interrogating alleged war criminals accused of murdering American soldiers and civilians. He managed to extract a number of confessions, and, in the final judgment, all but one of the defendants was found guilty to some degree. Forty-three of them were sentenced to death by hanging; the rest received prison sentences ranging from ten years to life. As commanding officer of the Sixth Panzer Army, Josef "Sepp" Dietrich received a twenty-year sentence.

The trial's chief defense lawyer, Colonel Willis M. Everett Jr. of Atlanta, initially appealed the convictions, saying that the men's confessions had been coerced through torture. In 1949, a subcommittee of three US senators was convened to investigate the matter. Senator Joseph McCarthy of Wisconsin gained permission to attend the meetings, spoke up frequently and vociferously, and demanded that Perl be given a lie detection test. When the subcommittee members demurred, they were widely accused of whitewashing the whole affair. Still, politics dictated that the forty-three death sentences be commuted to life sentences, and then to time served. Whether the defendants' claims were true or not, they left a stain on the proceedings and, in particular, on Perl's role as chief interrogator.

Although denazification was a priority of nearly all the men from Ritchie, many expressed doubts about the validity and effectiveness of the trials. Walter Rapp, who worked as chief of the Evidence Division at Nuremberg, strongly defended them, arguing that the absence of trials at the close of World War I had created an impression in Germany that the German generals "were or are kind, highly educated old gentlemen who would never have considered doing the kinds of things of which they were accused." Now, however, "the generals' true faces have . . . been exposed . . . for what they really are." This revelation would ensure "that in the future the population will never place blind trust in a general."[19]

Werner Michel, who had supplied prisoners and documents for the Nuremberg and Dachau trials, felt that this tactic misfired. Since the top echelon of the German military and political figures were proven guilty, he said, the average German now considered himself guiltless.[20]

George Bailey found the trial "Kafkaesque," since the crimes of a state were being pinned on a few individuals. He was especially outspoken in his defense of the German generals. He considered it hypocritical of the tribunal to sentence General Jodl to death simply for performing his duties as a good soldier. Bailey had studied Jodl at Reims as well as at the IMT trial, and he had determined that Jodl was "a soldier bound by oath to obey; he had not been allowed to resign; he could protest, as he had, but then he was bound to obey." Bailey claimed that the professional Allied military men sensed this truth from the first. At the very time Jodl was being tried and sentenced to death for performing his duty, for example, Bailey and his cohorts in Russian Liaison were facing their own conflict of conscience: "Just when the 'civilized world' was sitting in judgment of the major war criminals whose crime consisted in failing to disobey the orders of the führer, we in Russian Liaison were plagued by our consciences for obeying the directive to turn back all Soviet defectors to the Red Army." As a consequence, when Jodl was sentenced to death as a war criminal, "I met more than a few American and British officers at Nuremberg who swore a blue streak when they learned of the sentence."[21]

The International Military Tribunal became a major bone of contention among legal scholars. The Hague Convention of 1907 had criminalized the murder of foreign citizens and of prisoners of war, thereby making actions that the Germans took against civilians in France or in Poland crimes. But there was not—before Nuremberg—any international convention that punished a state, or individuals of a state, for murdering its own citizens.

Nuremberg changed all that. Under the auspices of the United Nations, two ad hoc International Criminal Tribunals were established in response to the war atrocities committed during the Yugoslav wars (1993) and to the Rwandan genocide (1994). In 2002, a permanent International Criminal Court was established at the Hague to "[try] individuals for genocide, war crimes, crimes against humanity, and aggression." As a legacy of Nuremberg, it, too, has had a contentious history.

German rocket scientists (104 in total) are brought to the United States in "Operation Paperclip" in 1946. SOURCE: IMPERIAL WAR MUSEUM

Hans Habe, seated at his desk surrounded by his core of newspaper men. From left to right: #2 Ernst Wynder, #3 Konrad Kellen, #5 Stefan Heym, #6 Louis Atlas, #7 Peter Wyden, #9 Joseph Eaton. SOURCE: UNITED STATES HOLOCAUST MEMORIAL MUSEUM; GIFT OF JOSEPH EATON

Edward Harriman and his wife shopping at the PX in Bremen.
SOURCE: NATIONAL ARCHIVES AND RECORDS ADMINISTRATION

Staff Sergeant George Sakheim (lower left) worked as a translator at the International Military Tribunal in Nuremberg. COURTESY OF DAVID SAKHEIM

Postwar Activities in the Pacific

Grandmother was still alive during the war. And so I decided to visit her. And she had evacuated to a village up in the hills called Yatsuo in Toyama. . . . And I remember the feeling I had. You know, here I'm visiting Grandma as a sort of a conquering soldier, but at the same time, I want her to accept me—all the people around her—to accept me as one of them, you know, that kind of complex kind of feeling.[1]

ALTHOUGH THE FOCUS AT CAMP RITCHIE WAS ON THE WAR IN THE European theater, there had been a rising Japanese presence at the camp for some time. The Pacific Military Intelligence Research Section—PACMIRS—had been set up there in September 1944 to coordinate document research services in the Pacific theater. In addition to the Nisei assigned to PACMIRS, thirty-three Nisei joined a few Japanese-speaking Caucasians as members of Ritchie's twenty-ninth class. The camp also made instructors and training aids available to the Military Intelligence Service Japanese Language School at Fort Snelling, Minnesota.

After V-E Day, Camp Ritchie shifted the emphasis of all its training programs from the European war to the war in the Pacific. Ritchie's thirty-first class began on July 26, 1945; this was the last of the large, traditional eight-week classes at Ritchie and the last to have a concentration on Japanese Order of Battle. In May and June, however, Camp Ritchie had already formed sixteen new Mobile Intelligence Training Units (MITUs). These replaced the old Composite School Unit; their assignment was to study Japanese weaponry, uniforms, and battle techniques and to learn the material well enough to communicate it to the GIs who were going to fight in the Pacific. They would then be sent out as demonstration teams to infantry replacement centers around the country.

In summer 1945, everyone was anticipating an Allied invasion of Japan, but the bombing of Hiroshima and Nagasaki on August 6 and August 9, respectively, brought a speedy conclusion to the war. All at once the Nisei who had not been allowed to fight in the Pacific were in high demand for all aspects of military occupation. In September 1945, a new two-week course was given at Camp Ritchie to orient German Order of Battle teams in Japanese Order of Battle for Occupational Redeployment in the Pacific, while a new four-week course trained new CIC (Counterintelligence Corps) personnel for Occupational Duties in the Far East. About half the Nisei who had been assigned to the MITUs took this course and then were sent on to Camp Holabird for more intense training in counterintelligence. The other half were sent to the MIS school at Fort Snelling for concentrated language training.

The men who had been assigned to the special Mobile Intelligence Training Units at Camp Ritchie had varying degrees of fluency. Some could speak, read, and write Japanese with little difficulty. Others, like Maya Miyamoto, knew only those few Japanese words and phrases they had picked up in their demonstrations of weaponry and battle tactics at Camp Ritchie. Miyamoto would be sent to the CIC course at Camp Holabird and then serve as head of the army's motor pool in Tokyo.

Meanwhile, as supreme commander of all US Army forces in the Pacific, General Douglas MacArthur held the Japanese surrender ceremony on board the USS *Missouri* battleship in Tokyo Bay on September 2, 1945.

The postwar situation in Japan differed from Germany's in several important respects. First, the Allied forces had never had to invade Japan prior to Japan's surrender. Also, Japan's supreme leader, Emperor Hirohito, did not commit suicide as Hitler had; rather, he had gone on the radio to legitimize Japan's surrender. This was the first time the Japanese population had ever heard the emperor's voice, and the effect was electrifying.

And finally, despite Soviet attempts to the contrary, the US military did not have to share postwar governance with its allies. There was some minor Allied involvement in postwar Japan—the British Commonwealth provided an occupation force, a few Allied troops were stationed there, and there was some multinational judicial involvement in the International Military Tribunal in Tokyo—but the reality was that General MacArthur, as supreme commander for the Allied powers, dictated the reshaping of Japan. And as Allied commander of the Japanese occupation, it was MacArthur who directed the demobilization of the Japanese military forces and the prosecution of war criminals.

In October 1945, the PACMIRS Nisei arrived in Tokyo to collect books and military documents to add to the stateside collections and to identify anything that could be used as evidence of Japanese war crimes. Yoshiaki Fujitani related that many of the books had been collected from Japanese libraries, mostly university libraries, and brought to one of the larger halls in the First Tokyo Arsenal. These were all kinds of books, not just military ones. "These books were just thrown on the floor, and we went through them," he said. "And we all wondered what's going to happen to them, those that we didn't select. And we suspected that they would all be thrown away, you know, just discarded. And so we had raided the libraries . . . of all the books there, selected what we wanted, and just discarded the rest."[2]

This assignment took five to six months. Then the lower-grade soldiers returned to the United States to work with these materials in the Washington Document Center, which had absorbed the PACMIRS collections while the men had been in Tokyo. The PACMIRS WACs moved to Washington as well. The PACMIRS master sergeants remained in Tokyo to assist in the International Military Tribunal for the Far East, better known as the Tokyo War Crimes Tribunal.

Stateside, Camp Ritchie contributed directly to the trials as well. Before its merger with the Washington Document Center, the Ritchie PACMIRS staff had begun publishing a War Crimes Information Series, beginning in mid-November 1945. By the time of the merger with the Washington Document Center in April 1946, PACMIRS had produced twenty issues; in some of these cases, specific materials were translated and published at the request of the War Crimes Office.

Meanwhile, the Japanese emperor presented MacArthur with a problem: Hirohito was personally responsible for giving many of the orders for actions that were clearly provable war crimes. For all those angered by MacArthur's decision that Hirohito and his sons would not be put on trial, MacArthur had to create a diversion. He did this by mounting show trials in Manila almost immediately after the surrender. While later trials of war criminals would be held in Tokyo with the cooperation and participation of the United States' allies, the Manila trials were held solely under US auspices or, rather, under General MacArthur's tight control. Hampton Sides described the situation in writing about the Manila trial of Masaharu Homma, the general who had forced the American surrender of the Philippines on May 6, 1942: "As the Supreme Allied Commander of the Pacific Theater, Douglas MacArthur was responsible for selecting the venue, the defense, the prosecution, the jury, and the rules of evidence in the trial of a man who had beaten him on the battlefield."[3]

The earlier trial of Tomoyuki Yamashita established the precedent. On October 9, 1944, Yamashita had assumed command of the Fourteenth Area Army to defend the Japanese-occupied Philippines. Although it was clear at the time that he could not defeat the American forces, he was determined to use delaying tactics as long as possible in order to prevent the Americans from landing on the Japanese mainland. After losing three-quarters of his forces, he surrendered on September 3, 1945, and, on October 29, he was put on trial for crimes and atrocities committed in the Philippines against civilians and prisoners of war.

Baldwin Eckel interrogated Yamashita soon after he was taken prisoner. Since leaving the German program at Camp Ritchie, Eckel had become one of the army's most proficient interrogators. Yamashita's trial was rushed; MacArthur wanted him to be convicted on December 7— the fourth anniversary of the Japanese attack on Pearl Harbor. Yamashita's defense team pointed out that there was no evidence that Yamashita had approved of any atrocities or that he'd even known of them; indeed, the February Manila massacre, with its brutal mutilations, rapes, and murders of thousands of Philippine civilians, had been carried out by naval forces not under his command. Nevertheless, he was found guilty and sentenced to death. Appeals to MacArthur, to the Philippine and the United States Supreme Courts, and to President Truman were fruitless; they all allowed the conviction to stand.

Yamashita was hanged on February 23, 1946. The action—or inaction—of the US Supreme Court set a precedent, known as the Yamashita Standard, which stated that a commander could be held accountable for the crimes committed by his troops even if he did not order or permit them, and even if he did not have the means to stop them. This standard is now part of the Geneva Conventions and has been adopted by the International Criminal Court at the Hague.

It was a decision deeply disturbing to those Ritchie men who knew the true situation. Lieutenant Stephen B. Ives Jr. had served as the responsible Japanese Order of Battle officer in the G-2 section of the US Sixth Army, and he had closely followed the actions of the Japanese military on Luzon. He stated, "I was troubled that Yamashita was to be held responsible for actions I knew he couldn't possibly have known of or prevented. I knew of nothing that reflected dishonorably on him." Ives was, in fact, so concerned that he told his commanding officer of his willingness to help Yamashita's defense team. "He strongly discouraged me," Ives reported, "saying the conviction was already settled and there was nothing I could do. To my continuing regret, I accepted his advice." What followed, he said, "was a predictable travesty of justice." Ives knew that Yamashita's conviction was "designed primarily to reduce pressure to try the [Japanese] emperor." As a consequence, "this prior objective led the US military to reach a political, rather than legal, decision."[4]

MacArthur dealt with the emperor in a different way. Hirohito was now fully subservient to the wishes of the American occupying forces. Since MacArthur was convinced that it would create chaos if the Americans were to remove Hirohito from his throne, Japan's new constitution kept the monarchy but reduced Hirohito's role from emperor/god to that of a mere symbol of state. As a figurehead, the once-distant Hirohito now toured the country, ostensibly to oversee reconstruction efforts. MacArthur was clearly the man in charge. As one of the Ritchie men, Victor

Matsui, put it, the Japanese "regarded [him] as a kind of shogun."⁵ Before the International Military Tribunal for the Far East—or Tokyo War Crimes Tribunal—convened on April 29, 1946, the Americans worked behind the scenes to make sure that the defendants did not implicate the emperor in their testimony. As a result, General Hideki Tōjō, who had served as Japan's prime minister and war minister from 1941 until 1944, was made to bear sole responsibility for the attack on Pearl Harbor and for the conduct of the war. He was one of seven defendants hanged for war crimes and crimes against humanity. Sixteen others were sentenced to life imprisonment.

In Japan, as in Germany, some war criminals managed to negotiate a deal and receive immunity from prosecution. The most notable of these, Shiro Ishii, had been the director of Unit 731, a biological warfare unit of the Imperial Japanese Army. He and his unit had engaged in forced experiments on civilians and prisoners of war, resulting in the deaths of more than ten thousand people. Hundreds of thousands more had died as a result of Japan's unleashing of deadly chemical weapons on civilian populations. Toward the end of the war, Ishii had even developed a plan to send fifteen planes on a nighttime mission to drop plague-infected fleas over San Diego, California, in an effort to spread the bubonic plague throughout the area; this was an action that had already been performed successfully on the Chinese cities of Changde and Ningbo. Now, however, Ishii was offering the Americans full access to his research materials, and American microbiologists were eager to take him up on the offer. As Dr. Edwin Hill, head of the US Biological Weapons Program at Fort Detrick, Maryland, put it, Ishii's "absolutely invaluable" information "could never have been obtained in the United States because of scruples attached to experiments on humans." By providing immunity, Hill said, Ishii's information was obtained "fairly cheaply." None of the judges at the Tokyo trials were informed of the matter.⁶

The Japanese people paid little heed to the proceedings of the tribunal, since they were preoccupied with their own personal survival. Yoshiaki Fujitani was struck by the fact that, although the young busboys working in the soldiers' cafeteria "all looked like me," they were malnourished. "I mean, they're under-nourished. They looked a little bit skinnier than they should be. And they'd go around, in fact, begging for food, and so on. And that was pretty sad to see."[7] Because of the nearly total destruction of Japan's major cities and its lack of government agencies, food shortages raged throughout the country; this problem was aggravated by the influx of more than 5.1 million repatriated Japanese who began pouring back into the country as soon as the war was over. Two of MacArthur's first decrees, issued immediately upon his arrival in Tokyo on August 30, 1945, were that no Allied personnel were to assault any of the Japanese, and no Allied personnel were to eat the scarce Japanese food.[8] He immediately set up a food distribution network, but millions of people continued to live on the brink of starvation for several years. One incident struck Fujitani with particular force:

One day, I visited the PX and bought a can of candy which I thought of giving to my cousins who lived there in Tokyo. . . . And I was walking down the street, I was approached by a man begging for food. Saying, "Can you give me something."

And all I had was the can, so I said, "Well, have this." And so I gave it to him. And the thought in my mind was, wow, it's so sad that he's begging for his family, and all I can give is this can of candy which will be gone in maybe a day. How much they must be suffering. . . . And I thought [that], well, maybe because— . . . because they're Japanese—because I look like them, or they look like me.[9]

Many of the Camp Ritchie men assigned to postwar Japan worked as interrogators. Baldwin Eckel and Masaru J. "Mas" Jinbo interviewed high-ranking Japanese military officers and government officials in preparation for the Tokyo Tribunal. Woodrow Wakatsuki tracked down black marketeers and confiscated their goods. Fred Nishizawa worked at a repatriation camp just outside the port city of Maizuru as an interrogator of Japanese citizens returning from China and other Asian countries. Roy T. Takai also served there; his team processed the first shipload of Japanese repatriates from Siberia. Ralph Yoohachi Nishime, who had a ham operator's license, was assigned to investigate former Japanese POWs who had been captured by the Soviets and then returned to Japan as radio agents.

There were, of course, cases of scapegoating. George S. Guysi, a graduate of Camp Ritchie's seventh class with a specialization in counterintelligence, was made the case officer of the Tokyo Metropolitan CIC detachment in charge of the investigations concerning Allied personnel who had broadcast for the Japanese during wartime over Radio Tokyo. One of the men he interrogated at length was a British-born Australian army captain, Charles Cousens, who had been captured during the fall of Singapore and shipped to Japan. There he'd been pressured to work as propaganda broadcaster, script writer, and producer at Radio Tokyo. He was put in charge of a propaganda variety program called *Zero Hour*. For this show Cousens enlisted the services of Iva Toguri D'Aquino. She had been working in the office as a typist; Cousens had known her from her actions of smuggling food into the nearby prison camp where he had been held. She agreed to serve as a program announcer as long as he did not force her to say anything against the United States. He agreed. After the war, Cousens was ordered to stand trial for treason, and Guysi was recalled to Australia as a witness. Before the trial could begin, the charges were dropped.

Toguri did not fare as well. She was named by two newsmen as the infamous "Mata Hari of the Airwaves" popularly known as Tokyo Rose. She was arrested but released after a year for lack of evidence. However, when Toguri applied to return to the United States, gossip columnist Walter Winchell lobbied against her and anti-Japanese sentiments in California were reawakened; although Cousens spoke out at the trial in her defense, she was sentenced to ten years in prison. Guysi had interviewed Toguri and also spoke in her defense. "It was and is inconceivable to me," he wrote in 1976, "that the United States would try Mrs. D'Aquino for treason without first trying others whose conduct was far more questionable to matters of degree." "[T]here were quite a few women announcers on Radio Tokyo, some of whom at one time held American citizenship," he added. "Only Mrs. D'Aquino was tried."[10] That same year Guysi went on the CBS news program *60 Minutes* to speak on her behalf. It was partly because of Guysi's and Cousens's efforts and the extensive labors of an investigative reporter for the *Chicago Tribune* that President Gerald Ford gave Toguri a full and unconditional pardon on his last full day of office. And in January 2006, the World War II Veterans Committee awarded Toguri its annual Edward J. Herlihy Citizenship Award for "her indomitable spirit, love of country, and the example of courage she has given her fellow Americans."[11]

Other Ritchie Boys protested the United States' eager embrace of anticommunist leaders. Just as some of them criticized America's handling of postwar Europe and its eager entrance into a Cold War with Russia, some with a more intimate knowledge of Asia criticized America's zealous support of unpopular leaders in its efforts to contain the spread of Communism in East Asia.

Frank Church, whose military service included one year serving as an Order of Battle specialist in China, wrote from Shanghai in December 1945:

> *The coming of peace and the return of the Chungking [nationalist] government, ironically enough, have served to aggravate more serious problems. Inflation, bad enough during the war, has become progressively worse during the past three months. The housing shortage is acute as a consequence of the arrival of large numbers of Chinese and American troops. The municipal government is practically impotent, and akin to its big brother, the national government [under Chiang Kai-shek] notoriously corrupt. It seems capable of nothing other than throwing its weight around by imposing exorbitant taxes, and enforcing annoying curfews. Chiang is fast losing prestige among the people.*

The fault, as Church saw it, lay with Chiang's infatuation with the West. He and his inner circle had "lost touch with the pulse beat of China. Mao was out in the provinces with the peasants, scorning foreign influence and preaching a gospel . . . shaped to the contour of indigenous aspirations."[12] US policy, however, was no longer influenced by the views of knowledgeable intelligence officers, and Church's words, like those of the men in the Dixie Mission, went unheeded. Church's insights into China later caused him to foresee clearly the futility of US participation in the Vietnam War and, as a US senator from Idaho, to oppose it. In 1975, Church would also chair a US Senate select committee, the Church Committee, that investigated abuses in the national intelligence agencies: the CIA, NSA, FBI, and IRS. This investigation led to the establishment of the US Senate Select Committee on Intelligence that provides oversight of these committees.

Like most Americans, the Ritchie Boys were divided in their views of the United States' unleashing the atomic bomb against Japan. Many felt that the United States had taken war to a horrifying new level by knowingly killing thousands of civilians and causing lasting suffering to thousands of others. Sergeant Klaus Mann described the agony he felt as a German turned American when he wrote in an unfinished novel shortly before his death:

> *I want to die because we dropped that accursed Bomb on a small town in Japan. I say "we," even though I personally had nothing to do with it. But it's my people who did it, my country is responsible for the outrage, yes we are guilty—all of us! . . .*
>
> *I want to die because we killed those Jews—how many of them? Five million, or six?—in the gas chambers. . . . It is true, I left Germany long before the Germans committed those ghastly crimes. . . . But I used to be one of them. It's my fault.*[13]

But those with a deeper knowledge of the Japanese mentality maintained that the war would have gone on for years and caused the deaths of many thousands of American fighting men if the bomb had not been deployed. Baldwin Eckel confirmed this belief. As one of the first American interrogators on Japanese soil, he inquired of army officers, government officials, and businessmen what had made them willing to surrender. Every one of them, he said, answered, "Atomic bomb." Eckel explained, "Japan's spiritual fabric was destroyed. It wasn't the Americans who did it. It was the atomic bomb, something supernatural. They could emotionally live with that explanation."[14]

This outlook may help explain why the Japanese did not commit ritual hara-kiri when faced with the defeat of their nation—and why

Japanese citizens did not greet the American occupying forces with the same bitter resentment that the Germans had expressed. Victor Matsui was sent to Japan immediately after the surrender to establish a secure area for the Allies; this was, he said, a period of uncertainty for both the Allies and the Japanese who feared mistreatment, physical attack, and rape. He was also to figure out categories of Japanese who might cause problems for the Americans. "But," he said, "they didn't."[15] Because Japanese-US military relations were generally amicable, Matsui's job eventually evolved into one of keeping track of the Japanese labor unions.

Probably none of the occupying forces were more relieved than the Nisei to find little hostility from the Japanese. When he was growing up in Hawaii, Ralph Yoohachi Nishime had suffered discrimination as the son of Okinawan parents. Now he was pleasantly surprised by the reception he received in Japan. As he wrote, some forty years later, "Perhaps the most important thing for me to come out of the military experience was my ability to develop rapport with Japanese officials and leaders of the community and gain their respect, primarily while stationed in Tottori and Sapporo. . . . To this day I have maintained contact with some of the Japanese nationals I worked with during the occupation."[16]

On a closer, familial level, Woodrow Wakatsuki had particular reason to dread meeting his relatives, since they lived on the outskirts of Hiroshima. In her book *Farewell to Manzanar*, Wakatsuki's youngest sister described his state of mind:

> *Woody has postponed this visit many times, postponed the train ride south from Tokyo, afraid of how he'd be received. Being an American is hard enough; being a Nisei among these occupying forces is sometimes agony. He dreads those looks that seem to call him traitor to his homeland or his race. And if he sees such looks in Tokyo, what might he not see in the eyes of those who survived the leveling and the ash heap of Hiroshima?*

Because of the extreme shortage of sugar in that country, Wakatsuki packed as much as he could into a large suitcase. "But he knew, as soon as he arrived, that he did not need the sugar to cancel out his GI crewcut and his American smile. Being Ko's son was enough, being family. That was all they saw."[17]

As occupying forces, the Americans encouraged the locals to participate in sports as a means of channeling aggression into friendly competition. The Americans had tried, without success, to introduce baseball into Germany. The Japanese, however, had been playing baseball for decades and were ardent fans of the sport. So were the Nisei. While Ralph Yoohachi Nishime was stationed in Tottori, he and the men stationed with him formed a baseball team and played against civilian teams in the area. These games doubtless contributed to the good will Nishime found among the local leaders.

Perhaps no Nisei soldier personifies the reconciliatory power of baseball better than Maya Miyamoto. He had grown up in Monterey, California, where he and his four brothers had played on the Monterey Minato team of the Japanese American baseball league. Leagues were then segregated by race, but the Minato team traveled all through northern and southern California to play against other Japanese American squads. When Miyamoto and his teammates were rounded up and sent to the Poston Internment Camp in Arizona, they regrouped and continued to play against other league teams in the camp. "We played on Sundays to big crowds there," one of these players has commented, "just like we did at home."[18] Small wonder, then, that Miyamoto and his fellow Nisei formed unit teams during the US occupation of Japan. "Every unit had a baseball team," he remembered, "that practiced in the big area stadiums and drew big crowds."[19] For Miyamoto, baseball had proved to be a big morale booster when he was imprisoned in an internment camp in the United States. Now it proved to be an equally important morale booster for the conquered Japanese. With the full support of General MacArthur, Japanese pro baseball started up again within the first nine months of occupation. The healing had begun.

One Ritchie Boy played a particularly critical role in the healing of American-Japanese relations, even though his background initially seemed to mitigate against it. Victor Delnore, whose family name was originally Abdelnour, was born in Jamaica to Lebanese parents, and when he came to Camp Ritchie, he entered and completed its second class with a specialization in Arabic. He had been sent to the European front as commander of the Thirteenth Armored Division's Forty-Sixth Tank Battalion and earned a Silver Star by taking out the German headquarters for antiaircraft units near Mudlinghoven, Germany.

In Europe, Delnore acquired a reputation for empathy. He refused to shoot up German towns as he passed through them because he did not want to risk killing women and children. And at the end of the war, he released German women prisoners to local German officials instead of putting them beside men in concentration camps.

This empathy continued when, on September 23, 1946, Delnore arrived in Japan as military governor of the country's political subdivision of Nagasaki. During his first month there, Delnore attended a Buddhist ceremony commemorating the war dead. He was deeply moved on two counts: First, because, when he was in Europe, he had not been able to confirm the status of his brother, who had been reported as missing, presumed dead. But, as he wrote his parents, he was also moved by the grief he saw in the Japanese faces, which "looked no different than the faces of the people at church back home; the war widows and the war mothers looked just as bereaved as any of our womenfolk." He added, "Honestly, I was deeply moved. Whether it was the strangeness of the ceremony, the numerous mourning womenfolk, or the boxes of the ashes of the 10,000 unclaimed and unidentified victims of the atom bomb that were piled all around the altar, I'll never know. All I do know is that I prayed for [my brother's] soul as I have never prayed before."[20]

During his three-year tenure in Japan, Delnore established a warm rapport with the Japanese citizenry as he helped rebuild Nagasaki from the ground up. He attributed his remarkable success there to the fact that, because he trusted the Japanese, they trusted him in return. It was also clear to them that his service to the Japanese people was neither condescending nor perfunctory. When his tour ended, the street below his Nagasaki home was renamed Delnore Road in his honor.

Yoshiaki Fujitani was assigned to work at PACMIRS at Camp Ritchie after a football injury prevented him from entering basic training. COURTESY OF YOSHIAKI FUJITANI

The 1945 Yamashita trial in Manila created a new definition of war crimes. General Yamashita is the second figure from the right. SOURCE: NATIONAL ARCHIVES AND RECORDS ADMINISTRATION

An American GI poses with Japanese baseball players during the American occupation. SOURCE: WRIGHT MUSEUM OF WWII PERMANENT COLLECTION

Victor Delnore and his wife Catherine stand by the street sign erected in his honor by the citizens of Nagasaki. SOURCE: GORDON W. PRANGE COLLECTION, UNIVERSITY OF MARYLAND

CHAPTER TWENTY-ONE

Ritchie Remembrances

Peacetime has finally returned to the mountains this summer. Last year there was still a certain atmosphere of uncertainty. Residents at Cascade, Pen Mar and Blue Ridge Summit were still getting used to not having the Army at Ritchie anymore.

This year, however, things are different. With the approach of summer, people threw open their doors to the country summer tourists. The Hiram Hotel (formerly the Chapman Manor) . . . now offers very comfortable rooms, excellent meals and seems to be expertly run. . . .

Drive through the country where you will see acres of rolling orchards in full bloom. Peach orchards of beautiful pink—apple and cherry orchards which, except for the gentle warm sun and strips of green grass separating row from row, one would think he were viewing great banks of snow.[1]

AFTER THE WAR WAS OVER AND THEY HAD BEEN DISCHARGED, THE MEN and women who had studied at Camp Ritchie scattered to the winds. Some, of course, did return for a brief holiday in Blue Ridge Summit. Some may even have stayed in the Camp Ritchie Club House, where, for $12 a day, a couple could get a room and hot meals while sharing bathroom and toilet facilities with the other guests.

Some may have reacted to the tourism pitch with the cynicism of one Ritchie Boy, who wrote, "Ah, what memories—those gorgeous hills, fragrant of chards, babbling brooks—late at night, no moon, no stars and a map printed in Italian, a compass, and five miles to go cross-country to your objective."[2]

We know that some Ritchie alums returned to marry local girls. We also know that at least one Camp Ritchie WAC, Gertrude D. Kramer, married a soldier from Blue Ridge Summit and spent the rest of her life there. She worked for fifteen years as an employee at Mountain Gate Restaurant in Thurmont and served as chaplain to the Women's Auxiliary of the American Legion Camp Ritchie Unit No. 229, in what had formerly been the camp's United Service Organizations (USO) center. It is unclear just how many Camp Ritchie vets (women and men) remained in the area—or how many returned there.

Some, unfortunately, didn't live to decide their futures. Lieutenant Jack Collette, graduate of the sixth Camp Ritchie class and of the Third Mobile Radio Broadcasting Company trained at Camp Sharpe, had married popular Hagerstown vocalist Merle Belle Snyder in February 1944 before shipping overseas. He saw action on the European front from D-Day onward, and he earned three Bronze Stars while serving in the Psychological Warfare Branch of Patton's Third Army. On March 21, 1945, Collette set out on a hog-calling mission near Mainz, Germany, despite warnings against putting himself in immediate danger. He was shot and killed. His widow found belated closure when his body was returned to the United States in April 1949 and reburied in the Knoxville National Cemetery in Tennessee. Merle Collette remained active in Hagerstown society as a frequent vocal performer, award-winning archer, bowler, and Grand Matron of the Eastern Star. She remarried in 1952.

Other Ritchie/Hagerstown couples were more fortunate. Major Edward A. Caskey, a Baltimore native, relocated to Hagerstown when he married Ruth Rhodes, a Hagerstown native. Caskey remained in the army until 1951, all the while maintaining his expertise and interest in psychological warfare. In spring 1945, he delivered a series of lectures on the topic with Colonel Donald F. Hall, the American military director of psychological warfare for North Africa and Italy, at the US Army War College. In January 1947, he addressed the Hagerstown Kiwanis Club about the training that had gone on at Ritchie. While giving full credit to such specialties as photo interpretation, aerial photography, and counterintelligence work, he devoted most of his lecture to combat psychology and propaganda, not only by giving coverage to his activities as commanding officer of the First Mobile Radio Broadcasting Company but also by providing a history of combat psychology all the way back to the days of Gideon in the Bible. And, in March 1949, Caskey took part in the most realistic and gigantic naval maneuvers ever staged in peacetime. In these maneuvers, he assumed the role of head of psychological warfare of enemy forces "occupying" the island of Vieques, off the Puerto Rico mainland, and was "captured" by American forces in training.

After retiring from the army in 1951, Caskey took the position of system and procedures analyst for Fairchild Aircraft Division in Hagerstown. He also pursued his interest in theater. Throughout his army service, Caskey had appeared in plays staged by local drama clubs. Now that he was free of army duties, Caskey returned to the theater and took on major roles in productions mounted by the Potomac Playmakers.

Former OSS (Office of Strategic Services) member and Camp Ritchie instructor Douglas Van Eyklebosch stayed on in Hagerstown after the Ritchie closing in order to study at Hagerstown Junior College. There he met his wife, an employee at the Fairchild Aircraft Corporation. They married in June 1947 and then moved to South Dakota, where he received a BS degree from the South Dakota School of Mines and Technology and served as assistant city engineer in Rapid City, South Dakota. When the Hagerstown mayor appointed him city engineer in 1965, Eyklebosch and his wife returned to the city, where he remained until his early death in 1973.

Sergeant Edward Harriman had spent the first twenty-five years of his life in Hamburg, Germany, but he became a Marylander after the war. While a member of the twenty-second class at Camp Ritchie, he had fallen in love with Marguerite (Peg) Schmidt, who was director of hostesses at the USO center in Hagerstown. They married, and Harriman made a solid career in financial management. He became a prominent figure in Hagerstown through his work as a Washington County commissioner, church teacher, and director of the Hagerstown Community Concert Associations. In addition, he served as member and officer in the Lions Club, the Elks Lodge, Order of Moose, and Jaycees.

Sergeant Albert E. Davis, a graduate of one of Camp Ritchie's special courses in counterintelligence, had met and fallen in love with local girl Mary Jane Elliot, who was, herself, a WAC. As soon as the war was over, they married, and he took a teaching position at the North Hagerstown High School, teaching English, history, physical education, and health sciences. He also served as assistant coach of the football team and manager of Hagerstown's municipal swimming pool. Like Harriman, he was heavily involved in civic activities: in the church, the American Legion, the Lions Club, the Washington County chapter of the Red Cross, and various Masonic organizations.

John Robert Strauss also married a local girl. Although he had flunked out of the Ritchie training program, he remained at the camp throughout the war years as head chef. He had held previous positions at exclusive restaurants throughout the country, including the Drake Hotel and the Palmer House in Chicago, the Netherland Plaza in Cincinnati, and the Town House in Los Angeles. But it was the position he had held at Antoine Restaurant in New Orleans that shaped the menu of the restaurant that he opened in Hagerstown in December 1946. He built his restaurant in the old Hagerstown Colonial Movie Theater, a grand old structure with an elaborate Beaux-Arts facade. It featured a dining room with a capacity of 250 and multicolored fluorescent lighting arrangements, as well as a small orchestra stage and a dance floor. The menu featured French Cajun cooking, "the delight of the epicurean," as well as seafood and raw oysters.[3] The former Camp Ritchie commandant, Charles Banfill, was a southerner who had served in the Louisiana National Guard; for him, French Cajun cooking had, indeed, been an epicurean delight, but this was apparently not true of a town trying to return to normalcy from a long war. Strauss's restaurant did not pay off, and in July 1948, it was put up for sale and sold to the Loyal Order of Moose. Strauss was undeterred, however. He took over an old diner, renaming it the "(West) Washington Street Diner" and specializing in seafood dishes. This diner was successful. Later he moved on to establish the more upscale Gourmet House. Former Camp Ritchie officers, recalling the excellent cuisine they had enjoyed in the officers' mess, doubtless visited one of the John Strauss restaurants when paying a return visit to the area.

William Warfield, in fact, ate at Strauss's restaurant when he returned to Hagerstown in 1966 to perform in the town's community concert series. It was his first visit to the town in twenty years, and the townspeople turned out to "welcome him back as an old friend," in fond recollection of his performances at Camp Ritchie and, especially, of his rendition of "Ballad for Americans" at a Fourth of July program held at the USO center next to the camp.[4] Warfield told his hosts that he had visited the town of Hagerstown very little during the war years. One reporter, surprised by this fact, now recalled hearing that "Warfield didn't come down much because he didn't want to get his feelings hurt." During his 1966 visit, Warfield spoke fondly about Camp Ritchie, his fellow soldiers, and his performances at the camp and at the musical soirees held at the home of a Blue Ridge society woman. But, for a Black man at that time, Hagerstown had been hostile territory. "And I realized," the reporter wrote, that "we have come a long way. For now, the doors of The Alexander [Hotel] would be open to him as well as the USO. In this decade he would be welcomed without a second thought. . . . Now he is recognized as a famous personality. Then, he was afraid of being hurt."[5]

One Camp Ritchie officer, Lieutenant Paul G. H. Wolber, did more than visit: he returned to Camp Ritchie in 1977 as senior physician at the old Camp Ritchie hospital. Wolber had, in fact, always kept a toehold in the area. He was a graduate of the third class at Ritchie and returned briefly to the camp as an instructor. In 1943, he had married a local girl, Anna Jane Rudisill, whom he had met at one of the camp's social functions. After serving for a time as a camp instructor, and then serving in the Pacific Theater of Intelligence Operations at General MacArthur's headquarters in Hawaii, he returned to Hagerstown and opened a men's clothing store in partnership with his father-in-law. During this period, Wolber actively pursued his twin passions for hunting and fishing. He was a member of the Izaak Walton League and other conservation organizations, and he was cited by *Field and Stream* magazine for his efforts at combating water pollution.

In 1952, sometime after the death of his father-in-law, Wolber sold the clothing store and took advantage of the GI bill by enrolling in the medical school at Ohio State University. After practicing medicine in

Ohio for two years, he returned to Hagerstown to serve at W. F. Prior Medical Publishing Company as chief of publications for medical texts and journals. He held this position for seventeen years before joining the old Camp Ritchie hospital as post surgeon. "Doc Wolber," as he was known to staff and students, remained in the Army Ready Reserves from 1946 to 1975 and served as commanding officer of a Selective Service reserve unit in Hagerstown. By the time he joined the Ritchie hospital, he held the rank of colonel.

Meanwhile, another Camp Ritchie colonel, Shipley Thomas, who had served at Ritchie throughout the war as director of training, made a return visit to nearby Blue Ridge Summit in 1949 and then purchased a large, stately home there. Thomas was working as an architect with Ford, Bacon and Davis Engineers; he was also amassing a fine collection of Peale family lithograph portraits that he later donated to the Peale branch of the Baltimore City Life Museums. Together with Major Gunther ("Gary") Hartel, Thomas created a newsletter for all those who had been stationed at Camp Ritchie during the war years. Hartel was German born and a graduate of the sixth class at Camp Ritchie; he had been stationed with MIRS (Military Intelligence Research Section) in Washington during the war, and then he returned to Camp Ritchie after V-E Day to direct operations of the German Army Archives, or *Heeres-archiv*, that was housed in the German Military Document Section at Camp Ritchie. He was now back at the Pentagon.

The two men launched the newsletter in hopes of attracting a large and accurate mailing list that could be used to develop a Camp Ritchie Association "of Ritchie graduates and other intelligence personnel who worked together in the field." It should include many more people than Ritchie grads, Ritchie WACs, camp administrators, and members of the camp's Composite School Unit; they called upon "all 'Ritchie-minded' people"—"civilians, soldiers, instructors, pupils, fire-men, officers, fifth generation and no-generation"—to join the association.[6]

The mimeographed newsletter, the *Blue Ridge Bulletin*, incorporated the former *Balowa Newsletter* that had serviced those who had worked in the exploitation of German documents in Washington, London, and

North Africa. The editors of the *Blue Ridge Bulletin* were optimistic. Using the old camp rosters, they sent the first issue out to ten thousand men. By the third issue, which came out in December 1948, they reported that "the high percentage of returns 'Unknown' is very discouraging." Of the twenty thousand Ritchie-ites sought, they had just under thirteen hundred positive returns. The quarterly bulletin contained articles of interest as well as news notes from Ritchie graduates, telling of war work, weddings, babies, and postwar jobs. But there were plaintive comments as well. "I notice that the B.R.B. does not mention much of the first classes," one noted, while another asked, "Why don't you give some info about 'Ritchie' step-children of Camp Sharpe?"[7]

Like many ad hoc alumni news bulletins, it soon became clear that the same members of the anticipated "Camp Ritchie Association" were writing in regularly, while widespread support of the *Blue Ridge Bulletin* was meager. Thomas and Hartel begged for a subscription fee of $2 a year to keep the newsletter going, but they were forced to stop printing after the fourth issue because of "the surprising lack of interest" among potential subscribers. The editors noted that, as of May 26, 1949, only 265 of the contacted 1,500 Ritchie graduates had sent in their $2 subscription fee. "If the remaining 1200 are not interested to the extent of mailing in their $2.00, the next issues of the *Bulletin* may have to be limited only to the subscribers," they threatened.[8] They did not receive the necessary funding.

Why did the proposed Camp Ritchie Association fail? For one thing, the number of found veterans' addresses fell far below 1 percent of its prospective membership. The costs of tracking down more camp veterans were prohibitive, since this process required sending out inquiries to men and women located all over the world while knowing that the chances of these addresses still being valid were extremely low. One reader suggested another problem with funding the project. "I think if you have dues, too many fellows may shy away from it," he wrote, "considering today's many requests for all types of contributions as well as fees for clubs, etc., which many of us have."[9]

After the war, the Ritchie alums were embarking on new lives—in the army, in intelligence, in business, in academe, on farms, and in shops in their old hometowns. They were using the GI bill to further their education; they were establishing families and focusing on the future, not the past. It is likely that many wanted to push the whole war experience from their minds.

But another, more compelling explanation for the low number of newsletter subscribers might be the relatively short time the Ritchie grads had spent at the training center in Maryland as opposed to the months and years spent elsewhere. The Ritchie Boys had been dispersed all over the world for the duration of the war: to South America, North Africa, and Europe, as well as an immense Pacific theater that included Burma, New Guinea, India, Indochina, Okinawa, China, and the Philippines. They had been assigned to offices headquartered in Washington, DC; London; Brisbane, Australia; and Hawaii. They had served on small teams (three to twelve men) with other Ritchie men but also with members of British intelligence and with Americans in the OSS and CIC. Small wonder, then, that they would identify themselves most strongly with the comrades with whom they'd served, such as men in MIRS London or in Patton's Third Army. Especially for those who had bled and suffered in the field, Camp Ritchie had been an intense, idyllic chapter that had ended on the day they set sail for Europe and Asia.

Thus it is not surprising that the Ritchie grads had strong attachments to the other members of their teams but not to many other classmates. This explains Thomas and Hartel's call for an association that included the "Ritchie-minded"—that is, those "many others who were connected with Ritchie people here and in overseas stations." They reported hearing about mini-reunions held around the world:

> *There have been several reunions of Ritchie men in New York; three reunions have been held in Washington, consisting mainly of people still involved in the same old game; one meeting held in Paris in September, 1947—key personnel were present there; a dinner in London [that] included a number of U.S. Ritchie chaps and some personnel on active service with the British Army during the War; there has been a reunion in Tokyo of men in the Occupational Forces; there are chaps in Singapore, Ethiopia, Austria, Brazil, Hudson Bay and Turkey.*

All of them have had their get-togethers and communications with each other.[10]

After Thomas and Hartel's failed attempt to create a Camp Ritchie Association, the search to find and reunite the Camp Ritchie veterans had to wait until an exhibition held in July 2011 at the Holocaust Memorial Center in Farmington Hills, Michigan. This exhibition—*Secret Heroes*—was inspired by the popularity of Christian Bauer's 2004 documentary film *The Ritchie Boys*. Most of the information for it came from the head and heart of Ritchie Boy Guy Stern, who was assisted in its presentation by the center's director, Stephen Goldman. By this time, of course, many of the surviving veterans were in frail health and unable to travel. Still, twelve Ritchie Boys showed up for the opening of the exhibition. This prompted a follow-up reunion, in June 2012, for a two-day symposium in Washington, DC, complete with veteran panels, guest speakers, a tour of the United States Holocaust Memorial Museum, and a visit to the abandoned camp. Thirty-four Ritchie Boys came to this symposium from as far away as London. All were in their upper eighties and nineties, and many navigated with canes, walkers, and wheelchairs. These veterans found Camp Ritchie in a sad state of disrepair. Unfortunately, in the years that followed, the remaining structures at the site would become even more fragile.

The US Army had closed its operations at Camp Ritchie on June 19, 1946, four years to the day from when the camp had officially opened. In their first *Blue Ridge Bulletin*, the editors described the state of the camp as of April 1, 1948:

> *Camp Ritchie has the appearance of an asylum at present. There are the same grey buildings. The trees and bushes have grown taller, the high fence and closed gates look formidable.*
>
> *No busy feet scurry across the parade ground, no bugles blow, no canned music blares forth in the early morning hours. Everything is green and peaceful.*
>
> *There is activity though! Behind the scene one finds a guest house run by Mr. Prior, the ex-Fire Chief of Blue Ridge Summit. The old*

Officers' Club could be visited on week-ends by Baltimore and Wash-
ington residents at $4.00 a day plus meals. Boats on Lake Royer could
be rented at 50¢ an hour. Steak dinners cost $1.50.

Just across the lake, where the hospitals were located[,] one finds
old people strolling in the shade of the large tulip tress which fringe
the lake. . . . The old Waac [sic] area is used by the Maryland State
Guard. There are rifle matches for the National Guard and for boys
clubs, though the impact area has largely recuperated from the terrific
battering it used to get during the war years from M-1, machine guns
and simulated 75's.[11]

When the army returned Camp Ritchie to the State of Maryland
in June 1946, the site immediately reverted to its prewar activities. The
annual highlight was the two-week training exercises that were held
there every summer. These events drew hundreds of Maryland State and
National Guardsmen to the camp: sixteen hundred in 1946 and seventeen hundred in 1947.

Prior to 1942, the Guardsmen had been bivouacked in tents; they
now enjoyed the luxury of the wooden barracks that the army had constructed there. Civic groups also returned to the camp to enjoy its facilities. Boy Scouts and Boys Club members came there for summer camp.
A new tri-state program for underprivileged boys was set up by the Elks
Club; groups totaling six hundred came each summer and were housed
in the old WAC barracks.

In the meantime, the State of Maryland took over the old Camp
Ritchie hospital for use as Maryland's first hospital for patients with
chronic diseases. This was a temporary arrangement, since the state had
plans to build a new, larger facility. In the meantime, the Camp Ritchie
facility housed more than two hundred patients.

From 1946 to 1951, area residents benefited from programs offered
on the Camp Ritchie grounds. The Blue Ridge Sportsmen's Association
held an ox roast and carnival on the parade ground. A local rifle club held
competitions at the camp's firing range, movies were shown at the camp
theater, and local drama groups performed there as well.

In 1948, a basketball team for local girls—the "Ritchie-ites"—was formed at the Camp Ritchie gym. The University of Maryland offered summer art classes on the Camp Ritchie grounds, and the public was invited to come to Lake Royer every summer for swimming and boating.

By 1951, the activities of the Camp Ritchie Military Intelligence Training Center were nearly forgotten, except for the rare shell fragments and copper cartridges that the local boys still found in the area. Occasionally these discoveries made it into the newspapers. They reported in June 1950 that a twelve-year-old boy attending summer camp at Camp Ritchie had gone exploring in a restricted area and stepped on an unexploded shell. Shrapnel tore through one leg and lodged in his foot and stomach. He recovered after three months' hospitalization, but one leg had to be amputated.

On September 30, 1946, a more significant news item appeared on page 9 in the Hagerstown *Daily Mail* without attracting much public attention. Under the headline "Camp Ritchie Would Replace the Pentagon," this byline, dated July 27, reported, "An emergency communications center, apparently to be used in case the Pentagon is ever knocked out by enemy attack, is to be set up at this 1000-acre military reservation."

This newspaper item was the first indication to area residents that the Joint Chiefs of Staff saw a need for a protected location for a joint command post, should a coming war cause the destruction of the nation's capital. Five years later the project became a reality. Raven Rock Mountain was chosen as the location for the command post; it was identified as "Site R" and located just six and a half miles northeast of Camp Ritchie, in Pennsylvania. Since this mountain was formed of hard granite, it was a suitably impenetrable site for the construction of an underground Pentagon. Camp Ritchie was selected as its base for operations support. This time the US Army bought rather than rented the Camp Ritchie property from the State of Maryland after agreeing upon a price of $2,350,000. This purchase caused a change in name for the new government property: on November 1, 1951, the name "Camp Ritchie" was officially changed to "Fort Ritchie," and new "secret" operations commenced there. But that is another story.

Ritchie WAC Ellen Kaufmann and Ritchie graduate Melville Boucher married in 1946. In 1948, they returned to Camp Ritchie to pose again in front of the chapel where they were wed. COURTESY OF ANITA BOUCHER

William Warfield made a return visit to Hagerstown after achieving fame on Broadway and in Hollywood. SOURCE: 1964 PHOTO, AUTHOR'S COLLECTION

Reunion photo of Ritchie Boys taken at the US Navy Memorial in Washington, DC, on June 18, 2012. Front Row (12): Arthur Jaffe, Gerald Geiger, Heinz Bondy, Max Horlick, Ernest Wachtel, Joseph Eaton, Bill Hess, Peter Kaskel, Adolf Grunbaum, Guy Stern, Harry Ebert, Sy Steinberg; Second Row (13): Colonel Steve Kleinman, Congressman Roscoe Bartlett, _?_, Otto Frank, Harry Jacobs, _?_, Gunter Kosse, Herbert Schader, Werner Michel, _?_, RB Wannabe Dan Gross, Thomas Farmer, Ralph Baer; Third Row (4): _?_, Santo Asaro, Wolfgang Lehmann, _?_; Fourth Row (3): John Rothman, _?_, Henry Lowenstern; Fifth Row (2): _?_, George Kahn; Sixth Row (2): Peter Skala, Felix Warburg; Seventh Row (3): Jon Jarvis (National Park Service), Peter Earnest (Spy Museum), Lieutenant General Patrick M. Hughes (Army). SOURCE: AUTHOR'S COLLECTION

The Maryland State Guard returned in full force to the Camp Ritchie parade ground in summer 1946. SOURCE: WESTERN MARYLAND REGIONAL LIBRARY, MARYLAND STATE ARCHIVES

Acronyms

AFHQ	Allied Force Headquarters
AGAS	Air-Ground Aid Section
AGF	Army Ground Forces
API	Aerial Photo Interpreter
ASTP	Army Specialized Training Program
CI	Counterintelligence
CIA	Central Intelligence Agency
CIC	Counterintelligence Corps
CID	Criminal Investigation Division
CO	Commissioned Officer
COI	Coordinator of Information
CSU	Composite School Unit
DC	Division Class
DEML	Detached Enlisted Men's List
DP	Displaced Person
EAM	Ethnikó Apeleftherotikó Métopo (Greek: National Liberation Front)
EEIS	Enemy Equipment Intelligence Service
ETO	European Theater of Operations
ETOUSA	European Theater of Operations US Army

FBI	Federal Bureau of Investigation
FID	Field Interrogation Detachment
G-2	General Staff Intelligence Officer
GI	"Government Issue" = Anything having to do with the US Army or Army Air force; infantrymen and airmen
GMDS	German Military Document Section
HQ	Headquarters
ICD	Information Control Division
IMT	International Military Tribunal
INS	Immigration and Naturalization Service
IPW	Interrogation of Prisoners of War
IRS	Internal Revenue Service
KP	"Kitchen Police"; Kitchen Patrol
MI	Military Intelligence
MII	Military Intelligence Interpreter
MIRS	Military Intelligence Research Section
MITC	Military Intelligence Training Center (i.e., Camp Ritchie)
MITU	Mobile Intelligence Training Unit
MP	Military Police
MRB, MRBC	Mobile Radio Broadcasting (Company)
NARA	National Archives and Records Administration
NCO	Noncommissioned Officer
NSA	National Security Agency
OB	Order of Battle
OBI	Order of Battle Intelligence
OCS	Officer Candidate School

OG	Operational Group
OKH	Oberkommando des Heeres (High Command of the German Army)
OKW	Oberkommando der Wehrmacht (High Command of the German Armed Forces)
OMGUS	Office of Military Government, United States
OSS	Office of Strategic Services
PACMIRS	Pacific Military Intelligence Research Section
PI	Photo Interpretation/Intelligence
PIC	Photo Intelligence Center
PLA	Permanent Limited Assignment
POW, PW	Prisoner of War
PWD	Psychological Warfare Division
RCM	Radio/Radar Countermeasures
RIAS	Radio in the American Sector
S-2	Staff Intelligence Officer
SEATIC	Southeast Asia Translation and Interrogation Center
SHAEF	Supreme Headquarters Allied Expeditionary Force
SO	Special Operation
SOE	Special Operation Executive (British equivalent of OSS)
SS	Schutzstaffel (elite Nazi forces)
T/5	Technician Fifth Grade
TI	Terrain Intelligence
TIS	Theater Intelligence Section
USFET	US Forces European Theater
USO	United Service Organizations

Camp Ritchie Student Numbers: All Classes

MITC CLASSES

31 8-Week Classes	27 July 1942–22 September 1945	11,637 graduated
28 Graduate OB Classes	26 August 1943–14 July 1945	899 graduated
26 Other Graduate Training Classes	26 August 1943–14 July 1945	878 graduated
2 Special Intelligence Classes	11 November 1943– 24 November 1943	21 graduated

ARMY GROUND FORCE CLASSES

41 Photo Interpretation Classes (20-day)	1 February 1943–6 October 1945	1,888 graduated
6 Order of Battle Classes (4-week)	5 November 1942– 24 August 1945	70 graduated
19 Division Classes (4-week)	7 March 1944–15 December 1944	773 graduated
18 Mobile Intelligence Training Units (5–6-week)	1 September 1944– 15 August 1945	306 graduated
12 Redeployment Classes (10–14-day)	31 May 1945–20 September 1945	119 graduated

CIC CLASSES

22 Special CIC Classes (2-week; 2-day)	2,340 graduated
4 Redeployment Classes	111 graduated

OCCASIONAL INSTRUCTION

8 RCM Classes (2-day)	12 May 1943–15 November 1943	71 graduated
1 Special Intelligence Group—Signal	16 April 1944–28 April 1944	60 graduated
2 Instr. Prior to ASTP Russian Lang. Training	24 May 1945–27 June 1945	46 graduated
1 First Class for Instructors—Japanese	17 July 1945–24 August 1945	40 graduated
Special Groups—MITC		420 graduated

GRAND TOTAL ALL CLASSES   19,679 graduated*

* This total differs from the number given in George Le Blanc's official history of the MITC at Camp Ritchie, because of an error in adding the figures of graduates in the occasional instruction classes.

Student Numbers in the Mobile Radio Broadcasting Companies

Training for the 1st Mobile Radio Broadcasting (MRB) Company was given at Camp Ritchie. It was a rushed affair, running from April 19 to May 1, 1943:

Unit	Number of Students
1st Mobile Radio Broadcasting Company	128

Subsequent training was held at Camp Sharpe, a Camp Ritchie subcamp located in Gettysburg, Pennsylvania. Four Mobile Radio Broadcasting companies were activated at Camp Ritchie on December 29, 1943; the first men entered Gettysburg on January 3, 1944, and formal training for the 2nd and 3rd MRBs began there on February 2 and lasted for six weeks. The 4th and 5th MRBs followed. Because soldiers at this camp were frequently transferred from one unit to another, numbers given here are for each student's original assignment.

Unit	Dates	Number of Students
2nd Mobile Radio Broadcasting Company		194
3rd Mobile Radio Broadcasting Company		141
4th Mobile Radio Broadcasting Company		152
5th Mobile Radio Broadcasting Company		164
TOTAL NUMBER IN ALL 5 MRB COMPANIES		779

The students in the five Mobile Radio Broadcasting Companies are generally not included in the overall enrollment figures for the training programs offered at Camp Ritchie. If we include only the one MRBC that actually trained on the Camp Ritchie grounds, that would raise the total number of students trained at Camp Ritchie to:

19,807

Including all five companies as Camp Ritchie training programs, that figure rises to:

20,458

Camp Ritchie Eight-Week Classes: Dates and Graduation Numbers

Class 1	27 July–19 September 1942	32 of 36 graduated
Class 2	24 August–17 October 1942	125 of 256 graduated
Class 3	2 November–23 December 1942	300 of 341 graduated
Class 4	6 January–6 March 1943	359 of 454 graduated
Class 5	8 February–9 April 1943	471 of 555 graduated
Class 6	13 March–11 May 1943	426 of 559 graduated
Class 7	15 April–12 June 1943	537 of 609 graduated
Class 8	17 May–16 July 1943	402 of 556 graduated
Class 9	21 June –18 August 1943	413 of 602 graduated
Class 10	23 July–20 September 1943	537 of 645 graduated
Class 11	25 August–23 October 1943	427 of 511 graduated
Class 12	27 September–25 November 1943	394 of 461 graduated
Class 13	30 October–23 December 1943	460 of 516 graduated
Class 14	2 December 1943–31 January 1944	427 of 503 graduated
Class 15	4 January–3 March 1944	359 of 552 graduated
Class 16	6 February–5 April 1944	513 of 613 graduated
Class 17	11 March–8 May 1944	511 of 696 graduated
Class 18	13 April–10 June 1944	622 of 708 graduated
Class 19	16 May–13 July 1944	489 of 583 graduated

Class 20	19 June–16 August 1944	355 of 551 graduated
Class 21	21 July–18 September 1944	309 of 416 graduated
Class 22	23 August–21 October 1944	344 of 465 graduated
Class 23	25 September–23 November 1944	360 of 576 graduated
Class 24	26 October–29 December 1944	514 of 653 graduated
Class 25	30 November 1944–29 January 1945	579 of 779 graduated
Class 26	3 January–3 March 1945	418 of 580 graduated
Class 27	5 February–5 April 1945	237 of 329 graduated
Class 28	11 March–10 May 1945	257 of 344 graduated
Class 29	13 April–12 June 1945	265 of 548 graduated
Class 30	18 May–17 July 1945	121 of 148 graduated
Class 31	26 July–22 September 1945	74 of 108 graduated
GRAND TOTAL		11,637 of 15,253 graduated

APPENDIX 5

Camp Ritchie Eight-Week Class Content*

Each of the thirty-one basic Camp Ritchie classes ran over an eight-week period, with the first five weeks focused on "General Instruction" and the last three including specialized training. "General Instruction" covered the following areas:

Terrain Intelligence	50 hours
Signal Intelligence	25 hours
Staff Duties	51 hours
Counterintelligence in Theater of Operation	21 hours
Enemy Armies	42 hours
Aerial Photo Interpretation	28 hours
Military Intelligence Interpreters and Foreign Maps	28 hours
Combat and Operations	27 hours
Visual Demonstration	Included above
Order of Battle	Included above
TOTAL HOURS	272 hours

During the final three weeks, while continuing to take "General Instruction," students were enrolled in eighty-two hours of "Specialized

---

*As outlined in Charles Y. Banfill, "Brief of Pertinent Facts and Data Concerning the Military Intelligence Training Center, Camp Ritchie, Maryland," June 3, 1944, and reprinted in Center for Strategic Intelligence Research, *Interrogation World War II, Vietnam, and Iraq*, 39–40.

Instruction." All students in the first class specialized in the interrogation of German prisoners of war (IPW). Students in the later classes were enrolled in a variety of languages and areas of specialization. The number of students in these specialized fields fluctuated according to the exigencies of the war. Instruction concentrated, as a rule, on the following areas, although counterintelligence increasingly became an important focus of the Camp Ritchie curriculum:

Interrogation of Enemy Prisoners of War and Identification and Translation of Documents
Aerial Photo Interpretation
Military Intelligence Interpreters (Allied and neutral)
Terrain Intelligence
Signal Intelligence

Appendix 6 shows the emphases and shifts in specialized instruction for the thirty-one classes.

Finally, the students participated in an eight-day "terrain exercise," which involved the completion of twenty intelligence-related problems. They were also sent on a forty-eight-hour patrol and on night azimuth training.

APPENDIX 6

Eight-Week Courses by Specialties

Class	IPW-Ge	IPW-It	IPW-Other lang.	PI	CI	TI	SigInt	German Transl	Russian Interp	Chinese Interp	General Intell	Japanese Interp
1	32											
2	32	4	56	33								
3	53	11	100	36	100							
4	123	22	125	57	52							
5	86	37	194	52	80	22						
6	80	25	142	95	59	25						
7	109	43	155	47	165	18						
8	130	23	82	74	93							
9	133		73	60	36	79	32					
10	177	87	98	82	37	28	28					
11	184	74		136		33						
12	119		128	147								
13	189		69	166		36						
14	130		61	165		71						
15	61		95	168		35						
16	163		120	193		37						
17	127		116	231		37						
18	147		147	328								
19	140		107	242								
20	107		40	164	19	25						
21	96		51	134		28						
22	118		62	122	18	24						

Class	IPW-Ge	IPW-It	IPW-Other lang.	PI	CI	TI	SigInt	German Transl	Russian Interp	Chinese Interp	General Intell	Japanese Interp
23	70		45	85	128				32			
24	35			91	261	15			112			
25	76			71	356	13			63			
26	58			45	272	12		23	8			
27	47			31	99	16		33	11			
28	46			3	78	25		19	11	58	17 (Ge)	
29	4			44	96	56			9	39	17 (Ru)	
30				22	62	20				13		4
31				4	64					6		
Totals	2,872	326	2,066	3,108	2,011	719	60	75	246	116	34	4

Appendix 7

Camp Ritchie Student Numbers: Forty-Seven Graduate Training Classes

26 August 1943–14 July 1945

Whereas most students in the thirty-one eight-week classes took their specialty as part of that eight-week program, students being trained in Order of Battle were enrolled in a four-week graduate program after completing these classes.

Graduate Order of Battle Classes	Student Numbers
12 Pacific Theater OB Classes	326
3 European Theater OB Classes (held in Washington DC)	77
16 European Theater OB Classes (at Ritchie)	492
Special OB Class No. 3	4
TOTAL GRADUATE STUDENTS IN OB	899

In addition to graduate training in Order of Battle, courses were offered in Photo Interpretation, Military Intelligence, Interrogation of Prisoners of War, Counterintelligence, Translation, and Interpretation.

Other Graduate Training Classes	Student Numbers
14 Special Graduate Training Classes, PI	476
Special Graduate Training Class, MI (French)	32
2 Special Graduate Training Classes, IPW (German)	29
4 Special Graduate Training Classes, CIC	171
3 Special Graduate Training Classes, MI (Russian)	133
Special Graduate Training Class, German translators	32
Special Graduate Training Class, Chinese Interpreters	5
TOTAL GRADUATE STUDENTS IN NON-OB COURSES	878

TOTAL NUMBER OF GRADUATE STUDENTS	1,777

Appendix 8

CIC Classes

The first four of the two-day close combat classes (SC 1–SC 4) included Ritchie students, primarily students in Photo Interpretation. SC 5 and SC 6 were solely for men in CIC, as were the two-week Special B classes, the Special Graduate Training Classes, and the four-week Special CIC courses.

A. SPECIAL CIC GROUPS (Two-day Close Combat)

Class Number	Dates	CIC	PI & Others	Total
SC 1	23 July–24 July 1943	137	52	189
SC 2	29 July–30 July 1943	92	36	128
SC 3	6 August–7 August 1943	164	32	196
SC 4	13 August–14 August 1943	138	36	174
SC 5	20 August–21 August 1943	45		45
SC 6	27 August–28 August 1943	65		65

B. SPECIAL B CLASSES (Two-week)

Class Number	Dates	Total
B-1	5 September–18 September 1943	74
B-2	19 September–2 October 1943	119
B-3	3 October–16 October 1943	86
B-4	17. October–30 October 1943	214
B-5	31. October–13 November 1943	227

Class Number	Dates	Total
B-6	14 November–27 November 1943	223
B-7	28. November–11 December 1943	219
B-8	12 December–25 December 1943	146
B-9	27 December 1943–8 January 1944	179
B-10	10 January–22 January 1944	81
B-11	24 January–5 February 1944	219

C. SPECIAL GRADUATE TRAINING CLASSES
(10–14 DAYS)

Class Number	Date
SGTC 1	26 September–5 October 1944
SGTC 2	20 October–29 October 1944
SGTC 3	30 October–13 November 1944
SGTC 4	26 November–9 December 1944
TOTAL NUMBER OF GRADUATES FROM SGTCS	2,340

D. SPECIAL CIC REDEPLOYMENT COURSES
(FOUR-WEEK)

Class Number	Date
1	3 July–31 July 1945
2	2 August–18 August 1945
3	20 August–15 September 1945
4	20 August–15 September 1945
TOTAL NUMBER OF GRADUATES FROM REDEPLOYMENT CLASSES	111

OVERALL TOTAL OF CIC GRADUATES FROM CAMP RITCHIE	2,451

Appendix 9
Military Intelligence Training Center

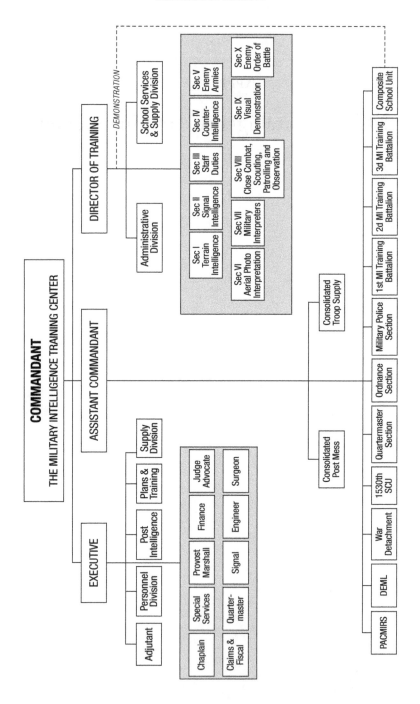

Appendix 10

Composite School Unit

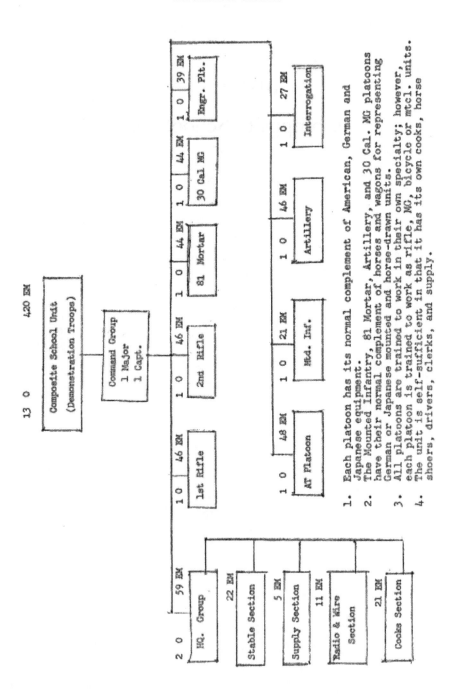

13 O   420 EM

Composite School Unit
(Demonstration Troops)

Command Group
1 Major
1 Capt.

		1 O 46 EM	1 O 46 EM
1st Rifle		2nd Rifle	

1 O 44 EM
81 Mortar

1 O 44 EM
30 Cal MG

1 O 39 EM
Engr. Plt.

1 O 48 EM
AT Platoon

1 O 21 EM
Md. Inf.

1 O 46 EM
Artillery

1 O 27 EM
Interrogation

59 EM
2 O
HQ. Group

22 EM
Stable Section

5 EM
Supply Section

11 EM
Radio & Wire Section

21 EM
Cooks Section

1. Each platoon has its normal complement of American, German and Japanese equipment.

2. The Mounted Infantry, 81 Mortar, Artillery, and 30 Cal. MG platoons have their normal complement of horses and wagons for representing German or Japanese mounted and horse-drawn units.

3. All platoons are trained to work in their own specialty; however, each platoon is trained to work as rifle, MG, bicycle or mtcl. units.

4. The unit is self-sufficient in that it has its own cooks, horse shoers, drivers, clerks, and supply.

358

Mobile Radio Broadcasting Company

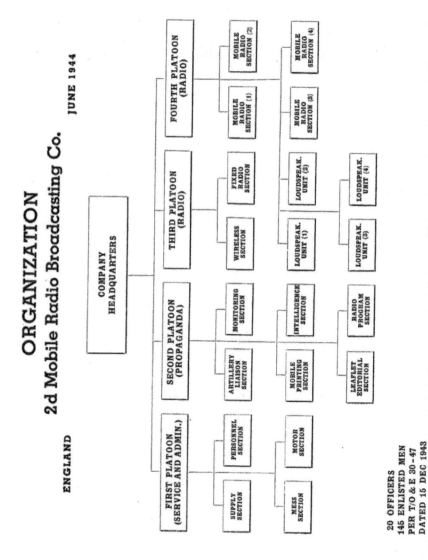

ORGANIZATION
2d Mobile Radio Broadcasting Co.

ENGLAND   JUNE 1944

COMPANY HEADQUARTERS

FIRST PLATOON (SERVICE AND ADMIN.)
- SUPPLY SECTION
- PERSONNEL SECTION
- MESS SECTION
- MOTOR SECTION

SECOND PLATOON (PROPAGANDA)
- ARTILLERY LIAISON SECTION
- MONITORING SECTION
- MOBILE PRINTING SECTION
- INTELLIGENCE SECTION
- LEAFLET EDITORIAL SECTION
- RADIO PROGRAM SECTION

THIRD PLATOON (RADIO)
- WIRELESS SECTION
- FIXED RADIO SECTION
- LOUDSPEAK. UNIT (1)
- LOUDSPEAK. UNIT (2)
- LOUDSPEAK. UNIT (3)
- LOUDSPEAK. UNIT (4)

FOURTH PLATOON (RADIO)
- MOBILE RADIO SECTION (1)
- MOBILE RADIO SECTION (2)
- MOBILE RADIO SECTION (3)
- MOBILE RADIO SECTION (4)

20 OFFICERS
145 ENLISTED MEN
PER T/O & E 30-47
DATED 15 DEC 1943

Pacific Military Intelligence Research Section

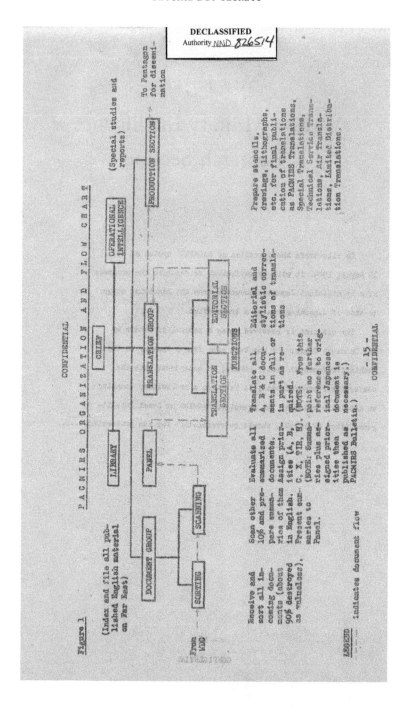

Appendix 13

German Military Document Section

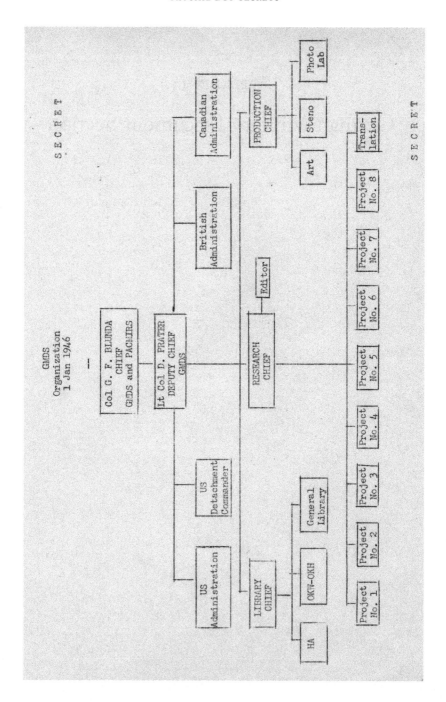

Specialized Training: Course Instruction (Class Syllabus)

11 March 1945
ENEMY ARMIES (IPW)—82 HOURS TOTAL

Instructional Section		Instructional Hours
V	**Germany Army Identification** (5 hours total)	
	Uniforms: Uniform Parade	1
	Distinguishing Colors of Arms; Ranks of Enlisted Men	1
	Ranks of Air Force; Ranks of Officers and Specialists	1
	Review and Test	1
	Identifications of German Semi-Military Uniforms	1
	German Map Reading Course (17 hours total)	
	Introduction	2
	German Map Reading	1
	Written Examination	1
	German Military Symbols	4
	Written Examination	1

Instructional Section	Instructional Hours
Reading German Military Situation Maps	2
Small Unit Leaders Sketches	1
Plotting of Information Extracted from German Document	1
Extraction of Information	1
Combined German Map and Document Exercise	2
Final Written Examination	1
German Documents (19 hours total)	
Introduction: Definition of Document	1
Technique of Translation; Military Abbreviations	1
Reading and Translation of Captured Documents	3
Practice in Reading Gothic Script	2
The German Paybook (Soldbuch)	2
German Identification Discs (Army, Navy, SS)	1
Principles of and Rules for Condensation	1
Practice in Condensation of Documents	1
Test	1
Recognition and Exploitation: Civilian and Military Documents	1
Lecture on Diaries	1
Exercise (UNTERGANG)	2
Lecture on Letters	1
Final Examination	1
Miscellaneous (3 hours total)	
Strong Point Demonstration	1
Medium Weapons Demonstration	1

Instructional Section		Instructional Hours
	Squad and Platoon in Attack	1
	Interrogation of Prisoners of War (38 hours total)	
	Introduction to Interrogation of Prisoners of War	1
	Evacuation of Prisoners of War	1
	How to Get Prisoners of War to Talk	1
	First Demonstration of Tactical Interrogation	1
	German Methods of Interrogation	1
	Interrogation Exercise	12
	IPW Techniques and Report Writing	1
	Report Writing Exercises	4
	Lecture on German Slang	1
	First-Hand Experiences	3
	Physical Interrogation Set-Up and Basic Type of Questions	1
	Lecture on IPW Administration	1
	Maps and IPW Exercises	2
	Lecture on Leading Questions and "Poor Interrogation"	1
	German Army Organization and IPW Exercise	2
	Demonstration of Detailed Interrogation	1
	IPW-PI Exercise	2
VI	**Aerial Photos and IPW Exercise**	2

Handout on Searching, Sorting, and Handling of Documents

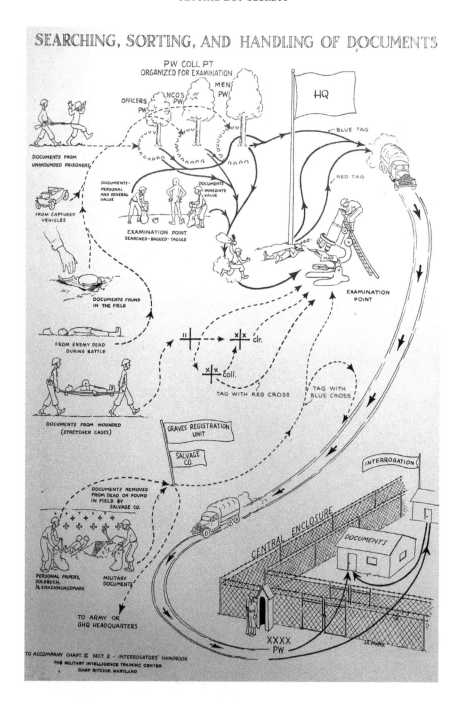

SEARCHING, SORTING, AND HANDLING OF DOCUMENTS

Handout on Evacuation and Interrogation of Prisoners of War

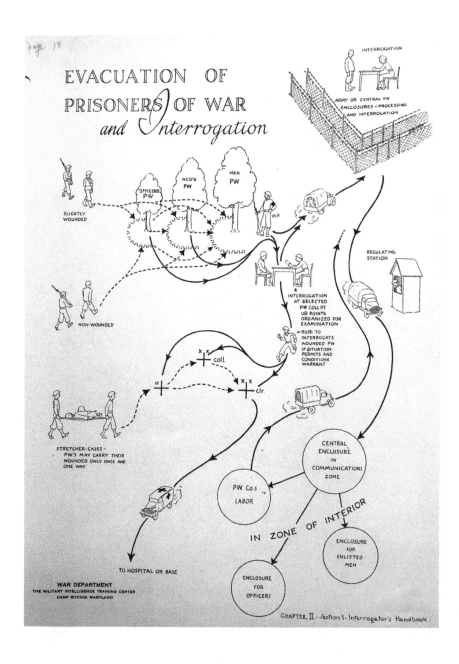

EVACUATION OF PRISONERS OF WAR and Interrogation

Exercise in Personality Analysis

One early IPW assignment involved studying a comic strip and, from that strip, analyzing the personality traits of its author. This assignment followed exercises in which the students had interviewed each other and, by following a set of guided questions, learned to determine traits that might be of assistance to an interrogator.

Exercise in Personality Analysis

To be turned in: _____   Tent No. _____

1. Name of comic strip?

2. Author of comic?

3. Intelligent or dumb?
Give reasons for your findings not to exceed ten lines:

4. Egotistical or not?
Reasons for your findings (not to exceed ten lines)

5. Good natured or grouchy?
Reasons for your findings (not to exceed ten lines)

6. Impulsive or reserved?
Reasons for your findings (not to exceed ten lines)

7. Brazen or timid?
Reasons for your findings (not to exceed ten lines)

8. Outstanding individuality or not?
Reasons for your findings (not to exceed ten lines)

Tactical Squeeze

Early on in their course, students were given handouts showing the kind of tactical information they were to extract from German prisoners, along with sample reports about various prisoners—all of them operating in the same battle area. Later on, they would write up their own reports taken from "prisoners" captured in a mock battlefield setting near the camp.

TACTICAL SQUEEZE

PERSONAL DETAILS (AGREES WITH IDENTITY DISC AND PAY-BOOK)

1. (a) NAME, (b) RANK, (c) NUMBER, (d) FIELD POST NUMBER, (e) COMPANY, (f) BATTALION, (g) REGIMENT, (h) DIVISION

2. PW's UNIT OR FORMATION IS ....

3. PW's UNIT CAME INTO ACTION) ON ....
   ONTO THE LINE) ON ....

4. PW's UNIT PRIOR TO COMING INTO ACTION/THE LINE WAS AT ....
   ON ....

5. SECTOR BOUNDARIES AND CRITICAL POINTS

6. UNITS ON FLANKS, IN SUPPORT, IN RESERVE

7. PW'S UNIT'S ORDERS WERE

8. PW'S OBJECTIVE WAS

9. ENEMY INTENTIONS WITH REGARD TO ATTACK, DEFENCE WITHDRAWAL, RELIEF

10. RECENT CASUALTIES IN PW'S UNIT AND MORALE

11. PRISONER HAS SEEN (WITHIN PAST THREE WEEKS) TANKS, GAS EQUIPMENT, AIRCRAFT EQUIPPED WITH COMBAT ARMS OR SPRAY PROJECTORS, FLAME THROWERS, A-T GUNS

12. PERSONNEL OF OTHER UNITS SEEN (WITHIN PAST 3 WEEKS), UNIT, WHERE, WHEN

13. P.W. APPEARS TO BE (a) TRUTHFUL/UNTRUTHFUL, (b) INTELLIGENT/IGNORANT, (c) COMMUNICATIVE/STUBBORN, (d) IN POSSESSION OF SPECIAL KNOWLEDGE

Situation Map for Practice in Tactical Interrogation

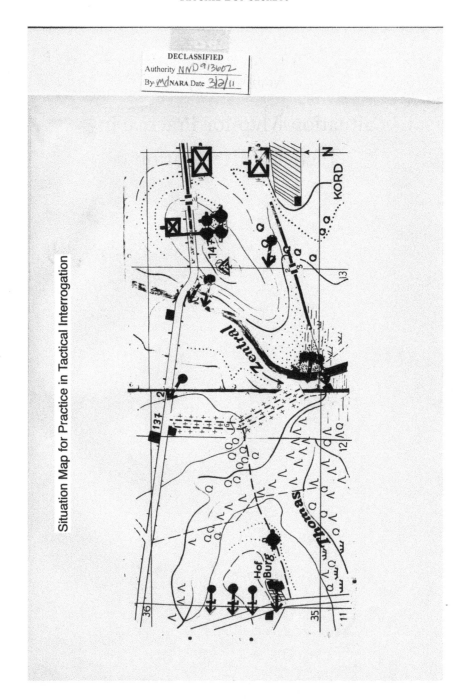

Awards

Name	Rank Held	Ritchie Class	Field of Action
MEDAL OF HONOR			
*Brostrom, Leonard C.	Private	10	Philippines
DISTINGUISHED SERVICE CROSS			
*Whittlesey, Henry C.	Captain	3	China
SILVER STAR RECIPIENTS			
Ackerman, Efraim	Master Sergeant	4	France
Arnold, David S.	1st Lieutenant	4	Italy
Axtell, Eugene N.	Captain	5	Germany
Bagby, Edward R.	T/5	17	Alaska
Bailey, Samuel L.	Sergeant	DC 28	Austria
Bongers, August L.	1st Lieutenant	29	Italy
Bothwell, Lyman	Major	7	Philippines
Brancato, Jacob S.	1st Lieutenant	8	France
Bronneck, Gary H.	1st Lieutenant	17	France
Burns, James D.	1st Sergeant	24	Tunisia
Buttery, Edwin B.	Captain	SC 6	Germany
Cahn, Herbert	Staff Sergeant	16	France
Canak, Dan	T/Sergeant	5	Austria
Cane, Lawrence	1st Lieutenant	6	France

Name	Rank Held	Ritchie Class	Field of Action
Cohn, Frederick G.	2nd Lieutenant	18	Germany
Cook, Harvey J.	Captain	9	France
Csasar, John F.	2nd Lieutenant	10	Germany
Defourneaux, Rene	2nd Lieutenant	14	France
Deka, Stanley J.	Sergeant	27	Tarawa
Delnore, Victor E.	Lt. Colonel	2	Germany
*Demetriou, Fotios D.	T/4	4	Italy
Duncan, Hoyt C. Jr.	Lieutenant	27	New Britain
Dunlay, Philip J.	Lieutenant	5	Sicily
Edgar, Bernhard G. F.	Master Sergeant	4	France
Ewald, William	Captain	8	Germany
**Frank, Peter R.	Master Sergeant	6	France (?)
Gilbert, Carl J.	Major	31	Philippines
Glenn, Edmund S.	Master Sergeant	8	France, Belgium
Grombacher, Gerd S.	Master Sergeant	18	France
Hadley, Arthur	1st Lieutenant	21	Germany
Harrington, Francis J.	T/3	15	France
Irving, Clark O.	1st Lieutenant	15	Philippines
Keeney, Barnaby C.	1st Lieutenant	15	Holland, Germany
Kittstein, Karl, Jr.	Captain	7	France
Komma, William M.	1st Lieutenant	29	Saipan
Landgraff, Alfred	2nd Lieutenant	13	France
LaVaux, Lloyd P.	Private	13	France
Lee, Glynn B.	Sergeant	4	Italy
Marsh, Louis V.	2nd Lieutenant	15	France
Midener, Walter	Master Sergeant	9	France
*Mills, Benjamin W., Jr.	1st Lieutenant	14	France
*Mosbacher, Stephen H.	Staff Sergeant	22	Germany

Name	Rank Held	Ritchie Class	Field of Action
Pendergast, James R.	1st Lieutenant	4	France
Phelps, Charles P.	1st Lieutenant	29	New Guinea
Pierce, Theodore L.	T/5	15	France
Pisarcik, John A.	1st Lieutenant	6	France
Robinow, Wolfgang F.	Master Sergeant	18	Germany
Scanlon, John H.	1st Lieutenant	7	Luxembourg
Skala, Peter H.	2nd Lieutenant	10	France
Smith, Norman	T/5	15	Holland
Sperl, Ferdinand P.	Captain	8	Czech., Germany
Streit, Pierre D.	Master Sergeant	15	France
Tomich, Alex	Corporal	5	France
Valtin, Ralph	2nd Lieutenant	13	Germany
Wells, Henry J.	T/3	11	Germany
White, Joseph E.	Corporal	24	Tunisia
**Wolf, Julius K.	T/3	10	Germany (?)

* Killed in action
** Undocumented

Notes

Introduction
1. DVD cover for the documentary film *The Ritchie Boys*.
2. George Bailey, *Germans: The Biography of an Obsession* (New York: World Publishing, 1972), 15.

Chapter 1: Building Camp Ritchie
1. Richard Seltzer, *One View of America in the World War II Generation: The Life and Times of Richard Warren Seltzer, Sr., Born June 5 1923*, part 1, *1923–1988*, Richard's Home Online, n.d., www.seltzerbooks.com/lifeandtimes.html.
2. *Baltimore Sun*, January 27, 1915, 21.
3. Information on the construction of the First Maryland Regiment summer camp (Camp Ritchie) is drawn from Becky Dietrich ("Camp Ritchie, Maryland—Development of the Intelligence Training Center," *K. Lang-Slattery* [blog]) and from the "Maryland Inventory of Historic Properties Form," Maryland Historical Trust Division of Historical and Cultural Programs, n.d., https://mht.maryland.gov/secure/medusa/PDF/Washington/WA-IV-262.pdf.
4. Joachim von Elbe, *Witness to History: A Refugee from the Third Reich Remembers* (Madison, WI: Max Kade Institute for German-American Studies, 1988), 259.
5. Author interview with Peter Burland, July 27, 2018.
6. Frank Woodring, "I Remember When: 'One of Last Cavalryman' [*sic*] Recounts Camp Ritchie Experience," *Maryland Cracker Barrel Magazine* (April–May 2007), 8.
7. Theodore A. Fuller, "Professional Summary," typescript, in private hands.

Chapter 2: The First Class
1. Theodore A. Fuller, "Professional Summary," typescript, in private hands.
2. Ann Redmon Diamant and Alfred Diamant, *Worlds Apart, Worlds United: A European-American Story: The Memoirs of Ann and Alfred Diamant* (Bloomington, IN: AuthorHouse, 2010), 211.
3. Steve Blizard and Kathy Fotheringham, *Fort Ritchie 1926–1998* (Gettysburg, PA: Herff Jones Yearbooks, 1998), 33–34.
4. Fuller, "Professional Summary."
5. Karen Ryser Newton, *Of Genuine Quality: The Biography of Sterling Ralph Ryser* (Scottsdale, AZ: Agreka Books, 2000), 53.

6. "Classroom and Field Instructions," Camp Ritchie, 1943, mimeograph sheet, private ownership.
7. Guy Stern, *Invisible Ink: A Memoir* (Detroit: Wayne State University Press, 2020), 58.
8. Newton, *Of Genuine Quality*, 54.
9. Newton, *Of Genuine Quality*, 54.
10. Vernon A. Walters, *Silent Missions* (Garden City, NY: Doubleday, 1978), 20–21.
11. Letter from Leroy H. Woodson to Truman N. Gibson, September 6, 1943, Library Archives and Museum Collections, Wisconsin Historical Society.
12. "Jovan M. Obradovic," HonorStates.org, n.d., https://www.honorstates.org/index .php?id=341118.

CHAPTER 3: THE MEN AT RITCHIE
1. "Ritchie-Bitchie," anonymous poem (courtesy of Paul Fairbrook).
2. Klaus Mann, *Der Wendepunkt: Ein Lebensbericht* (Munich: Edition Spangenberg im Ellermann Verlag, 1981), 512.
3. Klemens von Klemperer, *Voyage through the Twentieth Century: A Historian's Recollections and Reflections* (New York; Oxford: Berghahn Books, 2009), 49.
4. See George Bailey, *Germans: The Biography of an Obsession* (New York: World Publishing, 1972), 17.
5. Hans Habe, *All My Sins: An Autobiography* (London; Toronto: George G. Harrap, 1957), 324.
6. This figure is undoubtedly higher, since for 24.2 percent of the Camp Ritchie recruits there is no known religious affiliation. These percentage figures are based on those soldiers who graduated from one of the camp's thirty-one classes.
7. George Mandler, *Interesting Times: An Encounter with the 20th Century, 1924–* (Mahwah, NJ; London: Erlbaum, 2002), 95.
8. Bailey, *Germans*, 15–16.
9. Alfred G. Meyer, *My Life as a Fish* (Self-published typescript, 2000), 29–30.
10. Baldwin T. Eckel, "You're in the Army Now!" *Interpreter*, no. 78 [August 1, 2004]: 1–2.
11. Brandon Bies, Sam Swersky, and Doug Heimlich, "Interview with George Frenkel," 71, in *Fort Hunt Oral History*, National Park Service, December 5, 2006, and January 18, 2007, https://www.nps.gov/museum/exhibits/FOHU_oral_history/transcripts/PO%20 Box%201142_Frenkel,%20George_2016.pdf.
12. Bailey, *Germans*, 18.
13. Bailey, *Germans*, 18.
14. David Chavchavadze, *Crowns and Trenchcoats: A Russian Prince in the CIA* (New York: Atlantic International, 1990), 105.
15. Leon Edel, *The Veritable Past: A Wartime Memoir* (Honolulu: University of Hawaii, 2000), 17.
16. Chavchavadze, *Crowns and Trenchcoats*, 103–4.
17. William Sloane Coffin Jr., *Once to Every Man: A Memoir* (New York: Atheneum, 1977), 40.

18. Bailey, *Germans*, 20.

19. Daniel T. Skinner, *Ustaz Aswad (Black Professor)* (Baltimore: n.p., 1996), 59.

20. Max Horlick, unpublished memoirs, 47 (courtesy of Ruth Horlick).

21. Klaus Mann, "Giants at Home," *Town & Country* (January 1945), 90.

22. Chavchavadze, *Crowns and Trenchcoats*, 103.

23. Coffin, *Once to Every Man*, 39. In reality, Chavchavadze had already completed his training at the time of Coffin's arrival, and as a lieutenant, Guirey would not have been assigned to this detail.

24. Edel, *The Veritable Past*, 15.

25. Robert H. Sternberg, *From There to Here and Back Again* (New York: Carlton, 1995), 5.

26. Earl Prebezac, "Remembrances of CHIM from Camp Ritchie," CHIM, May 2008, https://davidseymour.com/writings-on-earl-prebezac/.

27. Prebezac, "Remembrances of CHIM from Camp Ritchie."

28. Archie Roosevelt, *For Lust of Knowing: Memoirs of an Intelligence Officer* (Boston; Toronto: Little, Brown, 1988), 118, 119.

29. Klemperer, *Voyage through the Twentieth Century*, 50.

30. Coffin, *Once to Every Man*, 41.

31. Edel, *The Veritable Past*, 16.

32. Stefan Heym, *Nachruf* (Frankfurt/Main: Fischer Taschenbuch, 1994 [1988]), 262–63.

33. United States Holocaust Memorial Museum, "Interview with Eric Heinz Bondy," by Ina Navazelskis, USHMM, August 30, 2012, https://collections.ushmm.org/search/catalog/irn47822.

34. Letter of May 12, 1944, cited in James W. Mims, *From Midland to Mindanao: Reminiscences of the War in the Pacific*, ed. Claudia Gravier Frigo (Buffalo Gap, TX: State House Press, 2016), 42.

35. Mims, *From Midland to Mindanao*, 39.

36. Igor Cassini, *I'd Do It All over Again* (New York: G. P. Putnam's Sons, 1977), 95.

37. Bailey, *Germans*, 22.

38. Joachim von Elbe, *Witness to History: A Refugee from the Third Reich Remembers* (Madison, WI: Max Kade Institute for German-American Studies, 1988), 261–62.

39. Prebezac, "Remembrances of CHIM from Camp Ritchie."

40. William Warfield, with Alton Miller, *William Warfield: My Music & My Life* (Champaign, IL: Sagamore, 1991), 63.

41. "Anti-Semitic Incident at This Post," confidential report cited in Beverley Driver Eddy, *Erika and Klaus Mann: Living with America* (New York: Peter Lang, 2018), 294.

42. Martin I. Selling, *With Rancor and Compassion: The Memoirs of a Jew Who Thought He Was a German* (New York: Vantage Press, 2003), 145.

43. Nina Wolff Feld, *Someday You Will Understand: My Father's Private World War II* (New York: Arcade, 2014), 97.

44. Walter Bodlander, *The Unauthorized Autobiography of W. B.: The War Years (1933–1945)*, ed. Betty Blair, Twentieth Century Book 1 (Los Angeles; Baku: Azerbaijan International, 2012), 136.

45. Warfield, *William Warfield*, 63.
46. Mandler, *Interesting Times*, 94.
47. Ed Linville, "Ed Linville's Life at Camp Ritchie, Md," http://reidcon.com/oldsite/frmd/linville.html (accessed April 8, 2019).
48. Sternberg, *From There to Here and Back Again*, 4.

CHAPTER 4: THE COMPOSITE SCHOOL UNIT

1. Hans Habe, *All My Sins: An Autobiography* (London; Toronto: George G. Harrap, 1957), 322–23.
2. J. E. Kaufmann and H. W. Kaufmann, *The American GI in Europe in World War II: The March to D-Day* (Mechanicsburg, PA: Stackpole Books, 2009), 120.
3. Frank Woodring, "I Remember When: 'One of Last Cavalryman' [*sic*] Recounts Camp Ritchie Experience," *Maryland Cracker Barrel Magazine* (April–May 2007), 6.
4. John Sullivan, "Resident Spotlight on Leonard McNutt," *Colony Voice* (April 2004), 19.
5. Joseph T. Simon, *Augenzeuge* (Vienna: Verlag der Wiener Volksbuchhandlung, 1979), 278.
6. Lillian Belinfante Herzberg, *Stephan's Journey: A Sojourn into Freedom* (Baltimore: Publish America, 2003), 116.
7. US Army, *What Is the C.S.U.?* (Camp Ritchie, MD: US Army, n.d.), 1. Most of the material regarding its organizational structure and the various demonstrations performed by its members is taken from this booklet.
8. US Army, *What Is the C.S.U.?*, 2.
9. Sullivan, "Resident Spotlight on Leonard McNutt."
10. Theodore A. Fuller, "Professional Summary," typescript, in private hands.
11. After the war, Russo continued his career as a vocalist under the name Todd Manners.
12. See http://www.e-yearbook.com/yearbooks/Swarthmore_College_Halcyon_Yearbook/1944/Page_57.html.
13. *Blue Ridge Bulletin* 4, March 1, 1949, 20.
14. Stefan Heym, *Nachruf* (Frankfurt/Main: Fischer Taschenbuch, 1994 [1988]), 214.
15. Christian Bauer and Rebekka Göpfert, *Die Ritchie Boys: Deutsche Emigranten beim US-Geheimdienst* (Hamburg: Hoffmann und Campe, 2005), 76.
16. Hanuš Burger, *Der Frühling war es wert: Erinnerungen* (Frankfurt/Main; Berlin; Vienna: Ullstein, 1981), 137.

CHAPTER 5: INTERROGATION OF PRISONERS OF WAR (IPW)

1. "POWs and Intel at Fort Hunt in World War II," National Park Service, n.d., https://www.nps.gov/articles/forthuntww2.htm.
2. Housed in the National Archives.
3. Brandon Bies, Sam Swersky, and Doug Heimlich, "Interview with George Frenkel," 55, in *Fort Hunt Oral History*, National Park Service, December 5, 2006, and January 18, 2007, https://www.nps.gov/museum/exhibits/FOHU_oral_history/transcripts/PO%20Box%201142_Frenkel,%20George_2016.pdf.
4. From a lecture delivered by Guy Stern at Fort Ritchie, Maryland, September 21, 2013.

5. United States Holocaust Memorial Museum, "Interview with Eric Heinz Bondy," by Ina Navazelskis, USHMM, August 30, 2012, https://collections.ushmm.org/search/catalog/irn47822.

6. Hans Habe, *All My Sins: An Autobiography* (London; Toronto: George G. Harrap, 1957), 335.

7. Christian Bauer and Rebekka Göpfert, *Die Ritchie Boys: Deutsche Emigranten beim US-Geheimdienst* (Hamburg: Hoffmann und Campe, 2005), 72.

8. George Mandler, *Interesting Times: An Encounter with the 20th Century, 1924–* (Mahwah, NJ; London: Erlbaum, 2002), 96.

9. Bies, Swersky, and Heimlich, "Interview with George Frenkel," 58–59.

10. Philip Glaessner recollection, cited in Bauer and Göpfert, *Die Ritchie Boys*, 68.

11. Nina Wolff Feld, *Someday You Will Understand: My Father's Private World War II* (New York: Arcade, 2014), 104.

12. George Bailey, *Germans: The Biography of an Obsession* (New York: World Publishing, 1972), 19.

13. Bauer and Göpfert, *Die Ritchie Boys*, 73. Michaels incorrectly gives Kaufmann's first name as Margarete.

14. Hans W. Vogel, *An Immigrant's Trek*, chapter 5, *Hans W. Vogel History* (blog), December 13, 2010, http://www.hanswvogelhistory.blogspot.com.

15. Bauer and Göpfert, *Die Ritchie Boys*, 73.

16. United States Holocaust Memorial Museum, "Interview with John Dolibois," by Joan Ringelheim, USHMM, May 11, 2000, https://collections.ushmm.org/search/catalog/irn507298.

17. United States Holocaust Memorial Museum, "Interview with Eric Heinz Bondy."

18. Victor Brombert, *Trains of Thought: Memories of a Stateless Youth* (New York; London: Norton, 2002), 265.

19. Bies, Swersky, and Heimlich, "Interview with George Frenkel," 74.

20. United States Holocaust Memorial Museum, "Interview with John Dolibois."

21. Brombert, *Trains of Thought*, 296.

22. Stephanie Harbaugh, "Dr. Guy Stern to Tell the Story of the Ritchie Boys," *Record Herald*, September 7, 2013.

23. "Student Interview with Walter Monasch," Telling Their Stories: Oral History Archives Project, February 10, 2008, https://www.tellingstories.org/liberators/monasch_walter/index.html.

24. Author interview with Richard Schifter, January 7, 2020.

25. Jane Cohen, "Interview with Rudolf Michaels," Veterans History Project, American Folklife Center, Library of Congress, May 29, 2003, http://memory.loc.gov/diglib/vhp-stories/loc.natlib.afc2001001.10008/transcript?ID=mv0001.

26. Studs Terkel, *"The Good War": An Oral History of World War Two* (New York: Ballantine Books, 1984), 472.

27. Mandler, *Interesting Times*, 102.

28. Ib Melchior, *Case by Case: A U.S. Army Counterintelligence Agent in World War II* (Novato, CA: Presidio, 1993), 110–11.

29. Mandler, *Interesting Times*, 103.

30. Wayne Clark, "Howard C. Bowman Interview," New York Military Museum, July 17, 2012, 9.

31. Ib Melchior, *Fire for Effect. The Unproduced Screenplay* (Duncan, OK: BearManor Media, 2012), 124. Melchior wrote this screenplay in tribute to his friend, remarking that it was "based on a true incident, the location is factual and the character of the IPW is based on the officer who lived the story and was decorated for his achievement, Leo Handel."

CHAPTER 6: AERIAL INTELLIGENCE AND PHOTO INTERPRETATION

1. Ib Melchior, *Case by Case: A U.S. Army Counterintelligence Agent in World War II* (Novato, CA: Presidio, 1993), 62.

2. James W. Mims, *From Midland to Mindanao: Reminiscences of the War in the Pacific*, ed. Claudia Gravier Frigo (Buffalo Gap, TX: State House Press, 2016), 40.

3. Melchior, *Case by Case*, 61.

4. Robert A. Potash, *Looking Back at My First Eighty Years: A Mostly Professional Memoir* (New York; Bloomington, IN: iUniverse, 2018), 46–47.

5. Brandon Bies and Sam Swersky, "Interview with Henry Kolm," 9, in *Fort Hunt Oral History*, National Park Service, May 7 and 8, 2007, https://www.nps.gov/museum/exhibits/FOHU_oral_history/transcripts/PO%20Box%201142_Kolm,%20Henry_2016.pdf.

6. Potash, *Looking Back at My First Eighty Years*, 47.

7. Mims, *From Midland to Mindanao*, 40.

8. Melchior, *Case by Case*, 65–66.

9. Mims, *From Midland to Mindanao*, 40, 65.

10. Jim Oldham, "Interview of David E. Feller, May 26, 1994," ed. Gilda Feller and James Oldham, 2006–2007, National Academy of Arbitrators, History Committee Interview, https://naarb.org/interviews/DavidFeller.PDF.

11. Oldham, "Interview of David E. Feller."

12. [Theodore A. Fuller], *Map and Aerial Photograph Reading*, 2nd rev. ed. (Harrisburg, PA: Military Service Publishing, 1943), 186.

13. Bies and Swersky, "Interview with Henry Kolm," 13.

14. Author interview with Peter Burland, July 25, 2018.

15. *Capital Journal* (Salem, OR), July 31, 1944, 8.

16. John Thompson, "Racine Airman Helps Spot Foe for Yank Guns," *Chicago Tribune*, August 1, 1944, 2.

17. "Hugh D. Jones," HonorStates.org, https://www.honorstates.org/index.php?id=67174 (accessed February 22, 2021).

CHAPTER 7: ORDER OF BATTLE AND THE MILITARY INTELLIGENCE RESEARCH SECTION (MIRS)

1. *History and Operation MIRS, London and Washington Branches, 1 May 1943–14 July 1945*, 94. This mimeographed history is the primary source of material for this section.

2. Lillian Belinfante Herzberg, *Stephan's Journey: A Sojourn into Freedom* (Baltimore: Publish America, 2003), 115.

3. *History and Operation MIRS*, 59.

4. Brandon Bies, Matthew Virta, and Vince Santucci, "Interview with John Kluge," 17–18, in *Fort Hunt Oral History*, National Park Service, May 16, 2008, https://www.nps.gov/museum/exhibits/FOHU_oral_history/transcripts/PO%20Box%201142_Kluge_John_2016.pdf.

5. *History and Operation MIRS*, 5.

6. Bies, Virta, and Santucci, "Interview with John Kluge," 15.

7. *History and Operation MIRS*, 61.

8. Carolyn Chandler, ed., *Autobiography of Paul Fairbrook, 1923–2017* (Typescript, 2018).

9. Bies, Virta, and Santucci, "Interview with John Kluge," 12.

10. I. V. Hogg, introduction to *German Order of Battle 1944: The Directory, Prepared by Allied Intelligence, of Regiments, Formations and Units of the German Armed Forces* (London: Greenhill Books; Mechanicsburg, PA: Stackpole Books, 1994), viii.

11. *German Order of Battle 1944: The Directory, Prepared by Allied Intelligence, of Regiments, Formations and Units of the German Armed Forces* (London: Greenhill Books; Mechanicsburg, PA: Stackpole Books, 1994), D 39.

12. Chandler, *Autobiography of Paul Fairbrook.*

13. Bies, Virta, and Santucci, "Interview with John Kluge," 17–18.

14. *History and Operation MIRS*, 66.

15. *History and Operation MIRS*, 86.

16. *History and Operation MIRS*, 96.

CHAPTER 8: FIELD MANEUVERS AND CLOSE COMBAT TRAINING

1. "Ritchie-Bitchie," anonymous poem (courtesy of Paul Fairbrook).

2. John M. Fuss, "Training at Emmitsburg in World War II—the Ritchie Boys," Emmitsburg Area Historical Society, n.d., http://www.emmitsburg.net/archive_list/articles/history/ww2/stories/ritchie_boys.htm.

3. William Sloane Coffin Jr., *Once to Every Man: A Memoir* (New York: Atheneum, 1977), 39–40.

4. Hanuš Burger, *Der Frühling war es wert: Erinnerungen* (Frankfurt/Main; Berlin; Vienna: Ullstein, 1981), 133.

5. Baldwin T. Eckel, "You're in the Army Now!" *Interpreter*, no. 78 [August 1, 2004], 1.

6. Daniel Teeter's son Bob relayed this anecdote to the author on September 29, 2019.

7. Stefan Heym, *Nachruf* (Frankfurt/Main: Fischer Taschenbuch, 1994 [1988]), 253.

8. Burger, *Der Frühling war es wert*, 136.

9. Fuss, "Training at Emmitsburg."

10. Henry Bretton, *A Dream, Shadows and Fulfillment* (Bloomington, IN: Xlibris, 2017), 24.

11. Martin I. Selling, *With Rancor and Compassion: The Memoirs of a Jew Who Thought He Was a German* (New York: Vantage Press, 2003), chapter 6, 3.

12. Robert A. Potash, *Looking Back at My First Eighty Years: A Mostly Professional Memoir* (New York; Bloomington, IN: iUniverse, 2018), 47.

13. Brandon Bies, Matthew Virta, and Vince Santucci, "Interview with John Kluge," in *Fort Hunt Oral History*, National Park Service, May 16, 2008, https://www.nps.gov/museum/exhibits/FOHU_oral_history/transcripts/PO%20Box%201142_Kluge_John_2016.pdf.

14. Lawrence Cane, *Fighting Fascism in Europe: The World War II Letters of an American Veteran of the Spanish Civil War*, ed. David E. Cane, Judy Barrett Litoff, and David C. Smith (New York: Fordham University Press, 2003), 48.

15. "Soldier Missing When Trapped in Maryland Flood," *Gettysburg Times*, November 12, 1943.

16. Fuss, "Training at Emmitsburg."

17. Wayne Clark, "Howard C. Bowman Interview," New York Military Museum, July 17, 2012, 9, http://dmna.ny.gov/historic/veterans/transcriptions/Bowman_Howard_C.pdf.

18. Bretton, *A Dream, Shadows and Fulfillment*, 23.

19. Maximilian Lerner, *Flight and Return: A Memoir of World War II* (Self-published, 2013), 140.

20. Lillian Belinfante Herzberg, *Stephan's Journey: A Sojourn into Freedom* (Baltimore: Publish America, 2003), 116.

21. Clark, "Howard C. Bowman Interview."

22. Burger, *Der Frühling war es wert*, 136.

23. George Bailey, *Germans: The Biography of an Obsession* (New York: World Publishing, 1972), 19.

24. Rex Applegate, *Kill or Get Killed: Riot Control, Techniques, Manhandling, and Close Combat, for Police and the Military* (Boulder, CO: Paladin Press, 1976 [1943]), 278.

25. John Whiteclay Chambers II, *OSS Training in the National Parks and Service Abroad in World War II* (Washington, DC: US National Park Service, 2008), 186–87.

26. Burger, *Der Frühling war es wert*, 136.

27. Applegate, *Kill or Get Killed*, 285–86.

28. Applegate, *Kill or Get Killed*, 179.

29. Author interview with Peter Burland, July 25, 2018.

30. Sandor Sigmond, *Greenhorn* (Bel Air, CA: Lion's Pride, 2003), 164.

31. Author interview with Arthur H. Jaffe, August 1, 2013.

32. Kevin Fagan, "War Stories from a Nazi Interrogator, Now a Mill Valley Retiree," *SFGATE*, last updated June 21, 2014, https://www.sfgate.com/world/article/War-stories-from-a-Nazi-interrogator-now-a-Mill-5568737.php.

33. Bretton, *A Dream, Shadows and Fulfillment*, 23.

34. Author interview with Peter Burland, July 25, 2018.

35. Beverley Driver Eddy, *Camp Sharpe's "Psycho Boys": From Gettysburg to Germany* (Bennington, VT: Merriam, 2014), 30.

36. Eddy, *Camp Sharpe's "Psycho Boys,"* 31.

37. Peter N. Carroll, *The Odyssey of the Abraham Lincoln Brigade* (Palo Alto, CA: Stanford University Press, 1994), 256.

CHAPTER 9: INSTRUCTIONAL UNITS

1. "Ritchie-Bitchie," anonymous poem (courtesy of Paul Fairbrook).

2. John E. Dolibois, *Pattern of Circles: An Ambassador's Story* (Kent, OH; London: Kent State University Press, 1989), 64.

3. Lawrence Cane, *Fighting Fascism in Europe: The World War II Letters of an American Veteran of the Spanish Civil War*, ed. David E. Cane, Judy Barrett Litoff, and David C. Smith (New York: Fordham University Press, 2003), 52, 53.

4. Author interview with Peter Burland, July 25, 2018.

5. Cane, *Fighting Fascism in Europe*, 43.

6. Ib Melchior, *Case by Case: A U.S. Army Counterintelligence Agent in World War II* (Novato, CA: Presidio, 1993), 108–9.

7. Hanuš Burger, *Der Frühling war es wert: Erinnerungen* (Frankfurt/Main; Berlin; Vienna: Ullstein, 1981), 135.

8. Melchior, *Case by Case*, 111–12.

9. Leon Edel, *The Visitable Past: A Wartime Memoir* (Honolulu: University of Hawaii, 2000), 17.

10. "Composite School Unit," addendum to *History of Military Intelligence Training at Camp Ritchie, Maryland* by George J. Le Blanc (n.p.: n.p., July 1945).

11. Class handout (from the Karl Hornung papers, US Army Heritage & Education Center, Carlisle, PA).

12. Author interview with Peter Burland, July 25, 2018.

13. George Mandler, *Interesting Times: An Encounter with the 20th Century, 1924–* (Mahwah, NJ; London: Erlbaum, 2002), 96.

14. Joe Razes, "Pigeons of War," American Pigeon Museum, December 27, 2019, https://www.theamericanpigeonmuseum.org/post/pigeons-of-war-by-joe-razes (originally published in *America in WWII* [August 2007]).

15. See Margalit Fox, "Richard Topus, a Pigeon Trainer in World War II, Dies at 84," *New York Times*, December 14, 2008.

16. Razes, "Pigeons of War."

17. Michael E. Ruane, "A Camp Ritchie Soldier's Encounter with a Top Nazi Officer at the End of WWII," *Washington Post*, June 30, 2012.

18. Author interview with Peter Burland, July 25, 2018.

CHAPTER 10: THE CAMP RITCHIE WACS

1. Esther Louise Severs, "Life in 1944," *Des Moines Register*, September 10, 1944, 10.

2. Bettie J. Morden, *The Women's Army Corps, 1945–1978* (Washington, DC: Center of Military History, United States Army, 1990), 10–11.

3. Mary Rasa, "The Women's Army Corps," National Park Service, n.d., https://www.nps.gov/gate/learn/education/upload/WAC%20pdf.pdf.

4. Rasa, "The Women's Army Corps."

5. Ruth Mills Bradley, "Activation of the WAC Detachment at Camp Ritchie," 1, Ruth Mills Bradley Collection, Fairfield Museum and History Center Library, Fairfield, CT.

6. Morden, *The Women's Army Corps, 1945–1978*, 15–16.

7. See Ruth Mills Bradley, "The WAC Day," manuscript, Ruth Mills Bradley Collection, Fairfield Museum and History Center Library, Fairfield, CT.

8. Ruth Mills Bradley, "Training and Recreation Program," Ruth Mills Bradley Collection, Fairfield Museum and History Center Library, Fairfield, CT.

9. Bradley, "Training and Recreation Program."

10. *Daily Mail* (Hagerstown), May 16, 1944, 1.

11. *Morning Herald* (Hagerstown), August 2, 1945, 8.

12. *Morning Herald* (Hagerstown), April 3, 1945, 2.

13. "MIS-X: The U.S. Escape and Evasion Experts," National Museum of the United States Air Force, May 1, 2015, https://www.nationalmuseum.af.mil/Visit/Museum -Exhibits/Fact-Sheets/Display/Article/197474/mis-x-the-us-escape-and-evasion -experts/.

14. Judith A. Bellafaire, "The Women's Army Corps: A Commemoration of World War II Service," CMH Publication 72-15, https://history.army.mil/brochures/WAC/WAC .HTM.

15. Bellafaire, "The Women's Army Corps."

16. Paul Audley, ed., *Ruth Bradley: 20th-Century Pioneer*, 18, Ruth Mills Bradley Collection, Fairfield Museum and History Center Library, Fairfield, CT.

17. Audley, *Ruth Bradley: 20th-Century Pioneer*, 19.

CHAPTER 11: INTERACTIONS WITH CIVILIANS

1. *Daily Mail* (Hagerstown), December 26, 1942, 2.

2. John M. Fuss, "Training at Emmitsburg in World War II—the Ritchie Boys," Emmitsburg Area Historical Society, n.d., http://www.emmitsburg.net/archive_list/ articles/history/ww2/stories/ritchie_boys.htm.

3. John A. Miller, "Camp Ritchie during World War Two," Emmitsburg Area Historical Society, n.d., http://www.emmitsburg.net/archive_list/articles/history/ww2/ camp_ritchie.htm.

4. Fuss, "Training at Emmitsburg in World War II."

5. Richard Happel Jr., "Waynesboro Man Recalls Growing Up Near Fort Ritchie," *Maryland Cracker Barrel Magazine* (August–September 1999), 22.

6. Cited in "Major Barrick Praises Local Man for Role at Camp Ritchie," *Maryland Cracker Barrel Magazine* (August–September 1999), 21.

7. Max Horlick, unpublished memoirs, 47–48 (courtesy of Ruth Horlick).

8. Cited in John Strausbaugh, *Victory City: A History of New York and New Yorkers during World War II* (New York; Boston: Twelve, 2018), 299.

9. *Morning Herald* (Hagerstown), July 23, 1942, 1.

10. *Morning Herald* (Hagerstown), January 15, 1943, 1, 16.

11. *Daily Mail* (Hagerstown), January 15, 1943, 1, 8.

12. *Daily Mail* (Hagerstown), April 6, 1943, 1, 8.

13. *Daily Mail* (Hagerstown), April 6, 1943, 1.

14. *Daily Mail* (Hagerstown), May 9, 1946, 9.

15. *Daily Mail* (Hagerstown), July 21, 1942, 2.

16. *Morning Herald* (Hagerstown), August 26, 1946, 9.

17. *Morning Herald* (Hagerstown), May 10, 1946, 12.

18. William Warfield, with Alton Miller, *William Warfield: My Music & My Life* (Champaign, IL: Sagamore, 1991), 67.

19. Libbie Powell, "Feminine Perspective," *Daily Mail* (Hagerstown), February 11, 1966, 6.

20. Jack Rutledge, "In Our Valley," *Brownsville Herald* (Texas), December 19, 1943, 4.

21. Powell, "Feminine Perspective," 6.

22. *Daily Mail* (Hagerstown), April 24, 1943, 5.

23. *Morning Herald* (Hagerstown), December 8, 1944.

24. *Morning Herald* (Hagerstown), January 31, 1945, 8.

25. Dick Kelly, "Spotlight on Sports," *Daily Mail* (Hagerstown), October 9, 1965, 10.

26. James Rada Jr., "The Mystery of the Masons and Their History," TheCatoctin Banner.com, July 1, 2015, https://www.thecatoctinbanner.com/category/history-2/.

27. Poem by Paul Schoenbach [Fairbrook], in private collection.

28. Hans Weinberger, "Frustrations," manuscript (courtesy of Paul Fairbrook).

29. *Morning Herald* (Hagerstown), February 21, 1945, 2.

30. "Indian Soldier Held for House Breaking," *Morning Herald* (Hagerstown), September 17, 1945, 1.

31. Miller, "Camp Ritchie during World War Two."

32. *Daily Mail* (Hagerstown), June 4, 1943.

33. *Daily Mail* (Hagerstown), April 7, 1943.

34. *Daily Mail* (Hagerstown), March 10, 1943, 12.

35. *Morning Herald* (Hagerstown), May 21, 1945, 8.

36. *Morning Herald* (Hagerstown), May 21, 1943, 1.

37. "Record Class Is Naturalized," *Morning Herald* (Hagerstown), April 22, 1943, 4.

38. Klemens von Klemperer, *Voyage through the Twentieth Century: A Historian's Recollections and Reflections* (New York; Oxford: Berghahn Books, 2009), 49–50.

39. Martin I. Selling, *With Rancor and Compassion: The Memoirs of a Jew Who Thought He Was a German* (New York: Vantage Press, 2003), 144. In those cases where soldiers were shipped out unexpectedly, these naturalization ceremonies were performed abroad.

40. Henry Bretton, *A Dream, Shadows and Fulfillment* (Bloomington, IN: Xlibris, 2017), 24, 25.

41. *Daily Mail* (Hagerstown), June 8, 1946, 3.

Chapter 12: The First Mobile Radio Broadcasting Company

1. Darrell T. Rathbun, "History 1st MRBC by Major Darrell T. Rathbun," WWII Operations Report, Army AGO, Entry 427 RG 407/270/61/31/7, Box 18468, National Archives and Records Administration.

2. Alfred de Grazia, *A Taste of War, Soldiering in World War Two: Memoirs* (Princeton, NJ: Metron, 2011), 134.

3. Hans Habe, *All My Sins: An Autobiography* (London; Toronto: George G. Harrap, 1957), 323.

4. Klaus Mann, *Der Wendepunkt: Ein Lebensbericht* (Munich: Edition Spangenberg im Ellermann Verlag, 1981), 512.

5. de Grazia, *A Taste of War*, 130.

6. Martin F. Herz, "Autobiographical Sketch," in *Psychological Warfare against Nazi Germany: The Sykewar Campaign, D-Day to VE-Day*, ed. Daniel Lerner (Cambridge, MA; London: MIT Press, 1971), 82.

7. de Grazia, *A Taste of War*, 134–35.

8. de Grazia, *A Taste of War*, 134–35.

9. Rathbun, "History 1st MRBC by Major Darrell T. Rathbun."

10. Herz, "Autobiographical Sketch," 83.

11. Habe, *All My Sins*, 335.

12. Habe, *All My Sins*, 336.

13. Daniel Lerner, ed., *Psychological Warfare against Nazi Germany: The Sykewar Campaign, D-Day to VE-Day*, 198.

14. de Grazia, *A Taste of War*, 141, 142.

CHAPTER 13: THE COUNTERINTELLIGENCE CORPS AND THE OFFICE OF STRATEGIC SERVICES

1. From Patrick Anderson, "Military Camp," Poetry Foundation, n.d., https://www.poetryfoundation.org/poetrymagazine/browse?contentId=23467.

2. Ian Sayer and Douglas Botting, *America's Secret Army: The Untold Story of the Counter Intelligence Corps* (London: Fontana, 1989), 33.

3. Sayer and Botting, *America's Secret Army*, 40.

4. Sayer and Botting, *America's Secret Army*, 40–41.

5. Sayer and Botting, *America's Secret Army*, 41.

6. Ib Melchior, *Case by Case: A U.S. Army Counterintelligence Agent in World War II* (Novato, CA: Presidio, 1993), 244. Melchior's book tells how an agent's gut instincts often led to the uncovering of enemy activities, even when subjects gave entirely credible testimony under questioning.

7. Unpublished material, cited in Scott Andrew Selby, *The Axmann Conspiracy: The Nazi Plan for a Fourth Reich and How the U.S. Army Defeated It* (New York: Berkley Caliber, 2013), 47–48.

8. Sayer and Botting, *America's Secret Army*, 48.

9. Melchior, *Case by Case*, 30.

10. Melchior, *Case by Case*, 60.

11. Dana Kennedy, "WWII Spy Hunters Gather for Overt Convention," *Arizona Republic*, September 4, 1989, A-6.

12. Melchior, *Case by Case*, 136.

13. Konrad Mitchell Lawson, "Wartime Atrocities and the Politics of Treason in the Ruins of the Japanese Empire, 1937–1953" (PhD diss., Harvard University, 2012), 145–46, https://dash.harvard.edu/bitstream/handle/1/9795484/Lawson_gsas.harvard_0084L_10577.pdf?sequence=3&isAllowed=y.

14. *The Evolution of American Military Intelligence* (Fort Huachuca, AZ: US Army Intelligence Center and School, May 1973), https://fas.org/irp/agency/army/evolution.pdf.

15. Sayer and Botting, *America's Secret Army*, 41.

16. Melchior, *Case by Case*, 7.

17. Melchior, *Case by Case*, 20.

18. Melchior, *Case by Case*, 22.

19. John Whiteclay Chambers II, "Office of Strategic Services Training during World War II," *Studies in Intelligence* 54, no. 2 (June 2010), 9–10.

20. This information is taken from Fred Eden, *An Untold War Story: A Novel* (CreateSpace Independent Publishing Platform, 2015).

21. The Jedburgh name may possibly refer to a small Scottish border town where, in the twelfth century, Scots conducted guerrilla warfare against the invading English.

22. Annie Jacobsen, *Surprise, Kill, Vanish: The Secret History of CIA Paramilitary Armies, Operators, and Assassins* (New York: Little, Brown, 2019), https://www.itseyeris.com/book/surprise-kill-vanish.

23. "Activity Report of Lieutenant Robert F. Cutting," October 31, 1944, NARA, RG 226, Entry A1-210, Box 270, Folder 12382.

24. René J. Défourneaux, *The Winking Fox: Twenty-Two Years in Military Intelligence* (Indianapolis: Indiana Creative Arts, 2003 [1998]), 167.

Chapter 14: Camp Sharpe

1. Philip Pines letter to author, January 2, 2020.

2. Maximilian Lerner, *Flight and Return: A Memoir of World War II* (Self-published, 2013), 143.

3. *Gettysburg Compiler*, November 13, 1943, 6.

4. Author interview with Gunter Kosse, January 18, 2014.

5. Lerner, *Flight and Return*, 144.

6. [US Army], introduction to *PWB Combat Team . . .* (Washington, DC: US Army, 1944), 5; 2.

7. Hans Habe, *All My Sins: An Autobiography* (London; Toronto: George G. Harrap, 1957), 342.

8. Stefan Heym, *Nachruf* (Frankfurt/Main: Fischer Taschenbuch, 1994 [1988]), 261.

9. [Arthur H. Jaffe], *History, Second Mobile Radio Broadcasting Company, December 1943–May 1945* (n.p.: n.p., n.d.), 20.

10. Author interview with Arthur Jaffe, August 1, 2013.

11. Heym, *Nachruf*, 264. "Habe" was an adopted name, based on the German pronunciation of "H.B."—Bekessy's initials. He was not nobility, despite the "de" that he added to his real last name.

12. Cited in Jessica Gienow-Hecht, *Transmission Impossible: American Journalism as Cultural Diplomacy in Postwar Germany 1945–1955* (Baton Rouge: Louisiana State University Press, 1999), 21.

13. Hanuš Burger, *Der Frühling war es wert: Erinnerungen* (Frankfurt/Main; Berlin; Vienna: Ullstein, 1981), 144.

14. Heym, *Nachruf*, 265.

15. United States Holocaust Memorial Museum, "Interview with Joseph Eaton," by Judith Cohen and Stephen Luckert, 36, USHMM, August 1, 2010, https://collections .ushmm.org/oh_findingaids/RG-50.030.0581_trs_en.pdf.

16. [Jaffe], *History, Second Mobile Radio Broadcasting Company*, 20.

17. [US Army], *PWB Combat Team* . . ., 28–29.

18. [US Army], *PWB Combat Team* . . ., 107.

19. [US Army], *PWB Combat Team* . . ., 147–48.

20. Burger, *Der Frühling war es wert*, 142.

21. [US Army], *PWB Combat Team* . . ., 35.

22. Konrad Kellen, *Katzenellenbogen: Erinnerungen an Deutschland* (Vienna: Edition Selene, ca. 2003), 111.

23. [US Army], *PWB Combat Team* . . ., 61.

24. Si Lewen, *Reflections and Repercussions: The Memoirs of Si Lewen*, Art of Si Lewen, n.d., chapter 18, http://www.silewen.com/script/.

25. [Jaffe], *History, Second Mobile Radio Broadcasting Company*, 51. Si Lewen was his artist's name. In the army, he was Simon Lewin.

26. Heym, *Nachruf*, 303.

27. David Hertz, "The Radio Siege of Lorient," *Hollywood Quarterly* 1, no. 3 (April 1946), 295.

28. Hertz, "The Radio Siege of Lorient," 296.

29. Hertz, "The Radio Siege of Lorient," 293.

30. Hertz, "The Radio Siege of Lorient," 294–95.

31. [Ray K. Craft], *Psychological Warfare in the European Theater of Operation*, Study no. 131 (Bad Nauheim, Germany: The General Board, U.S.F.E.T., 1945), 30.

32. *Boston Globe*, March 21, 1947, 25.

33. Arthur T. Hadley, "Firing Potent Words, from a Tank," Op-Ed, *New York Times*, September 25, 2006.

34. S. J. Woolf, "Battle of Bulletins Frays Enemy Nerves," *Geneva Daily Times* (New York), July 11, 1944.

CHAPTER 15: THE NISEI (PACMIRS AND MITUs)

1. Haruko (Sugi) Hurt, cited in "Japanese American Women in the US Military during WWII," Go for Broke National Education Center, n.d., http://www.goforbroke.org/ learn/history/combat_history/world_war_2/ja_women_us_military_ww2.php.

2. Bill Yenne, *Rising Sons: The Japanese American GIs Who Fought for the United States in World War II* (New York: St. Martin's Press, 2007), 42.

3. Terry Shima, "Interview with Masao Matsui," Veterans History Project, American Folklife Center, Library of Congress, n.d.

4. Ken Tagami, "Recollections of the Japanese Occupation," Discover Nikkei, May 1, 2005, http://www.discovernikkei.org/en/journal/2005/5/1/japanese-occupation/.

5. Yenne, *Rising Sons*, 51.

6. Michi Kodama-Nishimoto and Warren Nishimoto, "Oral History Interview with Yoshiaki Fujitani," Hawai'i Nisei Story, April 7, 2005, and May 16, 2005, nisei.hawaii. edu/object/io_1153458308905.html.

7. George J. Le Blanc, "PACMIRS," addendum to *History of Military Intelligence Training at Camp Ritchie, Maryland* by George J. Le Blanc (n.p.: n.p., July 1945), 3.

8. Quote from Pat Nagano, MISNorCal Bio, cited in James C. McNaughton, *Nisei Linguists: Japanese Americans in the Military Intelligence Service during World War II* (Washington, DC: Department of the Army, 2006), 219–20.

9. Gayle K. Yamada, "Kazuo Yamane Interview Segment 05," Gayle K. Yamada Collection, January 8, 2001, https://archive.org/details/ddr-densho-1004-20-5.

10. Le Blanc, "PACMIRS," 4.

11. "Kazuo Yamane Story," in *MIS: America's Secret Weapon: Japanese Americans in the Military Intelligence Service in World War II*, MIS Veterans Club, n.d., http://www.misveteranshawaii.com/page-3-kazuo-yamane/.

12. "Masaru J. 'Mas' Jinbo," Discover Nikkei, n.d., http://www.discovernikkei.org/en/resources/military/167/.

13. Kodama-Nishimoto and Nishimoto, "Oral History Interview with Yoshiaki Fujitani," 56.

14. "Haruko Sugi (Maiden Name) Hurt," Discover Nikkei, n.d., http://www.discovernikkei.org/en/resources/military/113/.

15. Le Blanc, "PACMIRS," 8.

16. Greg Bradsher, "Exploitation of Captured and Seized Japanese Records by the Pacific Military Intelligence Research Service (PACMIRS) 1945–Spring 1946," *The Text Message* (blog), October 23, 2014, https://text-message.blogs.archives.gov/2014/10/23/exploitation-of-captured-and-seized-japanese-records-by-the-pacific-military-intelligence-research-service-pacmirs-1945-spring-1946/.

17. "Ralph Yoohachi Nishime," Discover Nikkei, n.d., http://www.discovernikkei.org/en/resources/military/365/?first_name=ralph&last_name=Nishime.

18. Moorhouse underestimated the figures. As of April 30, 1946, forty-eight men had been awarded the Distinguished Service Cross, while 2,022 men had received Purple Hearts (a number later increased to 9,486) and 343 had received Silver Stars. See Yenne, *Rising Sons*, 247–48.

19. *Daily Mail* (Hagerstown), May 22, 1945, 4.

20. "Mamoru 'John' Fujioka," Discover Nikkei, n.d., http://www.discovernikkei.org/en/resources/military/50/?first_name=Mamoru&last_name=Fujioka.

21. *Daily Mail* (Hagerstown), August 6, 1945, 1.

22. *Daily Mail* (Hagerstown), August 25, 1945, 1.

23. "Ralph Yoohachi Nishime."

24. "Ralph Yoohachi Nishime."

25. "Mobile Intelligence Training Unit, E.T.O.," folder, Administrative History Collection, ADM 561, National Archives and Records Administration.

26. "Yoshiaki Fujitani," Discover Nikkei, n.d., http://www.discovernikkei.org/en/resources/military/55/?first_name=Yoshiaki&last%20name-Fujitani.

27. Gene Santoro, "The Story of Two Japanese Americans Who Fought in World War II," HistoryNet, n.d., https://www.historynet.com/the-story-of-two-japanese-americans-who-fought-in-world-war-ii.htm.

28. Cited in McNaughton, *Nisei Linguists*, 231.

29. "Hiroshi Sakai," Discover Nikkei, n.d., http://www.discovernikkei.org/en/resources/military/16991/?keywords=les&page=32.

30. William Warfield, with Alton Miller, *William Warfield: My Music & My Life* (Champaign, IL: Sagamore, 1991), 70.

31. "Ralph Yoohachi Nishime."

32. "Hiroshi Sakai."

33. Warfield, *William Warfield*, 70.

34. "Hiroshi Sakai."

35. "Ralph Yoohachi Nishime."

36. James Gatewood, "Haruko (Sugi) Hurt," in *REgenerations Oral History Project: Rebuilding Japanese American Families, Communities, and Civil Rights in the Resettlement Era: Los Angeles Region*, vol. 2, http://content.cdlib.org/view?docId=ft358003z1;NAAN=13030&doc.view=frames&chunk.id=d0e6290&toc.depth=1&toc.id=d0e6290&brand=calisphere.

37. Brenda L. Moore, *Serving Our Country: Japanese American Women in the Military during World War II* (New Brunswick, NJ: Rutgers University Press, 2003), 117.

38. *Morning Herald* (Hagerstown), December 28, 1945, 7.

CHAPTER 16: THE GERMAN "HILLBILLIES"

1. "Der Papierkrieg was verpönt, / Doch gewöhnt / Hat man sich an ihn so sehr, / Daß nicht mehr / Man von ihm sich trennen kann. / Denn mal ran!" "Uns're Arbeit," Camp Ritchie Prisoner Newsletter (1945), Homer W. Schweppe Papers, Box 3-6, Special Collections, Musselman Library, Gettysburg College, Gettysburg, PA.

2. Derek R. Mallett, *Hitler's Generals in America: Nazi POWs and Allied Military Intelligence* (Lexington: University Press of Kentucky, 2013), 146–47. Most of the material on organization and staffing of the Hill Project are taken from this work.

3. Mallett, *Hitler's Generals in America*, 140.

4. "Statement of Lt. Col. Gerald Duin," in *Forging an Intelligence Partnership: CIA and the Origins of the BND, 1945–1949: A Documentary History*, vol. 1, ed. Kevin C. Ruffner, cited in Mallett, *Hitler's Generals in America*, 161.

5. The Sinclair-Bissell Agreement of May 22, 1945, cited in Mallett, *Hitler's Generals in America*, 152.

6. German Military Document Section (Camp Ritchie, MD), "Report for the Month of December [1945]," January 10, 1946, 1, Homer W. Schweppe Papers, Box 3-7, Special Collections, Musselman Library, Gettysburg College, Gettysburg, PA.

7. German Military Document Section (Camp Ritchie, MD), "Report for the Month of December [1945]."

8. Mallett, *Hitler's Generals in America*, 150–51.

9. Mallett, *Hitler's Generals in America*, 159–60.

10. Author interview with Paul Fairbrook, June 6, 2019.

11. Ken Tagami, "Recollections of the Japanese Occupation," Discover Nikkei, May 1, 2005, http://www.discovernikkei.org/en/journal/2005/5/1/japanese-occupation/.

12. Administrative Control of the Hill Project, Camp Ritchie, MD, February 7, 1946, cited in Mallett, *Hitler's Generals in America*, 145.

13. See Mallett, *Hitler's Generals in America*, 145–46.

14. Homer W. Schweppe Papers, Box 3-8, Special Collections, Musselman Library, Gettysburg College, Gettysburg, PA.

15. "Trinkt, was Euch die Kantine gibt," "Denn wer nicht Coca-Cola trinkt, / Wird nie Amerikaner!" "Mahnung!" Homer W. Schweppe Papers, Box 3-8.

16. "Die Tage, die aus einem Blicke laugen / Den freud'gen Glanz vergang'ner schöner Zeiten, / Sie können ihn zum Stillstehn nur, zum Schreiten, / Zu müdem Warten und zur Sehnsucht taugen." "Sie eilen über blauer Berge Rand / Und über weite Meere, über Land / Dorthin, wo all die Seinen weilen."

17. Mallett, *Hitler's Generals in America*, 164–65.

18. Mallett, *Hitler's Generals in America*, 158.

CHAPTER 17: RITCHIE BOYS IN EUROPE

1. Lawrence Cane, *Fighting Fascism in Europe: The World War II Letters of an American Veteran of the Spanish Civil War*, ed. David E. Cane, Judy Barrett Litoff, and David C. Smith (New York: Fordham University Press, 2003), 117.

2. Boyd Jay Petersen, *Hugh Nibley: A Consecrated Life* (Salt Lake City, UT: Greg Kofford Books, 2002), 190.

3. Petersen, *Hugh Nibley*, 194.

4. Hugh Nibley and Alex Nibley, *Sergeant Nibley PhD: Memories of an Unlikely Screaming Eagle* (Salt Lake City, UT: Shadow Mountain, 2006), 168, 170.

5. Robert M. Bowen, from his memoir *Fighting with the Screaming Eagles*, cited in Nibley and Nibley, *Sergeant Nibley PhD*, 169.

6. Petersen, *Hugh Nibley*, 199.

7. Cane, *Fighting Fascism in Europe*, 94.

8. Cane, *Fighting Fascism in Europe*, 160, 161.

9. Victor Brombert, *Trains of Thought: Memories of a Stateless Youth* (New York; London: Norton, 2002), 278.

10. Richard Schifter, "Remarks," 52nd Jewish Historical Society of Greater Washington Annual Meeting, Washington Hebrew Congregation, Washington, DC, December 2, 2012.

11. Christian Bauer and Rebekka Göpfert, *Die Ritchie Boys: Deutsche Emigranten beim US-Geheimdienst* (Hamburg: Hoffmann und Campe, 2005), 148–49.

12. Bauer and Göpfert, *Die Ritchie Boys*, 168.

13. Cited in "Soldier, Known Locally, Writes of Joy over Being Liberated," *Daily Mail* (Hagerstown), April 26, 1945, 16.

14. "99th Infantry Division, 393rd Infantry Regiment," 99th Infantry Division Historical Society, https://www.99thinfantrydivision.com/393rd-infantry-regiment/.

15. Cited in "Soldier, Known Locally, Writes of Joy over Being Liberated."

16. "99th Infantry Division, 393rd Infantry Regiment."

17. Ib Melchior, introduction to *Fire for Effect: The Unproduced Screenplay* (Duncan, OK: BearManor Media, 2012), 3.

18. See "Stephen S. Mosbacher (1923–1945): Die Geschichte eines G.I. aus Nürnberg," Rijo, n.d., http://www.rijo.homepage.t-online.de/pdf_2/DE_NU_JU_mosbacher _stephen.pdf.

19. See "Paratroopers of the 505th Parachute Infantry Regiment: Page Dedicated to 2nd Lt. Raymond Paul Raux," 505th Regimental Combat Team, n.d., www.505rct.org/album2/raux_r.asp. See also *Brooklyn Daily Eagle*, September 10, 1943, 8.

20. See Headquarters First United States Army, APO 230, Office of the Staff Judge Advocate, "Review of Proceedings of Military Commission in the Case of United States v. Haup[t]mann (Captain) Curt Bruns, 2nd Battalion, 293rd Regiment, 18th Volks Grenadier Division, German Army," Headquarters First United States Army, APO 230, April 20, 1945. See also Bruce Henderson, *Sons and Soldiers* (New York: HarperCollins, 2017), 271–77, 346–51.

21. See, among other reports, John Taylor, "Bletchley Park," addendum to *Not Bletchley Park: The Other Secret Intelligence Stories*, http://www.mkheritage.co.uk.miha/mkha/projects/jt/misc/secret.html (accessed May 4, 2020); and Robin W. Winks, *Cloak and Gown: Scholars in the Secret War, 1939–1961* (New Haven, CT: Yale University Press, 1996), 278–79.

22. Melvin C. Helfers, "My Personal Experience with High Level Intelligence," typescript (Charleston, SC: The Citadel, November 1974).

23. "Radio: Operation Annie," *Time*, February 25, 1946. This story is based on a report by Hanuš Burger. I have found no other documentation to confirm this account.

24. Meier's participation in the work of the HOUGHTEAM is told in Greg Miller, "Behind the Lines: The Untold Story of the Secret U.S. Mission to Capture Priceless Mapping Data Held by the Nazis," *Smithsonian Magazine* (November 2019), 64–76, 78.

25. Akiva Bigman, "The Orthodox Jew in SS Uniform," Aish, June 22, 2019, https://www.aish.com/jw/s/The-Orthodox-Jew-in-SS-Uniform.html.

CHAPTER 18: RITCHIE BOYS IN THE PACIFIC

1. Lieutenant Roland B. Gittelsohn, Jewish chaplain, extracted from "Uncommon Valor," *Infantry Journal*, 1946, http://www.recordsofwar.com/iwo/dead/dead.htm.

2. "Editorial: 20 Years after John Chafee's Death—We Miss His Vision and Leadership the Most," *GOLOCALProv*, October 24, 2019, https://www.golocalprov.com/news/editorial-20-years-after-john-chafees-death-we-miss-his-vision-and-leadersh.

3. "Leonard C. Brostrom," Hall of Valor Project, n.d., https://valor.militarytimes.com/hero/2202.

4. A. R. Wichtrich, *MIS-X: Top Secret* (Raleigh, NC: Pentland Press, 1997), 57. This book provides the details of Whittlesey's achievements in China.

5. Connie Martinson, "1/04/2002," *Connie Martinson Talks Books*, January 4, 2002, http://www.conniemartinson.com/CMTB/013.html.

6. F. Forrester Church, *Father and Son: A Personal Biography of Senator Frank Church of Idaho by His Son* (New York: HarperCollins, 1985), 27, 28.

7. Martin Gilbert, *The Day the War Ended: May 8, 1945—Victory in Europe* (New York: Henry Holt, 2013), 101. His sister, Taya Zinkin, was a prolific author and journalist. For

an account of Ettinger's capture by the Viet Minh, see Dixee R. Bartholomew-Feis, *The OSS and Ho Chi Minh: Unexpected Allies in the War against Japan* (Lawrence: University Press of Kansas, 2006), 254–59.

8. William R. Peers and Dean Brelis, *Behind the Burma Road* (New York: Avon Books, 1963), 207.

9. *The Ohio Alumnus, May 1945*, Internet Archive, 2010, https://archive.org/stream/ ohioalumnusmay19228ohio/ohioalumnusmay19228ohio_djvu.txt.

10. Abbie Alford, "Veterans in Cardiff-by-the-Sea Honored for Service during WWII," CBS8, June 6, 2019, last updated June 7, 2019, https://www.cbs8.com/article/ news/local/veterans-in-cardiff-by-the-sea-honored-for-service-during-wwii/509 -9499ac3f-4bef-4edc-b83f-3330f17b7cf6.

11. Frederick Aandahl, "Interview with Robert F. Goheen," 2, Association for Diplomatic Studies and Training Foreign Affairs Oral History Project, 1988, https://adst.org/ OH%20TOCs/Goheen,%20Robert%20F.toc.pdf.

12. James W. Mims, *From Midland to Mindanao: Reminiscences of the War in the Pacific*, ed. Claudia Gravier Frigo (Buffalo Gap, TX: State House Press, 2016), 81.

13. Office of Director of Intelligence, Army Service Forces, *The Battle of Enemy Equipment: A Story of ASF Enemy Equipment Intelligence Service Teams*, Special Technical Intelligence Bulletin no. 5, March 13, 1945.

14. "Interview, Signal Corps History Section, with Lt Col Robert E. Meeds, EEIS Team CBI, 10 May 45," SigC Hist Sec file, 7f, cited in George Raynor Thompson and Dixie R. Harris, *The Signal Corps: The Outcome (Mid-1943 through 1945)* (Washington, DC: US Army, 1991), 176–77.

15. Robert A. Potash, *Looking Back at My First Eighty Years: A Mostly Professional Memoir* (New York; Bloomington, IN: iUniverse, 2018), 55, 56.

CHAPTER 19: POSTWAR ACTIVITIES IN EUROPE

1. Lawrence Cane, *Fighting Fascism in Europe: The World War II Letters of an American Veteran of the Spanish Civil War*, ed. David E. Cane, Judy Barrett Litoff, and David C. Smith (New York: Fordham University Press, 2003), 165.

2. Hans A. Schmitt, *Lucky Victim: An Ordinary Life in Extraordinary Times 1933–1946* (Baton Rouge; London: Louisiana State University Press, 1989), 203–4.

3. Victor Brombert, *Trains of Thought: Memories of a Stateless Youth* (New York; London: Norton, 2002), 312–13.

4. Studs Terkel, *"The Good War": An Oral History of World War Two* (New York: Ballantine Books, 1984), 474, 475.

5. "A Wayne State University Faculty Member Says Nazi Fugitive ..." UPI Archives, February 6, 1983.

6. *Washington Post*, February 12, 1983.

7. Jack Anderson, "Those Who Helped Klaus Barbie," *Washington Post*, October 21, 1984.

8. Henry H. Kolm, "Paperclip (1945–1946)," Henry H. Kolm, n.d., https://henrykolm .weebly.com/paperclip-1945-46.html.

9. Kolm, "Paperclip (1945–1946)."

10. Hans Habe, *All My Sins: An Autobiography* (London; Toronto: George G. Harrap, 1957), 361.

11. Cited in Habe, *All My Sins*, 362.

12. Habe, *All My Sins*, 367.

13. Letter from Peter van Eyck to Watson Webb, November 2, 1948, in private hands.

14. John E. Dolibois, *Pattern of Circles: An Ambassador's Story* (Kent, OH; London: Kent State University Press, 1989), 89.

15. George A. Sakheim, "The Nuremberg Diary: A Front Row Seat to Evil," *Jerusalem Post*, December 14, 2015, https://www.jpost/com/magazine/the-nuremberg-diary-434645.

16. "Subsequent Nuremberg Proceedings, Case #3: The Justice Case," *Holocaust Encyclopedia*, United States Holocaust Memorial Museum, n.d., https://encyclopedia.ushmm.org/content/en/article/subsequent-nuremberg-proceedings-case-3-the-justice-case.

17. Kim Christian Priemel, *The Betrayal: The Nuremberg Trials and German Divergence* (Oxford: Oxford University Press, 2016), 265.

18. Linda Feldman, "Bound by History: 2 Friends Recorded Grim Testimony at Dachau Trials," *Los Angeles Times*, July 6, 1993.

19. Cited in Wolfram Wette, *The Wehrmacht: History, Myth, Reality*, trans. Deborah Lucas Schneider (Cambridge, MA; London: Harvard University Press, 2007), 221.

20. Werner Michel, in conversation with Daniel Gross, n.d.

21. George Bailey, *Germans: The Biography of an Obsession* (New York: World Publishing, 1972), 97, 98.

CHAPTER 20: POSTWAR ACTIVITIES IN THE PACIFIC

1. Michi Kodama-Nishimoto and Warren Nishimoto, "Oral History Interview with Yoshiaki Fujitani," Hawai'i Nisei Story, April 7, 2005, and May 16, 2005, nisei.hawaii.edu/object/io_1153458308905.html.

2. Kodama-Nishimoto and Nishimoto, "Oral History Interview with Yoshiaki Fujitani."

3. Hampton Sides, "The Trial of General Homma," *American Heritage* 58, no. 1 (February/March 2007), https://www.americanheritage.com/trial-general-homma.

4. Stephen B. Ives Jr., "Vengeance Did Not Deliver Justice," *Washington Post*, December 30, 2001.

5. Terry Shima, "Interview with Victor Masao Matsui," Veterans History Project, American Folklife Center, Library of Congress, n.d.

6. "Biology at War: A Plague in the Wind," *BBC Horizon*, October 29, 1984.

7. Kodama-Nishimoto and Nishimoto, "Oral History Interview with Yoshiaki Fujitani."

8. "Occupation of Japan," *New World Encyclopedia*, December 17, 2018, https://www.newworldencyclopedia.org/entry/Occupation_of_Japan.

9. Kodama-Nishimoto and Nishimoto, "Oral History Interview with Yoshiaki Fujitani."

10. George S. Guysi, "More on Tokyo Rose," letter to the editor, *Wall Street Journal*, February 23, 1976, 9.

11. "Setting the Record Straight," American Veterans Center, January 15, 2006, https://www.americanveteranscenter.org/avc-media/magazine/wwiichronicles/issue -xxxiii-winter-200506/setting-the-record-straight/.

12. F. Forrester Church, *Father and Son: A Personal Biography of Senator Frank Church of Idaho by His Son* (New York: HarperCollins, 1985), 30.

13. Klaus Mann, *The Last Day*, novel fragment, n.d., Münchner Stadtbibliothek/Monacensia.

14. Cited in Louise Steinman, *The Souvenir: A Daughter Discovers Her Father's War* (Chapel Hill, NC: Algonquin Books, 2001), 140.

15. Shima, "Interview with Victor Masao Matsui."

16. "Ralph Yoohachi Nishime," Discover Nikkei, n.d., http://www.discovernikkei.org/ en/resources/military/365/?first_name=ralph&last_name=Nishime.

17. Jeanne Wakatsuki Houston and James D. Houston, *Farewell to Manzanar* (New York: Bantam Books, 1973), 144.

18. Geoffrey F. Dunn, "Japanese American Baseball Teams Thrived in Local Area before World War II," *Monterey Herald* (California), May 31, 2010.

19. Richard Hawkins, "Maya Miyamoto, Oral History, 2011-04-27," Go for Broke National Education Center Collection, USC Digital Library, http://digitallibrary.usc .edu/cdm/compoundobject/collection/p15799coll110/id/5996/rec/1.

20. Patricia Delnore Magee, ed., *Victor's War: The World War II Letters of Lt. Col. Victor Delnore* (Paducah, KY: Turner, 2001), 169–70.

CHAPTER 21: RITCHIE REMEMBRANCES

1. *Blue Ridge Bulletin* 2, July 1, 1948.

2. *Blue Ridge Bulletin* 2.

3. *Daily Mail* (Hagerstown), December 20, 1946, 20, 2.

4. *Daily Mail* (Hagerstown), February 3, 1966, 8.

5. Libbie Powell, "Feminine Perspective," *Daily Mail* (Hagerstown), February 11, 1966.

6. *Blue Ridge Bulletin* 1, April 1, 1948.

7. Arthur W. Gutenberg, in *Blue Ridge Bulletin* 3, December 1, 1948; Joseph de Chimay, in *Blue Ridge Bulletin* 4, March 1, 1949. (Although this last issue was dated March 1, it was not completed and released until late May.)

8. *Blue Ridge Bulletin* 4.

9. Herman W. Modinger, in *Blue Ridge Bulletin* 2.

10. *Blue Ridge Bulletin* 1.

11. *Blue Ridge Bulletin* 1.

Bibliography

"99th Infantry Division, 393rd Infantry Regiment." 99th Infantry Division Historical Society. https://www.99thinfantrydivision.com/393rd-infantry-regiment/.

Aandahl, Frederick. "Interview with Robert F. Goheen," 2. Association for Diplomatic Studies and Training Foreign Affairs Oral History Project, 1988. https://adst.org/OH%20TOCs/Goheen,%20Robert%20F.toc.pdf.

Alford, Abbie. "Veterans in Cardiff-by-the-Sea Honored for Service during WWII." CBS8, June 6, 2019. Last updated June 7, 2019. https://www.cbs8.com/article/news/local/veterans-in-cardiff-by-the-sea-honored-for-service-during-wwii/509-9499ac3f-4bef-4edc-b83f-3330f17b7cf6.

"Americanism Day Is Observed Here." *Morning Herald* (Hagerstown), May 21, 1945, 1, 8.

Anderson, Jack. "Those Who Helped Klaus Barbie." *Washington Post*, October 21, 1984.

Anderson, Patrick. "Military Camp." Poetry Foundation, n.d. https://www.poetryfoundation.org/poetrymagazine/browse?contentId=23467.

Applegate, Rex. *Kill or Get Killed: Riot Control, Techniques, Manhandling, and Close Combat, for Police and the Military.* Boulder, CO: Paladin Press, 1976 [1943].

"Army Officer Asks Hagerstown to Treat Nisei G.I.s Like Americans." *Daily Mail* (Hagerstown), May 22, 1945, 4.

"Army Statistics Show 'Amateurs' as Source of Venereal Infection." *Daily Mail* (Hagerstown), April 6, 1943, 1, 8.

"Artist's Exhibit to Close Sunday." *Morning Herald* (Hagerstown), February 21, 1945, 2.

Audley, Paul, ed. *Ruth Bradley: 20th-Century Pioneer.* Ruth Mills Bradley Collection, Fairfield Museum and History Center Library, Fairfield, CT.

Bailey, George. *Germans: The Biography of an Obsession.* New York: World Publishing, 1972.

Bartholomew-Feis, Dixee R. *The OSS and Ho Chi Minh: Unexpected Allies in the War against Japan.* Lawrence: University Press of Kansas, 2006.

Bauer, Christian, and Rebekka Göpfert. *Die Ritchie Boys: Deutsche Emigranten beim US-Geheimdienst.* Hamburg: Hoffmann und Campe, 2005.

Bellafaire, Judith A. "The Women's Army Corps: A Commemoration of World War II Service." CMH Publication 72-15. https://history.army.mil/brochures/WAC/WAC.HTM.

Bies, Brandon, and Sam Swersky. "Interview with Henry Kolm." In *Fort Hunt Oral History.* National Park Service, May 7 and 8, 2007. https://www.nps.gov/museum/

exhibits/FOHU_oral_history/transcripts/PO%20Box%201142_Kolm,%20Henry
_2016.pdf.

Bies, Brandon, Sam Swersky, and Doug Heimlich. "Interview with George Frenkel." In
Fort Hunt Oral History. National Park Service, December 5, 2006, and January 18,
2007. https://www.nps.gov/museum/exhibits/FOHU_oral_history/transcripts/
PO%20Box%201142_Frenkel,%20George_2016.pdf.

Bies, Brandon, Matthew Virta, and Vince Santucci. "Interview with John Kluge." In
Fort Hunt Oral History. National Park Service, May 16, 2008. https://www.nps
.gov/museum/exhibits/FOHU_oral_history/transcripts/PO%20Box%201142_
Kluge_John_2016.pdf.

Bigelow, Michael E. "A Short History of Army Intelligence." *Military Intelligence* (July–
September 2012): 1–59. https://fas.org/irp/agency/army/short.pdf.

Bigman, Akiva. "The Orthodox Jew in SS Uniform." Aish, June 22, 2019. https://www
.aish.com/jw/s/The-Orthodox-Jew-in-SS-Uniform.html.

"Biology at War: A Plague in the Wind." *BBC Horizon*, October 29, 1984.

Blizard, Steve, and Kathy Fotheringham. *Fort Ritchie 1926–1998*. Gettysburg, PA: Herff
Jones Yearbooks, 1998.

Blue Ridge Bulletin 1, April 1, 1948. Ernst Solinger Family Collection (AR 25395). Box
1. Folder 12. Item 14-21. Leo Baeck Institute.

Blue Ridge Bulletin 2, July 1, 1948. In private collection.

Blue Ridge Bulletin 3, December 1, 1948. In private collection.

Blue Ridge Bulletin 4, March 1, 1949. In private collection.

Bodlander, Walter. *The Unauthorized Autobiography of W. B.: The War Years (1933–1945)*.
Edited by Betty Blair. Twentieth Century Book 1. Los Angeles; Baku: Azerbaijan
International, 2012.

"Body of Soldier Is Removed to Ritchie." *Morning Herald* (Hagerstown), November 2,
1945, 1.

Bradley, Ruth Mills. "Activation of the WAC Detachment at Camp Ritchie." Ruth
Mills Bradley Collection. Fairfield Museum and History Center Library, Fairfield, CT.

———. "Training and Recreation Program." Ruth Mills Bradley Collection. Fairfield
Museum and History Center Library, Fairfield, CT.

———. "The WAC Day." Manuscript. Ruth Mills Bradley Collection. Fairfield
Museum and History Center Library, Fairfield, CT.

Bradsher, Greg. "Exploitation of Captured and Seized Japanese Records by the Pacific
Military Intelligence Research Service (PACMIRS) 1945–Spring 1946." *The
Text Message* (blog), October 23, 2014. https://text-message.blogs.archives.
gov/2014/10/23/exploitation-of-captured-and-seized-japanese-records-by-the
-pacific-military-intelligence-research-service-pacmirs-1945-spring-1946/.

Brady, James. *The Coldest War: A Memoir of Korea*. New York: St. Martin's Griffin,
2007.

Bretton, Henry. *A Dream, Shadows and Fulfillment*. Bloomington, IN: Xlibris, 2017.

Brombert, Victor. *Trains of Thought: Memories of a Stateless Youth*. New York; London:
Norton, 2002.

Burger, Hanuš. *Der Frühling war es wert: Erinnerungen.* Frankfurt/Main; Berlin; Vienna: Ullstein, 1981.

"Camp Ritchie Closing." *Morning Herald* (Hagerstown), May 10, 1946, 12.

"Camp Ritchie Would Replace the Pentagon." *Daily Mail* (Hagerstown), September 30, 1946, 9.

Cane, Lawrence. *Fighting Fascism in Europe: The World War II Letters of an American Veteran of the Spanish Civil War.* Edited by David E. Cane, Judy Barrett Litoff, and David C. Smith. New York: Fordham University Press, 2003.

Carlisle, Rodney P., and Dominic J. Monetta. *Brandy, Our Man in Acapulco: The Life and Times of Colonel Frank M. Brandstetter.* Denton: University of North Texas Press, 1999.

Carroll, Peter N. *The Odyssey of the Abraham Lincoln Brigade.* Palo Alto, CA: Stanford University Press, 1994.

Caskey, Edward A. Introduction to *PWB Combat Team . . .* Washington, DC, 1944.

Cassini, Igor. *I'd Do It All over Again.* New York: G. P. Putnam's Sons, 1977.

Center for Strategic Intelligence Research. *Interrogation World War II, Vietnam, and Iraq.* Washington, DC: National Defense Intelligence College, 2008.

Chambers, John Whiteclay, II. "Office of Strategic Services Training during World War II." *Studies in Intelligence* 54, no. 2 (June 2010): 1–25.

———. "The OSS in Catoctin Mountain Park." *Catoctin History*, no. 12 (2014): 2–9. https://pdfslide.net/documents/issue-12-catoctin-frederick-community-co-t -began-with-a-cryptic-notice-in-a-local.html.

———. *OSS Training in the National Parks and Service Abroad in World War II.* Washington, DC: US National Park Service, 2008.

Chandler, Carolyn, ed. *Autobiography of Paul Fairbrook, 1923–2017.* Typescript, 2018.

Chavchavadze, David. *Crowns and Trenchcoats: A Russian Prince in the CIA.* New York: Atlantic International, 1990.

Church, F. Forrester. *Father and Son: A Personal Biography of Senator Frank Church of Idaho by His Son.* New York: HarperCollins, 1985.

Clark, Wayne. "Howard C. Bowman Interview." New York Military Museum, July 17, 2012, 9. http://dmna.ny.gov/historic/veterans/transcriptions/Bowman_Howard _C.pdf.

"Closing Party for USO Club Slated." *Daily Mail* (Hagerstown), May 9, 1946, 9.

Coffin, William Sloane, Jr. *Once to Every Man: A Memoir.* New York: Atheneum, 1977.

Cohen, Jane. "Interview with Rudolf Michaels." Veterans History Project, American Folklife Center, Library of Congress, May 29, 2003. http://memory.loc.gov/ diglib/vhp-stories/loc.natlib.afc2001001.10008/transcript?ID=mv0001.

"Couple Married at St. John's Church." *Morning Herald* (*Hagerstown*), December 28, 1945, 7.

"Cpl. Nichols Is Speaker at Zonta." *Morning Herald* (Hagerstown), May 8, 1945, 6.

[Craft, Ray K.] *Psychological Warfare in the European Theater of Operation.* Study Number 131. Bad Nauheim, Germany: The General Board, U.S.F.E.T., 1945.

Défourneaux, René J. *The Winking Fox: Twenty-Two Years in Military Intelligence.* Indianapolis: Indiana Creative Arts, 2003 [1998].

de Grazia, Alfred. *A Taste of War, Soldiering in World War Two: Memoirs*. Princeton, NJ: Metron, 2011.

Delnore Magee, Patricia, ed. *Victor's War: The World War II Letters of Lt. Col. Victor Delnore*. Paducah, KY: Turner, 2001.

Diamant, Ann Redmon, and Alfred Diamant. *Worlds Apart, Worlds United: A European-American Story: The Memoirs of Ann and Alfred Diamant*. Bloomington, IN: AuthorHouse, 2010.

Dietrich, Becky. "Camp Ritchie, Maryland—Development of the Intelligence Training Center." *K. Lang-Slattery* (blog). https://klangslattery.com/camp-ritchie-maryland -development-of-the-intelligence-training-center/.

Dolibois, John E. *Pattern of Circles: An Ambassador's Story*. Kent, OH; London: Kent State University Press, 1989.

Dunn, Geoffrey F. "Japanese American Baseball Teams Thrived in Local Area before World War II." *Monterey Herald* (California), May 31, 2010.

Eckel, Baldwin T. "You're in the Army Now!" *Interpreter*, no. 78 [August 1, 2004]: 1–2.

Eddy, Beverley Driver. *Camp Sharpe's "'Psycho Boys": From Gettysburg to Germany*. Bennington, VT: Merriam, 2014.

———. *Erika and Klaus Mann: Living with America*. New York: Peter Lang, 2018.

Edel, Leon. *The Veritable Past: A Wartime Memoir*. Honolulu: University of Hawaii, 2000.

Eden, Fred. *An Untold War Story: A Novel*. CreateSpace Independent Publishing Platform, 2015.

"Editorial: 20 Years after John Chafee's Death—We Miss His Vision and Leadership the Most." *GOLOCALProv*, October 24, 2019. https://www.golocalprov.com/ news/editorial-20-years-after-john-chafees-death-we-miss-his-vision-and -leadersh.

Eisenkraft, Albert, as told to Abby Weingarten. "A Story of Love despite Conflict." *Herald-Tribune*, October 9, 2009. http://www.heraldtribune.com/news/20091009/ a-story-of-love-despite-conflict.

Elbe, Joachim von. *Witness to History: A Refugee from the Third Reich Remembers*. Madison, WI: Max Kade Institute for German-American Studies, 1988.

The Evolution of American Military Intelligence. Fort Huachuca, AZ: US Army Intelligence Center and School, May 1973. https://fas.org/irp/agency/army/evolution .pdf.

"Ex-Language Teacher on New Missing List." *Brooklyn Daily Eagle*, September 10, 1943, 8.

Fagan, Kevin. "War Stories from a Nazi Interrogator, Now a Mill Valley Retiree." *SFGATE*. Last updated June 21, 2014. https://www.sfgate.com/world/article/ War-stories-from-a-Nazi-interrogator-now-a-Mill-5568737.php.

Feld, Nina Wolff. *Someday You Will Understand: My Father's Private World War II*. New York: Arcade, 2014.

Feldman, Linda. "Bound by History: 2 Friends Recorded Grim Testimony at Dachau Trials." *Los Angeles Times*, July 6, 1993.

Foley, Sean. "When the Qur'an Was America's Weapon for Freedom in the Middle East: Muhammad Siblini and the Defeat of the Axis in North Africa." In *Shifting Borders: America and the Middle East / North Africa*, edited by Alex Lubin, 281–93. Beirut: American University of Beirut, 2014.

Fox, Margalit. "Richard Topus, a Pigeon Trainer in World War II, Dies at 84." *New York Times*, December 14, 2008. https:www.nytimes.com/2008/12/14/us/14topus .html?_r=1&ref=obituaries.

"From Our Reporters' Notebook." *Daily Mail* (Hagerstown), August 25, 1945, 1.

[Fuller, Theodore A.] *Map and Aerial Photograph Reading.* 2nd rev. ed. Harrisburg, PA: Military Service Publishing, 1943.

Fuller, Theodore A. "Professional Summary." Typescript, in private hands.

Fuss, John M. "Training at Emmitsburg in World War II—the Ritchie Boys." Emmitsburg Area Historical Society, n.d. http://www.emmitsburg.net/archive_list/ articles/history/ww2/stories/ritchie_boys.htm.

Gatewood, James. "Haruko (Sugi) Hurt." In *REgenerations Oral History Project: Rebuilding Japanese American Families, Communities, and Civil Rights in the Resettlement Era: Los Angeles Region*, vol. 2. http://content.cdlib.org/view?docId=ft358003z1 ;NAAN=13030&doc.view=frames&chunk.id=d0e6290&toc.depth=1&toc .id=d0e6290&brand=calisphere.

"German General Believed Killed by Allied Bombers." *Capital Journal* (Salem, OR), July 31, 1944, 8.

German Military Document Section (Camp Ritchie, MD). "Report for the Month of December [1945]," January 10, 1946, 1. Homer W. Schweppe Papers, Box 3-7. Special Collections, Musselman Library, Gettysburg College, Gettysburg, PA.

German Order of Battle 1944: The Directory, Prepared by Allied Intelligence, of Regiments, Formations and Units of the German Armed Forces. London: Greenhill Books; Mechanicsburg, PA: Stackpole Books, 1994.

Gienow-Hecht, Jessica. *Transmission Impossible: American Journalism as Cultural Diplomacy in Postwar Germany 1945–1955.* Baton Rouge: Louisiana State University Press, 1999.

Gilbert, Martin. *The Day the War Ended: May 8, 1945—Victory in Europe.* New York: Henry Holt, 2013.

"GI's Once Stationed Near City, Want Return Ticket." *Morning Herald* (Hagerstown), March 23, 1945, 1, 4.

"Guardsmen Dig in to Stop 'Foe.'" *Daily Mail* (Hagerstown), August 19, 1947, 12.

Guysi, George S. "More on Tokyo Rose." Letter to the Editor. *Wall Street Journal*, February 23, 1976, 9.

Habe, Hans. *All My Sins: An Autobiography.* London; Toronto: George G. Harrap, 1957.

Hadley, Arthur T. "Firing Potent Words, from a Tank." Op-Ed, *New York Times*, September 25, 2006. https://www.nytimes.com/2006/09/25/opinion/25hadley.html.

"Hager House, Swank New Eating Place Here, to Open Saturday." *Daily Mail* (Hagerstown), December 20, 1946, 20, 2.

Happel, Richard, Jr. "Waynesboro Man Recalls Growing Up Near Fort Ritchie." *Maryland Cracker Barrel Magazine* (August–September 1999): 22, 24, 26.

Harbaugh, Stephanie. "Dr. Guy Stern to Tell the Story of the Ritchie Boys." *Record Herald*, September 7, 2013. http://www.therecordherald.com/article/20130907/news/130909920.

"Haruko Sugi (Maiden Name) Hurt." Discover Nikkei, n.d. http://www.discovernikkei.org/en/resources/military/113/.

Hawkins, Richard. "Maya Miyamoto, Oral History, 2011-04-27." Go for Broke National Education Center Collection. USC Digital Library. http://digitallibrary.usc.edu/cdm/compoundobject/collection/p15799coll110/id/5996/rec/1.

Headquarters First United States Army, APO 230, Office of the Staff Judge Advocate, "Review of Proceedings of Military Commission in the Case of United States v. Haup[t]mann (Captain) Curt Bruns, 2nd Battalion, 293rd Regiment, 18th Volks Grenadier Division, German Army." Headquarters First United States Army, APO 230, April 20, 1945. https://www.online.uni-marburg.de/icwc/dachau/000-006-0056.pdf.

Helfers, Melvin C. "My Personal Experience with High Level Intelligence." Typescript. Charleston, SC: The Citadel, November 1974.

Henderson, Bruce. *Sons and Soldiers*. New York: HarperCollins, 2017.

Hertz, David. "The Radio Siege of Lorient." *Hollywood Quarterly* 1, no. 3 (April 1946): 291–302.

Herz, Martin F. "Autobiographical Sketch." In *Psychological Warfare against Nazi Germany: The Sykewar Campaign, D-Day to VE-Day*, edited by Daniel Lerner, 81–84. Cambridge, MA; London: MIT Press, 1971.

Herzberg, Lillian Belinfante. *Stephan's Journey: A Sojourn into Freedom*. Baltimore: Publish America, 2003.

Heym, Stefan. *Nachruf*. Frankfurt/Main: Fischer Taschenbuch, 1994 [1988].

"Hiroshi Sakai." Discover Nikkei, n.d. http://www.discovernikkei.org/en/resources/military/16991/?keywords=les&page=32.

History and Operation MIRS, London and Washington Branches, 1 May 1943–14 July 1945. NARA, mimeograph.

Hogg, I. V. Introduction to *German Order of Battle 1944: The Directory, Prepared by Allied Intelligence, of Regiments, Formations and Units of the German Armed Forces*. London: Greenhill Books; Mechanicsburg, PA: Stackpole Books, 1994.

Horlick, Max. Unpublished memoirs. Text shared with author by Ruth Horlick.

"Hugh D. Jones." HonorStates.org. https://www.honorstates.org/index.php?id=67174 (accessed February 22, 2021).

Hutt, David. *The Boy Who Wore White Stockings: From Hitler's Austria to Patton's Third Army*. Leicestershire, UK: Matador, 2013.

"Indian Soldier Held for House Breaking." *Morning Herald* (Hagerstown), September 17, 1945, 1.

Ives, Stephen B., Jr. "Vengeance Did Not Deliver Justice." *Washington Post*, December 30, 2001.

Jacobsen, Annie. *Surprise, Kill, Vanish: The Secret History of CIA Paramilitary Armies, Operators, and Assassins*. New York: Little, Brown, 2019. https://www.itseyeris.com/book/surprise-kill-vanish.

Jacobson, Mark. *The Lampshade: A Holocaust Story from Buchenwald and New Orleans.* New York: Simon & Schuster, 2010.

[Jaffe, Arthur H.] *History, Second Mobile Radio Broadcasting Company, December 1943– May 1945.* N.p.: n.p., n.d.

"Japanese American Women in the US Military during WWII." Go for Broke National Education Center, n.d. http://www.goforbroke.org/learn/history/combat_history/ world_war_2/ja_women_us_military_ww2.php.

Jellinek, George. *My Road to Radio and the Vocal Scene: Memoir of an Opera Commentator.* Jefferson, NC; London: McFarland, 2007.

"Jovan M. Obradovic." HonorStates.org, n.d. https://www.honorstates.org/index. php?id=341118.

Karras, Steven. *The Enemy I Knew: German Jews in the Allied Military in World War II.* Minneapolis, MN: Zenith Press, 2009.

Kaufman, Ernest. "Holocaust—Survivor or Escapee?" Medford Leas Residents Association, May 14, 2014. https://mlra.org/photo-essays/ernest-kaufman/.

Kaufmann, J. E., and H. W. Kaufmann. *The American GI in Europe in World War II: The March to D-Day.* Mechanicsburg, PA: Stackpole Books, 2009.

"Kazuo Yamane Story." In *MIS: America's Secret Weapon: Japanese Americans in the Military Intelligence Service in World War II.* MIS Veterans Club, n.d. http://www .misveteranshawaii.com/page-3-kazuo-yamane/.

Kellen, Konrad. *Katzenellenbogen: Erinnerungen an Deutschland.* Vienna: Edition Selene, ca. 2003.

Kelly, Dick. "Spotlight on Sports." *Daily Mail* (Hagerstown), October 9, 1965, 10.

Kennedy, Dana. "WWII Spy Hunters Gather for Overt Convention." *Arizona Republic*, September 4, 1989, A-6.

Klemperer, Klemens von. *Voyage through the Twentieth Century: A Historian's Recollections and Reflections.* New York; Oxford: Berghahn Books, 2009.

Kodama-Nishimoto, Michi, and Warren Nishimoto. "Oral History Interview with Yoshiaki Fujitani." Hawai'i Nisei Story, April 7, 2005, and May 16, 2005. nisei .hawaii.edu/object/io_1153458308905.html.

Kollander, Patricia, with John O'Sullivan. *"I Must Be a Part of This War": A German American's Fight against Hitler and Nazism.* New York: Fordham University, 2005.

Kolm, Henry H. "Paperclip (1945–1946)." Henry H. Kolm, n.d. https://henrykolm .weebly.com/paperclip-1945-46.html.

Lawson, Konrad Mitchell. "Wartime Atrocities and the Politics of Treason in the Ruins of the Japanese Empire, 1937–1953." PhD diss., Harvard University, 2012. https://dash.harvard.edu/bitstream/handle/1/9795484/Lawson_gsas.harvard _0084L_10577.pdf?sequence=3&isAllowed=y.

"Learn Army to Prefer Charges." *Daily Mail* (Hagerstown), June 4, 1943.

[Le Blanc, George J.] "Composite School Unit." Addendum to *History of Military Intelligence Training at Camp Ritchie, Maryland* by George J. Le Blanc. N.p.: n.p., July 1945.

———. *History of Military Intelligence Training at Camp Ritchie, Maryland.* N.p.: n.p., July 1945.

———. "PACMIRS." Addendum to *History of Military Intelligence Training at Camp Ritchie, Maryland* by George J. Le Blanc. N.p.: n.p., July 1945.

"Lectures Given at FBI Meeting Here." *Morning Herald* (Hagerstown), July 23, 1942, 1.

"Leonard C. Brostrom." Hall of Valor Project, n.d. https://valor.militarytimes.com/hero/2202.

Lerner, Daniel, ed. *Psychological Warfare against Nazi Germany: The Sykewar Campaign, D-Day to VE-Day.* Cambridge, MA; London: MIT Press, 1971.

Lerner, Maximilian. *Flight and Return: A Memoir of World War II.* Self-published, 2013.

Lewen, Si. *Reflections and Repercussions: The Memoirs of Si Lewen.* Art of Si Lewen, n.d. http://www.silewen.com/script/.

Linville, Ed. "Ed Linville's Life at Camp Ritchie, Md." http://reidcon.com/oldsite/frmd/linville.html (accessed April 8, 2019).

"Local Girls Are WAC Enlistees." *Daily Mail* (Hagerstown), May 16, 1944, 1.

"Major Barrick Praises Local Man for Role at Camp Ritchie." *Maryland Cracker Barrel Magazine* (August–September 1999): 20–22.

Mallett, Derek R. *Hitler's Generals in America: Nazi POWs and Allied Military Intelligence.* Lexington: University Press of Kentucky, 2013.

"Mamoru 'John' Fujioka." Discover Nikkei, n.d. http://www.discovernikkei.org/en/resources/military/50/?first_name=Mamoru&last_name=Fujioka.

Mandler, George. *Interesting Times: An Encounter with the 20th Century, 1924–.* Mahwah, NJ; London: Erlbaum, 2002.

Mann, Klaus. *Der Wendepunkt: Ein Lebensbericht.* Munich: Edition Spangenberg im Ellermann Verlag, 1981.

———. "Giants at Home." *Town & Country* (January 1945): 90.

———. *The Last Day.* Novel fragment, n.d. Münchner Stadtbibliothek/Monacensia.

Martinson, Connie. "1/04/2002." *Connie Martinson Talks Books,* January 4, 2002. www.conniemartinson.com/CMTB/013.html.

"Maryland Inventory of Historical Properties Form." Maryland Historical Trust Division of Historical and Cultural Programs, n.d. https://mht.maryland.gov/secure/medusa/PDF/Washington/WA-IV-262.pdf.

"Masaru J. 'Mas' Jinbo." Discover Nikkei, n.d. http://www.discovernikkei.org/en/resources/military/167/.

"Masashi Royden 'Mush' Uriu." Discover Nikkei, n.d. http://www.discovernikkei.org/en/resources/military/578/.

McNaughton, James C. *Nisei Linguists: Japanese Americans in the Military Intelligence Service during World War II.* Washington, DC: Department of the Army, 2006.

Melchior, Ib. *Case by Case: A U.S. Army Counterintelligence Agent in World War II.* Novato, CA: Presidio, 1993.

———. *Fire for Effect: The Unproduced Screenplay.* Duncan, OK: BearManor Media, 2012.

Meyer, Alfred G. *My Life as a Fish.* Self-published typescript, 2000.

Miller, Greg. "Behind the Lines: The Untold Story of the Secret U.S. Mission to Capture Priceless Mapping Data Held by the Nazis." *Smithsonian Magazine* (November 2019): 64–76, 78.

Miller, John A. "Camp Ritchie during World War Two." Emmitsburg Area Historical Society, n.d. http://www.emmitsburg.net/archive_list/articles/history/ww2/camp_ritchie.htm.

Mims, James W. *From Midland to Mindanao: Reminiscences of the War in the Pacific.* Edited by Claudia Gravier Frigo. Buffalo Gap, TX: State House Press, 2016.

"Miss Weller Enters Military Service." *Hagerstown Morning Herald* (Hagerstown), August 2, 1945, 8.

"MIS-X: The U.S. Escape and Evasion Experts." National Museum of the United States Air Force, May 1, 2015. https://www.nationalmuseum.af.mil/Visit/Museum-Exhibits/Fact-Sheets/Display/Article/197474/mis-x-the-us-escape-and-evasion-experts/.

"Mobile Intelligence Training Unit, E.T.O." Folder. Administrative History Collection, ADM 561. National Archives and Records Administration.

Moore, Brenda L. *Serving Our Country: Japanese American Women in the Military during World War II.* New Brunswick, NJ: Rutgers University Press, 2003.

Morden, Bettie J. *The Women's Army Corps, 1945–1978.* Washington, DC: Center of Military History, United States Army, 1990.

"More Homes for Soldiers Needed." *Morning Herald* (Hagerstown), August 26, 1946, 9.

Newton, Karen Ryser. *Of Genuine Quality: The Biography of Sterling Ralph Ryser.* Scottsdale, AZ: Agreka Books, 2000.

Nibley, Hugh, and Alex Nibley. *Sergeant Nibley PhD: Memories of an Unlikely Screaming Eagle.* Salt Lake City, UT: Shadow Mountain, 2006.

"Nisei Soldiers Make Friends in Hagerstown, Prefer East to West." *Daily Mail* (Hagerstown), August 6, 1945, 1, 2.

"N.Y. Awards Medal to Bridgewater Vet." *Boston Globe*, March 21, 1947, 25.

"Occupation of Japan." *New World Encyclopedia*, December 17, 2018, https://www.newworldencyclopedia.org/entry/Occupation_of_Japan.

Office of Director of Intelligence, Army Service Forces. *The Battle of Enemy Equipment: A Story of ASF Enemy Equipment Intelligence Service Teams.* Special Technical Intelligence Bulletin no. 5, March 13, 1945.

The Ohio Alumnus, May 1945. Internet Archive, 2010. https://archive.org/stream/ohioalumnusmay19228ohio/ohioalumnusmay19228ohio_djvu.txt.

"Oilers Face an Acid Test." *Morning Herald* (Hagerstown), January 31, 1945, 8.

Oldham, Jim. "Interview of David E. Feller, May 26, 1994." Edited by Gilda Feller and James Oldham, 2006–2007. National Academy of Arbitrators, History Committee Interview. https://naarb.org/interviews/DavidFeller.PDF.

"Our Reporters' Notebooks." *Daily Mail* (Hagerstown), June 8, 1946, 1, 3.

"Paratroopers of the 505th Parachute Infantry Regiment: Page Dedicated to 2nd Lt. Raymond Paul Raux." 505th Regimental Combat Team, n.d. www.505rct.org/album2/raux_r.asp.

"Patricia 'Pat' Liell" [Obituary]. *Indianapolis Star*, March 21, 2004.

Peers, William R., and Dean Brelis. *Behind the Burma Road.* New York: Avon Books, 1963.

Petersen, Boyd Jay. *Hugh Nibley: A Consecrated Life.* Salt Lake City, UT: Greg Kofford Books, 2002.

"Plan Service Men's Dance." *Daily Mail* (Hagerstown), July 21, 1942, 2.

"Police Question Officer Charge." *Daily Mail* (Hagerstown), April 6, 1943, 1.

Potash, Robert A. *Looking Back at My First Eighty Years: A Mostly Professional Memoir.* New York; Bloomington, IN: iUniverse, 2018.

Powell, Libbie. "Feminine Perspective." *Daily Mail* (Hagerstown), February 11, 1966, 6.

———. "William Warfield Returned Last Evening in Concert and Held a Friendly Audience in the Palm of His Hand." *Daily Mail* (Hagerstown), February 9, 1966, 8.

"POWs and Intel at Fort Hunt in World War II." National Park Service, n.d. https://www.nps.gov/articles/forthuntww2.htm.

Prebezac, Earl. "Remembrances of CHIM from Camp Ritchie." CHIM, May 2008. https://davidseymour.com/writings-on-earl-prebezac/.

Priemel, Kim Christian. *The Betrayal: The Nuremberg Trials and German Divergence.* Oxford: Oxford University Press, 2016.

"Problem of Social Diseases Debated." *Morning Herald* (Hagerstown), January 15, 1943, 1, 16.

Proctor, K. Harvey. *Credible and True.* London: Biteback, 2016.

"Pvt. Patrekeyeva Is Zonta Speaker." *Morning Herald* (Hagerstown), April 3, 1945, 2.

Rada, James, Jr. "The Mystery of the Masons and Their History." TheCatoctinBanner.com, July 1, 2015. https://www.thecatoctinbanner.com/category/history-2/.

"Radio: Operation Annie." *Time*, February 25, 1946.

"Ralph Yoohachi Nishime." Discover Nikkei, n.d. http://www.discovernikkei.org/en/resources/military/365/?first_name=ralph&last_name=Nishime.

Rasa, Mary. "The Women's Army Corps." National Park Service, n.d. https://www.nps.gov/gate/learn/education/upload/WAC%20pdf.pdf.

Rathbun, Darrell T. "History 1st MRBC." WWII Operations Report, Army AGO. Entry 427 RG 407/270/61/31/7. Box 18468. National Archives and Records Administration.

Razes, Joe. "Pigeons of War." American Pigeon Museum, December 27, 2019, https://www.theamericanpigeonmuseum.org/post/pigeons-of-war-by-joe-razes. Originally published in *America in WWII* (August 2007).

"Record Class Is Naturalized." *Morning Herald* (Hagerstown), April 22, 1943, 4.

"Record Class to Take Oath." *Daily Mail* (Hagerstown), March 10, 1943, 12.

Roosevelt, Archie. *For Lust of Knowing: Memoirs of an Intelligence Officer.* Boston; Toronto: Little, Brown, 1988.

Ruane, Michael E. "A Camp Ritchie Soldier's Encounter with a Top Nazi Officer at the End of WWII." *Washington Post*, June 30, 2012.

Rutledge, Jack. "In Our Valley." *Brownsville Herald* (Texas), December 19, 1943, 4.

Sakheim, George A. "The Nuremberg Diary: A Front Row Seat to Evil." *Jerusalem Post*, December 14, 2015. https://www.jpost/com/magazine/the-nuremberg-diary-434645.

Santoro, Gene. "The Story of Two Japanese Americans Who Fought in World War II." HistoryNet, n.d. https://www.historynet.com/the-story-of-two-japanese-americans-who-fought-in-world-war-ii.htm.

Sayer, Ian, and Douglas Botting. *America's Secret Army: The Untold Story of the Counter Intelligence Corps*. London: Fontana, 1989.

Schifter, Richard. "Remarks." 52nd Jewish Historical Society of Greater Washington Annual Meeting. Washington Hebrew Congregation, Washington, DC, December 2, 2012.

Schmitt, Hans A. *Lucky Victim: An Ordinary Life in Extraordinary Times 1933–1946*. Baton Rouge; London: Louisiana State University Press, 1989.

Schoenbach [Fairbrook], Paul. Untitled poem. Manuscript courtesy of Paul Fairbrook.

Selby, Scott Andrew. *The Axmann Conspiracy: The Nazi Plan for a Fourth Reich and How the U.S. Army Defeated It*. New York: Berkley Caliber, 2013.

Selling, Martin I. *With Rancor and Compassion: The Memoirs of a Jew Who Thought He Was a German*. New York: Vantage Press, 2003.

Seltzer, Richard. *One View of America in the World War II Generation: The Life and Times of Richard Warren Seltzer, Sr., Born June 5 1923*. Part 1, *1923–1988*. Richard's Home Online, n.d. www.seltzerbooks.com/lifeandtimes.html.

"Sergeant Pawlak Speaks Here Tomorrow." *Daily Mail* (Hagerstown), April 24, 1943, 5.

"Setting the Record Straight." American Veterans Center, January 15, 2006. https://www.americanveteranscenter.org/avc-media/magazine/wwiichronicles/issue-xxxiii-winter-200506/setting-the-record-straight/.

Severs, Esther Louise. "Life in 1944." *Des Moines Register*, September 10, 1944, 10.

Shima, Terry. "Interview with Victor Masao Matsui." Veterans History Project, American Folklife Center, Library of Congress, n.d.

Sides, Hampton. "The Trial of General Homma." *American Heritage* 58, no. 1 (February/March 2007). https://www.americanheritage.com/trial-general-homma.

Sigmond, Sandor. *Greenhorn*. Bel Air, CA: Lion's Pride, 2003.

Simon, Joseph T. *Augenzeuge*. Vienna: Verlag der Wiener Volksbuchhandlung, 1979.

Skinner, Daniel T. *Ustaz Aswad (Black Professor)*. Baltimore: n.p., 1996.

"Social Diseases Must Be Fought Like T.B. Is, Says Health Chief." *Daily Mail* (Hagerstown), January 15, 1943, 1, 8.

"Soldier, Known Locally, Writes of Joy over Being Liberated." *Daily Mail* (Hagerstown), April 26, 1945, 16.

"Soldier and Girl Found in Hotel." *Daily Mail* (Hagerstown), April 7, 1943.

"Soldier Drowned at Nearby Camp." *Daily Mail* (Hagerstown), July 10, 1943, 1.

"Soldier Is Found Hanging in Hotel." *Daily Mail* (Hagerstown), October 3, 1944, 1.

"Soldier Missing When Trapped in Maryland Flood." *Gettysburg Times*, November 12, 1943.

"Soldiers Are Yule Guests." *Daily Mail* (Hagerstown), December 26, 1942, 2.

Steinman, Louise. *The Souvenir: A Daughter Discovers Her Father's War*. Chapel Hill, NC: Algonquin Books, 2001.

"Stephen S. Mosbacher (1923–1945): Die Geschichte eines G.I. aus Nürnberg." Rijo, n.d. http://www.rijo.homepage.t-online.de/pdf_2/DE_NU_JU_mosbacher_stephen.pdf.

Stern, Guy. *Invisible Ink: A Memoir.* Detroit: Wayne State University Press, 2020.

Sternberg, Robert H. *From There to Here and Back Again.* New York: Carlton, 1995.

Strausbaugh, John. *Victory City: A History of New York and New Yorkers during World War II.* New York; Boston: Twelve, 2018.

"Student Interview with Walter Monasch." Telling Their Stories: Oral History Archives Project, February 10, 2008. https://www.tellingstories.org/liberators/monasch_walter/index.html.

"Stunt Flyer Coming." *Biloxi Daily Herald* (Mississippi), June 3, 1930, 6.

"Subsequent Nuremberg Proceedings, Case #3: The Justice Case." *Holocaust Encyclopedia,* United States Holocaust Memorial Museum. https://encyclopedia.ushmm.org/content/en/article/subsequent-nuremberg-proceedings-case-3-the-justice-case.

Sullivan, John. "Resident Spotlight on Leonard McNutt." *Colony Voice* (April 2004).

Tagami, Ken. "Recollections of the Japanese Occupation." Discover Nikkei, May 1, 2005. http://www.discovernikkei.org/en/journal/2005/5/1/japanese-occupation/.

"'Tanker' Practice? Man Mountain Dean Joins Up with Tanks." *Star Tribune* (Minneapolis), June 8, 1942, 14.

Taylor, John. "Bletchley Park." Addendum to *Not Bletchley Park: The Other Secret Intelligence Stories.* http://www.mkheritage.co.uk.miha/mkha/projects/jt/misc/secret.html (accessed May 4, 2020).

"Technique Used in Training of Soldiers Described by Officer." *Morning Herald* (Hagerstown), December 8, 1944.

Terkel, Studs. *"The Good War": An Oral History of World War Two.* New York: Ballantine Books, 1984.

Thompson, George Raynor, and Dixie R. Harris. *The Signal Corps: The Outcome (Mid-1943 through 1945).* Washington, DC: US Army, 1991.

Thompson, John. "Racine Airman Helps Spot Foe for Yank Guns." *Chicago Tribune,* August 1, 1944, 2.

"Uncommon Valor." *Infantry Journal,* 1946. http://www.recordsofwar.com/iwo/dead/dead.htm.

United States Holocaust Memorial Museum. "Interview with Eric Heinz Bondy," by Ina Navazelskis. USHMM, August 30, 2012. https://collections.ushmm.org/search/catalog/irn47822.

———. "Interview with John Dolibois," by Joan Ringelheim. USHMM, May 11, 2000. https://collections.ushmm.org/search/catalog/irn507298.

———. "Interview with Joseph Eaton," by Judith Cohen and Stephen Luckert. USHMM, August 1, 2010. https://collections.ushmm.org/oh_findingaids/RG-50.030.0581_trs_en.pdf.

[US Army.] *PWB Combat Team . . .* Washington, DC: US Army, 1944.

US Army. *What Is the C.S.U.?* Camp Ritchie, MD: US Army, n.d.

US Citizenship and Immigration Services. "Military Naturalization during WW II." USCIS, n.d. https://www.uscis.gov/history-and-genealogy/our-history/agency-history/military-naturalization-during-wwii.

"U.S. Protected Nazi Hunted." *Washington Post*, February 12, 1983.

"Veteran Leatherneck Learning Judo on the Riviera." *Rocky Mount Sunday Telegram* (North Carolina), June 6, 1954, 4.

Vogel, Hans W. *An Immigrant's Trek. Hans W. Vogel History* (blog), December 13, 2010. http://www.hanswvogelhistory.blogspot.com.

Vournas, George C. Introduction to *OSS with the Central Committee of EAM* by Costa G. Couvaras. San Francisco, CA: Wire Press, 1982. https://web.stanford.edu/~ichriss/Couvaras.htm.

Wakatsuki Houston, Jeanne, and James D. Houston. *Farewell to Manzanar*. New York: Bantam Books, 1973.

Walters, Vernon A. *Silent Missions*. Garden City, NY: Doubleday, 1978.

Warfield, William, with Alton Miller. *William Warfield: My Music & My Life*. Champaign, IL: Sagamore, 1991.

"A Wayne State University Faculty Member Says Nazi Fugitive . . ." UPI Archives, February 6, 1983.

Weinberger, Hans. "Frustrations." Manuscript courtesy of Paul Fairbrook.

Wette, Wolfram. *The Wehrmacht: History, Myth, Reality*. Translated by Deborah Lucas Schneider. Cambridge, MA; London: Harvard University Press, 2007.

Wichtrich, A. R. *MIS-X: Top Secret*. Raleigh, NC: Pentland Press, 1997.

Winks, Robin W. *Cloak and Gown: Scholars in the Secret War, 1939–1961*. New Haven, CT: Yale University Press, 1996.

Woodring, Frank. "I Remember When: 'One of Last Cavalryman' [*sic*] Recounts Camp Ritchie Experience." *Maryland Cracker Barrel Magazine* (April–May 2007): 4–8.

Woolf, S. J. "Battle of Bulletins Frays Enemy Nerves." *Geneva Daily Times* (New York), July 11, 1944.

Yamada, Gayle K. "Kazuo Yamane Interview Segment 05." Gayle K. Yamada Collection, January 8, 2001. https://archive.org/details/ddr-densho-1004-20-5.

Yenne, Bill. *Rising Sons: The Japanese American GIs Who Fought for the United States in World War II*. New York: St. Martin's Press, 2007.

"Yoshiaki Fujitani." Discover Nikkei, n.d. http://www.discovernikkei.org/en/resources/military/55/?first_name=Yoshiaki&last%20name-Fujitani.

Index of Names